THE BYZANTINE FATHERS OF THE FIFTH CENTURY

ABOUT THE COLLECTED WORKS

Fr. Florovsky devoted much attention to his *Collected Works*. Until shortly before his death, he had continued to supply a variety of materials. These included suggestions for the structuring of the volumes; changes in certain texts; new materials; updated materials; notes; revisions; suggestions for revisions; updated bibliography; and several outlines for a new structure to his work on the Byzantine Fathers. Substantial time has been expended to implement his suggestions and instructions. Some materials will be included in the final volume, a volume which also contains an Index to the entire *Collected Works*, Appendices, Notes, Bibliography, and Miscellanea. To publish *The Collected Works* in English has entailed the translation of his works from several languages, including Russian, Bulgarian, Czech, Serbian, German and French.

THE BYZANTINE FATHERS
OF THE
FIFTH CENTURY

VOLUME EIGHT
in *THE COLLECTED WORKS* of

GEORGES FLOROVSKY
Emeritus Professor of Eastern Church History
Harvard University

General Editor
RICHARD S. HAUGH
Visiting Scholar
Andover Newton Theological School

Translated by
RAYMOND MILLER
AND
ANNE-MARIE DÖLLINGER-LABRIOLLE
HELMUT WILHELM SCHMIEDEL

BÜCHERVERTRIEBSANSTALT
Postfach 461, FL - 9490 Vaduz, Europa
[Exclusive Sales Agent: Notable & Academic Books
P. O. Box 470, Belmont, MA {USA} 02178]

THE BYZANTINE FATHERS OF THE FIFTH CENTURY
ISBN 3-905238-08-X

THE COLLECTED WORKS OF GEORGES FLOROVSKY

[Additional forthcoming volumes. The final volume contains an Index to the entire *Collected Works*, Bibliography, Appendices, and Miscellanea]

BX
260
.F55
1987 / 56,209
V.8

SECOND PRINTING

TABLE OF CONTENTS

ESSENTIAL THOUGHTS OF THE EARLY APOLOGISTS

• The Apostolic Deposit • On the Nature and the Knowledge
of God • The Apologists and the Logos • The Influence of
Philo • The Immanent and Expressed Logos • The Problem
of Terminology •

CHAPTER SEVEN   92

MONARCHIANISM

•Dynamic Monarchianism in the Latin West • The Alogi •
Theodotus of Byzantium • Artemas and the Lingering of
Dynamic Monarchianism in Rome • Modalistic
Monarchianism •Noëtus • Praxeas • Sabellius •

CHAPTER EIGHT   102

TERTULLIAN AND HIPPOLYTUS

CHAPTER NINE   118

ORIGENISM AND ARIANISM

CHAPTER TEN   137

NICAEA AND THE ECUMENICAL COUNCIL

•The Theological Nature of a Council in the First Three
Centuries • Constantine and the Ecumenical Council •The
Role of the Byzantine Emperor • Constantine and the
Distinction of Two Authorities • The Fifth Canon of the
Council of Nicaea – Ecclesiastical Elitism or Tradition? •
The Silent Presence at the Ecumenical Councils • The
Guiding Hermeneutical Principle at the Ecumenical Councils
• The Meaning of "the Fathers" and "Scripture" • The
Council of Nicaea •

CHAPTER ELEVEN   156

FROM NICAEA TO EPHESUS

•The Dogmatic Meaning of Nicaea • St. Athanasius •
Anomoeanism • St. Basil • St. Gregory of Nazianzus • St.
Gregory of Nyssa • The Holy Spirit • Apollinarianism • The

Second Ecumenical Council • The Road to Ephesus •
Diodore of Tarsus •

CHAPTER TWELVE   194

THEODORE OF MOPSUESTIA

LIFE

• St. John Chrysostom's *Letter to Theodore of Mopsuestia*
• Theodore's Reputation During His Life and His
Posthumous Condemnation

WORKS

•Knowledge and Preservation of the Works of Theodore of
Mopsuestia • Theodore's *Commentaries* on the Old
Testament • Theodore's *Commentaries* on the New
Testament • Theodore's *Catechetical Homilies* • *De
Incarnatione* and His *Disputatio cum Macedonianis* •
Theodore's Ascetical Works • Theodore's *Contra Eunomium*
• Theodore's Work Against Apollinarius • Theodore's Work
Against St. Augustine • Theodore's Works Against Magic •
Liber Magaritarum • *Adversus Allegoricos* , *De Obscura*, and
De Legislatione •

THEOLOGICAL THOUGHT

•Christ as Perfect Man United with God • The Indwelling of
God in Christ • Theodore's Concept of the Unity of Person
• Theodore's Objection to the Term *Theotokos* • Theodore's
Anthropological Design •

CHAPTER THIRTEEN   210

NESTORIUS

LIFE

• The Condemnation of Apollinarius at the Second
Ecumenical Council • The Selection of Nestorius as
Patriarch of Constantinople • Nestorius' Character •
Nestorius' Agenda upon Becoming Patriarch • Nestorius and
the Term *Theotokos* • The Significance of the Term
Theotokos • St. John Chrysostom and Nestorius • The
Reaction to Nestorius • Nestorius' First *Letter to Pope
Celestine* • Nestorius' Diplomatic Blunder • Pope Celestine I

and the Authority of the Roman See • St. Cyril's Second
Letter to Nestorius • St. Cyril and Pope Celestine I • St.
Cyril's Third *Letter to Nestorius* • The *Twelve Anathemas* of
St. Cyril Against Nestorius • Nestorius' Reaction to the
Decisions of Rome and Alexandria •

WORKS

•The Bazaar of Heraclides of Damascus • Tragedy •
Theopaschites • Sermons • The Letters of Nestorius •

THEOLOGICAL TENDENCY OF NESTORIUS

LIFE

•Cyril's Early Years as Patriarch • The Storm Cloud in
Constantinople • The Alliance of Cyril and Pope Celestine
• The Reaction to St. Cyril's *Twelve Anathemas* in the
East • Behind the Scenes at the Council of Ephesus • St.
Cyril and the Aftermath of the Council of Ephesus • St.
Cyril's *Letter to John of Antioch* • The Confession of
Faith of John of Antioch and the Easterners • The
Difficulties of Reunion with the Easterners •

WORKS

• The Early Exegetical Works • *The Commentary on the
Gospel of St. John* • *The Commentary on the Gospel of
St. Luke* • Fragments of Other Works on the New
Testament • Dogmatic Writings Before the Nestorian
Controversy • Writings During the Nestorian Controversy
• *The Letters* of St. Cyril • *For the Holy Religion of the
Christians Against the Books of the Impious Julian* •

THEOLOGY OF ST. CYRIL

• The Limits of Logical Consciousness • The Importance
of Faith As a Necessary Prerequisite for Understanding •
The Mystery of the Knowledge of Complete Truth • The
Ontological Character of the Trinitarian Hypostases • The
Church as the Perfect Reflection of the Unknowable
Trinity • The Revelation of God as Father and Its
Trinitarian Significance • The Logos or Word of the Father
• The Holy Spirit • The Procession of the Holy Spirit •
The Difference Between St. Cyril and St. Augustine on the

Doctrine of the Procession of the Holy Spirit • The Incarnation • The Incarnation and the Eucharist • The Single Person or Hypostasis of Christ from Faith and Experience • Nestorius and the Denial of the Ontological Unity of Christ • The En-Hypostasis in Christ • Cyril's Early Rejection of Apollinarianism • The Basis and Essence of His Attack on Antiochene Christology • Imprecision and Unclarity in His Theological Terminology •

x *Contents*

THE THEOLOGY OF THEODORET

IN MEMORIAM

FR. GEORGES FLOROVSKY
1893-1979

"Preeminent Orthodox Christian Theologian, Ecumenical Spokesman, And Authority on Russian Letters."

[All quotations are from pages 5 and 11 of the *Harvard Gazette* of October 1, 1982, written by George H. Williams, Hollis Professor of Divinity *Emeritus*, Harvard Divinity School and Edward Louis Keenan, Dean of the Graduate School of Arts and Sciences, Harvard University and "placed upon the records" at the Harvard Faculty of Divinity Meeting on September 16, 1982.]

"Archpriest Professor Georges Vasilyevich Florovsky (1893-1979), preeminent theologian of Orthodoxy and historian of Christian thought, ecumenical leader and interpreter of Russian literature . . . died in Princeton, New Jersey in his 86th year" on August 11, 1979.

Born in Odessa in 1893, Fr. Florovsky was the beneficiary of that vibrant Russian educational experience which flourished toward the end of the 19th century and produced many gifted scholars. His father was rector of the Theological Academy and dean of the Cathedral of the Transfiguration. His mother, Klaudia Popruzhenko, was the daughter of a professor of Hebrew and Greek. Fr. Florovsky's first scholarly work, "On Reflex Salivary Secretion," written under one of Pavlov's students, was published in English in 1917 in the last issue of *The Bulletin of the Imperial Academy of Sciences.*

In 1920, with his parents and his brother Antonii, Fr. Florovsky left Russia and settled first in Sophia, Bulgaria. He left behind his brother, Vasilii, a surgeon, who died in the 1924 famine, and his sister Klaudia V. Florovsky, who became a professor of history at the University of Odessa. In 1921 the President of Czechoslovakia, Thomas Masaryk, invited Fr. Florovsky and his brother Antonii to Prague. Fr. Florovsky taught the philosophy of law. Antonii later became a professor of history at the University of Prague.

In 1922 Georges Florovsky married Xenia Ivanovna Simonova and they resettled in Paris where he became cofounder of St. Sergius Theological Institute and taught there as professor of patristics (1926-1948). In 1932 he was ordained a priest and placed himself canonically under the patriarch of Constantinople.

In 1948 he came to the United States and was professor of theology at St. Vladimir's Theological Seminary from 1948 to 1955, and dean from 1950. From 1954 to 1965 he was professor of Eastern Church History at Harvard Divinity School and, concurrently (1962-1965) an associate of the Slavic Department and (1955-1959) an associate professor of theology at Holy Cross Theological School.

"Although Fr. Florovsky's teaching in the Slavic Department [at Harvard University] was only sporadic, he became a major intellectual influence in the formation of a generation of American specialists in Russian cultural history. His lasting importance in this area derives not from his formal teaching but from the time and thought he gave to informal "circles" that periodically arose around him in Cambridge among those who had read *The Ways of Russian Theology* [then only in Russian], for decades a kind of "underground book" among serious graduate students of Russian intellectual history, and had sought him out upon discovering that he was at the Divinity School . . . During a portion of his incumbency at Harvard . . . patristics and Orthodox thought and institutions from antiquity into 20th century Slavdom flourished. In the Church History Department meetings he spoke up with clarity. In the Faculty meetings he is remembered as having ener - getically marked book catalogues on his lap for the greater glory of the Andover Harvard Library! In 1964 Fr. Florovsky was elected a director of the Ecumenical Institute founded by Paul VI near Jerusalem." Active in both the National Council of Churches and the World Council of Churches, Fr. Florovsky was Vice President-at-Large of the National Council of Churches from 1954 to 1957.

"After leaving Harvard, Professor *Emeritus* Florovsky taught from 1965 to 1972 in Slavic Studies at Princeton University, having begun lecturing there already in 1964; and he was visiting lecturer in patristics at Princeton Theological Seminary as early as 1962 and then again intermittently after retirement from the University. His last teaching was in the fall semester of 1978/79 at Princeton Theological Seminary."

"Fr. Florovsky in the course of his career was awarded honorary doctorates by St. Andrew's University . . . Boston University, Notre Dame, Princeton University, the University of Thessalonica, St. Vladimir's Theological Seminary, and Yale. He was a member or honorary member of the Academy of Athens, the American Academy of Arts and Sciences, the British Academy, and the Fellowship of St. Alban and St. Sergius."

Fr. Florovsky personified the cultivated, well-educated Russian of the turn of the century. His penetrating mind grasped both the detail and depth in the unfolding drama of the history of Christianity in both eastern and western forms. He was theologian, church historian, patristic scholar, philosopher, Slavist, and a writer in comparative literature. "Fr. Florovsky sustained his pleasure on reading English novels, the source in part of his extraordinary grasp of the English language, which, polyglot that he was, he came to prefer above any other for theological discourse and general exposition. Thus when he came to serve in Harvard's Slavic Department, there was some disappointment that he did not lecture in Russian, especially in his seminars on Dostoievsky, Soloviev, Tolstoi, and others. It was as if they belonged to a kind of classical age of the Russian tongue and civilization that, having been swept away as in a deluge, he treated as a Latin professor would Terrence or Cicero, not presuming to give lectures in the tonalities of an age that had vanished forever."

Fr. Florovsky's influence on contemporary church historians and Slavists was vast. The best contemporary multi-volume history of Christian thought pays a special tribute to Fr. Florovsky. Jaroslav Pelikan of Yale University, in the bibliographic section to his first volume in *The Christian Tradition: A History of the Development of Doctrine*, writes under the reference to Fr. Florovsky's two works in Russian on the Eastern Fathers: "These two works are basic to our interpretation of trinitarian and christological dogmas" (p. 359 from *The Emergence of the Catholic Tradition: 100-600*). George Huntston Williams, Hollis Professor *Emeritus* of Harvard Divinity School, wrote: "Faithful priestly son of the Russian Orthodox Church . . . , Fr. Georges Florovsky – with a career-long involvement in the ecumenical dialogue – is today the most articulate, trenchant and winsome exponent of Orthodox theology and piety in the scholarly world. He is innovative and creative in the sense wholly of being ever prepared to restate the saving truth of Scripture and Tradition in the idiom of our contemporary yearning for the transcendent."

AUTHOR'S PREFACE (1978)

These four volumes on the Eastern Fathers of the fourth century and the Byzantine fathers from the fifth to eighth centuries were originally published in 1931 and 1933 in Russian. They contained my lectures given at the Institute of Orthodox Theology in Paris from 1928 to 1931 and were originally published in Russian more or less in the form in which they were originally delivered. They therefore lacked exact references and appropriate footnotes. Another reason for the omission of reference material in the 1931 and 1933 publications is that the books were originally published at my own expense and strict economy was therefore necessary. In fact, their publication was only the result of the generous cooperation and help of personal friends. These English publications must be dedicated to their memory. The initiative of the original publication was taken by Mrs. Elizabeth Skobtsov, who became an Orthodox nun and was later known under her monastic name of Mother Maria. It was she who typed the original manuscripts and she who was able to persuade Mr. Iliia Fondaminsky, at that time one of the editors of the renowned Russian review, *Sovremennye Zapiski* [*Annales Contemporaines*], to assume financial responsibility. Both these friends perished tragically in German concentration camps. They had been inspired by the conviction that books in Russian on the Fathers of the Church were badly needed, not only by theological students, but also by a much wider circle of those concerned with doctrinal and spiritual vistas and issues of Eastern Orthodox Tradition. Their expectation was fully justified: the volumes in Russian rapidly sold out and were warmly appreciated in the general press.

When I began teaching at the Paris Institute, as Professor of Patro - logy, I had to face a preliminary methodological problem. The question of the scope and manner of Patristic studies had been vigorously debated by scholars for a long time. (There is an excellent book by Fr. J. de Ghellinck, S.J., *Patristique et Moyen Age*, Volume II, 1947, pp. 1-180). The prevailing tendency was to treat Patrology as a history of Ancient Christian Literature, and the best modern manuals of Patrology in the West were written precisely in this manner: Bardenhewer, Cayré, Tixeront, Quasten, adherents to this school of thought, made only spor - adic reference to certain points of doctrine but their approach was no doubt legitimate and useful. However, another cognate discipline came into existence during the last century, *Dogmengeschichte*, or the school of the history of doctrine. Here scholars were concerned not so much with individual writers or thinkers but rather with what can be defined as the "internal dialectics" of the Christian "mind" and with types and trends of Christian thought.

In my opinion, these two approaches to the same material must be combined and correlated. I have tried to do precisely this with the re - vision of some of the material for the English publications. I have written some new material on the external history and especially on the ecumenical councils. But in essence Patrology must be more than a kind of literary history. It must be treated rather as a history of Christian doctrine, although the Fathers were first of all *testes veritatis,* witnesses of truth, of the faith. "Theology" is wider and more com - prehensive than "doctrine." It is a kind of Christian Philosophy. Indeed, there is an obvious analogy between the study of Patristics and the study of the history of Philosophy. Historians of Philosophy are as primarily concerned with individual thinkers as they are interested ultimately in the dialectics of ideas. The "essence" of philosophy is ex - hibited in particular systems. Unity of the historical process is assured because of the identity of themes and problems to which both phil - osophers and theologians are committed. I would not claim originality for my method, for it has been used occasionally by others. But I would underline the theological character of Patrology.

These books were written many years ago. At certain points they needed revision or extension. To some extent, this has been done. Re - cent decades have seen the rapid progress of Patristic studies in many directions. We now have better editions of primary sources than we had forty or even thirty years ago. We now have some new texts of prime importance; for example, the Chapters of Evagrius or the new Sermons of St. John Chrysostom. Many excellent monograph studies have been published in recent years. But in spite of this progress I do not think that these books, even without the revisions and additions, have been made obsolete. Based on an independent study of primary sources, these works may still be useful to both students and scholars.

GEORGES FLOROVSKY
SEPTEMBER, 1978

CHAPTER ONE

THE SOURCE OF BYZANTINE THEOLOGY

It is not at all easy to distinguish the borders between periods in the fluid and unbroken element of human life. Moreover, the incommensurability of successive historical cycles is quite manifestly revealed. New life themes come to light, new forces start to make themselves felt, new spiritual centers form. One's very first impression is that the late fourth century signifies some indisputable boundary in the history of the Church, in the history of Christian culture. One may conditionally define this boundary as the *beginning of Byzantinism.* The Nicene era closes the previous epoch and a new epoch begins, if not with Constantine (d. 337), then with Theodosius (emperor 379-395) in any case. It attains its zenith, its acme under Justinian (emperor 527-563). The failure of Julian the Apostate (332-363; emperor from 361 to 363) testifies to the decline of pagan Hellenism, but only its decline, not its eradication.

The epoch of Christian Hellenism has begun; it is a time when people try to construct Christian culture as a system. And in addition this is a time of painful and intense spiritual struggle. In the disputes and disquiet of earlier Byzantinism, it is not difficult to identify a common fundamental characteristic theme. This is the Christological theme, which is at the same time the theme of man. One can say that *what was really being discussed in these Christological disputes was the anthropological problem,* for it was a dispute over the Savior's humanity and over the sense of how the Only-Begotten Son and the Logos [or Word] receives human nature, and thus over the sense and limit of human life and activity. It is perhaps precisely for this reason that Christological disputes attained such exceptional poignancy and dragged on for three centuries. In them were revealed and laid bare a whole multitude of irreconcilable and mutually exclusive religious ideals. *These disputes ended with a great cultural and historical catas - trophe – the great defection of the East.* Almost all of the non-Greek East broke away, dropped out of the Church, and retired into heresy. If one accepts the late fourth century as a boundary, as the end of one epoch and the beginning of Byzantine theology proper, then more is involved, for Byzantine theology not only cannot be properly understood without understanding the theological controversies of the fourth century, without understanding the legacy of the fourth century. And more. The legacy which Byzantine theology was to inherit cannot be understood properly without an understanding of the entire legacy which it inherited. And here there is a special concern, for Byzantine theology – indeed Byzantium itself – has been understood but little in the West.

For several reasons Western Christianity somehow keeps pace, even if inadequately, with some of the Greek or "Byzantine" fathers of the fourth century – in a strictly historical sense Byzantine theology begins in 330, in that year in which the city of Byzantium was inaugurated, was christened Constantinople, the "New Rome." Those theologians writing in Greek after the year 330 can indeed be considered "Byzantine" theologians. But as the decades and centuries flow onward the Latin West appears incapable of keeping abreast with the vital work of Byzantine theologians. True, there is usually a small circle of persons in Rome who have contact with and some knowledge of Byzantine or Eastern theology but this circle is limited and their knowledge fragmented. It was a sore tragedy for the history of Christianity, for the life of the united Church, that this drift took place. There were certainly political and cultural reasons for the drift and often the blame can be placed on Byzantium. But in the realm of the Church, in the realm of theological thought, in the realm of vital issues concerning the essence of the faith such a drift should never have occurred. In modern terms one could say that Byzantium and Byzantine theology has had – and to a great extent still has – a "bad press" among Western Christians. And included in this "bad press" is not only an atmosphere of contempt for the Byzantine East but also a grave ignorance and lack of understanding. Byzantine theology was engaged in a struggle for the preservation of the truth – it was engaged in vital theological issues just as was St. Athanasius and as were the Cappadocian fathers in the fourth century. Western Christians kept abreast with the thought of St. Athanasius and the Cappadocians but, it must be regrettably acknowledged, that even that knowledge is not complete, that somehow ineluctably a curtain partially closes and prevents Western Christians from dealing with and understanding the totality of the thought of St. Athanasius and the Cappadocians.

Not only is a brief survey of the salient elements of fourth century Eastern theology necessary for a proper understanding of Byzantine theology but also necessary is an overview of certain patterns of thought in the earlier Patristic era. Moreover, it is almost scandalous that even a brief overview of Christological thought in the New Testament is a prerequisite for an understanding of Byzantine theology *precisely to demonstrate that Byzantine theology is organically related to the original deposit of the truth of the faith* , that Byzantine theology is, as it were, a Biblical theology and not a fabrication of sophistry, that Byzantine theology was dealing with burning issues of the Christian faith and of Christian life. The beginning of Byzantinism is not the beginning of a new Christianity. Rather it is the legitimate heir of the legacy of the New Testament, of early Christianity, of the Apostolic Fathers, of the Fathers of Church.

The Christological and Trinitarian definitions of the Council of Chalcedon – moreover, of all the definitions of the seven Ecumenical Councils – are not the result of philosophical intrusions into the

Biblical vision of God but rather – and precisely – the explication of what was originally revealed, of what was originally deposited, of what was experienced by the earliest Christians: that Jesus was the Christ, the Son of the Living God, that Jesus was both true God and true man, the God-Man, that God is God the Father, God the Son, and God the Holy Spirit.

The rationalism and, as it were, the arrogance of the eighteenth and nineteenth century scholars of the New Testament created more an exercise in eisegesis than exegesis of the New Testament. And this has made the understanding of Byzantine theology even more distant to Western Christians. If the Christ of the New Testament is one and the same with the Christ of Byzantine theology in its ultimate victory over heretical thought, and if the Christ of the New Testament has been misrepresented by schools of New Testament thought in the eighteenth and nineteenth century, some carrying over to the twentieth century, then the possibility of misunderstanding Byzantine theology is heightened, is increased. For this reason it is necessary to present textual material from the New Testament precisely as a legacy inherited by Byzantine theologians, a task that should not be necessary and that would not have been necessary in most periods of the history of Christianity. The twentieth century has witnessed to a great extent a reverse of this position – a considerable body of twentieth century scholarship on the New Testament has again discovered that the definitions of the Ecumenical Councils correspond to that truth present *ab initio*. There is no intention to present any comprehensive study of the New Testament. Moreover, there is no intention to present an exhaustive and comprehensive analysis of the Christology of the New Testament. Only some texts from various writers of the New Testament will be presented. These texts consist of those which are explicit and those in which many do not discern the Christological implications. It is merely a sampling, merely an overview to set the basis of the background, the core of the foundation in which and from which Byzantine theology worked. Moreover, it must not be forgotten that the Byzantine theologians were always conscience of being the heirs of the apostolic faith, heirs of the theology of the New Testament and the theology first delivered. They saw a continuous and cohesive link and bond between them and the earliest theology of the Church, between them and the Incarnation, Life, Death, Resurrection and Ascension of Jesus Christ, the eternal Only-Begotten Son of the Father. The very fact of the existence of the Christological controversies in Byzantium testifies that it was a vibrant and creative theological life rather than an ossified one. It is true that they also saw themselves as preservers of that faith once delivered but in the very process of preserving that original deposit they are of necessity creative.

CHAPTER TWO

THE LEGACY OF THE NEW TESTAMENT

THE WITNESS OF THE NEW TESTAMENT

The profound existential mystery of the earliest Christians has often been lost sight of – from the womb of Judaism, from a matrix of Hebraic thought whose most sacred principle was the oneness of God, a monotheism distinct from the pagan ethos of polytheism at that time – from this source of Hebraic monotheism came the Apostles. Yet they could not deny what they had witnessed: they had lived among Jesus and this Jesus was God yet not God the Father, this Jesus was man yet not merely a man. Chalcedonian Christology is present already with the Apostles. Indeed, for the Hebraic Peter, John, and Paul to write as they did about Jesus was blasphemy from the perspective of the strict monotheism of Judaism, from the sacred Hebraic principle of the transcendence of Yahweh.

And what did these sons of Judaism write about Jesus? It is sufficient to recall just a portion of what they wrote. In *Philippians* 2: 6-11 St. Paul writes: ὃς ἐν μορφῇ θεοῦ ὑπάρχων οὐχ ἁρπαγμὸν ἡγήσατο τὸ εἶναι ἴσα θεῷ ἀλλὰ ἑαυτὸν ἐκένωσεν μορφὴν δούλου λαβών, ἐν ὁμοιώματι ἀνθρώπων γενόμενος· καὶ σχήματι εὑρεθεὶς ὡς ἄνθρωπος ἐταπείνωσεν ἑαυτὸν γενόμενος ὑπήκοος μέχρι θανάτου, θανάτου δὲ σταυροῦ· διὸ καὶ ὁ θεὸς αὐτὸν ὑπερύψωσεν καὶ ἐχαρίσατο αὐτῷ τὸ ὄνομα τὸ ὑπὲρ πᾶν ὄνομα, ἵνα ἐν τῷ ὀνόματι Ἰησοῦ πᾶν γόνυ κάμψῃ ἐπουρανίων καὶ ἐπιγείων καὶ καταχθονίων, καὶ πᾶσα γλῶσσα ἐξομολογήσηται ὅτι κύριος Ἰησοῦς Χριστὸς εἰς δόξαν θεοῦ πατρός. ["Who, though he was in the form of God, did not count equality with God a thing to be grasped, but emptied himself, taking the form of a servant, being born in the likeness of men. And being found in human form he humbled himself and became obedient unto death, even death on a cross. Therefore God has highly exalted him and bestowed on him the name which is above every name, that at the name of Jesus every knee should bow, in heaven and on earth and under the earth, and every tongue confess that Jesus Christ is Lord, to the glory of God the Father"].

In *Colossians* 1:15ff. St. Paul writes that Jesus "ἐστιν εἰκὼν τοῦ θεοῦ τοῦ ἀοράτου, πρωτότοκος πάσης κτίσεως, ὅτι ἐν αὐτῷ ἐκτίσθη τὰ πάντα ἐν τοῖς οὐρανοῖς καὶ ἐπὶ τῆς γῆς, τὰ ὁρατὰ καὶ τὰ ἀόρατα, εἴτε θρόνοι εἴτε κυριότητες εἴτε ἀρχαὶ εἴτε ἐξουσίαι· τὰ πάντα δι' αὐτοῦ καὶ εἰς αὐτὸν ἔκτισται· καὶ αὐτός ἐστιν πρὸ πάντων καὶ τὰ πάντα ἐν αὐ - τῷ συνέστηκεν ." ["He is the image of the invisible God, the first-born of all creation; for in him all things were created, in heaven and on earth, visible and invisible, whether thrones or dominions or principalities or authorities – all things were created through him and for him. He is before all things, and in him all things hold together."].

This text, of course, will be used by the Arians but the point here is to present only some material from the New Testament expressions about Jesus to demonstrate that Patristic and Byzantine theology did not invent the teaching that Jesus was unique – truly God and truly man. In *Colossians* 2:9 St. Paul writes that ἐν αὐτῷ κατοικεῖ πᾶν τὸ πλήρωμα τῆς θεότητος σωματικῶς ["in him the whole fulness of the Godhead dwells bodily"]. In *II Corinthians* 4:4 St. Paul writes that Christ ἐστιν εἰκὼν τοῦ θεοῦ ["the image of God"]. In *I Corinthians* 8:6 St. Paul writes that ἀλλ᾿ ἡμῖν εἷς θεὸς ὁ πατήρ, ἐξ οὗ τὰ πάντα καὶ ἡμεῖς εἰς αὐτόν, καὶ εἷς κύριος Ἰησοῦς Χριστός, δι᾿ οὗ τὰ πάντα καὶ ἡμεῖς δι᾿ αὐτοῦ ["yet for us there is one God, the Father, from whom are all things and for whom we exist, and one Lord Jesus Christ, through whom are all things and through whom we exist."]. The author of *I Timothy* writes (3:16): καὶ ὁμολο-γουμένως μέγα ἐστὶν τὸ τῆς εὐσεβείας μυστήριον· ὃς ἐφανερώθη ἐν σαρκί. ["Great indeed, we confess, is the mystery of our religion: He was manifested in the flesh . . ."].

In *Hebrews* (1:2-3) there is explicit language: ὁ θεὸς . . . ἐπ᾿ ἐσχάτου τῶν ἡμερῶν τούτων ἐλάλησεν ἡμῖν ἐν υἱῷ, ὃν ἔθηκεν κληρονόμον πάντων, δι᾿ οὗ καὶ ἐποίησεν τοὺς αἰῶνας· ["God . . . who . . . in these last days has spoken to us by a Son, whom he appointed the heir of all things, through whom also he created the world."]; ὃς ὢν ἀπαύγασμα τῆς δόξης καὶ χαρακτὴρ τῆς ὑποστάσεως αὐτοῦ, φέρων τε τὰ πάντα τῷ ῥήματι τῆς δυνάμεως αὐτοῦ ["He reflects the glory of God and bears the very stamp of his *hypostasis*, upholding all things by his word of power."].

What is noteworthy about the epistles in the New Testament is that even without such explicit texts as those mentioned above the Divinity and Humanity of Christ are present. It comes through clearly in the very use of language, in the very names and titles given by the writers to Jesus Christ, in the very activity of Jesus Christ as Lord, as Redeemer, as the Risen One, as the Judge, as the Creator. It is not an exaggeration to say it is astonishing that any reader can fail to see the picture of Christ as it unfolds in the epistles of the New Testament. The same can be said about the Holy Spirit, for it is the description of the activity and interrelationship of the Spirit and Son with the Father that is impossible to hide.

The same applies to the Synoptic Gospels, although the form and presentation of the portrait of Jesus differs somewhat in each of the *Synoptics* and from the *Gospel of St. John* . The very beginning of the *Gospel of St. Mark* proclaims Jesus as the Christ; some manuscripts contain "the Son of God." The baptism of Jesus proclaims: "Thou art my beloved Son, in thee I was well pleased" – σὺ εἶ ὁ υἱός μου ὁ ἀγαπητός, ἐν σοὶ εὐδόκησα. Jesus is portrayed as having an author-ity – ὡς ἐξουσίαν ἔχων – hitherto not known, an authority of teaching which astounds the people – ἐξεπλήσσοντο ἐπὶ τῇ διδαχῇ αὐτοῦ. The demonic spirits recognize him: "I know who you are, the Holy One of God" – οἶδά σε τίς εἶ, ὁ ἅγιος τοῦ θεοῦ. An as-tonishing feature, one that almost passes us by, one that we pay little attention to, is the fact that Jesus forgives sin: "My son, your sins are forgiven" – τέκνον, ἀφίενταί σου αἱ ἁμαρτίαι. The spiritual, existential and ontological significance of this text resides in the question: who has the power to forgive the sins of another person, sins not even committed against the one forgiving? Yet there are two reactions to this, the same two reactions we find at many of the "hard sayings" of Jesus – one is that it is great blasphemy; the other is that it somehow belongs to the very character and nature of Jesus, and that leads to the inescapable conclusion that only God can forgive sins. Already, with the act of forgiving sins, we experience, are caught up in, the mystery of Jesus as God – "Why does this man speak thus? It is blasphemy! Who can forgive sins but God alone" (2:7). He completely violates the law of the Sabbath by healing on the Sabbath, exclaiming that "the Son of man is Lord even of the Sabbath." The implications are theologically significant. Here, as elsewhere, Jesus refers to himself as the "Son of man" and the "Lord," the implications of which, though perhaps lost on modern man, were not lost on those present. The titles "Son of man" and "Lord" had vast theological significance for the Jews. A relationship with God the Father is also expressed: "For whoever is ashamed of me and of my words . . . of him will the Son of man also be ashamed, when he comes in the glory of his Father with the holy angels" (8:38). The *Gospel of St. Mark* includes a description of the Transfiguration: "and he was transfigured before them, and his garments became glistening, intensely white, as no fuller on earth could bleach them." And the voice of God the Father is mentioned in this context: "This is my beloved Son" – οὗτός ἐστιν ὁ υἱός μου ὁ ἀγαπητός. Theologically significant is also the episode of the receiving children: "Whoever receives one such child in my name receives me; and whoever receives me, receives not me but him who sent me." By itself this text places one within the realm and atmosphere of the Councils of Nicaea and Chalcedon. Such texts tend to be overlooked Christologically because of the more explicit Christological texts elsewhere in the New Testament. There is a strong statement contained within Jesus' question to the man who called him "Good Teacher" – "Why do you call me good? No one is good but God alone" (10:18). This text does not disclaim Jesus' Divinity; rather, it affirms it in a most intriguing way. In this same *Gospel of St. Mark* Jesus says that "the Son of Man also came . . . to give his life as a ransom for many." Again he refers to himself by the theologically meaningful term of "Son of Man" and places the life of the "Son of Man" in a soteriological context. With all the references to his Divinity, Jesus responds to the question of which is the greatest commandment by reasserting the monotheism of

Judaism: "The first is, 'Hear, O Israel: The Lord our God, the Lord is one." The implication is interesting. The *Gospel of St. Mark* also includes words not uttered by a mere man: "Take, this is my body . . . This is my blood of the New Covenant, which is poured out for many." When asked by the High Priest if he is the Christ, the Son of the Blessed, Jesus answers with "I am" – ἐγώ εἰμι. In this same Gospel the centurion proclaims: "Truly this man was the Son of God." It is the *Gospel of St. Mark* that is usually singled out as the Gospel which lacks evidence of the Divinity of Christ, as the Gospel in which Jesus is portrayed as a man – indeed, to some, a great prophet and religious leader, but nevertheless not as God and man. But the totality of the textual evidence does not lead to that conclusion. The texts quoted above are but examples. It is not to be forgotten that in the *Gospel of St. Mark* the titles of "Son of Man," "Son of God," "Lord," and "Son of David" are used, the meaning of which was obvious for the Jews of that time.

In the *Gospel of St. Matthew* the baptism of Jesus contains the similar account as in the *Gospel of St. Mark*; that is, a voice from heaven identifies Jesus: "This is my beloved Son, in whom I was well pleased" – οὗτός ἐστιν ὁ υἱός μου ὁ ἀγαπητός, ἐν ᾧ εὐδόκησα (3:17). The description of the temptation of Jesus contains interesting elements. The devil addresses Jesus with "If you are the Son of God" – εἰ υἱὸς εἶ τοῦ θεοῦ (4.3,6). Jesus responds twice with "You shall not tempt the Lord your God" and "You shall worship the Lord your God." The text is, of course, open to more than one interpretation but the fact remains that one interpretation, consistent and contextual, is that Jesus refers to himself as the "Lord your God." One aspect of a text from the Beatitudes is striking (5:11): "Blessed are you when men reproach you and persecute and utter all kinds of evil against you falsely for my sake." The pivotal expression here is *for my sake* – ἕνεκεν ἐμοῦ. What person could have the virtue or power or capability of placing another into the category of "blessed" because the evil committed was "for his sake"? It is precisely outside the normal realm of moral and ethical values; it hinges precisely on the unique nature of this person. Hebrew Scripture had a sacred value for the Jews of that time – indeed as it still does. And yet Jesus, knowing that sacred value, speaks with such authority that he is able to reinterpret that Scripture in a rather scathing manner. Again and again Jesus exclaims: "You have heard it said . . . but I say to you." This by itself implies much. Another astonishing example is found in 7:21. In this text Jesus identifies himself as "Lord," asserts his power of judgment over the kingdom of heaven, and explicitly links his judgment with the will of his Father: "Not every one who says to me, 'Lord, Lord,' shall enter the kingdom of heaven, but he who does the will of my Father who is in heaven." In this Gospel, as in the *Gospel of St. Mark*, the demons know who he is" "What have you to do with us, O Son of God?" In this Gospel is also the striking act of forgiving the sins of others, sins which, were Jesus merely a man, would not be his prerogative to forgive, for they were not directed against him: "Take heart, my son; your sins are forgiven" (9:2). And the reaction? "This man is blaspheming." Had Jesus been a mere man, this accusation would have been accurate according to Hebraic law. In 11:27 we confront a text which is strikingly similar to the content of the *Gospel of St. John:* "All things have been delivered to me by my Father; and no one knows the Son except the Father, and no one knows the Father except the Son." An accusation brought against Jesus at his trial was what he had to say about the Temple, for the Temple was holy. In 12:6 Jesus says that "something greater than the Temple is here" and the reference is to himself. In 14:33 "those in the boat" proclaim: "Truly you are the Son of God." The *Gospel of St. Matthew* is often seen as the "Gospel of the Church" but the very reason for this is not merely the occurrence of the word ἐκκλησία (16:18; 18:17) but the very ecclesiology is founded upon Christology, upon the confession of St. Peter – σὺ εἶ ὁ χριστός ὁ υἱός τοῦ θεοῦ τοῦ ζῶντος ["You are the Christ, the Son of the Living God."]. It is only as a result of Peter's confession that Christ utters the famous Petrine statement – the foundation of the Church is an ontological impossibility without this Christological confession. As in the *Gospel of St. Mark*, so also here there is a description of the Transfiguration (17:2ff.): "And he was transfigured before them, and his face shone like the sun, and his garments became white as light . . . He was still speaking, when lo, a bright cloud overshadowed them, and a voice from the cloud said, 'This is my beloved Son, in whom I was well pleased'." A hint of Jesus' consubstantiality with both God and man is indicated in 18:5 in the text relating to children: "Whoever receives one such child in my name receives me." This text is impregnated with deep theological meaning. Another text which is more indicative but still not explicit, though its theological meaning is clear, is found in Jesus' discourse on "The Great Judgment" (25:31-46). Here Jesus clearly refers to himself as the "Son of Man" coming in glory. Here Jesus' consubstantiality with God the Father and with mankind is the overarching theme. "Come, O blessed of my Father, inherit the kingdom prepared for you from the foundation of the world; for I was hungry and you gave me food, I was thirsty and you gave me drink, I was a stranger and you welcomed me, I was naked and you clothed me, I was sick and you visited me, I was in prison and you came to me." In answering those perplexed because they had never done these things to or for Jesus, Jesus exclaims as "King": "Truly, I say to you, as you did it to one of the least of these my brethren, you did it to me." Judgment and entrance into the kingdom of heaven is predicated on the consubstantiality of Jesus with all humanity – to the "least of my brethren." They are "blessed of the Father" because the Son of the Father judges. Nicaea and Chalcedon are implicit even in such a seemingly remote text. In this Gospel also there is the description of the institution of the Eucharist (26:26 ff.): "Take, eat; this is my body.

. . Drink of it, all of you, for this is my blood of the New Covenant, which is poured out for the forgiveness of sins." Here the forgiveness of sins is not restricted to Jesus' forgiveness of one individual's sins but it is a universal, a cosmic forgiveness through his redemptive and life-giving death and resurrection. As the patristic writers point out again and again, no man is capable of such an ontological and existential redemptive activity – it is can only be accomplished by God. Caiaphas, the High Priest, says to Jesus at his trial: "I adjure you by the living God, tell us if you are the Christ, the Son of God." Skillfully, Jesus acknowledges it and adds: "But I tell you, hereafter you will see the Son of Man seated at the right hand of Power, and coming on the clouds of heaven." With this "confession" Caiaphas, tearing his clothes, exclaims: "He has uttered blasphemy. Why do we still need witnesses? You have heard his blasphemy" (26:63-65). And what is often forgotten is that Caiaphas was right, *if Jesus was not God*. The final command by Jesus in the *Gospel of St. Matthew* is explicitly Trinitarian: "All authority in heaven and on earth has been given to me. Go therefore and make disciples of all nations, baptizing them in the name of the Father and of the Son and of the Holy Spirit. . ."

Many of the texts presented above from the *Gospel of St. Mark* and the *Gospel of St. Matthew* are repeated in the *Gospel of St. Luke*. Approximately 350 of 661 verses are taken from the *Gospel of St. Mark*; approximately 325 verses come from the *Gospel of St. Matthew*. There is no need to repeat these texts. Approximately 548 of the 1149 verses in the *Gospel of St. Luke* are Lucan. In the Annun - ciation in the first chapter Jesus is called the "Son of the Most High," "holy," and "the Son of God." Simeon refers to Jesus as "salvation" (2:30). There are interesting implications in Jesus's statement that the "Son of Man is the Lord of the Sabbath" (6:5). There is an identity with the Father in 9:26 and 10:16. In 10:18 Jesus declares that he was present when Satan fell: "I saw Satan fall like lightning from heaven."

In the *Gospel of St. John* Christ is explicit about his relationship with God the Father. Even here, however, a "high Christology" exists even if the explicit statements were withdrawn, for again it is the activity of Jesus and the language used to describe this activity which leads to certain inescapable conclusions. But the explicit texts do exist. In the *Prologue* we read: ἐν ἀρχῇ ἦν ὁ λόγος, καὶ ὁ λόγος ἦν πρὸς τὸν θεόν, καὶ θεὸς ἦν ὁ λόγος· οὗ ἦν ἐν ἀρχῇ πρὸς τὸν θεόν· πάντα δι ' αὐτοῦ ἐγένετο, καὶ χωρὶς αὐτοῦ ἐγένετο οὐδὲ ἓν ὃ γέγονεν· ἐν αὐτῷ ζωὴ ἦν, καὶ ἡ ζωὴ ἦν τὸ φῶς τῶν ἀνθρώπων· καὶ τὸ φῶς ἐν τῇ σκοτίᾳ φαίνει, καὶ ἡ σκοτία αὐτὸ οὐ κατέλαβεν . . . ἦν τὸ φῶς τὸ ἀληθινόν, ὃ φωτίζει πάντα ἄνθρωπον, ἐρχόμενον εἰς τὸν κόσμον· ἐν τῷ κόσμῳ ἦν, καὶ ὁ κόσμος δι ' αὐτοῦ ἐγένετο, καὶ ὁ κόσμος αὐτὸν οὐκ ἔγνω· εἰς τὰ ἴδια ἦλθεν, καὶ οἱ ἴδιοι αὐτὸν οὐ παρέλαβον· . . . καὶ ὁ λόγος σὰρξ ἐγένετο καὶ ἐσκήνωσεν ἐν ἡμῖν, καὶ ἐθεασάμεθα τὴν δόξαν αὐτοῦ, δόξαν ὡς μονογενοῦς

παρά πατρός, πλήρης χάριτος καὶ ἀληθείας. English translations do not capture the dynamism of the Greek – especially of the
Greek verbal structures and of the dynamic inner relationship between
the Father and the Son expressed by the Greek πρὸς τὸν θεόν, the
dynamism of which the Old Slavonic preserved by translating πρὸς by
"к." ["In the beginning was the *Logos*, and the *Logos* was with God,
and the *Logos* was God. This one, the *Logos*, was in the beginning
with God. All things became through him, and without him not one
thing became which has become. In him was life, and the life was the
light of men. And the light shines in the darkness, and the darkness
overtook it not. . . He was the true light which enlightens every man
coming into the world. He was in the world and the world became
through him, and the world knew him not. He came to his own, and his
own people received him not. . . And the *Logos* became flesh and
dwelt among us, and we beheld his glory, the glory as of an Only-
Begotten from the Father, full of grace and of truth."]. In his *Prologue*
St. John mentions both the inner life and nature of God *ad se* and the
οἰκονομία of God's life *ad extra*, the *oikonomic* activity of God in
relation to the world.

In what can be considered the *Prologue* to *I John* we read something characteristic of that which is contained in the *Prologue* to the
Gospel of St. John – ὃ ἦν ἀπ ' ἀρχῆς, ὃ ἀκηκόαμεν, ὃ
ἑωράκαμεν τοῖς ὀφθαλμοῖς ἡμῶν, ὃ ἐθεασάμεθα καὶ αἱ
χεῖρες ἡμῶν ἐψηλάφησαν, περὶ τοῦ λόγου τῆς ζωῆς, καὶ ἡ
ζωὴ ἐφανερώθη, καὶ ἑωράκαμεν καὶ μαρτηροῦμεν καὶ
ἀπαγγέλλομεν ὑμῖν τὴν ζωὴν τὴν αἰώνιον, ἥτις ἦν πρὸς τὸν
πατέρα καὶ ἐφανερώθη ἡμῖν, ὃ ἑωράκαμεν καὶ ἀκηκόαμεν,
ἀπαγγέλλομεν καὶ ὑμῖν, ἵνα καὶ ὑμεῖς κοινωνίαν ἔχητε μεθ '
ἡμῶν· καὶ ἡ κοινωνία δὲ ἡ ἡμετέρα μετὰ τοῦ πατρὸς καὶ
μετὰ τοῦ υἱοῦ αὐτοῦ Ἰησοῦ Χριστοῦ. ["He who was from the beginning, whom we have heard, whom we have seen with our eyes,
whom we have looked upon and touched with our hands – concerning
the *Logos* of life. And the life was manifested, and we have seen and we
bear witness and we announce to you the life eternal, which was with
the Father and was manifested to us – Whom we have seen and we have
heard, we announce also to you in order that you also may have
fellowship with us. And indeed our fellowship is with the Father and
with his Son, Jesus Christ."]. In the same epistle of *I John* (2:23; 24)
the interrelationship and equality of the Father and the Son are linked:
πᾶς ὁ ἀρνούμενος τὸν υἱὸν οὐδὲ τὸν πατέρα ἔχει· ὁ
ὁμολογῶν τὸν υἱὸν καὶ τὸν πατέρα ἔχει· ὑμεῖς ὃ ἠκούσατε
ἀπ 'ἀρχῆς, ἐν ὑμῖν μενέτω· ἐὰν ἐν ὑμῖν μείνῃ ὃ ἀπ 'ἀρχῆς
ἠκούσατε, καὶ ὑμεῖς ἐν τῷ υἱῷ καὶ ἐν τῷ πατρὶ μενεῖτε.
["Everyone who is denying the Son, has neither the Father; he who is
confessing the Son has also the Father. Let remain in you what you
heard from the beginning. If what you heard from the beginning
remains in you, you will remain in the Son and in the Father." And

further in the same epistle (4:9) the thoughts of the *Gospel of St. John*
echo: ἐν τούτῳ ἐφανερώθη ἡ ἀγάπη τοῦ θεοῦ ἐν ἡμῖν, ὅτι τὸν
υἱὸν αὐτοῦ τὸν μονογενῆ ἀπέσταλκεν ὁ θεὸς εἰς τὸν κόσμον
ἵνα ζήσωμεν δι᾽ 'αὐτοῦ. ["By this the love of God was manifested
toward us because God has sent his Only-Begotten Son into the world
in order that we might live through him."].

The *Gospel of St. John* is replete with not only explicit statements
about the relationship of God the Father and God the Son but also with
those interesting formulations of language and usage that often reveal
more than the explicit texts. It is sufficient to recall the numerous ἐγώ
εἰμι/ἐγὼ εἰμί – "I am" – sayings: "I am the bread of life"; "I am the
living bread"; "I am from above"; "I am not of this world"; ". . . you
will know that I am"; "before Abraham became I am"; "I am the light
of the world"; "I am the door"; "I am the good shepherd"; "I am the Son
of God"; "I am the resurrection and the life"; "I am the way, the truth,
and the life"; "I am the true vine" – these "I am" sayings are striking.

Striking also are the "I" sayings, the sayings in the first person
singular, the "I/verb" sayings of Jesus. A few examples are enough – "I
will raise up [the Temple] in three days"; "I shall give water . . ·.
welling up into eternal life"; "I who speak to you am he [the
Messiah]"; "I have food to eat of which you know not"; "as I hear, I
judge"; "I do not receive glory from men"; "I have come in my Father's
name"; "I have come down from heaven"; "I will raise him up at the
last day"; "I shall give bread for the life of the world [and that bread] is
my flesh"; "I live because of the Father"; "I testify [of the world] that
its works are evil"; "I know him, for I have come from him"; "I shall
be with you a little longer, and then I go to him who sent me"; "I
know whence I have come and whither I am going"; "I alone do not
judge, but I and he who sent me"; "I bear witness to myself, and the
Father who sent me bears witness to me"; "You will die in your sins
unless you believe that I am he"; "I do nothing on my own authority
but speak thus as the Father taught me"; "I speak of what I have seen
with my Father"; "I came forth [ἐκ τοῦ θεοῦ ἐξῆλθον καὶ ἥκω] and
have come from God"; "I honor my Father, and you dishonor me"; "I do
not seek my own glory; there is One seeking and judging"; "I know the
Father"; "I lay down my life that I may take it again"; "I lay it down of
my own accord. I have authority to lay it down, and I have authority to
take it again; I have received this commandment from my Father"; "I
give [my sheep] eternal life"; "I said 'I am the Son of God' "; "I am in
the Father [and the Father is in me]"; "And I, if I am lifted up out of the
earth, will draw all men to myself"; "I have come as light into the
world, that everyone believing in me may not remain in darkness"; "I
came not that I might judge the world but that I might save the world;
he who is rejecting me and not receiving my words has the one judging
him – the word which I spoke, that will judge him in the last day"; "I
did not speak on my own authority but the Father who has sent me, he
has given me the commandment of what I may say and what I may

speak"; "Father, I desire that they also . . . may . . . behold my glory which thou hast given me in thy love for me before the foundation of the world" – ἣν δέδωκάς μοι ὅτι ἠγάπησάς με πρὸ καταβολῆς κόσμου; "I go to prepare a place for you"; "I will come again and will take you to myself"; "I am in the Father and the Father in me"; "I go to the Father"; "I will pray the Father, and he will give you another Counselor, that he may be with you forever, even the Spirit of Truth"; "I will not leave you desolate"; "because I live, you will live also"; "I am in my Father, and you in me, and I in you"; "I came from the Father and have come into the world"; "I am leaving the world and going to the Father"; "I am not alone, for the Father is with me"; "I have overcome the world."

Striking also are the "My/Mine" Sayings – "My hour has not yet come"; "My Father's house – you shall not make it a house of trade"; "My food is to do the work of him who sent me"; "My Father is working still, and I am working"; "he who is coming to me by no means hungers, and he who is believing in me by no means will ever thirst"; "My Father's will is that everyone seeing the Son and believing in him may have life eternal"; "he who is eating my flesh and drinking my blood has life eternal"; "My flesh is true food, and my blood is true drink"; "My teaching is not mine, but his who sent me"; "You know neither me nor my Father; if you knew me, you would know my Father also"; "My Father glorifies me, of whom you say that he is your God"; "My sheep hear my voice . . . my Father has given them to me"; "In my Father's house are many rooms"; "the Father dwells in me"; "he who loves me will be loved by my Father"; "My peace I give to you"; "My Father is the vinedresser"; "By this my Father is glorified, that you bear much fruit"; "My Father's commandments I have kept"; "He who hates me, hates my Father also"; "[The Spirit of truth] will glorify me, for he will take what is mine and declare it to you"; "All that the Father has is mine; . . . he will take what is mine and declare it to you"; "all mine are thine, and thine are mine"; "Thou, Father, art in me, and I in thee"; "My kingship is not of this world"; "I am ascending to my Father."

It is difficult to imagine anything more explicit than what Jesus says in the following texts. In the *Gospel of St. John* (10:30) he declares that ἐγὼ καὶ ὁ πατὴρ ἕν ἐσμεν – "I and the Father – we are one." The response in verse 33 is clear: ἀπεκρίθησαν αὐτῷ οἱ Ἰουδαῖοι· περὶ καλοῦ ἔργου οὐ λιθάζομέν σε ἀλλὰ περὶ βλασφημίας, καὶ ὅτι σὺ ἄνθρωπος ὢν ποιεῖς σεαυτὸν θεόν – "The Jews answered him: we do not stone you because of a good work but because of blasphemy; because you, being a man, make yourself God." The oneness with the Father is explicitly stated again in 17:11: ἵνα ὦσιν ἓν καθὼς ἡμεῖς – "that they may be one, even as we are one." The thought continues in 17:21: ἵνα πάντες ἓν ὦσιν, καθὼς σύ, πατήρ, ἐν ἐμοὶ κἀγὼ ἐν σοί, ἵνα καὶ αὐτοὶ ἐν ἡμῖν ὦσιν, ἵνα ὁ κόσμος πιστεύῃ ὅτι σύ με ἀπέστειλας – "that they may all be one, even as thou, Father, art in me, and I in thee, that they also may be in us, so that the world may believe that thou has sent me." In 5:18 we read: διὰ τοῦτο οὖν μᾶλλον ἐζήτουν αὐτὸν οἱ Ἰουδαῖοι ἀποκτεῖναι, ὅτι οὐ μόνον ἔλυεν τὸ σάββατον, ἀλλὰ καὶ πατέρα ἴδιον ἔλεγεν τὸν θεόν, ἴσον ἑαυτὸν ποιῶν τῷ θεῷ – "This was why the Jews sought all the more to kill him, because he not only broke the Sabbath but also called God his Father, making himself equal with God." In 17:5 Jesus refers to his existence with the Father before the creation of the world: καὶ νῦν δόξασόν με σύ, πάτερ, παρὰ σεαυτῷ τῇ δόξῃ ᾗ εἶχον πρὸ τοῦ τὸ κόσμον εἶναι παρὰ σοί – "and now, Father, glorify thou me with thyself with the glory which I had with thee before the world was."

The personhood of the Holy Spirit is present also throughout the New Testament. It is enough to recall the texts of "the sin against the Holy Spirit," the command to "baptize in the name of the Father, the Son, and the Holy Spirit," the "breathing of the Holy Spirit upon the Apostles," the descent of the Holy Spirit at Pentecost, the conception of Jesus by the power of the Holy Spirit. The nature and work of the Holy Spirit in the theology of St. Paul is indeed extraordinarily deep and rich. It is enough to recall what Christ says of the Holy Spirit. In the *Gospel of St. John* (16:13 ff.) we read: ὅταν δὲ ἔλθῃ ἐκεῖνος, τὸ πνεῦμα τῆς ἀληθείας, ὁδηγήσει ὑμᾶς εἰς τὴν ἀλήθειαν πᾶσαν· οὐ γὰρ λαλήσει ἀφ᾽ ἑαυτοῦ, ἀλλ᾽ ὅσα ἀκούει λαλή – σει, καὶ τὰ ἐρχόμενα ἀναγγελεῖ ὑμῖν. ἐκεῖνος ἐμὲ δοξάσει, ὅτι ἐκ τοῦ ἐμοῦ λήμψεται καὶ ἀναγγελεῖ ὑμῖν. πάντα ὅσα ἔχει ὁ πατὴρ ἐμά ἐστιν· διὰ τοῦτο εἶπον ὅτι ἐκ τοῦ ἐμοῦ λαμβάνει καὶ ἀναγγελεῖ ὑμῖν. – "When the Spirit of truth comes, he will guide you into all the truth; for he will not speak on his own authority, but whatever he hears he will speak, and he will declare to you the things that are to come. He will glorify me, for he will take what is mine and declare it to you. All that the Father has is mine; therefore I said that he will take what is mine and declare it to you." In 15:26 the inner nature of the Holy Trinity is glimpsed: ὅταν ἔλθῃ ὁ παράκλητος ὃν ἐγὼ πέμψω ὑμῖν παρὰ τοῦ πατρός, τὸ πνεῦμα τῆς ἀληθείας ὃ παρὰ τοῦ πατρὸς ἐκπορεύεται, ἐκεῖνος μαρ- τυρήσει περὶ ἐμοῦ. – "But when the Counselor comes, whom I shall send to you from the Father, *who proceeds from the Father*, he will bear witness to me." And in 14:26 the Holy Spirit teaches and evokes memory: ὁ δὲ παράκλητος, τὸ πνεῦμα τὸ ἅγιον ὃ πέμψει ὁ πατὴρ ἐν τῷ ὀνόματί μου, ἐκεῖνος ὑμᾶς διδάξει πάντα καὶ ὑπομνήσει ὑμᾶς πάντα ἃ εἶπον ὑμῖν ἐγώ. – "But the Counselor, the Holy Spirit, whom the Father will send in my name, he will teach you all things, and bring to your remembrance all that I have said to you."

This brief overview presents Jesus in the fulness of his Divinity. We have – for the purpose at hand – deliberately excluded texts dealing with Messianic prophecies, for the Messiah in Hebraic thought was not necessarily God; excluded also are the numerous miracles because the performance of a miracle does not necessitate the Divinity of the performer. The vast and rich body of material from the parables were of necessity excluded. And further, it was not considered necessary to demonstrate the humanity of Jesus. It is however noteworthy that St. John is very careful to demonstrate both the Humanity and Divinity of Jesus Christ – that is precisely why he emphasizes the flow of water and blood at the crucifixion. Already in the time of the composition of the *Gospel of St. John* there were doubters of both the Humanity and the Divinity of Jesus.

Such, however, is the glimpse we gather from a brief presentation of Jesus in the New Testament. This view of Jesus is the same as that of Byzantine theology – it is the same as that of the Council of Nicaea, the same as the Council of Chalcedon. The link is organic and the Byzantine theologians are exceedingly, yet naturally, aware of their inner, organic link with apostolic Christianity, with the very earliest of Christian thought.

THE SOURCE OF THE NEW TESTAMENT

Thus far concentration has been on the New Testament's image of Jesus but there is something which precedes, something the reality of which is the foundation of the Church: there were no New Testamental writings for the earliest Christians and yet they possessed the fulness of the truth and faith of Christianity. On the day of Pentecost the Church was born and yet there was no New Testament in a written form. For decades there were no Gospels as we know them today. It would not be a theological exaggeration to assert that the Church would be the Church in her fulness even if it did not possess the New Testament. For many raised on the Reformational principal of *sola scriptura* this may seem a radical – even heretical – statement. But the fact is that we do possess the New Testament and, as such, it is a part of the sacred history of Christianity. But there was a time when the Church did not possess this corpus of inspired writing and yet the Church existed in her fulness, Christians experienced the truth of the faith in all its fulness. The historical fact, the historical reality is that the Church existed before anything was written, that the Church preceded the existence of the New Testament, that it was the Church precisely which gave birth to the New Testament and it was the Church out of which the New Testamental writings emerged and the Church which determined ultimately which of these writings would be accepted as canonical. The authority of the writing and the authority of acceptance was the Church. Christian faith is centered on Christ. The mystery of God become man is the holy truth of the Church. Christianity is Christ – our entire religion stands or falls with belief in Christ. The sermons of Christ and those of the first apostles were the living "word" which first planted the seed of faith – long before a Christian literature existed. Hence, this literature did not produce faith but was the product of faith. As Karl Adam has correctly observed: "It is missionary literature. And thus the most superior source of Christianity is not the word of the Bible, but the living word of the Church's proclamation of faith. Even if the Bible did not exist, a Christian religious movement would be conceivable." But without the firm support of the written documents, of the New Testament, the faith would constantly be in danger of obscuring the abundance of concrete detail "in the unique and mighty experience of Christ." But the Church would have been capable of conveying the faith to us even without the written documents, as it did in the beginning. St. Paul writes in *I Corinthians* 11:23: ἐγὼ γὰρ παρέλαβον ἀπὸ τοῦ κυρίου, ὃ καὶ παρέδωκα ὑμῖν – "For I received from the Lord what I also delivered to you "

The historical reality is the fact that God through the Church provided us with the New Testament and hence there is an obvious and sacred purpose in that gift. The New Testament is the revelation of and about God. But, at the same time, revelation is always a Word addressed to man, a summons and an appeal to man. The highest objectivity in the hearing and understanding of Scripture is achieved through the greatest exertion of the creative personality, through spiritual growth, through the transfiguration of the personality, which overcomes in itself "the wisdom of the flesh," ascending to "the measure of the stature of the fulness of Christ" – εἰς μέτρον ἡλικίας τοῦ πληρώ- ματος τοῦ Χριστοῦ [*Ephesians* 4:13]. From man it is not self-abnegation which is demanded but a victorious forward movement, not self-destruction but a rebirth or transformation. Without man Revelation would be impossible – because no one would be there to hear and God would then not speak. And God created man so that man would hear his words, receive them, and grow in them and through them become a participator of "eternal life." "And the Logos became flesh and dwelt among us . . . and we have beheld his glory, glory as of the only Son from the Father, full of grace and truth" [*John* 1:14]. The way of life and light is open. And the human spirit has anew become capable of hearing God completely and of receiving his words.

REVELATION AND THE LANGUAGE OF DOGMA

The unalterable truths of experience can be expressed in different ways. Divine reality can be described in images and parables, in the language of devotional poetry and of religious art – the Church preaches this way even now in her liturgical hymns and in the symbolism of her sacramental acts. That is the language of proclamation, the language of prayer and of mystical experience, the language of *kerygmatic* theology. But there is another language, the language of comprehending thought, the language of dogma. Dogma is a witness of experience. The entire pathos of dogma lies in the fact that it points to Divine Reality – in this the witness of dogma is symbolic. Dogma is the testimony of thought about what has been seen and revealed, about what has been contemplated in the experience of faith – and this testimony is expressed in concepts and definitions. Dogma is an "intellectual vision," a truth of perception. One can say that it is the logical image, a "logical ikon" of Divine Reality. And at the same time a dogma is a definition – that is why its logical form is so important for dogma, that "inner word" which acquires force in its external expression. This is why the external aspect of dogma – its wording – is so essential.

Dogma is by no means a new Revelation. Dogma is only a witness. The whole meaning of dogmatic definition consists of testifying to unchanging truth, truth which was revealed and has been preserved from the beginning. Thus it is a total misunderstanding to speak of the "development of dogma." Dogmas do not develop; they are unchanging and inviolable, even in their external aspect – their wording. Least of all is it possible to change dogmatic language or terminology. As strange as it may appear, one can indeed say: dogmas arise, dogmas are established, but they do *not develop*. And once established, a dogma is perennial and already an immutable "rule of faith" – ὁ κανὼν τῆς πίστεως. Dogma is an intuitive truth, not a discursive axiom which is accessible to logical development. The whole meaning of dogma lies in the fact that it is *expressed* truth. Revelation *discloses itself* and is received in the silence of faith, in silent vision – this is the first and apophatic step of the knowledge of God. The entire fulness of truth is already contained in this apophatic vision, but truth *must be expressed*. Man, however, is called not only to be silent but also to speak, to communicate. The *silentium mysticum* does not exhaust the entire fulness of the religious vocation of man. There is also room for the expression of praise. In her dogmatic confession the Church expresses herself and proclaims the apophatic truth which she preserves. The quest for dogmatic definitions is therefore, above all, a quest for terms. Precisely because of this the doctrinal controversies will be a dispute over terms. One will have to find accurate and clear words to describe and express the experience of the Church.

This is necessary because *the truth of faith* is also the truth *for* reason and *for* thought – this does not mean, however, that it is the truth of thought, the truth of pure reason. The truth of faith is fact, reality – *that which is*. In this "quest for words" human thought changes, the essence of thought itself is transformed and sanctified. The Church indirectly testifies to this in rejecting the heresy of Apollinarius. Apollinarianism is, in its deepest sense, a false anthropology, it is a false teaching about man and therefore it is also a false teaching about the God-Man Christ. Apollinarianism is the negation of human reason, the fear of thought – "it is impossible that there be no sin in human thoughts" – ἀδύνατον δέ ἐστιν ἐν λογισμοῖς ἀνθρωπίνοις ἁμαρτίαν μὴ εἶναι – St. Gregory of Nyssa, *Contra Apollinarium* II, 6, 8; I, 2]. And that means that human reason is incurable – ἀθεράπευτόν ἐστι – that is, it must be cut off. The rejection of Apollinarianism meant therefore the fundamental jus - tification of reason and thought. Not in the sense, of course, that "natural reason" is sinless and right by itself but in the sense that it is open to transformation, that it can be healed, that it can be renewed. And not only can but also must be healed and renewed. Reason is summoned to the knowledge of God. The "philosophizing" about God is not just a feature of inquisitiveness or a kind of audacious curiosity. On the contrary, it is the fulfillment of man's religious calling and duty. Not an extra-achievement, not a kind of *opus supererogatorium* – but a necessary and organic moment of religious behavior. And for this reason the Church "philosophized" about God – "formulated dogmas which fishermen had earlier expounded in simple words" [from the service in honor of the Three Hierarchs]. The "dogmas of the Fathers" present again the unchanging content of "apostolic preaching" in intellectual categories. The experience of truth does not change and does not even grow; indeed, thought penetrates into the "understanding of truth" and transforms itself through the process.

In establishing dogmas the Church expressed Revelation in the language of Greek philosophy – or, if preferable, the Church translated Revelation from the poetic and prophetic language of Hebrew into Greek. That meant, in a certain sense, a "Hellenization" of Revelation. But in reality it was a "Churchification" of Hellenism This theme has been discussed and disputed too much and too often. Here it is essential to raise only one issue. The Old Covenant has passed. Israel did not accept the Divine Christ, did not recognize him or confess Him and "the promise" passed to the Gentiles. We must acknowledge this basic fact of Christian history in humility before the will of God. The "calling of the Gentiles" meant that Hellenism became blessed by God. In this there was no "historical accident" – no such accident could lie therein. In the religious destiny of man there are no "accidents." The fact remains that the Gospel is given to us all and for all time in the Greek language. It is in this language that we hear the Gospel in all its entirety and fulness. That does *not* and cannot, of course, mean that it is untranslatable – but we always translate it from the Greek. And there was precisely as little "chance" or "accident" in this "selection" of the Greek language – as the unchanging proto-language of the Christian Gospel – as there was in God's "selection" of the Jewish people – out of all the people of antiquity – as "His" People. There was as little "accident" in the "selection" of the Greek language as there was in the fact that "salvation comes from the Jews" [*John* 4:22].

We receive the Revelation of God as it occurred. And it would be pointless to ask whether it could have been otherwise. In the selection of the "Hellenes" we must acknowledge the hidden decisions of God's will. The presentation of Revelation in the language of historical Hellenism in no way restricts Revelation. It rather proves precisely the opposite – that this language possessed certain powers and resources which aided in expounding and expressing the truth of Revelation.

The words of dogmatic definitions are not "simple words," they are not "accidental" words which one can replace by other words. They are eternal words, incapable of being replaced. This means that certain words – certain concepts – are eternalized by the very fact that they express divine truth. But this does not mean that there is an "eternalization" of one specific philosophical "system." To state it more correctly – Christian dogmatics itself is the only true philosophical "system." Dogmas are expressed in philosophical language but not at all in the language of a specific philosophical school. One can, indeed, speak of a philosophical "eclecticism" of Christian dogmatics. And this "eclecticism" has a much deeper meaning than one usually assumes. Its entire meaning consists of the fact that particular themes of Hellenic philosophy are received and, through this reception, they change essentially – they change and are no longer recognizable because now, in the terminology of Greek philosophy, a new, a totally new experience is expressed. Although themes and motives of Greek thought are retained, the answers to the problems are quite different, for they are given out of a new experience. Hellenism, for this reason, received Christianity as something foreign and alien, and the Christian Gospel was "foolishness" to the Greeks – ἔθνεσιν δὲ μωρίαν [*I Corinthians* 1:23].

Usually we do not sufficiently perceive the entire significance of this transformation which Christianity introduced into the realm of thought. This is so, partially because we too often remain ancient Greeks philosophically, not yet having experienced the baptism of thought by fire. And in part, on the contrary, because we are too accustomed to the new world-view, retaining it as an "innate truth" when, in actuality, it was given to us only through Revelation. It is sufficient to point out just a few examples: the idea of the createdness of the world, not only in its transitory and perishable aspect but also in its primordial principles. For Greek thought the concept of "created ideas" was impossible and offensive. And bound up with this was the Christian intuition of history as a unique – once-occurring – creative fulfillment, the sense of a movement from an actual "beginning" up to a final end, a feeling for history which in no way at all allows itself to be linked with the static pathos of ancient Greek thought. And the understanding of man as person, the concept of personality, was entirely inaccessible to Hellenism which considered only the mask as person. And finally there is the message of Resurrection in glorified but real flesh, a thought which could only frighten the Greeks who lived in the hope of a future dematerialization of the spirit. These are just some of the new vistas disclosed in the new experience of Christianity. Hellenism, forged in the fire of a new experience and a new faith, is renewed, is transformed. These are the presuppositions and categories of a new Christian philosophy, a new philosophy enclosed in Church dogmatics.

Revelation is not only Revelation about God but also about the world, for the fulness of Revelation is in the image of the God-Man, in the fact of the ineffable union of God and Man, of the Divine and human, of the Creator and the creature – in the indivisible and unmerged union of God and Man in Jesus Christ.

The path to Chalcedon is present in the New Testament. It is precisely the Chalcedonian dogma of the unity of the God-Man – *despite what we shall see as great imprecision in the language of the councils and in the language of the "Fathers"* – which is the true, decisive point of Revelation, of the experience of faith and of Christian vision. Modern man is in general very critical of the definition of the Council of Chalcedon. It fails to convey any meaning to him. The "imagery" of the creed is for him nothing more than a piece of poetry, if anything at all. The whole approach, I think, is wrong. The "definition" of Chalcedon is a statement of faith and therefore cannot be understood when taken out of the total experience of the Church. It is precisely for that reason that I have included an overview of the statements about Christology in the New Testament and it is precisely for that reason that an overview of the Christological thought of the early centuries must be presented as a background not only for Chalcedon but for the whole of Byzantine theology.

The definition of the Council of Chalcedon is, in fact, an "existential statement." It is, as it were, an intellectual contour of the mystery which is apprehended by faith. Our Redeemer is *not* a man, but God *himself*. Here lies the existential emphasis of the definition of Chalcedon and of the work of Byzantine theology accepted by the Church. Our Redeemer is one who "came down" and who, by "be - coming man," identified himself with men in the fellowship of a truly human life and nature. Not only was the initiative Divine but the "captain of our salvation" was a Divine Person. The fulness of the human nature of Christ means, as we shall see, precisely the adequacy and truth of this redeeming identification. God enters human history and becomes an historical person. This sounds paradoxical. Indeed, there is a mystery. But this mystery is a revelation – the true character of God is disclosed in the Incarnation. God was so much and so intimately concerned with he destiny of man – and precisely with the destiny of every one of "the little ones" – as to intervene *in person* in the chaos and misery of the lost life. God is therefore not merely an omnipotent ruling of the universe from an august distance by divine majesty. Rather, there is the Divine *kenosis*, a "self-humiliation" of the God of glory. There is a *personal* relationship between God and Man.

There is an amazing coherence in the body of the traditional doctrine of Christ – from the earliest Christians to the New Testament to the Councils and to the positive contributions of Byzantine theology. True, the definitions of the Council of Nicaea and the Council of Chalcedon will cause a sore disruption in the Church, for not only is truth preserved and defined but also there is *an imprecision in the human language* used by the councils, an imprecision that gravely wounded the body of the Church. But the truth was there, the truth was defined. It can be apprehended and understood only in the living context of faith, by a personal communion with the personal God. Faith alone makes formulas convincing; faith alone makes formulas live, for Christ is not a text but a living Person and He abides in his body, the Church.

It may seem ridiculous to modern man to suggest that we should accept and preach the doctrine of Chalcedon "in a time such as this." Yet it is precisely this doctrine, already contained on the pages of the New Testament, that can change the whole spiritual outlook of modern man, that reality to which this doctrine bears witness. It brings man a true freedom. The Christological disputes of the past are unfortunately continued and repeated in the controversies of our own age. Modern man, deliberately or subconsciously, is tempted by the Nestorian extreme – modern man does not take the Incarnation in earnest, he does not dare to believe that Christ is a Divine Person, he wants to have a human redeemer, one assisted by God. Modern man is more interested in the human psychology of the Redeemer than in the mystery of Divine love precisely because, in the last resort, he believes optimistically in the dignity of man.

On the other extreme we have in our age a revival of "Monophysite" tendencies in theology and religion – man is reduced to complete passivity and is allowed only to listen and to hope. The present tension between "liberalism" and "neo-orthodoxy" is in fact a reenactment of the old Christological struggle, albeit on a new existential level and in a new spiritual guise. Unless a wider vision is acquired the conflict will never be settled or solved. In the early Church the preaching was emphatically theological. The New Testament itself is a theological book. Neglect of theology, of the theology of the God-Man, is responsible both for the decay of personal religion and for that sense of frustration which dominates the modern mood. The whole appeal of the "rival gospels" in our time is that they offer some sort of pseudo-theology, a system of pseudo-dogmas. They are gladly accepted by those who cannot find any theology in the reduced Christianity of "modern" style, by those who have been cut off from the organic Christology of the New Testament, of the definitions of the Councils, and of the work of the Eastern and Byzantine Fathers.

I have often a strange feeling. When I read the ancient classics of Christian theology, the fathers of the Church, I find them more relevant to the troubles and problems of my own time than the production of modern theologians. The fathers were wrestling with existential problems, with those revelations of the eternal issues which were described and recorded in Holy Scripture. It is precisely the Chalcedonian dogma of the unity of the God-Man which is the true, decisive point of Revelation, of the experience of faith, and of the Christian vision.

A clear knowledge of God – that for which Byzantine theology was striving and striving to protect – is impossible for man, if he is committed to vague and false conceptions of the world and of himself. That is precisely why St. Athanasius' distinction between *creation* and *generation* is so important as a prelude to, as a background for, as a legacy received by Byzantine theology. There is nothing surprising about a false conception of the world leading to an unclear knowledge of God, for the world is the creation of God and therefore, if one has a false understanding of the world, one attributes to God a work which God did not create – one therefore casts a distorted judgment on God's activity and will. In this respect a true philosophy is necessary for faith. And, on the other hand, faith is committed to specific metaphysical presuppositions. Dogmatic theology, as the explanation of Divinely revealed truth in the realm of thought, is precisely the basis of a Christian philosophy, of a sacred philosophy, of a philosophy of the Holy Spirit.

Dogma, a word disliked by modern man, presupposes experience, and only in the experience of vision and faith does dogma reach its fulness and come to life. And dogmas do not exhaust this experience, just as Revelation is not exhausted in "words" or in the "letter" of Scripture. The experience and knowledge of the Church are more comprehensive and fuller than her dogmatic pronouncement. The Church witnesses to many things which are not in "dogmatic" statements but rather in images and symbols. Dogmatic theology can neither dismiss nor replace "*kerygmatic*" theology. In the Church the fulness of knowledge and understanding is given but this fulness is only gradually and partially disclosed and professed. In general, the knowledge in this world is always only a "partial" knowledge, and the fulness will be revealed only in the *Parousia* – ἄρτι γινώσκω ἐκ μέρους ["Now I know in part" (*I Corinthians* 13:12)]. This "incompleteness" of knowledge results from the fact that the Church is still "in pilgrimage," still in the process of "pilgrimage." The Church witnesses to the mystical essence of time in which the growth of mankind is being accomplished according to the measure of the image of Christ. Nevertheless, this "incompleteness" of our knowledge here and now does not weaken the authentic and apodictic character of the Church. The definition of Chalcedon is precisely a definition of that truth which we do here and now possess. Without the definitions of the Ecumenical Councils, always following the fathers and Holy Scripture, that truth which was revealed in the God-Man, Jesus Christ, would be distorted, would threaten our redemption, indeed, would strike at the very core and heart of the ontological reality of redemption. These definitions are a vital part of that truth which we do possess and Byzantine theology's contribution to the definitions and to the elucidation of the definitions of the truth of the God-Man is vital to the life of the Christian faith.

CHAPTER THREE

PRESERVATION OF THE LEGACY

If the teaching about Christ in the New Testament is so clear, a fundamental question arises. Why all the historical struggle over Christology? Why the divisions, why the disruptions, why the apparent damage to the Body of Christ, the Church? Why such controversy over that which was the cornerstone of our very redemption? It is a legitimate question. It must never be forgotten that we are warned again and again in the New Testament to guard the faith, to beware of false teachers, to hold fast to that which we have received. It is a constant theme expressed in a variety of ways throughout the New Testament. *II Timothy* 4:3-4 warns that "the time is coming when people will not endure sound teaching, but having itching ears they will accumulate for themselves teachers to suit their own likings, and will turn away from listening to the truth and wander into myths" – ἔσται γὰρ καιρὸς ὅτε τῆς ὑγιαινούσης διδασκαλίας οὐκ ἀνέξονται, ἀλλὰ κατὰ τὰς ἰδίας ἐπιθυμίας ἑαυτοῖς ἐπισωρεύσουσιν διδασκάλους κνηθόμενοι τὴν ἀκοήν, καὶ ἀπὸ μὲν τῆς ἀληθείας τῆς ἀκοὴν ἀποστρέψουσιν, ἐπὶ δὲ τοὺς μύθους ἐκτραπήσονται. *Colossians* 2:8 warns: "See to it that no one makes a prey of you by philosophy and empty deceit, according to human tradition, according to the elemental spirits of the universe, and not according to Christ" – βλέπετε μὴ τις ὑμᾶς ἔσται ὁ συλαγωγῶν διὰ τῆς φιλοσοφίας καὶ κενῆς ἀπάτης κατὰ τὴν παράδοσιν τῶν ἀνθρώπων, κατὰ τὰ στοιχεῖα τοῦ κόσμου καὶ οὐ κατὰ Χριστόν. In *I Timothy* 1: 3-4; 6-7 we read: "that you may charge certain persons not to teach any different doctrine, nor to occupy themselves with myths and endless genealogies which promote speculations rather than the divine training that is in faith . . . certain persons by swerving from these have wandered away into vain discussion, desiring to be teachers of the law, without understanding either what they are saying or the things about which they make assertions" – ἵνα παραγγείλῃς τισὶν μὴ ἑτερο - διδασκαλεῖν μηδὲ προσέχειν μύθοις καὶ γενεαλογίαις ἀπε - ράντοις, αἵτινες ἐκζητήσεις παρέχουσιν μᾶλλον ἢ οἰκονομίαν θεοῦ τὴν ἐν πίστει· ὧν τινες ἀστοχήσαντες ἐξετράπησαν εἰς ματαιολογίαν, θέλοντες εἶναι νομοδιδάσ - καλοι, μὴ νοοῦντες μήτε ἃ λέγουσιν μήτε περὶ τίνων διαβε - βαιοῦνται. In *I Timothy* 6: 3 ff. we read: "If any one teaches otherwise and does not agree with the sound words of our Lord Jesus Christ and the teaching which accords with godliness, he is puffed up with conceit, he knows nothing; he has a morbid craving for controversy and for disputes about words . . ." – εἴ τις ἑτεροδιδασκαλεῖ καὶ μὴ προσέρχεται ὑγιαίνουσιν λόγοις τοῖς τοῦ κυρίου ἡμῶν Ἰησοῦ Χριστοῦ, καὶ τῇ κατ᾽ εὐσέβειαν διδασκαλίᾳ, τετύφωται, μηδὲν ἐπιστάμενος, ἀλλὰ νοσῶν περὶ ζητήσεις καὶ λογομαχίας. In

the same chapter (20) Timothy is exhorted: "O Timothy, guard what
has been entrusted to you. Avoid the godless chatter and contradictions
of what is falsely called knowledge, for by professing it some have
missed the mark as regards the faith" – ὦ Τιμόθεε, τὴν παραθήκην
φύλαξον, ἐκτρεπόμενος τὰς βεβήλους κενοφωνίας καὶ ἀντι -
θέσεις τῆς ψευδωνύμου γνώσεως, ἥν τινες ἐπαγγελλόμενοι
περὶ τὴν πίστιν ἠστόχησαν. In *II Peter* 2:1 ff. we read: "there will
be false teachers among you, who will secretly bring in destructive
heresies, even denying the Master" – ἐν ὑμῖν ἔσονται ψευδοδι -
δάσκαλοι, οἵτινες παρεισάξουσιν αἱρέσεις ἀπωλείας, καὶ . . .
δεσπότην ἀρνούμενοι. Similar warnings occur in the epistles and the
Gospels of the New Testament. It is clear that already in the earliest
days of the Christian Church there were divisions, that the truth had to
be preserved and guarded from the very beginning.

Christ encourages his disciples that the Holy Spirit will guide
them into all truth – ὁδηγήσει ὑμᾶς εἰς τὴν ἀλήθειαν (*John* 16:
13), and the implication is that, though truth is present, though truth
has been revealed and given, "all" aspects of truth will be explicated
under the guidance of the Holy Spirit in the Church.

And the very created nature of man allows for the possibility of
corrupting that which has been revealed. But the promise that the truth
shall be preserved by the Holy Spirit reveals that, despite controversy
and dispute already present within the early life of the Church,
theological work is still to be active in the ongoing life of the Church
– the explication and definition of the redemptive activity of the God-
Man.

The Church is "Apostolic" indeed. But the Church is also
"Patristic." She is intrinsically "the Church of the Fathers." There are,
as it were, two basic stages in the proclamation of the Christian faith.
"Our simple faith had to acquire composition." There was an inner urge,
an inner logic, an internal necessity, in this transition from *kerygma* to
dogma. Indeed, the teaching of the Fathers and the dogma of the Church
are still the same "simple message" which has been once delivered and
deposited, once for ever. But now it is, as it were, necessary for this
"simple message" to be properly and fully articulated.

The main distinctive mark of Patristic and Byzantine theology is
its "existential" character, if we may borrow this current neologism.
The Fathers theologized, as St. Gregory of Nazianzus puts it, "in the
manner of the Apostles, not in that of Aristotle" – ἀλιευτικῶς, οὐκ
ἀριστοτελικῶς (*Homily* 23, 12). Their theology is still a "message,"
a *kerygma*. Their theology is still "*kerygmatic theology*," even if it is
often logically arranged and supplied with intellectual arguments. The
ultimate reference is still to the vision of faith, to spiritual knowledge
and experience. Apart from life in Christ theology carries no conviction
and, if separated from the life of faith, theology may degenerate into
empty dialectics, a vain polylogia, without any spiritual consequence.
Patristic and Byzantine theology is existentially rooted in the decisive

commitment of faith. It is not a self-explanatory "discipline" which could be presented argumentatively, that is ἀριστοτελικῶς, without any prior spiritual engagement. In the age of the theological strife and incessant debates which we will be discussing, the Fathers – especially the Cappadocian Fathers – formally protested against the use of dialectics, of "Aristotelian syllogisms," and endeavored to refer theology back to the vision of faith. Patristic and Byzantine theology could be only "preached" or "proclaimed" – preached from the pulpit, proclaimed also in the words of prayer and in sacred rites, and indeed manifested in the total structure of Christian life. Theology of this kind can never be separated from the life of prayer and from the exercise of virtue. "The climax of purity is the beginning of theology," as St. John Klimakos puts its – τέλος δὲ ἁγνείας ὑπόθεσις θεολογίας (*Scala Paradisi*, grade 30).

On the other hand, Patristic and Byzantine theology is always, as it were, "propaideutic," since its ultimate aim and purpose is to ascertain and to acknowledge the Mystery of the Living God, to bear witness to it, in word and deed. "Theology" is not an end in itself. It is always but a way. Theology, and even the "dogmas," present no more than an "intellectual contour" of the revealed truth, and a "noetic" testimony to it. Only in the act of faith is this "contour" filled with content. Christological formulas are fully meaningful only for those who have encountered the Living Christ, and have received and acknowledged Him as God and Saviour, and are dwelling by faith in Him, in His body, the Church. In this sense, theology is never a self-explanatory discipline. It is constantly appealing to the *vision of faith*. "What we have seen and heard we announce to you." Without this "announcement" theological formulas are empty and of no consequence. For the same reason these formulas can never be taken "abstractly," that is, out of total context of belief. It is misleading to single out particular statements of the Fathers and to detach them from the total perspective in which they have been actually uttered, just as it is misleading to manipulate with detached quotations from the Scripture. It is a dangerous habit "*to quote*" the Fathers; that is, *to quote* their isolated sayings and phrases outside of that concrete setting in which only they have their full and proper meaning and are truly alive. "*To follow*" the Fathers does *not* mean just "*to quote*" them. "*To follow*" the Fathers means to acquire their "mind," their *phronema*.

The name of "*the Fathers of the Church*" is usually restricted to the teachers of the ancient Church. And it is currently assumed that their authority depends upon their antiquity, upon their comparative nearness to the "primitive Church," to the initial age of the Church. Already St. Jerome had to contest this idea. Indeed, there was no decrease of "authority" and no decrease in the immediacy of spiritual competence and knowledge in the course of Christian history. In fact, however, this idea of "decrease" has strongly affected our modern theological thinking. In fact, it is too often assumed, consciously or unconsciously, that the

Early Church was, as it were, closer to the spring of truth. As an admission of our own failure and inadequacy, as an act of humble self-criticism, such an assumption is sound and helpful. *But it is dangerous to make of it the starting point or basis of our "theology of Church history," or even of our theology of the Church.* Indeed, the Age of the Apostles should retain its unique position. Yet it was just a beginning. It is widely assumed that the "Age of the Fathers" has ended. Accordingly, it is regarded just as an ancient formation, "antiquated" in a sense and "archaic."

The limit of the "Patristic Age" is variously defined. It is usual to regard St. John of Damascus as the "last Father" in the East and St. Gregory the Dialogos or Isidore of Seville as "the last" in the West. This periodization has been justly contested in recent times. Should not, for example, St. Theodore of Studium, at least be included among "the Fathers"? Mabillon has suggested that Bernard of Clairvaux, the Doctor Mellifluous, was "the last of the Fathers, and surely not unequal to the earlier ones."

Actually, it is more than a question of periodization. *From the Western point of view "the Age of the Fathers" has been succeeded, and indeed superseded, by "the Age of the Schoolmen," which was an essential step forward.* Since the rise of Scholasticism, "Patristic theology" has been antiquated, has become actually a "past age," a kind of archaic prelude. This point of view, legitimate for the West, has been, most unfortunately, accepted also by many in the East, blindly and uncritically. Accordingly, one has to face the alternative. *Either* one has to regret the "backwardness" of the East which never developed any "Scholasticism" of its own. *Or* one should retire into the "Ancient Age," in a more or less archeological manner, and practice what has been wittily described recently as a "theology of repetition." The latter, in fact, is just a peculiar form of imitative "scholasticism."

And often it is suggested that the "Age of the Fathers" has ended much earlier than St. John of Damascus. Very often one does not proceed further than the Age of Justinian or the Council of Chalcedon. Was not Leontius of Byzantium already "the first of the Scholastics"? Psychologically, this attitude is quite comprehensible, although it cannot be theologically justified. Indeed, the Fathers of the Fourth century are impressive and their unique greatness cannot be denied. Yet, the Church remained fully alive also after Nicaea and Chalcedon. The current overemphasis on the "first five centuries" dangerously distorts theological vision and prevents the right understanding of the Chalcedonian dogma itself. The decree of the Sixth Ecumenical Council is often regarded as a kind of an "appendix" to Chalcedon, interesting only for theological specialists, and the great figure of St. Maximus the Confessor is almost completely ignored. Accordingly, the theological significance of the Seventh Ecumenical Council is dangerously obscured and one is left to wonder why the Feast of Orthodoxy should be related to the commemoration of the Church's victory over the

Iconoclasts. Was it not just a "ritualistic controversy"? We often forget that the famous formula of the *Consensus quinquesaecularis* [*Agreement of Five Centuries*], that is, actually, up to Chalcedon, was a Protestant formula, and reflected a peculiar Protestant "theology of history." It was a *restrictive* formula, as much as it seemed to be too inclusive to those who wanted to be secluded in the Apostolic Age. The point is, however, that the current Eastern formula of the "Seven Ecumenical Councils" is hardly much better, if it tends, as it usually does, *to restrict* or to limit the Church's spiritual authority to the first eight centuries, as if "the Golden Age" of Christianity has already passed and we are now, probably, already in an Iron Age, much lower on the scale of spiritual vigor and authority. Our theological thinking has been dangerously affected by *the pattern of decay*, adopted for the interpretation of Christian history in the West since the Reformation. The fulness of the Church was then interpreted in a static manner, and the attitude to Antiquity has been accordingly distorted and misconstrued. After all, it does not make much difference whether we *restrict* the normative authority of the Church to one century, or to five, or to eight. *There should be no restriction at all.* Consequently, there is no room for any "theology of repetition." The Church is still fully authoritative as she has been in the ages past, since the Spirit of Truth quickens her now no less effectively than in the ancient times.

One of the immediate results of our careless periodization is that we simply ignore *the legacy of Byzantine theology*. We are prepared, now more than only a few decades ago, to admit the perennial authority of "the Fathers," especially since the revival of Patristic studies in the West. But we still tend to limit the scope of admission, and obviously "Byzantine theologians" are not readily counted among the "Fathers." We are inclined to discriminate rather rigidly between "Patristics" – in a more or less narrow sense – and "Byzantinism." We are still inclined to regard "Byzantinism" as an inferior sequel to the Patristic Age. We have still doubts about its normative relevance for theological thinking. Now, Byzantine theology was much more than just a "repetition" of Patristic theology. Nor was that which was new in it of an inferior quality in comparison with "Christian Antiquity." *Indeed, Byzantine theology was an organic continuation of the Patristic Age.* Was there any break? Has the ethos of the Eastern Orthodox Church been ever changed at a certain historic point or date, which, however, has never been unanimously identified so that the "later" development was of lesser authority and importance, if of any?

CHAPTER FOUR

THE EARLIEST CHRISTIAN WRITERS

THE CHURCH'S STRUGGLE WITH TWO EXTREME VIEWS OF JESUS

One of the earliest confrontations over the nature of Christ was the Church's encounter with two extreme views, two very different views, two views which Gregory Dix refers to as the Syriac and Hellenistic. There were points of agreement even with these two groups – they believed that God was one and that Jesus was God's Messiah. We witness this encounter already in the *Gospel of St. John*, for there we are aware that the author is fighting on two fronts. One group is not convinced that Christ is in the full sense Divine. The other group cannot grasp the full humanity of Christ. For one group Jesus is a mere man; for the other Jesus the Christ is a divine apparition. Against the former the *Gospel of St. John* addresses the words: "but these are written that you may believe that Jesus is the Christ, the Son of God, and that believing you may have life in his name" (20:31). Against the other group, believing that God appeared on earth in human form but without any actual flesh and blood, the *Gospel of St. John* directs these words: "But one of the soldiers pierced his side with a spear, and at once there came out blood and water. He who saw it has borne witness – his testimony is true, and he knows that he tells the truth – that you also may believe" (19:34-35).

There exists independent knowledge of these two heretical schools of thought. One is represented by a Jewish-Christian sect known as the Ebionites. In short, they taught that Jesus was a mere man who scrupulously observed the Law of Judaism and became the Messiah. The opposite extreme was represented by the Docetists. The term comes from the Greek δοκεῖν [to seem]. Serapion of Antioch (fl. 200) was the first to mention the Docetists by name – δοκηται. Docetism is much more a tendency, an attitude, than a unified doctrine or a unified group. The numerous Gnostic sects will all contain within their system the Docetist heretical tendency. In brief, the Docetists viewed the humanity and the sufferings of the earthly Christ as apparent rather than real. St. Justin Martyr refers to them as those "who claim that Jesus Christ did not come in flesh but only as spirit, and revealed an appearance – φαντασίαν – of flesh." What is significant is that these two heretical schools of thought embrace two different views of Christology and these two different views are pointedly challenged already by the Christology of the Church as evidenced in the *Gospel of St. John*. One overemphasizes the manhood of Christ; the other overemphasizes the Divinity of Christ. Here, already, we see, though in a different historical context and in a different doctrinal context, the *two emphases* which will be present later in a more sophisticated form in Nestorianism and Monophysitism – in terms of *emphases*, not of doctrinal content. It was Harnack who applied the term "Adoptionists" to the Ebionites and the term "Pneumatic" to the Docetists. The early Christian writers are constantly challenging these two tendencies.

The early Christian writers have the tendency to explicate God in His οἰκονομία, *ad extra*, in his revelatory self-disclosure and not to reflect at length on the nature of God in and of itself – *ad se*. To understand God in his revelatory self-disclosure is not incorrect but it is one-sided and ultimately inadequate. The understanding of the inner life of God is not only also necessary but it must presuppose the explication of God's self-revelation, of God's relation to the created world. From an historical perspective, from an understanding of the living reality in which the early Christian writers found themselves, their *oikonomic* approach is understandable. But because of this tendency, because of the lack of balance between a theology of God in himself and a theology of God in his relation to created existence, and because of imprecision in terminology certain problems inevitably occur – conflicting tendencies of Christological and Trinitarian thought arise already in the late second and third century. The theological breakthrough comes in a forceful presentation only with St. Athanasius. It is sufficient to call attention to that aspect of the early Christian writers which reflects the understanding of Christ as God and hence provides the common ground for the definitions of the Ecumenical Councils, especially the Council of Chalcedon – Jesus Christ as fully God and fully Man.

ST. CLEMENT OF ROME

St. Clement of Rome's *First Letter to the Corinthians* is one of the oldest extra-Biblical documents of the Church. It was probably written in 96 or 97. The letter is primarily a pragmatic document, an exhortation to the Corinthian Church to obey the "rule of tradition," the deposit which the apostles received from the Lord Jesus Christ – οἱ ἀπόστολοι ἡμῖν εὐηγγελίσθησαν ἀπὸ τοῦ κυρίου Ἰησοῦ Χριστοῦ, Ἰησοῦς ὁ χριστὸς ἀπὸ τοῦ θεοῦ ἐξεπέμφθη. ὁ Χριστὸς οὖν ἀπὸ τοῦ θεοῦ, καὶ οἱ ἀπόστολοι ἀπὸ τοῦ Χριστοῦ ἐγένοντο οὖν ἀμφότερα εὐτάκτως ἐκ θελήματος θεοῦ (42). But it is clear that the entire pragmatic exhortation of this letter is based upon, assumes, the Divinity of Christ. This is all the more significant when one considers the "Judaistic and Stoic tone" of his letter. He writes (7): "We ought to . . . turn to the glorious and sacred rule of our tradition. Let us observe that which is good, that which is pleasing and acceptable to Him who made us. Let us fasten our eyes on the blood of Christ and let us realize how precious it is to his Father because it was shed for our salvation and it brought the grace of repentance to the whole world." This text speaks of cosmic redemption and connects the redemptive work of Christ to *his* Father. Implicit in this text is the fact that "his Father" refers to a unique relationship between Father and Son and not a general Fatherhood of God with all men, precisely because no man is capable of shedding blood that will redeem and bring the "grace of repentance" to the entire world. In chapter 21 St. Clement repeats the same idea: "Let us reverence the Lord Jesus Christ whose blood was given for us." In chapter 12 he writes similarly: "it was by the blood of the Lord that redemption was going to come to all who believe and hope . . ." In chapter 49 the same idea is expressed but this time with an emphasis that may have reference to the Docetists: "Jesus Christ, our Lord, gave his blood for us, his flesh for our flesh, and his life for ours."

In chapter 16 St. Clement refers to "the Lord Jesus Christ" as "the scepter of God's majesty." Referring to God as Father, Creator, and Master of the universe, St. Clement writes: "he poured forth his gifts on them all, but most abundantly on us who have taken refuge in his compassion through our Lord Jesus Christ, to whom be glory and majesty forever and ever." Again there is the connection between God the Father and Creator and "our Lord Jesus Christ." He then attributes eternal glory and majesty to "our Lord Jesus Christ," something that does not cohere if Jesus is not Divine – indeed, it would be bordering on blasphemy. In general, throughout the letter St. Clement centers everything on Christ – the expression ἐν Χριστῷ and the expression διὰ Ἰησοῦ Χριστοῦ are repeated often in the letter.

St. Clement refers to Christ as the image or mirror or reflection of God the Father: "This is how . . . we found our salvation, Jesus Christ, the high priest of our offerings . . . Through him we fix our gaze on the heights of heaven. In him we see the mirror of God's pure and transcendent face. Through him the eyes of our hearts are opened. Through him our foolish and darkened comprehension wells up to the light. Through him the Master has willed that we should taste immortal knowledge." In this chapter (36) St. Clement continues with explicit thought: "For, because he reflects the splendor of God, he is as superior to the angels as his title is more distinguished than theirs. . . But of his Son this is what the Master said: 'You are my Son: today I have begotten you'." Here St. Clement clearly states that Christ is not of the angelic order, that he is the "begotten Son" of the Father. St. Clement distinguishes between his human descent – τὸ κατὰ σάρκα – and, implicitly, his Divine nature. In this pragmatic, moral, non-speculative letter one encounters a "high" Christology precisely because it is the basis and presupposition of the Christian faith and of all that St. Clement writes from a moral perspective, of keeping the laws and commandments – νόμοι καὶ προστάγματα – of Christ.

In this early Christian document the Father, Son, and Holy Spirit are mentioned throughout, although from the perspective of their *oikonomic* activity. Nevertheless, that the Father is God, that the Son is God, and that the Holy Spirit is God is a presupposition of St.

Clement's thought – θεὸς καὶ ὁ κύριος Ιησοῦς Χριστὸς καὶ τὸ πνεῦμα τὸ ἅγιον (46 and 58). But it is not only in the explicit state - ments that one finds an affirmation of the Holy Trinity. Rather, it is in the language, context, and thought-structure that a belief in the Holy Trinity is exhibited in St. Clement's letter.

ST. IGNATIUS OF ANTIOCH

The commonly accepted seven letters of St. Ignatius in their shorter form are exceedingly important documents in the history of Christian theology. They were written before 107, the commonly accepted time of his matyrdom in Rome. His letters are therefore an undisputed witness to the faith of the early Church. Those who find the definitions of the Ecumenical Councils difficult to accept will encounter difficulty with the thought of St. Ignatius. Again it must be noted that these are not theological treatises but rather letters written by St. Ignatius, the bishop of Antioch, on his way to Rome to be thrown to the wild beasts. They are in a very real sense existential letters written by one about to die, existential letters which just happen to touch on theological subjects as well as moral ones. It was indeed the so-called "developed doctrine" contained in St. Ignatius' letters that caused some Protestant theologians to question their authenticity until Lightfoot and Harnack established the authenticity of the seven epistles. It was especially the 1885 edition by Lightfoot which established permanently the authenticity of the seven letters in their Greek shorter versions.

In his *Letter to the Ephesians* (7) St. Ignatius writes: "There is only one physician – of flesh yet spiritual, born yet uncreated – γέννητος καὶ ἀγέννητος – God become man, true life in death, sprung from both Mary and from God – καὶ ἐκ Μαρίας καὶ ἐκ θεοῦ – first subject to suffering and then incapable of it – Jesus Christ our Lord." He is God Incarnate – ἐν σαρκὶ γενόμενος θεός and θεοῦ ἀνθρωπίνως φανερουμένου. In the same letter he writes (18-20): "For our God, Jesus the Christ, was conceived by Mary, in God's plan being sprung forth from both the seed of David and from the Holy Spirit. He was born and baptized that by His Passion he might sanctify water. . . for God was revealing himself as a man to bring newness of eternal life. What God had prepared was now beginning. Therefore everything was in confusion because the destruction of death was being executed." "The New Man – ὁ καινὸς ἄνθρωπος – Jesus Christ . . . is Son of man and Son of God." In his *Letter to the Romans* he writes that Jesus Christ is the "only Son of the Father" – ὁ μόνος υἱὸς τοῦ πατρός and he is the Father's thought – γνώμη.

In his *Letter to the Magnesians* St. Ignatius writes of the co-eternality of Jesus Christ (6): ". . . Jesus Christ, who was with the Father from all eternity and in these last days has been made manifest." The union of the Father and Son is explicitly stated (1): "I desire that they confess the union of Jesus with the Father." "The Lord was completely one with the Father and never acted independently of him" (7). "Make speed, all of you, to one temple of God, to one altar, to one Jesus Christ, who came forth from the one and only Father, is eternally with that One, and to that One is now returned" (7). "God is one . . . he has revealed himself in his Son Jesus Christ, who is his Logos issuing from the silence" (8).

In his *Letter to the Trallians* he poignantly describes the reality of the humanity of Jesus: "Be deaf, then, to any talk that ignores Jesus Christ, of David's lineage, of Mary. he was truly – ἀληθῶς – born, ate, and drank. He was truly persecuted under Pontius Pilate. He was truly crucified and died in the sight of heaven and earth and of the powers of the nether world. He was truly raised from the dead, the Father having raised him, who in like manner will raise us also who believe in him – his Father, I say, will raise us in Christ Jesus, apart from whom we have no true life" (9).

He writes more forcefully in his *Letter to the Smyrnaeans* : "I extol Jesus Christ, the God who has granted you such wisdom. . . Regarding our Lord, you are absolutely convinced that on the human side he was actually sprung from David's line, Son of God according to God's will and power, actually born of a virgin, baptized by John and actually crucified for us in the flesh, under Pontius Pilate and Herod the Tetrarch. We are part of his fruit which grew out of his most blessed Passion. And thus, by his resurrection, he raised a standard to rally his saints and faithful forever, whether Jews or Gentiles, in one body of his Church – ἐνόησα ὑμᾶς κατηρτισμένους ἐν ἀκινήτῳ πίστει, ὥσπερ καθηλωμένους ἐν τῷ σταυρῷ τοῦ κυρίου Ἰησοῦ Χριστοῦ σαρκί τε καὶ πνεύματι καὶ ἡδρασμένους ἐν ἀγάπη ἐν τῷ αἵματι Χριστοῦ, πεπληροφορημένους εἰς τὸν κυρίου ἡμῶν, ἀληθῶς ὄντα ἐκ γένους Δαβὶδ κατὰ σάρκα, υἱὸν θεοῦ κατὰ θέλημα καὶ δύναμιν θεοῦ, γεγενημένον ἀληθῶς ἐκ παρθένου, βεβαπτισμένον ὑπὸ Ἰωάννου, ἵνα πληρωθῇ πᾶσα δικαιοσύνη ὑπ αὐτοῦ, ἀληθῶς ἐπὶ Ποντίου Πιλάτου καὶ Ἡρώδου τετράρχου καθηλωμένον ὑπὲρ ἐν σαρκί, ἀφ ' οὗ καρποῦ ἡμεῖς, ἀπὸ τοῦ θεομακαρίτου αὐτοῦ πάθους, ἵνα ἄρῃ σύσσημον εἰς τοὺς αἰῶνας διὰ τῆς ἀναστάσεως εἰς τοῦ ἁγίους καὶ πιστοὺς αὐτοῦ εἴτε ἐν Ἰουδαίοις εἴτε ἐν ἔθνεσιν ἐν ἑνὶ σώματι τῆς ἐκκλησίας αὐτοῦ He truly suffered, just as he truly raised himself. It is not as some unbelievers say, that his Passion was a sham. It is they who are a sham! For myself, I am convinced and believe that even after the resurrection he was in the flesh. Indeed, when he came to Peter and his friends, he said to them, 'Take hold of me, touch me and see that I am not a bodiless phantom'. And they at once touched him and were convinced, clutching his body and his very breath. For this reason they despised death itself, and proved its victors. Moreover, after the resurrection he ate and drank with them as a real human being, though even then he and the Father were spiritually – πνευματικῶς – one." In this same letter he writes that Jesus Christ is Perfect Man – τέλειος.

In his *Letter to Polycarp* St. Ignatius writes: "You must not be panic-stricken by those who have an air of credibility but who teach heresy. Stand your ground like an anvil under the hammer." He refers to Jesus Christ as the "Timeless, the Unseen, the One who became visible for our sakes, who was beyond touch and passion, yet who for our sakes became subject to suffering, and endured everything for us" (3). These are indeed a collection of powerful and explicit statements on the reality of the full humanity and the full Divinity of Jesus Christ. It is, as it were, a preamble to Chalcedon already at the turn of the first cen - tury. It is not an exaggeration to claim that his expressions foreshadow the later doctrine of ἀντίδοσις τῶν ἰδιωμάτων.

Such are some of St. Ignatius' explicit comments on Christology. If one looks carefully at what he writes about the Eucharist, the hierarchy of the Church, the unity of the Church and the Church's unity with the unity of God the Father, God the Son, and God the Holy Spirit, a deeper and even more vital Christology obtains. Everything, for example, that he writes about the Eucharist becomes meaningless without his belief in the Divinity of Christ. The Church is the "place of sacrifice" – θυσιαστήριον – and the Eucharist is θυσία. He writes in his *Letter to the Ephesians* (19-20): "Meet together in common – every single one of you – in grace, in one faith and on Jesus Christ (who was of David's line in his human nature, son of man and son of God) that you may obey the bishop and presbytery with undistracted mind; breaking one bread, which is the medicine of immortality, our antidote to ensure that we shall not die but live in Jesus Christ forever" – ἕνα ἄρτον κλῶντες ὅς ἐστιν φάρμακον ἀθανασίας, ἀντί - δοτος τοῦ μὴ ἀποθανεῖν ἀλλὰ ζῆν ἐν Ἰησοῦ Χριστοῦ διὰ παντός. In his *Letter to the Philadelphians* (3) he writes: "Take great care to keep one Eucharist. For there is one flesh of our Lord Jesus Christ and one cup to unite us by his blood; one sanctuary, as there is one bishop, together with the presbytery and the deacons." And in his *Letter to the Smyrnaeans* he writes (8): "All of you follow the bishop, as Jesus Christ followed the Father, and the presbytery as the Apostles. Respect the deacons as the ordinance of God. Let no one do anything that pertains to the Church apart from the bishop. Let that be considered a valid Eucharist which is under the bishop or one whom he has delegated. Wherever the bishop shall appear, there let the people be, just as wherever Christ Jesus may be, there is the Catholic Church."

This is the first written use which has come down to us of the term "Catholic" Church – ὅπου ἂν ᾖ Χριστὸς Ἰησοῦς ἐκεῖ καθολικὴ Ἐκκλησία. The word "catholic" means in Greek "universal" but the conception of catholicity cannot be measured by its world-wide expansion – "universality" does not express the Greek meaning exactly. Καθολικὴ comes from καθ᾽ ὅλου which first of all means the inner wholeness, not only of communion, and in any case not of a simple empirical communion. Καθ᾽ ὅλου is not the same as κατὰ παντός. It belongs not to the phenomenal and empirical, but to the noumenal and ontological plane. It describes the very essence and not the external manifestations. If "catholic" also means "universal," it certainly is not an empirical universality but rather an ideal one: the communion of ideas, not of facts, is what is meant. St. Ignatius' use of the word is precisely this. This word gives prominence to the orthodoxy of the Church, to the truth of the Church in contrast with the spirit of sectarian separatism and particularism. He is expressing the idea of integrity and purity.

Grillmeier correctly observes that St. Ignatius foreshadows the later definitions of the Ecumenical Councils. Grillmeier writes that from "Christ's Godhead and manhood . . . there arises the antithetic, two-membered formula, so well loved in the later history of the dogma of Christ," which emphasizes the distinction between the Divine and human nature in the *one* Lord. Grillmeier presents an antithetical schematic from St. Ignatius: σαρκικός καὶ πνευματικός; γεννητός καὶ ἀγέννητος; ἐν ἀνθρώπῳ . . . θεός; ἐν θανάτῳ . . . ζωὴ ἀληθινή; καὶ ἐκ Μαρίας . . . καὶ ἐκ θεοῦ; πρῶτον παθητός . . . καὶ τότε ἀπαθής . . . ἐστιν Ἰησοῦς Χριστός ὁ Κύριος ἡμῶν.

There is a tendency among some scholars to assume that if some - thing is not mentioned in a text, the author had no knowledge of it. This is a fundamentally erroneous presupposition and hence an er - roneous methodology. The assumption of this methodological approach or perspective misses the prime reality – a living Church was already in existence since Pentecost and that living Church knew the deposit about which they preached, knew the tradition which they had received and continued to impart in their missionary activity. Again the statement by Karl Adam is significant: "Even if the Bible [the New Testament] did not exist, a Christian religious movement would be conceivable." Indeed, not only conceivable but it actually existed without the New Testament as we know it for decades. And during that time the Apostolic and Sub-Apostolic Church flourished with and in the fulness of faith. St. Ignatius is an excellent example of this precisely because his seven occasional letters were written so early and especially because of what he has to say about the "documents," "the archives." In his *Letter to the Philadelphians* St. Ignatius writes (8): "When I heard some people saying, 'If I do not find it in the original documents, I do not believe it'." Here the essence of the dispute was that the Old Testament, the Bible for the early Christians in its Greek Septuagint version, was the reference point of validity. The New Testament is not the criterion, precisely because it was still in process in the days of the early Church and it was certainly not used as a canonical authority in the earlier days of the life of St. Ignatius. It is the reality of the living Church which gives rise to the New Testament and it is the Church which determines the "canon" of the New Testament – there were numerous writings circulating which claimed apostolic authorship and it was the Church which determined which of those were authentic. St. Ignatius then makes a statement which confirms how the early Church understood its reality, its faith, its tradition, its authority: "To my mind it is Jesus Christ who is the original documents. The inviolable archives are his Cross and Death and his Resurrection and the faith that came by him." St. Ignatius needs no written "documents," needs no written "archives." The historical, existential and ontological reality of the God-Man Jesus Christ and his redemptive work is the truth of the faith – he is oral "document" of the living God. He knows of this through the tradition, through that which was delivered, through the deposit which was preserved and handed down in its original purity of content and fulness.

It is historically interesting to take even a casual look at St. Ignatius' occasional, *ad hoc*, non-systematic, hastily written letters, for in these seven brief letters St. Ignatius just happens to touch on many of the basic principles of the faith of the living Church, a faith not recorded in a "document" but a faith that has been preserved and delivered faithfully from Christ to the Apostles to the episcopate. The main purpose of all seven letters is two-fold: it is to urge unity and also to convince the churches to which he writes not to interfere with his desire for martyrdom, his desire to "imitate the Passion of Christ God." And yet we find in these brief pages a rather broad Christian theology in skeletal form. The reality of God the Father, God the Son, and God the Holy Spirit is mentioned (in "Son, Father, and Spirit"; "to Christ, to the Father, and to the Spirit"; the Spirit "comes from God"; "the most High Father and Jesus Christ, his only Son"). He has no hesitation to speak of grace and deeds, of a justification by grace and one of deeds, implying an existential understanding of the synergistic relationship between grace and spiritual freedom, between grace and "works." And from the totality of his seven brief letters it is clear that everything is a gift from God. It is also clear that man participates in this gift, in his salvation. St. Ignatius also has no hesitation in speaking about predestination, election, and freedom. They all cohere for him in one theological vision. For him there is no tension between predestination and freedom. This is not a result of his inability to see a potential theological problem. Rather it is natural, instinctive, intuitive and apostolic understanding of the vision of salvation, a salvation which comes from God and in which man participates, a salvation which is a gift but one which must be received.

St. Ignatius speaks equally of the spiritual nature and the external structure of the Church – the bishops, presbytery, deacons (the "bishops reflect the mind of Jesus Christ"; the Church has a unique "intimacy" with Jesus Christ, as Jesus Christ has with the Father; the Church is "a choir, so that in perfect harmony and with a pitch taken from God," it "may sing in unison and with one voice to the Father through Jesus Christ"). Jesus Christ is our inseparable life – τὸ ἀδίακριτον ἡμῶν ζῆν, without whom we have no true life – τὸ ἀληθινὸν ζῆν οὐκ ἔχομεν.

St. Ignatius' stress on the "imitation of Christ" is a theme that will be repeated often in the history of Christian spirituality. His specific idea of the "imitation of the Passion of Jesus Christ" is expressed in vivid, fervid terms ("Let me be fodder for wild beasts – that is how I can attain to God. I am God's wheat and I am being ground by the teeth of wild beasts to make a pure loaf for Christ"; "Come fire, cross, battling with wild beasts, wrenching of bones, mangling of limbs, crushing of my whole body, cruel tortures of the devil – only let me get to Jesus Christ!"). This has struck many as an exaggerated form of spirituality, as one of arrogance. Yet, St. Ignatius is quite humble in this respect. For him the process of salvation is dynamic and he in no sense sees his desire as a superior spirituality ("I am only beginning to be a disciple"; "I am going through the pangs of being born . . . Do not stand in the way of my coming to life").

He is ever conscious of the importance, the necessity of a spiritual solidarity among Christians ("I needed your coaching in faith, encouragement"; "Do not try to convince yourselves that anything done on your own is commendable. Only what you do together is right. Hence, you must have one prayer, one petition, one mind, one hope, dominated by love and unsullied joy – that means you must have Jesus Christ!"). He knows the pain he is to face, yet he is ever mentioning the God-given joy and the overflowing mercy of God. He is on guard against pride and boasting: "I keep my limits, lest boasting should be my undoing. For what I need most at this point is to be on my guard and not to heed flatterers. Those . . . are my scourge." He is fully aware that his desire is an "impetuous ambition" and this causes "all the more a struggle" within him. He exclaims that what he needs is "gentleness." For those who think his desire is extreme, it must be admitted that his attitude towards it is spiritually balanced: "I endure all things because he gives me the power who is Perfect Man."

St. Ignatius stresses that we must "not only be called Christians but we must be Christians." For him the Christian life was Christocentric, for through the God-Man all things come from the Father and return to the Father. The Christocentric emphasis of the Christian life is a constant motif in his letters – the constant mention of "the blood of Christ"; "love" as a hymn to Jesus Christ; the "mind of Christ" is "the Father's mind"; "Jesus Christ is God's knowledge"; the "Name" of Jesus is sacred; the Cross, the Passion, the Death, the Resurrection of Christ are the foundations of our "Hope," creating, through the Incarnation, the path to our redemption; "if we live in union with him now, we shall gain eternal life," we shall rise with him. Through "initiation" into the mysteries [sacraments], through faith, love, continual prayer, and fasting, we can have Christ "within us." And, through union with Christ, "in faith and love in the Son and Father and Spirit" we shall have "increasing insight" and we shall rise with him, for true freedom is only in union with the Risen Christ.

St. Ignatius highlights a basic theology of worship and sacramental, liturgical life. The Eucharist is for him "the medicine of immortality." He has, as is apparent, a developed theology of the unity of the Church. Conversely, he has a theological attitude towards heresy: "He who fails to join in your worship shows his arrogance by the very fact of becoming a schismatic . . . If then, those who act carnally suffer death, how much more shall those who by wicked teaching corrupt God's faith for which Jesus Christ was crucified. Such a vile creature will go to the unquenchable fire along with anyone who listens to him."

A theology of faith and love weaves its way through his letters: "Your faith is what lifts you up, while love is the way you ascend to God . . . Faith is the beginning and love the end." The dynamism in the process of salvation is constantly emphasized: "For what matters is not a momentary act of professing, but being persistently motivated by faith."

St. Ignatius has an interesting theological insight into the spiritual importance of silence: "It is better to keep quiet and be real than to chatter and be unreal . . . He who has really grasped what Jesus said can appreciate his silence. Thus he will be perfect: his words will mean action and his very silence will reveal his character."

The great exclamatory Easter hymn in the Byzantine liturgy – Χριστὸς ἀνέστη ἐκ νεκρῶν, θανάτῳ θάνατον πατήσας – is adumbrated by St. Ignatius: Christ's death is described as "the destruction of death." This realism carries over to the sanctification of the material world in the theology of St. Ignatius: Christ's baptism "sanctifies water" and the pouring of ointment on the Lord's head passes on "the aroma of incorruption to the Church."

The deepest parts of the interior life of a person are not neglected in his thought: "all secrets are known and will be revealed." But repentance and forgiveness by the overflowing mercy of the grace of God are not neglected either: "The Lord forgives all who repent."

It is clear that the Church already at the time of St. Ignatius believed that marriage must be approved and blessed by the Church: "it is right for men and women who marry to be united with the bishop's approval." Already there is implicit here the sacramental nature of marriage.

Simultaneous with his theology of the active Christian spiritual life of continual prayer, humility, love, faith, constant participation in the sacramental life of the Church, simultaneous with his theology of the "imitation of the Passion of Christ God" is a theology of the "social gospel." He places great stress on concern and care for widows, orphans, the oppressed, those in prison, those released from prison who are in need of help and guidance, those who are hungry and thirsty. His social concern extends to slaves who must not be treated "con-temptuously." He even emphasizes the spiritual importance of "taking an interest in those to whom you talk."

This sketch of some of the subjects St. Ignatius just happens to address in his seven occasional letters reveals that he certainly had a grasp of the fulness of the Christian life and faith. The early date of these letters and their spontaneous, occasional nature cannot be overstressed. They are vital "documents" of a faith that was not rooted in "documents" or "archives" but rather rooted in the delivered tradition about the living person of Jesus Christ, divine and human, yet One Lord and One Eternally with the Father. It is not an exaggeration to point out that the definition of the Council of Chalcedon can is foreshadowed in general idea in the brief, occasional letters of St. Ignatius, letters which predate 107.

ST. POLYCARP

St. Irenaeus tells us that he sat at the feet of St. Polycarp, that St. Polycarp had been personally acquainted with St. John, that St. Polycarp was consecrated bishop by the apostles – Tertullian claims by St. John – that St. Polycarp was held in great esteem, and that he was the last witness of the Apostolic Age. That he was held in great esteem is attested by his visit to Rome to discuss ecclesiastical matters with Pope Anicetus, especially the problem of the date of celebration of Easter. It was in Rome where St. Polycarp apparently met Marcion. Marcion, it is claimed, asked St. Polycarp if he recognized him whereupon St. Polycarp is recorded as having replied: "I recognize you as the first-born of Satan."

St. Polycarp was born about 70, consecrated bishop before 110, and died probably in 155 or 156. What is historically important is that St. Irenaeus claims that St. Polycarp wrote many letters, letters to Christian communities as well as to fellow-bishops. But of these "many letters" only one has come down to us. Once again we find ourselves in the reality of history, in that encounter of an age now past in which there was a vibrant, living faith and a busy exchange of letters, the nature of which we shall never have knowledge. But it can be safely assumed that whatever the content of those lost letters they would in no way give us a full knowledge of that living Christian faith that was active and complete, that faith which prompted those letters. It is the deposit, the delivered faith, the handed down tradition which is the catalyst of the letters. But we do possess one letter – St. Polycarp's *Letter to the Philippians*.

The *Letter to the Philippians* is very brief and, again, it is an occasional letter. About that original, living deposit and that tradition which has been delivered St. Polycarp writes: "Let us turn back to the word delivered to us from the beginning . . . this is what we believed." The context in which St. Polycarp appeals to "the word delivered to us from the beginning" is in opposition to "false brethren," in opposition to those "who bear in hypocrisy the name of the Lord, who deceive empty-headed people." St. Polycarp becomes more concrete: "For whoever does not confess that Jesus Christ has come in the flesh is Antichrist, and whoever does not confess the testimony of the Cross is of the devil, and whoever perverts the sayings of the Lord to suit his own lusts and says there is neither resurrection nor judgment – such a one is the first-born of Satan" (7). And part of that "word delivered to us from the beginning" is to "hold steadfastly and unceasingly" to Christ "our Hope and our Pledge – ἀῤῥαβὼν – of righteousness," to Christ "who bore our sins in his own body on the Cross, who committed no sin, on whose lips no guile was found," to Christ who "for our sakes endured everything that we might live in him." As with St. Ignatius, St. Polycarp can speak of the deeds of the Christian life, of the "works," so to speak, of righteousness and simultaneously know that all grace initiates with God through Christ – χάριτι ἐστε σεσωσ-μένοι οὐκ ἐξ ἔργων, ἀλλὰ θελήματι θεοῦ, διὰ Ἰησοῦ Χριστου [*Letter to Ephesians* 2: 8 ff.].

And what is St. Polycarp's theology of Christ? He writes: "May God and the Father of our Lord Jesus Christ, and the Eternal High Priest himself, the Son of God, Jesus Christ, build you up in faith and truth and in all gentleness" (12). This Christological statement is quite consonant with the understanding of Christ in the New Testament documents and with the definitions of the later Ecumenical Councils. St. Polycarp upholds the concrete humanity of Jesus, the Divinity of Jesus Christ, and his eternality.

THE MARTYRDOM OF ST. POLYCARP

The Letter of the Church of Smyrna to the Church of Philomelium – and "to all those of the holy and catholic Church everywhereæ – is an important document in early Christian literature. It was written shortly after St. Polycarp's matyrdom in probably 156. It too is brief and an occasional letter. When asked by the the Proconsul to renounce Christ, St. Polycarp's reply is: "For eighty-six years I have served Christ, nor has He ever done me any harm. How, then, could I blaspheme my King who has saved me – τὸν βασιλέα μου τὸν σώσαντά με (9). It is St. Polycarp's last prayer that is of prime importance here. If the prayer is not precisely as St. Polycarp delivered it, then it may contain much of what he did say. What is certain is that it reflects the "mind of the Church" at Smyrna and hence its content is important: "O Lord, God Almighty, Father of Thy beloved and blessed Son Jesus Christ, through whom we have received the perfect knowledge of Thee, God of angels and powers and all creation and of the entire race of saints who live in Thy presence. I bless Thee because Thou hast found me worthy of this day and hour that I may participate with the number of the martyrs in the cup of Thy Christ in the resurrection to eternal life both in soul and in body by virtue of the immortality of the Holy Spirit. May I be received in Thy presence this day as a rich and pleasing sacrifice, just as Thou, the true God incapable of falsehood, hast prepared and revealed in advance and consummated. For this and for everything I bless Thee, I glorify Thee through the Eternal and Heavenly High Priest, Jesus Christ, Thy beloved Son, through whom be glory to Thee together with Him and the Holy Spirit, both now and unto the ages to come. Amen" (14). The Christological and Trinitarian nature of this prayer is unambiguous. God is the Creator of all things. Through Jesus Christ, who is eternal, a "perfect knowledge" of God the Father has been revealed. Immortality is a gift of the Holy Spirit and it is an immortality that is a resurrection of both body and soul. Absent here is the Platonic idea of the immortality of the soul by nature – and this is precisely the Christian teaching: the soul is not, as the Platonists held, immortal by nature but rather immortal by grace, by the free will and merciful gift of God. Glory is given to God the Father, God the Son, and to the Holy Spirit.

One other aspect of this letter deserves brief comment. It is the first time that we encounter the "veneration of the saints" in a document of this type in the early Church. Polycarp, the "apostolic and prophetic teacher and bishop of the Catholic Church in Smyrna," is now "crowned with the wreath of immortality." "Many" who knew St. Polycarp wanted "to have fellowship with his holy flesh." This is not described or portrayed as a *novelty* but rather as that which would be expected, as something natural. Indeed, it is fortuitous that the context affords the writer of the letter an explanation. The authorities hesitated to give the remains of St. Polycarp's corpse to the Christians precisely because "Nicetas, the father of Herod and brother of Alce" pleaded with the authorities "not to give up his body, 'else', he said, 'they will abandon the Crucified and begin worshipping this one'." This prompts the author of the letter to write that the opposition was "ignorant that we can never forsake Christ, who suffered for the salvation of the entire world of those who are saved, the blameless one for the sinners, nor can we ever worship any other. *For we worship only One as Son of God, while we deservedly love the martyrs as disciples and imitators of the Lord because of their unsurpassable devotion to their own King and Teacher.*" Out of love for the man and out of respect for the body which suffered for the sake of Christ the Christians in Smyrna "took up his bones, more precious than costly stones and more valuable gold, and laid them away in a suitable place. There the Lord will permit us . . . to gather together in joy and gladness to celebrate the day of his martyrdom as a birthday, in memory of those athletes who have gone before, and for the training and preparation of those yet to walk in their steps." Love, respect, joy, gladness, celebration, remembrance and memorial, a physical but holy relic from the real body of a real martyr to be used as a spiritual focus to train and to prepare others – these are the elements that comprise the love of the early Christians for the bodies of the saints. St. Polycarp "was not only a noble teacher but also a distinguished martyr, *whose martyrdom all desire to imitate as one according to the gospel of Christ.*"

THE DIDACHE

The Didache, known in Greek under two titles – Διδαχὴ τῶν δώδεκα ἀποστόλων [*The Teaching of the Twelve Apostles*] and Διδαχὴ τοῦ κυρίου διὰ τῶν δώδεκα ἀποστόλων τοῖς ἔθνεσιν [*The Teaching of the Lord to the Gentiles through the Twelve Apostles*], was put into its present form between 70 and 150. Indeed, some parts of it may be the earliest records we possess of early Christianity. *The Didache* does not offer us much Christological insight but we precisely should not expect this of any document from the early Church. The Christology was known, was delivered, and hence was a part – rather the base – of the Christian faith. It is because knowledge of Christ is assumed that no document must feel compelled to write on the subject. *The Didache* does, however, refer to Jesus – in an interesting context (16) – as "God's Son."

The document is in essence a moral exhortation, an ethical outline of certain Christian teachings which lead to "the way of life," a presentation of "what these maxims" of life, of Christianity teach. Presumed is the foundation of the faith, the corner-stone, Christ, without whom there could be no Christian faith, for it is Christ who has revealed God's saving will (10: 2): εὐχαριστοῦμέν σοι, πάτερ ἅγιε, ὑπὲρ τοῦ ἁγίου ὀνόματός σου, οὗ κατεσκήνωσας ἐν ταῖς καρδίας ἡμῶν καὶ ὑπὲρ τῆς γνώσεως καὶ πίστεως αἱ ἀθανασίας, ἧς ἐγνώρισας ἡμῖν διὰ Ἰησοῦ τοῦ παιδός σου. To walk in the "way of life" rather than the "way of death" the Christian sacraments are thought to be necessary. The Eucharist is a real sacrifice – θυσία – and it is referred to as spiritual food and drink – πνευματικὴ τροφὴ καὶ ποτόν. Only those who have been baptized are permitted "to eat and drink of" the Eucharist, which is considered "holy." The Christological nature of the Eucharist is assumed: "We give thanks to Thee, our Father, for the Holy Vine of David, Thy child, which you have revealed through Jesus, your child. . . We give thanks to Thee, our Father, for the life and knowledge which you have revealed through Jesus, your child." That there is no direct reference to the body and blood of Christ is not surprising, for again it must be emphasized that the early Christians certainly knew that the "cup" referred to the blood of Christ and that the bread – the broken bread, κλάσμα – referred to the body of Christ. Through the broken bread, the body of Christ, Jesus has "revealed" a certain and specific "life and knowledge" which is contextually clearly new. Elsewhere the author declares that "through Jesus" "knowledge and faith and immortality" have been "revealed." In contrast to the "food and drink" that God has given mankind, the author specifies "but to us you have given spiritual food and drink and eternal life through Jesus, your child." In context the "spiritual food and drink" is linked with "immortality." And in this sense, the idea is quite similar to St. Ignatius' description of the Eucharist as "the medicine of immortality." Confession is required before partaking of the Eucharist. The inner connection between the Eucharist and Baptism is clear. Baptism is not just Christological but Trinitarian. Twice the author speaks of the Trinitarian nature of Baptism. "Now about baptism: this is how to baptize. Give public instruction on all these points, and then baptize in running water 'in the name of the Father and of the Son and of the Holy Spirit'. If you do not have running water, baptize in some other. If you cannot in cold, then in warm. If you have neither, then pour water on the head three times 'in the name of the Father, Son, and Holy Spirit'."

As in all early Christian literature, *The Didache* warns against the twisting of the faith, against false prophets – ψευδοπροφήτης. "Multitudes of false prophets and seducers will appear. Sheep will turn into wolves and love into hatred" (16. The preservation of the faith as it was received is stressed: "You must not forsake 'the Lord's commandments', but 'observe' the ones you have been given, 'neither adding nor subtracting anything'." This is the seriousness of the faith that they have received, the foundation of which is Jesus Christ. They must always be on guard against false teachers and, as is implied, false documents masquerading as Christian.

THE OLDEST EXTANT CHRISTIAN HOMILY

The oldest extant Christian homily has come down to us as *The Second Letter of Clement*. That it was not written by St. Clement of Rome is certain and even the ancients did not accept it as such. St. Jerome in his *De viris illustribus* (15) writes " that a second letter under Clement's name circulates but the men of antiquity did not acknowledge this as such." Eusebius in his Ἐκκλησιαστικὴ ἱστορία (3, 38, 4) in - forms us that there is "a second letter attributed to Clement but we do not have the same confidence of its acceptance as the other. We are not even certain if the ancient writers used it." Of all the scholarly conjectures on the origin, only two have much of a force. One view, shared by Lightfoot, Krüger, and Funk, is that it originated in Corinth. Another view, which has valid considerations, is that it originated in Alexandria. Harnack's argument that it was a letter of Pope Soter (165-173) to the Church at Corinth is not well-founded. Where the homily originated is not an important issue – it is its content that is important. All that can safely be said of this valuable document is that it is a homily, not a letter, and that it was probably delivered in the first half of the second century. If it is a homily given in Corinth, then its connection with St. Clement's *Letter to the the Corinthians* is understandable but the textual linking of the two could have taken place in Alexandria also. It is known that it was included among the Scriptures by the Syrian Church. Whether this homily was delivered in 120, 130 or 150 is not important. What is important is that it is early, that it is a homily, and that it gained a good reputation in the early Church.

As a homily, it provides us with a glimpse of what the early Church preached to its flock. Here on one occasion we encounter what was the reality of the early Church – that the Church knew its faith. In the course of the homily (14) the speaker reveals this when he says: "I do not suppose that you are ignorant that the living 'Church is the body of Christ'." Explicit here is the fact that there was a body of truth once delivered which the faithful knew. Although there is no necessity for the speaker to discuss Christology, the fact that there is mention of Christology is nothing more than the preacher's occasional comments, comments which whether spoken – or written in documents – were the very foundation of the Church. Christ is the "author of incorruptibility" – ἀρχηγὸς τῆς ἀφθαρσίας, he has "willed our existence from nothing," he has given us "light" and has "rescued us" from perishing. He took pity on us and "in his tenderness" he "willed to save that which was perishing." There is "no hope of salvation unless it comes" from Christ. Through Christ we "have come to know the Father of truth" and we must "think of Christ as God." Christ the Lord, who "saved us," "became flesh." The "living Church is the body of Christ," it has "existed from the beginning," and "was made manifest in the flesh of Christ." The Church, the "body of Christ" – if we participate in it through "the Holy Spirit" – will bring us to eternal life.

The essence of this homily is precisely what one would expect of a homily – a call to repentance and Christian living.We are urged to guard, to protect our baptismal gift, for baptism is the seal – σφραγίς – of our new life in Christ. Redemption has come. Man no longer must die. A totality of new life has come in Jesus Christ, new life here on earth through the the reality of the Church, Christ's body, and new life for eternity. "Our whole life was nothing else but death . . . we were encompassed in darkness and our eyes were full of great mist." But redemption has now been given by God, in Jesus Christ, and through the Holy Spirit. The objective reality of redemption is presented in brief glimpse, is ejected into the homily, and then the emphasis, as consonant with the essence of a homily, is how we participate in this objective reality of redemption. We must "acknowledge him through whom we are saved" by our actions, by repentance and by living a "holy and upright life." The spiritual life is a contest, a struggle, a warfare and only those "who have struggled hard and competed well" will gain the victory of eternal life. "So while we are on earth, let us repent." "While we have an opportunity to be healed, let us give ourselves over to God, the physician . . . How? By repenting with a sincere heart." "Let us do the will of the Father who called us, so that we may have life." There is no pretension of superior spiritual life on the part of the preacher: "I too am a grave sinner and have not yet escaped temptation. I am still surrounded by the devil's devices. But I am anxious to pursue righteousness. My aim is to manage at least to approach it." Here is expressed that dynamic spiritual life so common in early Christianity – the spiritual life is a process, it is one in which intent, desire, and continual striving play a necessary, existential role in the ongoing path to salvation.

Much has been made about the fact that the preacher of this homily quotes a few times from the *Gospel of the Egyptians*. What must not be lost sight of is the fact that the quotations from the *Gospel of the Egyptians* are in essence the same as those found in the canonical Gospels. The quotations are consonant with the original deposit, with the tradition of the Church and not at variance with anything in the *kerygmatic* deposit.

THE LETTER OF BARNABAS

The Letter of Barnabas was in all probability not written by Barnabas, the disciple of St. Paul, whose name, originally Joseph, was given to him and, according to the *Acts of the Apostles* (4: 36), means the "son of consolation" – υἱὸς παρακλήσεως. What can be said con - cerning *The Letter of Barnabas* is that it was written between 70 and 138 and hence is one of the older documents of early Christianity. Regardless of what one thinks about his allegorical interpretation of the Old Testament, the fact remains that this letter was held in high esteem in the early Church. In the *Codex Sinaiticus* from the fourth century it is considered canonical. Origen refers to it as a catholic epistle – καθολικὴ ἐπιστολή. Eusebius in his Ἐκκλησιαστικὴ ἱστορία refers to it first as spurious (3,25) – ἐν τοῖς νόθοις . . . ἡ φερομένη Βαρνάβα ἐπιστολή – and then as doubtful – ἀντιλεγόμενα. Jerome in his *De viris illustribus* (6) considered it apocryphal – *inter apocryphas scripturas*. Still, the fact remains that it was highly regarded and used often – Clement of Alexandria quotes from it frequently.

The author stresses that he is not addressing anyone as a teacher but as one with them – οὐχ ὡς διδάσκαλος, ἀλλὰ ' ὡς εἷς ἐξ ὑμῶν and πολλὰ θέλων γράφειν, οὐχ ὡς διδάσκαλος. The central theological focus of the letter is the "New Law of our Lord Jesus Christ" – ὁ καινὸς νόμος τοῦ Κυρίου ἡμῶν. It is a law without co - ercion – ἄνευ ζυγοῦ ἀνάγκης ὤν – and it is a Sacrifice not made by human hands. "It is necessary for us to inquire very carefully into this matter of our salvation."

Christ is the "Lord of all the earth, to whom at the foundation of the world God said 'Let us make man in our image and likeness'. For the Scripture says concerning us, when [God the Father] speaks to the Son, 'Let us make man in our image and likeness'." (5, 5; 6, 11). Not only is the pre-existence of Christ taught but also his divine creative activity. And he will come again as Judge in divine omnipotence (15, 5).

He "manifested himself as the Son of God" in a non-Docetic sense: "the Son of God came in the flesh . . . He was about to be manifested and to suffer in the flesh." "The Son of God suffered that by his suffering he might win life for us. Let us believe that the Son of God could not have suffered except for our sakes." the Lord "delivered his body" to corruption and death with the purpose "of sanctifying us by the remission of our sins," with the purpose "of destroying death." He embraced his Passion "willingly" and through his redemptive work has made us "completely new," as though he had recreated us, "for you and I have actually been made completely new creatures." We have "entered into new life."

THE LETTER OF DIOGNETUS

The *Epistula ad Diognetum* has been one of the puzzles of early Christian documents. It is in the form of a letter to a highly placed pagan, Diognetus. Nothing is known of the author and scholars have exercised much creativity in attempting to ascribe it to someone. In its present form it could very well be the work of two writers, Quadratus and Hippolytus. Authorship is not the important issue but rather content. The letter has been praised by many scholars as the single, most impressive document of early Christianity. It was written probably between 120 and 150.

Unlike the literature which sprang from within the Christian Church to other Christians, this letter is written to a pagan. Hence, one would expect that distinctive doctrines of the Christian faith would be mentioned. And we are not disappointed. The heart of Christian faith is spoken: "It is not an earthly discovery that was committed [to the Christians]; it is not a mortal thought that they think of a worth guarding with such care; it is not merely human mysteries with which they have been entrusted. On the contrary, it was really the Ruler of all, the Creator of all, the Invisible God himself, who from heaven established the truth and the holy, incomprehensible word among men, and fixed it firmly in their hearts. And, as might be assumed, he did not do this by sending to men some subordinate – an angel, or a principality, or one of those to whom the government of things in heaven is entrusted – οὐ, καθάπερ ἄν τις εἰκάσειεν ἄνθρωπος, ὑπηρέτην τινὰ πέμψας ἢ ἄρχοντα ἢ τινα τῶν διεπόντων τὰ ἐπίγεια ἢ τινα τῶν πεπιστευμένων τὰς ἐν οὐρανοῖς διοι-κήσεις, ἀλλ αὐτὸν τὸν τεχνίτην καὶ δημιουργὸν τῶν ὅλων. Rather, he sent the Designer and Maker of the universe himself, by whom he created the heavens and confined the sea within its own bounds – him whose hidden purposes all the elements of the world faithfully carry out . . . He sent him by whom all things have been set in order and distinguished and placed in subjection . . . God sent him to men. . . He sent him out of kindness and gentleness. . . He sent him as God; he sent him as man to men. He willed to save man by persuasion, not by compulsion, for compulsion is not God's way of working. . . he sent him in love, not in judgment. Yet he will indeed send him someday as our Judge. . . And when he had planned a great and unutterable design, he communicated it to his Child alone. . . he revealed it through his beloved Child and made known the things that had been prepared from the beginning . . . He had planned everything by himself in union with his Child. . . Then, when we had proven ourselves incapable of entering the Kingdom of God by our own efforts, the power of God made it possible for us to do so. . . O, the overflowing kindness and love of God toward man! God did not hate us or drive us away or bear us ill will. Rather, he was long-suffering and forbearing. In his mercy, he took up the burden of our sins. He himself gave up his own Son as a ransom for us – the Holy One for the unholy, the Innocent One for the guilty, the Righteous One for the unrighteous, the Incorruptible One for the corruptible, the Immortal One for the mortal. For what else could cover our sins except his righteousness? In whom could we, lawless and impious as we were, be made holy except in the Son of God alone? O, most sweet exchange! O, unfathomable work of God! O, blessings beyond expectation! The sinfulness of many is hidden in the One Holy and the holiness of One sanctifies the countless sinners. . . He sent his Only-Begotten Son. . . he showed the Savior's power to save even the powerless with the intention that . . . we should have faith in his goodness and look on him as Nourisher, Father, Teacher, Counselor, Healer, Mind, Light, Honor, Glory, Might, Life."

After this brief presentation of the Christian teaching of the redemptive work of Christ, the author turns to the subject of how one acquires, of how one appropriates, of how one takes hold of this faith. "If you too yearn for this faith, then first of all you must acquire full knowledge of the Father. . . And once you have acquired this knowledge, think with what joy you will be filled! Think how you will love him, who first loved you so! And when you love him, you will be an imitator of his goodness." Once again we encounter the "imitation of Christ," the constant motif in early Christian literature. "And do not be surprised to hear that a man can become an imitator of God. He can because God wills it."

ST. JUSTIN THE MARTYR

St. Justin was born about 100 to 110 in Flavia Neapolis, the former Shechem in Palestinian Samaria and the present Nablus. The old city of Shechem had been razed to the ground by Vespasian in the Jewish war and rebuilt as the Graeco-Roman city of Flavia Neapolis. He tells us in his *Dialogue with Trypho* that he was a pagan in quest of truth, that he first was a Stoic, then a Peripatetic, and then a Pythagorean. He was deeply influenced by Plato when, according to his account in his *Dialogue with Trypho* (8), he had a discussion with an old man who gave him convincing reasons that Platonism could never strike to the heart of man and brought St. Justin's attention to the

Prophets. "When he had spoken these and many other things . . . he went away, suggesting that I pay attention to this. I have not seen him since then. But at once a flame was kindled in my soul and developed into a love of the prophets and of those men who are friends of Christ. I found this philosophy alone to be safe and profitable."

His conversion to Christianity might have taken place in Ephesus. Thereafter he spent the rest of his life explicating and defending the Christian faith, wearing always, as did Aristides, Athenagoras, Tertullian and other Apostolic Fathers, his philosopher's cloak – τριβώνιον or *pallium*, a threadbare cloak worn by philosophers and later by monks as a sign of severe study or austere life. During the reign of Antoninus Pius (138-161) St. Justin came to Rome and established a school there. St. Justin was beheaded probably in 165. The account of his death in the *Martyrium S. Justini et Sociorum* is based on the official court transcript when Junius Rusticus was prefect (163-167) during the reign of Emperor Marcus Aurelius Antoninus, the Stoic philosopher. The sentence pronounced against St. Justin and six other Christians reads: "Let those who will not sacrifice to the gods and yield to the command of the Emperor be scourged and led away to be beheaded in accordance with the law."

St. Justin wrote prolifically but only three of his works have come down to us – his two *Apologies* (which may be one work) and his *Dialogue with Trypho*, the oldest extant apology against the Jews. We possess only fragments – often only a title – of the other works written by St.Justin. One book, to which he himself refers in his *First Apology* (26), was written against "all heresies" – *Liber contra Omnes Haereses*. Another, mentioned by Eusebius (4, 11) and used by St. Irenaeus, was in opposition to Marcion – *Adversus Marcionem*. Eusebius claims that St. Justin wrote a *Psalter*, of which nothing remains. He also wrote a *Discourse against the* Greeks, *A Confutation* (to the Greeks), *On the Soul, On the Sovereignty of God*, and *On the Resurrection*. Three substantial fragments of the latter were preserved in St. John Damascene's *Sacra Parallela*. Several works have been attributed to St. Justin which most probably were not written by him – *Cohortatio ad Graecos, Oratio ad Graecos, De Monarchia, Quaestiones et Responsiones ad Orthodoxos, Quaestiones Christianorum ad Gentiles, Quaestiones Graecorum ad Christianos, Confutatio Dogmatum Quorumdam Aristotelicorum, Expositio Fidei seu De Trinitate* and *Epistola ad Zenam et Serenum*.

St. Justin is in dialogue with the pagan thinkers and hence it would be expected that he would touch upon most of the teachings of the Christian faith, unlike the earlier Christian documents which were written within the Christian community and assumed a knowledge of the faith on the part of the reader. St. Justin presents Christianity as a philosophy, as a reality of thought that embraces all of life and death, as the reality of philosophy. In his *First Apology* (5) he writes that the Logos "took form and became man and was called Jesus Christ." The "most true God" is the "Father of righteousness," the "unbegotten and impassible God." Christians worship and adore him "and the Son who came from him . . . and the prophetic Spirit" (6). The Logos is Divine (10), "begotten by God" (12).

The historical Jesus is emphasized: "It is Jesus Christ who has taught us these things. He was born for this purpose and was crucified under Pontius Pilate, who was procurator in Judea in the time of Tiberius Caesar" (13). "Christ was born one hundred and fifty years ago under Quirinius, and taught what we say he taught still later, under Pontius Pilate" (46). He is "the Son of the true God himself . . . in the second place and the prophetic Spirit in the third rank." We follow the "only Unbegotten God through his Son," who "was begotten by God as the Logos of God in a unique manner beyond ordinary birth . . . he was "born of a virgin . . . he came among men as man . . . he was crucified" and "his passion" is "unique." He is God's offspring (21) – γέννημα. "Jesus Christ alone was really begotten as Son of God, being his Logos and First-Begotten and Power, and becoming man by his will . . for the reconciliation and restoration of the human race" (22-23).

St. Justin sharply denies that "Christ was a man, of human origin [who only] appeared to be God's Son" (30). He is not only really called the Son of God but really is the Son of God (31). Christ is "the First-Begotten of God," the "First-Begotten of the Unbegotten God" (46 and 52) and is the Logos "of which every race of man partakes" (46). "For those who identify the Son and the Father are condemned, as neither knowing the Father nor recognizing that the Father of the universe has a Son, who being the Logos and the First-Begotten of God is also Divine.

In reference to baptism St. Justin writes: "They are brought by us where there is water and are made new – καινοποιηθέντες – by the same manner of rebirth by which we ourselves were made new, for they are then washed in the water in the name of God the Father and Master of all, and of our Savior Jesus Christ, and of the Holy Spirit" (61). Baptism, he writes in his *Dialogue with Trypho* (19) is the washing for the remission of sins and unto regeneration – τὸ ὑπὲρ ἀφέσεως ἁμαρτιῶν καὶ εἰς ἀναγέννησιν λουτρόν and can allow us the pos - sibility of becoming perfect – τέλειον γίνεσθαι (*Dialogue with Trypho*, 8). In reference to the Eucharist St. Justin writes that "praise and glory" is given "to the Father of the universe through the name of the Son and of the Holy Spirit" (65). "This food we call Eucharist, of which no one is allowed to partake except one who believes that the things we teach are true, and has received baptism for forgiveness of sins and for rebirth, and who lives as Christ handed down to us. For we do not receive these things as common bread or common drink. But as Jesus Christ our Savior being incarnate by God's word took flesh and blood for our salvation, so also we have been taught that the food consecrated by the word of prayer which comes from him, from which our flesh and blood are nourished by transformation – κατὰ μεταβολήν, is the flesh and blood of that incarnate Jesus" (66). At the end of a service they "bless the Maker of all things through his Son Jesus Christ and through the Holy Spirit" (67). It is significant that when St. Justin is discussing Christian worship, he writes that a ser - mon is delivered. Here again we confront the communication within the Christian community and the content of the sermon is precisely the same as we have observed in the earlier Christian documents – it "urges and invites us to the imitation of these noble things" (67). This is precisely the living Christian faith, the life of active Christian striving, the ethical and moral dimension of Christian teaching.

In his *Second Apology* (which may be a part of the *First Apology)* St. Justin declares that "to the Father of all, who is Unbegotten, no name is given . . . the words Father, and God, and Creator, and Lord, and Master, are not names but appellations coming from the goodness of his deeds and activity" (6). "And his Son, who alone is properly called Son, the Logos, who also was with him and was Begotten before he created and arranged all things by him, is called Christ because of his being anointed and because of God's ordering all things through him" "But 'Jesus', his name as man and Savior, also has significance, for he became man also" (6). "Christ . . . became the whole rational being, both body, and reason, and soul" (10) – διὰ τοῦ τὸ λογικὸν τὸ ὅλον τὸν φανέντα δι 'ἡμᾶς Χριστὸν γεγονέναι, καὶ σῶμα καὶ λόγον καὶ ψυχήν. Christ is the "power of the ineffable Father and not the mere instrument of human reason" (10). Together with God the Father Christians "worship and love the Logos who is from the Unbegotten and Ineffable God and became man for our sakes so that, in becoming a partaker of our sufferings, he might also bring us healing" (13).

St. Justin has much to say about the nature of Christ in his lengthy *Dialogue with Trypho* . In brief, however, he writes (128) that "Christ is Lord and God, the Son of God" and Christ it is who brings the gospel from the Father to men but he "remains indivisibly and inseparably" with the Father. He is "begotten from the Father" with no division in the essence of the Father" and yet he is "numerically distinct" – καὶ ἀριθμῷ ἕτερον. He is the Only-Begotten Son (105) – ὁ μονογενής.

ATHENAGORAS OF ATHENS

Athenagoras of Athens, the most lucid and eloquent writer among the Apologists, was most probably a pagan who converted to Christianity. Bossuet considered him the author "of one of the finest and earliest apologies of the Christian religion." Almost nothing is known of his life except that he was an Athenian and considered himself "a Christian philosopher." St. Photius held that he was the same Athenagoras to whom Boethos, the Platonist, dedicated his work *On Difficult Expressions in Plato (Bibl. Cod.* 154 f.). He is mentioned by

Methodius in *De resurrectione* (I, 36) and by Philip Sidetes in his lengthy Χριστιανικὴ ἱστορία. About 177 Athenagoras wrote his *Plea Regarding Christians* – πρεσβεία περὶ τῶν χριστιανῶν. A second work, *On the Resurrection of the Dead* – περὶ ἀναστάσεως νεκρῶν – has been attributed to him and he was most probably the author.

Athenagoras is the first to write so penetratingly about the unity of God. "All philosophers, then, even if unwillingly, reach complete agreement about the unity of God when they come to inquire into the first principles of the universe" (7). God is "uncreated" and "eternal" (6). God is "uncreated, impassible, and indivisible. He does not, therefore, consist of parts" (8). God is the "Creator" (8). "I have sufficiently shown that we are not atheists since we acknowledge one God, who is uncreated, eternal, invisible, impassible, incomprehensible, illimitable. He is grasped only by mind and intelligence, and surrounded by light, beauty, spirit, and indescribable power. By him the universe was created through his Logos, was set in order, and is held together. . . Let no one think it stupid for me to say that God has a Son. For we do not think of God the Father or of the Son in the way of poets . . . But the Son of God is his Logos in idea and in actuality – ἐν ἰδέᾳ καὶ ἐνεργείᾳ. For by him and through him all things were made, the Father and the Son being one. And since the Son is in the Father and the Father in the son by the unity and power of the Spirit, the Son of God is the mind and Logos – νοῦς καὶ λόγος – of the Father" (10). The Son is "the first offspring of the Father. I mean that he did not come into being – οὐχ ὡς γενόμενον, for, since God is eternal mind, he had his Logos within himself from the beginning, being eternally logical – ἀιδίως λογικός. Indeed we say that the Holy Spirit himself, who inspires those who utter prophecies, is an effluence – ἀπόρροιαν – from God, flowing from him and returning like a ray of the sun. Who, then, would not be astonished to hear those called atheists who admit God the Father, God the Son, and the Holy Spirit, and who teach their unity in power and their distinction in rank? – τὴν ἐν τῇ τάξει διαίρεσιν (10). Christians "are guided by this alone – to know the true God and his Logos, to know the unity of the Father with the Son, the fellowship of the Father with the Son, what the Spirit is, what union – ἕνωσις – exists between these three, the Spirit, the Son, and the Father, and what is their distinction – διαίρεσις – in union" (12).

TATIAN THE SYRIAN

Tatian the Syrian's conversion from paganism to Christianity is similar to a certain extent with that of St. Justin, who became Tatian's teacher in Rome. Tatian found in Christianity the only true philosophy. Unlike St. Justin, who sees elements of truth throughout the world and in all cultures, Tatian has a narrow view of Christianity – indeed he despises all "culture," anything that is not Christian. His tendency for extremism has more in common with Tertullian than with his teacher, St. Justin, whom he calls a "most admirable man" – θαυμασιώτατος. He was probably born in Eastern Syria about 120. Nothing is known about his death. He broke with the Church and became the founder of a sect called the Encratites – ἐγκρατεῖς ἐγκρατηταί, ἐγκρατῖται ("self-controlism"), a sect which rejected marriage as a form of adultery, as a service to the devil. St. Irenaeus tells us that Tatian "apostatized" after the martyrdom of St. Justin and that, "puffed up with conceit," he fell into Gnostic heresy little different than that of Valentinus and, like Marcion and Saturninus, taught that marriage was corrupt (St. Irenaeus, *Adversus Haereses*, 28). The Encratites survived well into the fifth century. They condemned the eating of any meat and the drinking of any wine. Because of their attitude toward wine they substituted water for wine in the Eucharist and were, accordingly, also known as the "Aquarii" and the "Hydroparastatae" – ὑδροπαραστάται. The term "Encratites" was later used to refer to all Gnostic ascetic groups – the Manichees used this term for themselves. This practice of using water instead of wine in the Eucharist was condemned by Clement of Alexandria, Cyprian, and St. John Chrysostom – it was prohibited in 382 by Emperor Theodosius.

Two of Tatian's works have come down to us – his *Oration* or *Discourse to the Greeks* [λόγος πρὸς Ἕλληνας or *Oratio adversus Graecos*] and his "harmony" of the Gospels, his "out of four" or *Diatessaron* – τὸ διὰ τεσσάρων εὐαγγέλιον. Tatian's *Diatessaron* was used in the liturgy of the Syrian Church for a long time, at least up to the fifth century when it was replaced by the four canonical Gospels. Tatian most probably wrote it originally in Greek; it was then translated into Syriac. Excavations at Dura Europos in Syria in 1934 uncovered a fourteen line fragment of the Greek text. The entire text can be reconstructed from the versions that exist in Latin, Arabic, and Franconian. St. Ephraem the Syrian wrote a commentary on the *Diatessaron* which is extant in an Armenian translation. In these two extant works there is not much of a trace of Gnosticism.

Christianity is a philosophy for Tatian – ἡ ἡμετέρα φιλοσοφία (31); οἱ βουλόμενοι φιλοσοφεῖν παρ᾽ ἡμῖν ἄνθρωποι – but a philosophy with doctrines, with dogmas – δόγματα. God is the necessary foundation – ὑπόστασις – of all being. No creature had as yet come into being. The Logos is not separate from God but belongs to God, is in God by essence. "He was all power, the necessary foundation of all things visible and invisible, with him were all things. The Logos himself was with him by the power of the Logos, was in him. And by his simple will the Logos issues forth. And the Logos, not issuing forth in vain, becomes the First-Begotten work of the Father. We know the Logos to be the beginning [or source] of the cosmos. But the Logos came into being by participation, not by abscission, for what is cut off is separated from the original but that which comes by participation . . . does not make him deficient from whom it is taken. For just as from one torch many fires are lighted but the light of the first torch is not lessened by the kindling of many torches, so the Logos, issuing forth from the logical power of the Father, has not divested of the logical power him who begat him" (5) –

Θεὸς ἦν ἐν ἀρχῇ, τὴν δὲ ἀρχὴν λόγου δύναμιν παρειλήφαμεν. ὁ γὰρ δεσπότης τῶν ὅλων, αὐτὸς ὑπάρχων τοῦ παντὸς ἡ ὑπόστασις, κατὰ μὲν τὴν μηδέπω γεγενημένην ποίησιν μόνος ἦν· καθὸ δὲ πᾶσα δύναμις, ὁρατῶν τε καὶ ἀοράτων αὐτὸς ὑπόστασις ἦν, σὺν αὐτῷ τὰ πάντα· σὺν αὐτῷ διὰ λογικῆς δυνάμεως αὐτὸς καὶ ὁ λόγος, ὃς ἦν ἐν αὐτῷ, ὑπέστησε. θελήματι δὲ τῆς ἁπλότητος αὐτοῦ προπηδᾷ λόγος, ὃν κατὰ κενοῦ χωρήσας, ἔργον πρωτότοκον τοῦ πατρὸς γίνεται. Τοῦτον ἴσμεν τοῦ κόσμου τὴν ἀρχήν. Γέγονε δὲ κατὰ μερισμόν, οὐ κατὰ ἀποκοπήν· τὸ γὰρ ἀποτμηθὲν τοῦ πρώτου κεχώρισται, τὸ δὲ μερισθὲν οἰκονομίας τὴν αἵρεσιν προσλαβὸν οὐκ ἐνδεᾷ τὸν ὅθεν εἴληπται πεποίηκεν. ὥσπερ γὰρ ἀπὸ μιᾶς δᾳδὸς ἀνάπτεται μὲν πυρὰ πολλά, τῆς δὲ πρώτης δᾳδὸς διὰ τὴν ἔξαψιν τῶν πολλῶν δᾳδων οὐκ ἐλαττοῦται τὸ φῶς, οὕτω καὶ ὁ λόγος προελθὼν ἐκ τῆς τοῦ πατρὸς δυνάμεως οὐκ ἄλογον πεποίηκε τὸν γεγεννηκότα.

God is "ineffable," "pefect," "in need of nothing," "without beginning," but "the beginning of all things." He is "invisible," "impalpable," and the creator of all things (4). Matter is "brought into existence" by God (5). He will "resurrect" our bodies after "the consummation of all things" but "not as the Stoics affirm" with their "return of certain cycles, the same things being produced and destroyed for no useful purpose." Rather, the Christian resurrection is a "resurrection once for all" at which time "judgment" will be passed by "the Creator, God himself" (6). From nothingness we have come into existence. We shall die but "shall exist again" in a restored body. The Logos, "in imitation of the Father from whom he is Begotten, made man an image of immortality" so that man, participating in the Divine, might have immortality (7).

That Tatian was an extremist, that he left the Church to establish a "purer" form of Christianity seems indisputable. But to judge Tatian's theology from his sole surviving theological work, his *Discourse to the Greeks*, is incorrect, unfair, and indeed impossible, precisely because this work is a very specific work, a very different work from all other early Christian documents. He has a special task to accomplish in this work and that he does extraordinarily well. His task is not to present Christian doctrine – indeed, he touches on the nature of God, on the Logos, on the Spirit, on the depth of created freedom, on the resurrection of the body and the immortality of the soul by grace, on the meaning of time and death, and on the coming judgment. But he touches on these subjects only parenthetically and only in relationship to his on-going commentary, which has a completely different purpose than the "apologies" of other early Christians. Tatian is engaged in a heated dispute with not only pagan Greek philosophy but also with all of pagan Greek culture. His knowledge of his subject is impressive. Indeed, Tatian's work is a rich source for a knowledge of all phases of pagan Greek culture – it is a penetrating look at all aspects of that life, culture, and society. One feels oneself present, one obtains an insider's glimpse into this society – its philosophy, its religious beliefs and practices, its laws, its literature, its inside gossip, its ranging attitudes, its public amusements, its scandals. Herein is its uniqueness. And Tatian, though it is not necessary, tells us that this is an insider's view: "The things I have thus set before you I have not learned at second hand. I have visited many lands. I have followed rhetoric, like yourselves. I have been captivated by many arts . . . I wish to give you a distinct account of what I myself have seen and felt" (35).

Tatian does not explicate the Christian faith except on occasion. He is in dialogue. Indeed, it appears he is in dialogue with persons whom he knows. His main objective is to prepare them that the "barbarian" philosophy which he has accepted, Christianity, should be given a hearing, especially in light of the fact that their entire culture is far inferior to this "barbaric" philosophy at which they scoff without knowing it. His logistical approach is to strike a serious blow to their entire culture so that they may be somewhat incapacitated, somewhat immobilized. And he strikes his blow in all directions and with that insider's knowledge which may cause them to reflect, that may cause them to wonder how Tatian, once one of them, has now found what he considers to be far superior, to be truth itself. In one instance Tatian compares quickly: "One of you asserts that God is body, but I assert that He is without body. You assert that the world is indestructible, but I assert that it is to be destroyed. You assert that a conflagration will take place at various times, but I assert that it will come to pass once for all. You assert that Minos and Rhadamanthus are judges, but I assert that God himself is Judge. You assert that the soul alone is endowed with immortality, but I assert that the flesh also is endowed with it" (25). "The soul is not in itself immortal, O Greeks, but mortal. Yet it is possible for the soul not to die" (13).

Tatian admits that he has neglected to speak of the doctrines of Christianity in order "to discuss matters that demanded more immediate attention." He then immediately writes that "it is time I should attempt to speak concerning the doctrines [of Christianity]" (35) but then falls immediately back into his commentary on the total dimensions of Greek pagan culture. By his closing words it appears that he intended to present himself to them and at that time to discuss and be examined on the teachings of Christianity: "Knowing who God is and what is his work, I present myself to you prepared for an examination concerning my doctrines" (42).

Those who expect to find a Christian theology miss the entire essence of this work. There is no mention of Christology except in the brief passages quoted above on the nature of God and the Logos. There is no mention or theology of the human and Divine nature of Christ precisely because the nature of this work does not require it. In his dialogue with the Greeks about their philosophy, religion, and culture, it is appropriate to speak briefly about the nature of God, of time, of the Logos. These are references to which they can relate. But if he began to present the deposit, the *kerygma*, the apostolic teaching, then that would be counterproductive. He has laid a groundwork for future discussion and a mightily interesting one. No more can be expected from this fascinating work that allows us a first hand look into the wide-ranging aspects of Greek pagan society and life.

Serious judgment of Tatian's theology from this work must be withheld. Indeed, there may be expressions at times which can be interpreted in more than one way. But Tatian is writing a deeply personal and impassioned critique and has no intention of presenting his theology of the faith in any detail. He is not writing to a Christian community, he is not writing a traditional "apology" to the pagans. Rather, he is engaged in a personal critique and intends to present himself for examination on Christian doctrines. Those who judge him or dismiss him on the basis of this work have missed the whole point of his critique. That he in essence says nothing about Christ becomes meaningless in context. That he was concerned about Christ, that he was focused on Christ becomes clear from his work on the Gospels. If he had no interest in the historical Christ would he have expended so much time to produce his "harmony" of the Gospels? But even in this work Tatian does mention the Incarnation: "We do not act as fools, O Greeks, nor utter idle tales when we announce that God was born in the form of a man – ἐν ἀνθρώπου μορφῇ γεγονέναι. I call on you who reproach us to compare your mythical accounts with our narrations" (21).

That he later fell prey to schism and heretical ideas is not disputed. So did Tertullian and yet what Tertullian wrote on Christology and the Trinity remained a precious part of Church literature and the beginning of Latin theological expressions that obtained in the Latin Church.

THEOPHILUS OF ANTIOCH

Eusebius in his Ἐκκλησιαστικὴ Ἱστορία (4, 20) informs us that Theophilus was the sixth bishop of Antioch, after Peter, Evodius, Ignatius, Heron, Cornelius, and Eros. St. Peter, although in the list, is not considered a bishop but an apostle. It is clear from his writings that he was born of pagan parents near the Euphrates and that he received a typically Hellenistic education. It was only later in life that he studied the Scriptures of the Church seriously and then became a convert. All we know about his dates is that he flourished around 180.

He wrote works against Marcion and Hermogenes, catechetical lectures, commentaries on Proverbs and the Gospels, a historical work known to us only from his own references to it – περὶ Ἱστοριῶν, and a harmony of the Gospels. But the only work that has come down to us is his *Ad Autolycum* in three books.

Theophilus' *Ad Autolycum* is an important work of early Christian literature. He is the first writer – from whom we have extant documents – to be explicit on a few important areas concerning Christianity. He is the first to write explicitly that the evangelists are θεοφόρητοι – divinely inspired as were the prophets (2, 22) and that St. Paul's *Letter to Romans* and the work of *I Timothy* are considered "the divine word" – διδάσκει ἡμᾶς ὁ θεῖος λόγος (3, 14). He is the first to use the word τριάς – Trinity –for the union of the three divine persons: "the three days which were before the luminaries are types of the Trinity – τριάδος – of God and His Word and His Wisdom" (2, 15). Here Theophilus uses the word Wisdom – σοφία – to refer to the Holy Spirit. But elsewhere he refers σοφία to the Son (2, 10). Theophilus is also the first to distinguish between the Logos ἐνδιάθετος and the Logos προφορικός – the Logos internal or immanent in God and the Logos uttered or emitted by God, a distinction in a terminology which will have an important role to play in the explication of later Trinitarian thought.

The knowledge of God was revealed in the past by the prophets and is fulfilled and contained in the Gospel – καὶ γὰρ ἐγὼ ἠπίστουν τοῦτο ἔσεσθαι, ἀλλὰ νῦν κατανοήσας αὐτὰ πιστεύω, ἅμα καὶ ἐπιτυχὼν ἱεραῖς γραφαῖς τῶν ἁγίων προφητῶν, οἳ καὶ προ – εῖπον διὰ πνεύματος θεοῦ τὰ προγεγονότα ᾧ τρόπῳ γέγονεν καὶ τὰ ἐνεστῶτα τίνι τρόπῳ γίνεται, καὶ τὰ ἐπερχόμενα ποίᾳ τάξει ἀπαρτισθήσεται. ἀπόδειξιν οὖν λαβὼν τῶν γινο – μένων καὶ προαναπεφωνημένων οὐκ απιστῶ (I, 14). But Revel – ation is necessary precisely because the wisdom of the philosophers and poets is wisdom inspired by demonic forces – ὑπὸ δαιμόνων δὲ ἐμπνευσθέντες καὶ ὑπ᾿αὐτῶν φυσιωθέντες ἃ εῖπον δι αὐτῶν εῖπον (II, 8).

God is "ineffable," "indescribable," "incapable of being seen by the eyes of flesh," "incomprehensible," "unfathomable," "inconceivable," "without being," "unbegotten," "unchangeable," and "eternal" (I, 3). "For if I say He is Light, I name but his own work. If I call him Logos, I name but his sovereignty. If I call him Mind, I speak but of his Wisdom. If I say he is Spirit, I speak of his breath. If I call him Wisdom, I speak of his offspring. If I call him Strength, I speak of his power. If I call him Power, I speak of his activity. If I call him Providence, I speak of his goodness. If I call him Kingdom, I but mention his glory. If I call him Lord, I speak of him as Judge. If I call him Judge, I speak of him as being just. If I call him Father, I speak of all things as coming from him" (I, 3).

God is Creator, not a "Fashioner" of primeval matter. "Plato and those of his school acknowledge indeed that God is uncreated, and the Father and Maker of all things. But then they maintain that matter as well as God in uncreated and claim that it is coexistent with God. But if

God is uncreated and matter uncreated, God is no longer, according to the Platonists, the Creator of all things, nor, according to their opinions, is the monarchy of God established. . . If matter too were uncreated, it also would be unalterable and equal to God, for that which is created is mutable and alterable but that which is uncreated is immutable and unalterable. And what great thing is it if God made the world out of existent materials? For even a human artist, when he gets material from some one, makes of it what he pleases. But the power of God is manifested in this, that out of the things that are not he makes whatever he pleases . . . out of things that are not he creates and has created things that are" (II, 4).

God, then, "having his own Logos internal – *ἐνδιάθετον* – begat him, emitting – *προφορικός* – him along with his own Wisdom before all things" (II, 10). "When God willed to make all that he determined, he begot his Logos, uttered – *προφορικόν* – the First-Born of all creation, not himself being emptied of the Logos but having begotten the Logos and always conversing with the Logos" (II, 22).

It must be kept in mind that Theophilus is addressing only those questions raised by Autolycus – the invisibility of the Christian God, the faith in the resurrection, the name of Christian, and the question of the alleged inferiority of Christian Scripture to Greek philosophy and literature. The very nature of this work precludes a presentation of the entirety of the Christian faith. Theophilus addresses only those issues in common. It must not be forgotten that Theophilus was a bishop and that he wrote other works which intrinsically would have dealt with the original deposit, with that which had been handed down.

MELITO OF SARDIS

Melito, bishop of Sardis in Lydia, was well-respected by his contemporaries. He flourished during the reign of Emperor Marcus Aurelius (161-180). Polycrates of Ephesus in a letter to Pope Victor (189-199) on the controversy over the date of Easter refers to Melito as one of the "great lights" of Asia. Very little is known of his life but he wrote prolifically, according to the list of his works given by Eusebius. Until recently only fragments of some of his works had come down to us. He wrote an *Apology* on behalf of the Christians to Emperor Marcus Aurelius and more than twenty other works: *On God Incarnate, On the Incarnation of Christ, On Christian Life and the Prophets, On the Church, On Hospitality, On Prophecy, On the Revelation of St. John, On Baptism, On Truth, On Faith and Christ's Birth, On the Devil, On the Senses, On Creation, On the Lord's Day, On the Faith of Man, On the Obedience of Faith, On the Soul and Body*, two books *On the Passover*, and six books *On the Law and Prophets* which contains the oldest list of the canonical books of the Old Testament – the preface of this is preserved by Eusebius. But until recently only fragments of some of these works had come down to us.

His *Homily on the Passion* has been discovered in an almost complete form – εἰς τὸπάθος. It is a powerful sermon written in a rich, rhythmic style that has an almost hypnotic aspect to it. The central theme is Christ's destruction of death, the "slayer of man." This theological hymn to the mystery of salvation emphasizes the Divinity and pre-existence of Christ. Christ is referred to as "our emperor or king" – ὑμῶν βασιλεύς; as God – θεός; as the Word or Logos – λόγος; as Son – υἱος; as the First-Born of God – ὁ πρωτότοκος τοῦ θεοῦ, as Lord – δεσπότης; as the King of Israel – ὁ βασιλεὺς Ἰσ - ραήλ, and quite oddly as Father – πατήρ. The reference to Father is in an important passage which portrays the many activities of Christ: "For born as a Son, and led forth as a Lamb, sacrificed as a Sheep, buried as a Man, he rose from the dead as God, being by nature God and Man. He is all things. He is Law because he judges. He is Logos because he teaches. He is Grace because he saves. He is Father because he begets. He is Son because he is begotten. He is the sacrificial Sheep because he suffers. He is Man because he is buried. He is God because he arises. This is Jesus Christ, to whom belongs the glory unto ages of ages" (8-10). It is possible to interpret this complete identification of Christ with the Godhead as a form of what later would be known as Monarchian Modalism.

But such an interpretation is dangerous. It could be nothing more than rhetorical usage. To judge him on this one text is inappropriate, especially since he wrote so prolifically and those writings are no longer extant. But even in this homily he is more specific: "This is he who became flesh in a Virgin, whose bones were not broken upon the tree, who in burial was not corrupted by earth, who arose from the dead and raised man from the grave below to the heights of the heavens. This is the Lamb who was slain, this is the Lamb who was dumb, this is he who was born of Mary the fair ewe" (70-71). Elsewhere Melito writes that Christ "took flesh from the Virgin Mary" – ἐκεῖνον ἔτι σαρκωθέντα διὰ παρθένου Μαρίας (66). In his *Homily* he clearly affirms both the Divine and human in Christ – φύσει θεὸς ὢν καὶ ἄνθρωπος. If the text conveyed by Anastasius Sinaita is authentic, then Melito introduced the word οὐσία into Christology – θεὸς γὰρ ὢν ὁμοῦ τε καὶ ἄνθρωπος τέλειος ὁ αὐτὸς τὰς δύο αὐτοῦ οὐσίας ἐπιστώσατο ἡμῖν. Melito, knowing that the Church has received an original deposit, refers to the Church as the "reservoir of truth" – ἀποδοχεῖον τῆς ἀληθείας (40).

CHAPTER FIVE

ST. IRENAEUS OF LYONS AND
CLEMENT OF ALEXANDRIA

ST. IRENAEUS OF LYONS

St. Irenaeus of Lyons was probably born in Asia Minor between 125 and 145, perhaps in Smyrna – in his letter to the Roman presbyter Florinus St. Irenaeus tells us that in his early youth he had listened to the sermons of Polycarp, bishop of Smyrna: "When I was still a boy, I knew you, Florinus, in lower Asia, in Polycarp's house . . . I remember the events of those days more clearly than those which happened recently . . . so that I can speak even of the place in which the blessed Polycarp sat and disputed, how he came in and went out, the character of his life, the appearance of his body, the discourses which he made to the people, how he reported his relationship with John and with the others who had seen the Lord, how he remembered their words, and what were the things concerning the Lord which he had heard from them, and about their miracles, and about their teachings, and how Polycarp had received them from the eye-witnesses of the Logos of Life, and reported all things in agreement with the Scriptures. I listened eagerly even then to these things through the mercy of God which was given me, and made notes of them, not on paper, but in my heart, and ever by the grace of God do I truly ruminate on them." This text is preserved by Eusebius in his Ἐκκλησιαστικὴ Ἱστορία 5, 20. But the fact that St. Irenaeus was in Smyrna as a boy does not necessitate that he was born there.

St. Irenaeus is one of the most important theologians or Church writers of the second century. Some scholars consider him "the most important of the theologians" of the second century. Nygren in his *Agape and Eros* asserts that "Irenaeus is chief of the anti-Gnostic Fathers." The fact remains that his importance is enormous. It is not known why St. Irenaeus left Asia Minor and went to Gaul. One conjecture is that he accompanied St. Polycarp to Rome in 155, stayed for a while, and then from Rome went to Gaul. What is known is that through Polycarp St. Irenaeus was in contact with the Apostolic Age.

The first historical mention of St. Irenaeus is in the year 177. At that time he was a priest of the Church of Lyons [Lugdunum] under the elder bishop, St. Pothinus. A certain group of Christians coming from Phrygia had come to Lyons with the news that, according to the Phrygian prophets, the second coming of Christ was at hand. At this time Pope Eleutherius (175-189) had been solicited to confirm the condemnations which the bishops of Asia had passed on the Montanists. The Church of Lyons wrote a letter on this subject to the pope and entrusted it to St. Irenaeus who was to take it to Rome. The letter contained an excellent recommendation, as found in Eusebius: "We have asked our brother and companion Irenaeus to bring this letter to you, and we beg you to hold him in esteem, for he is zealous for the covenant of Christ." It was fortuitous for St. Irenaeus because while he was gone a persecution broke out in Lyons (177-178), one of the victims of which was St. Pothinus. On his return from Rome St. Irenaeus was chosen to succeed St. Pothinus as bishop.

St. Irenaeus became involved with Rome once again when Pope Victor I (189-198) took a strong stand against the Church of Asia Minor – Proconsular Asia, the metropolis of which was Ephesus – in the Paschal controversy. The Church in Asia Minor, following a tradition alleged to come from St. John, celebrated the feast of the Christian Passover, Easter, on the day of the Paschal full moon, whether that day fell on a Sunday or on any other day of the week. The rest of the Church, both East and West, celebrated the Christian Pascha on the Sunday following the Paschal full moon. The Church at Rome, as the capital of the empire, had Christians living or visiting there from all parts of the empire. The Christians from Asia Minor celebrated Easter according to their tradition in Rome. This created disharmony in the liturgical life of the Church but it was tolerated by five popes from about 118 to 165 – Xystus, Telesphorus, Hyginus, Pius, and Anicetus. It was this liturgical and calendrical issue which was discussed in Rome in 155 by St. Polycarp and Pope Anicetus without a resolution of the problem. It appears that Pope Soter, who followed Anicetus, required all Christians in Rome to celebrate Easter simultaneously. But Pope Soter did not interfere with the custom in Asia Minor where that tradition continued. Pope Victor determined to bring uniformity to the entire Church. Such a step required the suppression of the custom of Asia Minor. It appears that Pope Victor sent letters from the Church of Rome to the metropolitans in Asia Minor requesting them to summon local councils to discuss the proper day for the celebration of Easter. That Pope Victor requested rather than commanded seems to be the meaning that Polycrates, bishop of Ephesus, attaches to the word ἠξιώσατε in his letter to Pope Victor, although ἀξιόω can be used in the sense of "to require." In compliance with the request from the Roman Church councils were held in many provinces – in Palestine, in Asia, in Pontus, in Osrhoene, in Gaul and elsewhere. Pope Victor held his own council in Rome. The decision was unanimous – except for Polycrates' province – that Easter should be celebrated on Sunday. It appears that Pope Victor, in communicating the result of his council to Polycrates, threatened to excommunicate the Church in Asia if they continued in their custom. Polycrates' reply is historical interesting in shedding light on the attitude of other churches to Rome at this time; it is also defiant. Eusebius relates that Pope Victor then "endeavored" to cut off the churches "of all Asia, along with their neighboring churches, as heterodox, from the common unity." Eusebius also relates that Victor sent letters to the other churches proclaiming that the Church in

Asia was "utterly – *ἀρδην* – separated from communion." Victor
received letters from other bishops exhorting him to pursue a policy of
unity, peace, and love. Some of these letters sharply upbraid Victor. St.
Irenaeus entered the conflict, admonishing Pope Victor. Eusebius relates
that Irenaeus lived up to his name, for he was a real "peace" maker –
εἰρηνοποιός. After this incident St. Irenaeus is not heard about again –
even the date of his death is unknown, although tradition fixes it about
202 or 203.

St. Irenaeus had a breadth of knowledge, a depth of faith, and a love
and knowledge of Scripture. In addition to his episcopal duties, he was,
as Tertullian writes about him, "a curious explorer of all doctrines." He
made it a kind of official duty to know all the heresies with the explicit
purpose of refuting them so that the received faith, the faith from the
tradition of the Apostles would triumph. He was highly educated and
had read numerous Greek writers, both literary and philosophical. But
he was not attracted to abstract speculation, precisely because he
believed this to be the main source of Gnosticism which at that time
was ravaging Gaul as it was also ravaging Italy and the East. For him,
the very fact of revealing the system of the Gnostics "was to vanquish
them." In addition to his episcopal duties and his writings, St. Irenaeus
worked to spread Christianity in the provinces adjacent to Lyons. The
Church at Besançon and at Valence claim that St. Irenaeus was the first
to announce the Gospel to them.

St. Irenaeus' main work is *ἔλεγχος καὶ ἀνατροπὴ τῆς ψευδο –
νύμου γνώσεως – The Detection and Overthrow of the Pretended but
False Gnosis*, more commonly known as the *Adversus Haereses*. This
work has been preserved not in its Greek original but in a Latin
translation which was in circulation soon after the original Greek
because not only St. Cyprian worked from it but also Tertullian.
Fragments of the Greek original have been preserved by Eusebius,
Hippolytus, and Epiphanius. From these three writers almost the entire
text can be reestablished. A literal translation of the fourth and fifth
books exists in an Armenian translation and fragments also exist in
Syriac translations. From Eusebius we knew that another work of his,
the *ἐπίδειξις τοῦ ἀποστολικοῦ κηρύγματος [The Demonstration
of the Apostolic Teaching]*, had been written by St. Irenaeus but
nothing more than the title was known until 1904 when the entire text
was discovered in an Armenian translation. Only fragments exist of the
other works by St. Irenaeus. Eusebius mentions a work called *Περὶ
ἐπιστήμης [On Knowledge]*, which he considers a "short but necessary
book." A substantial fragment from his work *On the Monarchy or How
God is Not the Cause of Evil* is preserved by Eusebius. This work was
directed against Florinus, a former friend who had become a Gnostic.
St. Irenaeus wrote another work against his former friend Florinus, the
closing words from which are preserved by Eusebius – *On the Ogdoad*
[of Valentinus]. The title of a letter St. Irenaeus wrote to Blastus, *On
Schism*, is found in Eusebius. A fragment is extant in Syriac of a letter

he wrote to Pope Victor requesting that he take measures against
Florinus and suppress Florinus' writings. Eusebius has preserved
excepts from St. Irenaeus' letter to Pope Victor on the Paschal
controversy.

St. Irenaeus clearly enunciates both his position of "apostolic
faith" and the Church's Trinitarian faith early on in *Adversus Haereses*.
"Now the Church, although scattered over the whole civilized world to
the end of the earth, received from the apostles and their disciples its
faith in one God, the Father Almighty . . . and in one Christ Jesus, the
Son of God, who was made flesh for our salvation, and in the Holy
Spirit . . . Having received this preaching and this faith . . . the
Church, although scattered in the whole world, carefully preserves it, as
if living in one house. She believes these things everywhere alike, as if
she had but one heart and one soul, and preaches them harmoniously,
teaches them, and hands them down, as if she had but one mouth. For
the languages of the world are different but the meaning of the tradition
is one and the same . . . For since the faith is one and the same, he who
can say much about it does not add to it, nor does he who can say little
diminish it. . . the real Church has one and the same faith everywhere
in the world" (I, 10). "For we learned the plan of salvation from no
others than from those through whom the gospel came to us. They first
preached it abroad, and then later . . . handed it down to us in writings"
(III, 1). How important the "received tradition" is for St. Irenaeus is
clear when he discusses "the writings." The Gnostic heretics attack "the
writings," saying they are "nor correct, or authoritative." St. Irenaeus
then turns to his defense from the received and preserved tradition, a
defense which becomes the crucial test for orthodoxy and heterodoxy.
He must present a specific defense because, as he writes, "what it comes
to is that they will not agree with either Scripture or tradition" (III, 2).
"The tradition of the apostles, made clear in all the world, can be clearly
seen in every church by those who wish to behold the truth. We can
enumerate those who were established by the apostles as bishops in the
churches, and their successors down to our time, none of whom taught
or thought anything like their mad ideas. Even if the apostles had
known of hidden mysteries, which they taught to the perfect secretly
and apart from others, they would have handed them down especially to
those to whom they were entrusting the churches themselves. . . But
since it would be very long in such a volume as this to enumerate the
successions of all the churches, I can by pointing out the tradition
which that very great, oldest, and well-known Church, founded and
established at Rome by those two most glorious apostles Peter and
Paul, received from the apostles, and its faith known among men,
which comes down to us through the successions of bishops, put to
shame all of those who in any way . . . gather as they should not. For
every church must be in harmony with [or resort to] this Church
because of its outstanding pre-eminence, that is, the faithful from
everywhere, since the apostolic tradition is preserved in it by those from

everywhere" (III, 20). St. Irenaeus uses the Church of Rome as the example because it was founded by Peter and Paul and was hence apostolic, because it possessed some type of "pre-eminence" or primacy, and because it was visited, as the capital city of the empire, by Christians from everywhere and therefore possessed the existential reality of knowing the faith of those from all parts of the world, a faith which was the same as that of Rome. He then continues by using the Church at Smyrna and the Church at Ephesus as further examples of the "apostolic tradition." "Since there are so many clear testimonies, we should not seek from others for the truth which can easily be received from the Church. There the apostles, like a rich man making a deposit, fully bestowed upon her all that belongs to the truth, so that whoever wishes may receive from her the water of life" (III, 2). St. Irenaeus raises the vital issue addressed by St. Ignatius, the issue about which Karl Adam has written – what if there were no Scriptures? "Even if the apostles had not left their writings to us, ought we not to follow the rule of the tradition which they handed down to those to whom they committed the churches?" St. Irenaeus gives an example of where this actually applies – among "many barbarian people" who follow the rule of tradition "written in their hearts by the Spirit without paper and ink." These Christians "diligently follow the old tradition." He then briefly summarizes the essence of this "old tradition": "they believe in one God, maker of heaven and earth and of all that is in them, through Christ Jesus the Son of God, who on account of his abundant love for his creation submitted to be born of a Virgin, himself by himself uniting man to God, and having suffered under Pontius Pilate, and risen. Those who believe in this faith without written documents are barbarians . . . if anyone should preach to them the inventions of the heretics . . . they would at once stop their ears and run far, far away, not enduring even to listen to such blasphemous speech." It is, writes St. Irenaeus, "the old tradition of the apostles" that preserves them in the true faith.

St. Irenaeus describes how the heretical Gnostics taught about Jesus – "according to none of the views of the heretics was the Logos of God made flesh" (III, 11). "Some say that this Jesus . . . incarnate and suffered, and that he had passed through Mary like water through a tube. Others say that it was the son of the Demiurge, on whom the Jesus . . . descended. Others again say that Jesus indeed was born of Joseph and Mary, and that Christ who came from above descended on him, being without flesh and free from suffering. . . If one should read over all their credal statements, he would find that they always bring in the Logos of God and the Christ who is from above as without flesh and free from suffering. Some think that he was manifested as a transfigured man but say that he was neither born nor incarnate. Others say that he did not even take the form of a man, but descended like a dove on that Jesus who was born of Mary" (III, 11). "Vain also are the Ebionites, who do not accept in their souls by faith the union of God and man, but remain in the old leaven of human birth – not wishing to understand that the Holy Spirit came upon Mary, and the power of the Most High overshadowed her, and so what was born of her is holy and the Son of God Most High, the Father of all who thus brought about his Incarnation and displayed the new birth so that as we by the former birth were heirs of death, by this birth we should be heirs of life" (V, 3).

St. Irenaeus delineates the legitimate areas of theology in his *Adversus Haereses*. The "basic idea" remains the same – by this he means that the original deposit remains always one and the same. Theology consists of "working out the things that have been said," of "building them into the foundation of faith." This is done by "expounding the activity and dispensation of God for the sake of mankind," by "showing clearly" God's long-suffering, by "declaring why one and the same God made some things subject to time, others eternal," by "understanding why God, being invisible, appeared to the prophets, not in one form, but differently to different ones," by "showing why there were a number of covenants with mankind," by "teaching the character of each of the covenants," by "searching out why God shut up all in disobedience that he might have mercy on all," by "giving thanks that the Logos of God was made flesh, and suffered," by "declaring why the coming of the Son of God was at the last times," by "unfolding what is found in the prophets about the end and the things to come," by "not being silent that God has made the forsaken Gentiles fellow heirs and of the same body and partners with the saints," and by "stating how this mortal and fleshly body will put on immortality, and this corruptible incorruption" (I, 10). Clearly St. Irenaeus does not consider this enumeration to be exhaustive and comprehensive. Rather, it is no more than a sketch, a guide of some of the areas in which speculative theology can be utilized. He himself discusses far more areas of theological concern.

God, for St. Irenaeus, is the Creator, the "Father of all," the "Source of all goodness." He is "simple, uncompounded, without diversity of parts, completely identical and consistent, beyond the emotions and passions" of created existence (II, 13). God as Creator gives existence to everything; creation was an act of his freedom, a free act, for "he was not moved by anything" (I, 1). God in his "greatness" cannot be known to man, he cannot be "measured" (IV, 20). It is God's love which brings man within the grasp of a knowledge of God but this knowledge is limited, it is not a knowledge of God's "greatness" or his "true being." Our knowledge of God comes from the revelation of the Logos of God (IV, 20; III, 24). God is without need. He did not create because he had need of man and creation. Neither does he need our love, obedience, and service. God gives, confers, grants (IV, 14).

God is "absolute and eternal." Creation is "contingent" and, being contingent, having their beginning in time, created beings "fall short of their maker's perfection" (IV, 38). Akin to the thought of Theophilus of

Alexandria and other Apologists, St. Irenaeus thinks of man at creation as "immature" – "being newly created they are therefore childlike and immature, and not yet fully trained for an adult way of life. And just as a mother is able to offer food to an infant, but the infant is not yet able to receive food unsuited to its age, so also God could have offered perfection to man at the beginning, but man, being yet an infant, could not have absorbed it" (IV, 38).

Not only is man's participation in the redemptive work of Christ a process but the very plan of redemption is a process and – moreover, the very Incarnation, the reality of God becoming man, begins a process in the life of the God-Man that sanctifies every aspect and stage in the life of man. This is his well-known teaching of "recapitulation", of *ἀνακεφαλαίωσις*. There is no notion in the thought of St. Irenaeus of any form of passive holiness or passive righteousness. Everything is process, everything is dynamic, everything is moving toward the goal of rebirth in Christ, of rebirth into incorruptibility, of rebirth into eternality, of rebirth leading to a vision and knowledge of God, of rebirth leading to transfiguration. The theme of the later Greek and then Byzantine fathers of the vision of God and of deification is also the thought of St. Irenaeus. As St. Irenaeus asks, what is the deification of created beings if not their participation in the divine life? Men will "see God in order to live; men will become immortal by the vision and will progress on the path to God" *per visionem immortales facti et peregrinantes usque in Deum*. St. Irenaeus writes that "it is impossible to live without life, and the foundation or existence – *ὕπαρξις* – of life comes from participating – *μετοχή* – in God. To participate in God is to know – *γιγνώσκειν* – him and to enjoy his goodness" (III, 20). In the thought of St. Irenaeus everything is accomplished by God and by the will of God and yet man participates by a spiritually free acceptance of everything accomplished and revealed by God.

Since God is the cause of the being of all things, these created things, in order to participate in "incorruptibility," must remain "subject to God." Subjection and obedience to God conveys incorruptibility and "continuance in incorruptibility is the glory of eternity." "Through such obedience and discipline and training, man, who is contingent and created, grows into the image and likeness of the eternal God. This process the Father approves and commands; the Son carries out the Father's plan, the Spirit supports and hastens the process – while man gradually advances and mounts towards perfection; that is, he approaches the eternal. The eternal is perfect and this is God. Man has first to come into being, then to progress, and by progressing come to manhood, and having reached manhood to increase, and thus increasing to persevere, and by persevering be glorified, and thus see his Lord. For it is God's intention that he should be seen: and the vision of God is the acquisition of immortality; and immortality brings man near to God" (IV, 38). It has been observed and commented upon that St. Irenaeus taught in *The Demonstration of the Apostolic Teaching* (15) that man before the Fall was immortal by nature. What appears to be contradictory is not necessarily the case if one analyzes the two different perspectives from which St. Irenaeus was writing in the respective texts. The interpretation involves that important "if" in St. Irenaeus – if man had kept the commandments of God, if man had remained subject to incorruptibility. But in his thought it is clear that this "if" is completely speculative and theoretical, not real and existential. The very nature of created existence and the depth of spiritual freedom in his thought renders this "if" existentially meaningless.

God, invisible by nature, reveals himself, manifests himself to man by the Logos, the principle of all manifestation. And here there is a simultaneity and reciprocity of knowledge and vision, for the Logos reveals God to man while simultaneously revealing man to God. And the Logos has become man so that men might become gods (V, preface).

Eternally the Son is the "Only-Begotten" of the Father. "His Begetting" is "in truth indescribable. . . Only the Father knows who begat him, and the Son who was Begotten" (II, 28). "The Son always co-exists with the Father" (II, 30). The "Son of God did not begin to be" (III, 18). "Through the Son who is in the Father and who has the Father in himself, He Who Is has been revealed" (III, 6). "The Son is the measure of the Father because he contains the Father" (IV, 4). "All saw the Father in the Son, for the Father is the invisible of the Son, the Son the visible of the Father" (IV, 6).

"There is one God, who by his Logos and Wisdom made and ordered all things . . . His Logos is our Lord Jesus Christ who in these last times became man among men so that he might unite the end with the beginning, that is, Man with God" (IV, 20). "God became man and it was the Lord himself who saved us" (III, 21). "He united man to God . . . If he had overcome man's adversary as man, the enemy would not have been justly overcome. If it had not been God who granted salvation, we should not have it as a secure possession. And if man had not been united to God, man could not have become a partaker of immortality. For the mediator between God and man had to bring both parties into friendship and harmony through his kinship with both, and to present man to God and to make God known to man. In what way could we share in the adoption of the sons of God unless through the Son we had received the fellowship with the Father, unless the Logos of God made flesh had entered into communion with us?" (III, 18). "The Lord redeemed us by his blood and gave his life for our life, his flesh for our flesh, and poured out the Spirit of the Father to unite us and reconcile God and man, bringing God down to man through the Spirit, and raising man to God through his Incarnation" (V, 1).

The Holy Spirit, the "unction," is referred to constantly by St. Irenaeus not only in credal forms but in terms of his activity – the "Spirit prepares man for the Son of God," the "Spirit supplies knowledge of the truth," the "Spirit has revealed the *oikonomiai* of the

Father and the Son towards man," the Spirit is the "living water" which the Lord pours forth.

CLEMENT OF ALEXANDRIA

Clement of Alexandria was born, according to St. Epiphanius, in Athens probably about 150. His parents were pagans and he at some point converted to Christianity. To increase his knowledge of Christianity Clement wandered throughout Syria, Palestine, and Italy. Finally, in 180, his soul "found rest" under the famous teacher St. Pantaenus in Alexandria. Pantaenus had travelled extensively in Arabia before coming to Alexandria where he became the first known teacher at the famous Didascalia, the "school of oral teaching" – τό τῆς κατηχήσεως διδασκαλεῖον. The Didascalia, like the school of cate - chumens, was probably in existence from the very beginnings of the Alexandrian Church. In the middle of the second century the Didascalia became an important and vital school of theology and its heads were appointed and dismissed by the bishop of Alexandria. The Didascalia, unlike St. Justin's school which was more of a private school, was an "official school." The students or "auditors" came from throughout the empire – there were catechumens, idolaters, philosophers representing a variety of schools of philosophy, and Gnostics of all types. The mission of the Didascalia was to react to these different philosophies, especially the Gnostics. The polemical perspective of the Didascalia was anti-Gnostic. Pantaenus' reputation as a teacher was one universally acclaimed, according to Clement and to Eusebius. That he wrote anything is doubtful, although Henri Marrou claims he is the author of the *Letter to Diognetus*.

Clement became Pantaenus' student, then his associate and assistant. He became the successor to Pantaenus, probably about 200. One of his students was Origen, according to Eusebius, although some modern scholars, especially Munck disagree – they also dispute whether the Didascalia was anything more than a private school. A few years later Clement had to flee from Alexandria because of the persecution of Septimius Severus. Clement died in Cappadocia, never again seeing Alexandria, between 211 and 216. He was considered St. Clement by Christian writers of the early centuries.

We may know very little about Clement's life but his character and personality come through quite vividly in his writings. He had a broad education – he possessed a good knowledge of philosophy, literature, mythology, and poetry and knew early Christian literature very well. His knowledge of the Bible and the post-apostolic literature, both orthodox and heretical, is exceedingly good. Clement realized that the Church had to be in dialogue with the world and that world was one of pagan philosophy and literature. For him all secular learning serves theology, if approached correctly. He presented the Christian faith as a system of thought to the world at that time.

Clement's three most important works are his *Exhortation to the Greeks* – Προτρεπτικὸς πρὸς Ἕλληνας; his *Tutor* – Παιδαγωγός; and his *Stromata* – Στρωματεῖς. One other work is extant. It is a "homily," preserved as a written work, on *The Gospel of St. Mark 10: 17-31*, and entitled *Who is the Rich Man Who is Saved* – Τίς ὁ σωζόμενος πλούσιος? It is in this latter work that Clement maintains that richness as such does not exclude one from the Kingdom of God. Rather it is one's attitude, for one must keep the heart from the desire for wealth and from any attachment to it. It is the passion, not the wealth, that must be renounced.

His most important lost work is his commentary on and sketches of the writings of both the Old and New Testament, including even all the disputed books, entitled *Hypotyposeis* – ὑποτυπώσεις. Most of the extant Greek excerpts are preserved in Eusebius. Other excerpts exist in the *Pratum spirituale* of John Moschus and in a Latin translation which goes back to the time of Cassiodorus (c. 540). St. Photius possessed in the entire *Hypotyposeis* in Greek and writes bitterly about it (*Bibl. Cod.* 109): "Correct doctrine is held firmly in some places but in other places he is carried away by odd and impious notions. He maintains the eternity of matter, produces a theory of ideas from the words of Holy Scripture, and reduces the Son to a mere creature. He relates incredible stories of metempsychosis and of many worlds before Adam. His teaching on the formation of Eve from Adam is blasphemous and scurrilous – and anti-Scriptural. He imagines that the angels had intercourse with women and begot children with them. He also writes that the Logos did not become man in reality but only in appearance. He has, it would appear, a fantastic idea of two Logoi of the Father, of which the inferior one appeared to men." Clement of Alexandria had a good reputation in Byzantium and for that reason St. Photius' conclusion is that the work is not authentically that of Clement. And in this case St. Photius is probably correct because what he writes about Clement is not consonant with the the extant works of Clement. He was no Docetist. Harnack has accused Clement, based on a text from the Hypotyposeis and from other texts, of actually believing in two Logoi, the originally existing Logos and the Logos who was the Son of God. Harnack has unfortunately misread Clement. There is in Clement no distinction between the λόγος ἐνδιάθετος and the λόγος προφορικός from an ontological perspective. His does distinguish between the two but only in the sense that the term λόγος προ – φορικός deprives the Son of the full majesty disclosed by the term λόγος ἐνδιάθετος. His idea is rather clear. The Logos is one and the same from eternity. But when the Logos is thought of only in his *oikonomic* activity and not in his eternal life there is a tendency to deprive the Logos of the full majesty of eternity. His point is precisely the opposite of Harnack's interpretation. Clement's central idea is that the Logos is eternally equal with but distinct from the Father and distinct precisely as the Son of the Father.

Other lost works are his *Ecclesiastical Canon or Against the Judaizers*, one fragment of which exists; his *On Providence*, a few fragments of which are extant; his *Exhortation to Endurance or To the Recently Baptized*, of which one fragment may be authentic; his *Discourses on Fasting* and *On Slander*, of which nothing is extant; his *On the Prophet Amos*, mentioned only by Palladius; and his *Letters*, of which none are extant.

Clement of Alexandria is in a very real sense the founder of speculative theology, the founder of Christian apologetics on a systematic basis. In this sense he is different from the Christian writers we have touched upon above and is quite different from St. Irenaeus, who was much more of a traditionally rooted writer and bishop. But Clement too believes in the deposit, in the oneness of the teaching of the Christian faith from the very beginning. "For just as the teaching is one, so also the tradition of the apostles was one" – μία ἡ πάντων γέγονε τῶν ἀποστόλων ὥσπερ διδασκαλία οὕτως δὲ καὶ ἡ παράδοσις (*Stromata* 7, 17). "It is my view that the true Church, that which is really ancient, is one. . . For from the very reason that God is one, and the Lord is one, that which is in the highest degree honorable is praised as a result of its oneness, for it is an imitation of the one first principle. In the nature of the One, then, the one Church is one . . . Therefore in substance and idea, in origin, in preeminence, we say that the ancient and Catholic Church is alone, gathering as it does into the unity of the one faith . . . in its oneness the preeminence of the Church, as the principle of union, surpasses all other things and has nothing like or equal to itself." Those who "pervert" the "divine words" have not the key but a counter key – ἀντικλεῖς – "by which they do not enter in as we enter in, through the tradition of the Lord" (7, 17). Clement discusses at length the relationship between this tradition and Scripture. The Church has, as "the source of teaching," both the Lord and the Scriptures (7, 16).

Clement's virtue is his courage, his fearless approach into dialogue with Hellenic philosophy and culture. He has been accused of the Hellenization of Christianity in the negative sense. A Christianity that is not Hellenized properly is not an authentic Christianity. But in this sense it is more proper to speak of the Christianization of Hellenism which produced an authentically Christian Hellenization of Christianity. But Clement ventured into new terrain and to a great extent he was successful. For example, instead of rejecting Gnosticism in totality, Clement attempted to create a true, an authentic Christian "Gnosis." This allowed Christianity to utilize truth wherever it was found. In this regard Clement is close to St. Justin and in sharp opposition to Tatian. For Clement the beginning of philosophy is faith. To confront philosophy from a Christian perspective is to realize that all philosophy without Christ is vain and without foundation (*Stromata* 1, 20). Clement believed that faith and knowledge were harmonious and that the proper combination produced the perfect Christian and the true

Gnostic. At times he may appear to wander too far into philosophy but his basic principle is that "faith is superior to knowledge and that faith is the criterion of knowledge" (*Stromata* 2, 4). Clement can write that philosophy possesses a pedagogical significance for every Christian who can rise above mere faith – ψιλή πίστις – to Gnosis. But at the same time this must be done "in accordance with the canon of the Church" – κατά κάνονα ἐκκλησιαστικόν (*Stromata* 7, 7; 6, 15). For Clement faith in Revelation is necessary for salvation but that very faith points beyond itself, almost in Tillichian terminology, to the ultimate which is Gnosis (*Stromata* 2, 2; 5, 1; 7, 10). Faith is the outward acceptance of God out of fear and respect (*Stromata* 2, 12; 5, 1; 7, 12). But the true Gnostic lives in "initiated vision" – ἐποπτική θεωρία – comprehending and apprehending salvation inwardly (*Stromata* 6, 10; 1, 2). Those who merely believe – ἁπλῶς πε - πιστευκώς – require the purifications – καθάρσια – or the "minor mysteries" – μικρά μυστήρια – of the Church but the Gnostic needs the "great mysteries" – μεγάλα μυστήρια, the ἐποπτεία (*Protrep - tikos* 1 ; 12 and *Stromata* 5, 11). Some scholars have sharply criticized Clement at this point because he seems to make a distinction between classes of Christians – on the one hand, there is the unsophisticated beginner who clings to the externalities of the faith; on the other hand, there is the advanced Gnostic Christian who beholds the mysteries of God and who abides in communion with God through a heart full of understanding. These critics detect a Stoic influence at this point, the Stoic discrimination of those who are advancing – προκόπτοντες. Such an interpretation, while observing a point correctly, interprets this not from within the early Christian exhortation to advance in Christian virtue, not from the perspective of the Biblical and early Christian call to perfection, call to striving, not from the inner dynamism of a realistic and existential struggle of spirituality, not from within the context of St. Paul's running the race. Rather, these critics look back into the phenomenon of early Christian spirituality from the perspective of Reformation theology. It is not only unfair to evaluate Clement of Alexandria in such a perspective but it is also a revisionist approach to intellectual history. The New Testament stresses the dynamism of spiritual growth, from being "babes" in Christ to constant growth in the faith spiritually and intellectually.

For Clement the One God is beyond nature – ἐπέκεινα τῆς οὐσίας – and approached apophatically (*Stromata* 5, 11; 5, 12). He is the Creator. "If, then, abstracting all that belongs to bodies and things called incorporeal, we cast ourselves into the greatness of Christ, and thence advance into immensity by holiness, we may reach somehow to the conception of the Almighty, knowing not what he is, but what he is not. And form and motion, or standing, or a throne, or place, or right hand or left, are not at all to be conceived as belonging to the Father of the cosmos, although it is so written . . . The First Cause is not then in space but is above both space and time and name and conception. . .

No one can rightly express God fully. Because of his greatness he is considered the All and is the Father of the cosmos. No parts can be predicated to him. For the One is indivisible . . . infinite in his being, without dimensions, without any limits. . . And if we name God, we do not do so properly, whether we call him the One, or the Good, or Mind, or Absolute Being, or Father, or God, or Creator, or Lord. We speak not as if we supply a name but because of our lack of a name. We use good names so that the mind may have these as points of support in order not to err in other respects. Each name by itself does not express God but all names combined are indicative of the power of the Omnipotent. For predicates are expressed either from what belongs to things themselves or from their mutual relation. But none of these are admissible in reference to God. Nor is he apprehended by the science of demonstration, for it depends on primary and better known principles. But there is nothing antecedent to the Unbegotten. *It remains that we understand, then, the Unknown, by divine grace*, and by the Logos alone who come forth from him."

God is "not a subject for demonstration and, therefore, cannot be the object of science. But the Son is Wisdom and Knowledge and Truth and all that is akin to these. The Son is also susceptible of demonstration and of description. All all the powers of the Spirit, becoming collectively one unity, terminate in the same point – that is, in the Son. But the Son is not completely expressed by our conception of each of his powers. He is not merely One, as Unity, nor Many, as having parts, but One as All. Hence, he is All. For he is the circle of all powers, which in him are rounded and united. To believe in him, and by him, is to participate in unity, being indissolubly united in him" (*Stromata* 4, 25).

The unity of the Father and Son is clearly expressed by Clement. "The Son is in him and the Father is in the Son" (*Paidagogos* 1, 7). He is "Jesus, the Logos, then, who leads the children to salvation. And he is appropriately called the Instructor – παιδαγωγός." "Our Instructor is the Holy God Jesus, the Logos, who is the guide of all humanity. The loving God himself is our Instructor." In the Old Testament the "Lord God was unnamed because he had not yet become man." "The face of God is the Logos by whom God is manifested and made known." Some critics call attention to Clement's reference to the Logos who "has appeared," to the statement: "the Logos was an angel but to the fresh and new people has also been given a New Covenant, and the Logos has appeared, and fear is turned to love, and that mystic angel is born – Jesus." But in this context Clement is merely discussing the theophanies of the Old Testament and making the claim that in these theophanies God really appeared but not God the Father. It was the Son of God, the Logos, who appeared to man in the theophanies. Hence, the reference to that "mystic angel." It is a realistic interpretation of the theophanies, as opposed to the later interpretation of the theophanies by St. Augustine who could not grasp that God actually appeared to man and hence interpreted these theophanies by a form of "created grace." St. Augustine in general has serious problems with God's relationship to the created world. Clement, on this point, is quite Biblical. "Eternal grace and truth were by Jesus Christ. Mark the expressions of Scripture: of the law only is it said 'was given'. But truth, being the grace of the Father, is the eternal work of the Logos, and it is not said 'be given' but 'to be' by Jesus without whom nothing was. (*Paidagogos* 1, 7).

The Lord, the Instructor, is "most good." He "sympathizes from the exceeding greatness of his love with the nature of each man. . . Nothing exists, the cause of whose existence is not supplied by God. Nothing, then, is hated by God, nor by the Logos. For both are one – that is, God. For he has said 'In the beginning the Logos was in God, and the Logos was God'. . . Therefore God is loving. Consequently the Logos is loving." (*Paidagogos* 1, 8). "As the Logos is the Son in the Father," he possesses both love and justice by the mutual relationship of the Father and the Son. . . Very clearly, then, we conclude him to be one and the same God. . . It is indisputable, then, that the Lord is the Son of the Creator. And if the Creator above all is confessed to be just, and the Lord to be the Son of the Creator, then the Lord is the Son of him who is just . . . For the sake of man the Logos became man."

Clement writes precisely about false Gnostics while concentrating on central aspects of Christology. "Of the Gnostic so much has been cursorily, as it were, written . . . There are some who draw the distinction that faith has reference to the Son and knowledge to the Spirit. But it has escaped their attention that, in order to believe truly in the Son, we must believe that he is the Son, and that he came, and how, and for what, and respecting his Passion. And we must know who is the Son of God. Now neither is knowledge without faith nor faith without knowledge. Nor is the Father without the Son, for the Son is with the Father. And the Son is the true teacher about the Father. . . In order that we may know the Father, we must believe in the Son, that it is the Son of God who teaches, for the Father brings us from faith to knowledge by means of the Son" (*Stromata* 5, 1). "Believe, O man, him who is man and God. Believe, O man, the living God who suffered and is adored" (*Protreptikos* 10).

Throughout his extant works Clement speaks of, refers to, and underpins his thought with the unity and oneness of the Father, Son, and Holy Spirit. "The all-loving, beneficent Father rained down his Logos and straightway did he become the spiritual nourishment for the good. O, the marvelous mystery! For one is the Father of all, one the Logos of all, and one is the Holy Spirit, one and the same everywhere" (*Paidagogos* 1, 6). "Be gracious, O Instructor, to us thy children, O Father, Charioteer of Israel, Son and Father, both one, O Lord. Grant to us who obey thy precepts that we may perfect the likeness of the image, and with all our power know the goodness of God and the kindness of his judgment. . . That we may give praise and thanksgiving to the only Father, and to the only Son, to Son and Father, Son our

Instructor and Teacher, together with the Holy Spirit, all in One, in whom are all things, through whom all things are one, through whom is eternity, of whom all men are members . . . all praise to the All-Good, the All-Lovely, the All-Wise, the All-Just One, to whom be glory both now and ever. Amen" (*Paidagogos* 3, 12). The Trinitarian praise ends Clement's *Who Is the Rich Man Who Is Saved?* "To whom, by his Son Jesus Christ, the Lord of the living and the dead, and by the Holy Spirit, be glory, honor, power, eternal majesty, both now and ever, from generation to generation, and from eternity to eternity. Amen" (42).

CHAPTER SIX

ESSENTIAL THOUGHTS OF THE EARLY APOLOGISTS

THE APOSTOLIC DEPOSIT

All the Apologists are immersed in and constantly refer to the "tradition," to the "rule of faith," to that which was received and safeguard, the "original deposit." Gebhardt collected most of the textual references – ἡ διδαχή, τὸ μάθημα, ἡ παράδοσις, ὁ κανὼν τῆς ἀληθείας, ὁ παραδοθεὶς λόγος, ἡ πίστις, ὁ κανών πίστεως, τὸ κήρηγμα, τὰ διδάγματα τοῦ χριστοῦ, ἡ παράδοσις τῶν ἀποστόλων, ὁ κανὼν ἐκκλησιαστικός, τὸ ἀρχαῖον τῆς ἐκκλη - σίας, regula fidei, regula veritatis, traditio apostolica, lex fidei, fides catholica. This was not merely a kind of rule to which the Apologists refer. Rather it was the living reality of how God revealed himself to man in the God-Man Jesus Christ, how this was an authoritative – indeed, a divine – "delivery" of the essence of the New Covenant to the apostles and through them to the Church. It was a reference to sacred reality. It is found in the New Testament, preserved by the Apologists as the basis of the living faith, and continually preserved in the Church – indeed, this is what is meant by the Ecumenical Councils when they declare: "Following the Fathers . . ." The depths of this adherence to the apostolic deposit is glimpsed in St. Ignatius and St. Irenaeus, both of whom declare that the Church exists even if there are no written documents. For St. Ignatius it is Jesus Christ who is the original document. St. Irenaeus refers to those barbarian tribes, who have the original faith – sine charta et atramento – written in their hearts through apostolic succession. This principle, this belief in the original deposit and its sacredness, is what St. Victor of Lérins uses to unveil the "novelty" of the thought of St. Augustine on predestination and original sin. This frame of reference will never leave the Church. St. Athanasius will write that "the true original tradition, faith and teaching of the Catholic Church, bestowed by the Lord, proclaimed by the apostles" was "safeguarded by the fathers" (*Ad Serapionem* I, 28). This not only forms but is the Church's consciousness of herself. The theological struggles of the Byzantine theologians come from the heart of the Church and are there ultimately resolved.

ON THE NATURE AND KNOWLEDGE OF GOD

When the Apologists consider the nature and knowledge of God, they speculate or theologize from within the framework of the apostolic deposit. If some of their language is philosophical, it does not mean that this philosophical language is in contradiction with that which has been revealed. Indeed, the Apologists in general believed that God had revealed elements of truth throughout history, that elements of truth, consonant always with the revelation in the Old Testament and with the apostolic deposit, were to be found in Greek philosophy and Greek culture in general – Tatian is an exception. It must not be forgotten that they believed that Plato had taken some of his ideas from Hebrew Scripture.

The unity – *εἷς θεός* – and monarchy of God – *τῶν ὅλων τὸ μοναρχικόν* were central doctrines taught by the Apologists. God is completely beyond all that is created – *τὸ ἄρρητον, τὸ ἀχώρητον, τὸ ἀνέκφραστον, τὸ ἀκατάληπτον, τὸ ἀπερινόητον, τὸ ἀσύγκριτον, τὸ ἀσυμβίβαστον, τὸ ἀνεκδιηγητόν*. God is begin - ningless – *ἄναρχος, ὅτι ἀγένητος*. He is perfect – *τέλειος* – and without any need – *ἀπροσδεής*. He is eternal and unchangeable – *ἀναλλοίωτος καθότι ἀθάνατος*. He is absolute causality – *αὐτὸς ὑπάρχων τοῦ παντὸς ἡ ὑπόστασις*. God is sovereign, the Father of everything – *δεσπότης τῶν ὅλων, πατὴρ διὰ τὸ εἶναι αὐτὸν πρὸ τῶν ὅλων, κτίστης τῶν πάντων*. God is wisdom, spirit, mind, and reason – *σοφία, πνεῦμα, νοῦς λόγος*. He is the Father of all righteousness and goodness – *πατὴρ τῆς δικαιοσύνης καὶ πασῶν τῶν ἀρετῶν χρηστότης* – and the *Pantocrator* – *παντοκράτωρ ὅτι αὐτὸς τὸ πάντα κρατεῖ καὶ ἐμπεριέχει*. The emphasis placed upon the unity and monarchy of God is there to protect God as the Uncreated, as the self-existing and cause of all existence, of all that is "created."

THE APOLOGISTS AND THE LOGOS

THE INFLUENCE OF PHILO

For the Apologists, as for St. John, God the Father reveals himself to mankind, relates to created existence, through his Logos. Both Greek philosophy and Hebraic thought had a theology of the Logos. The main spokesman for the Logos theology of Hebraic thought was Philo Judaeus, the Alexandrian Jewish philosopher and theologian. He was born sometime between 13 and 30 B.C. and died approximately around 45 A.D. For Philo, as for the Apologists, God is completely other, completely transcendent. He is pure being or "that which existingly exists" – *τὸ ὄντως ὄν*. He is without quality – *ἄποιος*. God is un - nameable – *ἀκατόνομαστος*; ineffable – *ἄρρητος*; incomprehensible – *ἀκατάληπτος*. Philo brings a new thought to philosophy, a distinc - tion that was never previously made but a distinction that will become vital for the Greek and Byzantine Fathers, culminating in the thought of St. Gregory Palamas (d. 1359). For Philo it was completely impossible that God could be known in his essence by any creature. All cataphatic terms for God in Hebrew Scripture must be understood apophatically. Even the Septuagint terms "God" and "Lord" do not refer to God's essence, to the τὸ ὄν. These terms can refer only to God's activities which are knowable, but not to the unknowable essence of τὸ ὄν. Θεός refers to the activity of τὸ ὄν in creating the world; κύριος refers to the presence of τὸ ὄν in the created world.

These divine activities are, for Philo, powers – δυναμεῖς. The "one who existingly exists" relates to created existence through the Logos. Philo's doctrine of the Logos is inconsistent and at times contradictory. Yet his main idea is clear. The Logos is the bond, the cohesive force – τόνος – which unites everything to the unknowable τὸ ὄντως ὄν, while simultaneously keeping the created order distinct from the τὸ ὄντως ὄν. Much of his Logos doctrine is taken from the Stoics but with the important distinction that for Philo reality is not material, not restricted to the physicality of the Stoics.

Stoicism reacted vigorously to the distinction in Platonic philosophy between the imperceptible, transcendent world and the world of the senses. For the Stoics reality was material, physical. Yet within their perspective of the world the Stoics distinguished between the "characterless, unformed matter" and the principle which organized this material – the dynamic reason, the Logos. Though the Stoics could refer to the Logos as πνεῦμα, this "spirit" was also material. The Logos, the *anima mundi*, penetrates as a higher form of matter, the reality of the "unformed matter." All reality is filled with microcosms of the whole. The Logos contains the "seminal seeds" – λόγοι σπερματικοί which reflect in some way the Logos, λόγος σπερματικός. Man too was a microcosm and within man the Stoics distinguished between two aspects of the soul. There is the "immanent Logos" – λόγος ἐνδιάθετος – which constitutes man's reason, the presence of the soul, its *Dasein*. But when the soul reveals itself, makes itself known to others, then it is the "expressed Logos" – λόγος προφορικός. The fact that these terms preceded Christian thought, the fact that they were first used by the Stoics, in no way lessens their importance when the Apologists utilize them in reference to the Logos, the eternal Son of God, for the origin of terms or ideas has nothing whatever to do with truth or falsity.

Philo drew on both the Greek and Hebraic philosophical tradition of the Logos and united it with his emphasis on the divine transcendence of τὸ ὄντως ὄν. Philo elevates the terms λόγος ἐνδιάθετος and λόγος προφορικός to a divine level, to the thoughts in the mind of God. At one point Philo speaks of the Logos as the "First-Begotten Son" but to claim any type of affinity with or adumbration of the Christian doctrine here is to misinterpret Philo. Philo's influence on the Apologists can neither be exaggerated nor underestimated. His influence on Clement of Alexandria is obvious. Philo's understanding of evil, of the disorder in man and in the world, influences the Apologists. Evil comes from self-love – φιλαυτία, from self-conceit – οἴησις, from sensual desires – ἐπιθυμίαι. Philo, just as the Apologists in general, claimed that all the best ideas of Greek philosophy were already either anticipated in or contained in Hebrew Scripture.

THE IMMANENT AND EXPRESSED LOGOS

For the Apologists the Logos is the Father's agent in creation and the Logos reveals the Father and the truth of the Father to all created existence. All existence, exclusive of God's uncreated existence, consists of "things made" – ποιήματα, or creatures – κτίσματα. But the Logos is God's "child" – τέκνον, God's "offspring" – γέννημα, and God's "Only-Begotten" – μονογενής. He is the eternally immanent Logos – ἐνδιάθετος, never coming into existence – οὐχ ὡς γενό – μενον. St. Justin writes in his *Second Apology* (6): ὁ υἱὸς τοῦ πατρὸς καὶ θεοῦ, ὁ μόνος λεγόμενος κυριῶς υἱός. It is impossible to conceive of God as without his Logos, for God is not ἄλογος. God, as the fulness of reason, has eternally had his Logos. And the Logos is of the essence of God – nowhere is this clearer than in Tatian (5) – θεὸς ἦν ἐν ἀρχῇ τὴν δὲ ἀρχὴν λόγου δύναμιν παρειλήφαμεν . . . In relation to created existence, to the world and to mankind, the Logos is "expressed" – προφορικός, and in this expres-sion the Logos reveals the Father, expresses himself and simultaneously the Father. This, however, does not mean nor imply that the Logos "becomes" a hypostasis for the first time in order to create. Such a view is a complete misreading of the Apologists.

THE PROBLEM OF TERMINOLOGY

It is quite correct that terminology is a problem for the Apologists, just as it will be in the coming centuries of theological controversy. The Apologists may not have always used precise terminology, especially when dealing with the eternal distinctions within the One Divine Being, but they knew, they believed in, and they attempted to explicate at times these distinctions. They knew that before creation the Logos was "with God" and "was God." Even the personhood of the Logos is constantly affirmed by the Apologists – they are constantly referring to the Father's communication with the Logos, with the Son, especially when discussing the *Genesis* account of "Let us make man in our image, after our likeness." When the Apologists refer to the Logos as a "second God" or "in second rank," they have little intention to introduce subordinationism. Rather, their intent is to protect the divine monarchy, to safeguard monotheism, to preserve the Oneness and Unity of God. Even Clement of Alexandria, accused by Harnack as "expressing himself in such a way that one can scarcely fail to notice a distinction between the Logos of the Father and the Logos of the Son," teaches that the Logos is One and the Same, from the beginning to the end of things. In fairness to Harnack there is one extant text from Clement's *Hypotyposeis* whose meaning is so unclear that it could – by itself – be interpreted as did Harnack. St. Photius also excoriated this work and considered it unauthentic. Exclusive of that one passage Clement's teaching on the Logos, often misrepresented and misinter - preted, is understandable from within the context of the mainstream orthodox thought of the Apologists.

It is, as it will be in the coming centuries, a problem of ter - minology with the Apologists. It is not an exaggeration to assert that the central problem in all the theological controversies will be that of terminology. The Church fathers had good reason for devoting so much attention to problems of terminology, for they were trying to find and establish words and terms that would be adequate to their conceptions of God and which would precisely express, and thus protect and preserve, the truths of the apostolic faith. Their concern for terminology will not be excessive but necessary, for it is the word, the terms, the phrases that give outer form to a thought and verbal precision is necessary for the full expression of intellectual conception. The patristic and Byzantine theologians will attempt to formulate their theology and their creeds with clarity because their hope is to establish the living traditions of the Church by expressing them in a versatile system of theology. This task will not be easily fulfilled and theological speculation, as in the age of the Apostolic Fathers, will develop in many different directions. But all will coincide in their basic principles and all will be united by the common experience of the Church, for "that is the mystery of the Church, that is the tradition of the fathers."

The Apologists emphasis on the divine unity and monarchy – their protection of monotheism – led to a somewhat exaggerated attempt to protect the divine monarchy and, in so doing, they tended to transfer focus from the distinction of the Father, the Son, and the Holy Spirit to the Divine Oneness. And yet the Apologists are often accused of stressing the distinction of the Son and Spirit *ad extra*, in οἰκονομία, so much that "subordinated" the Son and Spirit to the "real" God, God the Father. It is certainly true that the Apologists – quite understandably – write more about God's relation to the world than about the inner, eternal existence of God. It is understandable precisely because the Apologists were engaged in a dialogue with a non-Christian world and attempted to present the Christian teaching of God's action in redeeming mankind. Hence, the very nature of their task determined the content and focus of their writing. For this reason it is all the more significant that we do possess texts from the Apologists that do reflect, however briefly, on the inner, eternal existence of the Divine Being. Just as the earlier Christian documents were written to other Christian com - munities and hence assumed the knowledge of the faith, so also in the writings of the Apologists we should not expect to find much on the inner, eternal existence of God, precisely because that was not the central focus of their task, of their mission. Rather than being surprised by the paucity of their thought on the inner, eternal existence of God, we should be surprised that they wrote on that subject as often as they did. In this they, to a very great extent, exceeded their task.

As a reaction to both Gnostic ideas and the emphasis of the Apologists on a theology of God's *oikonomic* activity, a theology in which some detected a tendency to "subordinate" the Son and Spirit, a new emphasis of thought emerged – Monarchianism. In the early Church only Modalism was referred to as Monarchianism. Modern scholars, however, divide Monarchianism into two forms – Dynamic Monarchianism and Modalistic Monarchianism. They are two different thought patterns, both in origin and in purpose. However, the two thought patterns are common in that they both focus on divine oneness rather than on the distinctions of the Father, Son, and Holy Spirit. In these two thought patterns we encounter two tendencies which, in different forms, will challenge the faith of the Church in the coming centuries. Dynamic Monarchianism is actually Adoptionism, the notion that Christ was merely a man – ψιλὸς ἄνθρωπος – upon whom the Spirit somehow "descended" and took up an "indwelling." For the Adoptionists, or in modern terminology the Dynamic Monarchians, Jesus Christ was not always God. At some point a "power" of the Father or the "Spirit" descended upon the man Jesus – either at conception, or birth, or baptism, or at the resurrection. Modalism, or Modalistic Monarchianism, known in the East as Sabellianism, tended to consider the Father, Son, and Holy Spirit as "modes," aspects, or phases of the One Divine Person.

CHAPTER SEVEN

MONARCHIANISM

DYNAMIC MONARCHIANISM IN THE LATIN WEST

THE ALOGI

The first known opponents to the doctrine of the Logos set forth by the Apologists came from Asia Minor and were appropriately named the Alogi by Hippolytus. The Alogi were strict opponents of Mon - tanism and any type of prophetic movements within the Church – all prophecy should be excluded from the Church. Their opposition to prophecy was combined with an opposition to the "Spirit" which in turn led to opposition to the *Gospel of St. John* , especially to eradicate the announcement of the coming of the "Spirit" from that Gospel. They concluded that the *Gospel of St. John* was written "in St. John's name" – εἰς ὄνομα Ἰωάννου – by Cerinthus the Gnostic. The books attrib - uted to St. John should not be accepted in the Church – οὐκ ἄξια αὐτά φασιν εἶναι ἐν ἐκκλησία. For a variety of reasons the *Gospel of St. John* was considered unauthentic – it was accused also of being Docetic. As Epiphanius relates, the Alogi attacked the linking of the Logos with the Son of God – τὸν λόγον τοῦ θεοῦ ἀποβάλ - λονται τὸν διὰ Ἰωάννην κηρυχθέντα. The Alogi considered the *Gospel of St. John* to be tinged with Gnostic Docetism. Because the Alogi were anti-Gnostic and anti-Docetic they are treated rather mildly by St. Irenaeus and St. Hippolytus. In rejecting the Logos the Alogi emphasized the human life of Jesus. Implicit from what little we know of their views is that they apparently rejected the eternality of Christ and stressed a type of Adoptionism. Though there is no evidence that they used such a term, they apparently would have conceived of Jesus as a "mere man" – ψιλὸς ἄνθρωπος; a man in whom spiritual progress took place, probably from baptism. The Alogi were the first within the Church to adopt a critical approach to both Christian Scriptures and Christian tradition.

THEODOTUS OF BYZANTIUM

A more serious Adoptionism came from the city of Byzantium. The founder of Dynamic Monarchianism, the "founder, leader, and father of the God-denying revolt" of Adoptionism was, writes Hippolytus, the leather-merchant from Byzantium, Theodotus – the ἀπόσπασμα of the *Alogi*. Theodotus, described as exceedingly well-educated, came to Rome about 190. All that is known for certain is that Theodotus was excommunicated – ἀπεκήρυξε τῆς κοινωνίας – by Pope Victor (186-198) because of his Christology. St. Hippolytus informs us that he had taught that Jesus was a man who was born of a virgin through the power of the Holy Spirit by a special decree of God. But there was no divine being or person who had taken flesh in the virgin. His spirituality was tested and as a result the Holy Spirit descended upon him at his baptism, at which time he became the Christ.

The two most important disciples of Theodotus were his namesake, Theodotus the Banker or Money-Changer, and Asclepiodotus. It appears that under the influence of these two disciples of the founder of this group a separate Church was established with its own bishop. Hippol - ytus even gives the monthly salary of their bishop – 150 *denarii*. They too were appealing to apostolic tradition, claiming that their position had been accepted by the Church from the time of the apostles to the time of Pope Zephyrinus (198-217), at which time the true faith became corrupted. Their attempt to establish their own Church failed. In fact, what they had established was a "school of theology" not unlike those to appear in Alexandria and Antioch. They applied the exegesis of textual criticism to the Scriptures of the Church, along with a rationalism and an empiricism – they studied logic, mathematics, and the empirical sciences. They rejected the allegorical interpretation of Scripture and instead used the scholarly tools available to them to attempt to discover the "original text." They considered themselves scholars and Catholics but their scholarship was biased and unobjective and they found themselves cut off from the Catholic Church.

The position that the followers of Theodotus were merely at - tempting to preserve the "older, Roman Christology" contained in *The Shepherd* of Hermes misunderstands the very nature of the Roman Church and the significance of *The Shepherd* in Rome, even though there are some points of similarity between *The Shepherd* and the thought of the followers of Theodotus. But the author of *The Shepherd* was by no means a theologian. His mind focuses only on practical matters – especially penance – and whenever he discusses anything of any depth or significance in theology his mind is not capable of the task. It is not difficult to ascertain a confusion of the Son of God with the Holy Spirit in *The Shepherd*. But *The Shepherd* did not determine the main or central features of Roman theology, especially on Christology or Trinitarian thought. The Christology evident in *The Shepherd* is Adoptionist but the entire work is strange and belongs to the genre of apocryphal apocalypses. The differences between the followers of Theodotus and the author of *The Shepherd* are greater than is any similarity.

The followers of Theodotus attempted to distinguish between the eternal Son of God and the Crucified One, much of which was based on their extreme emphasis on Melchizedek, who was considered to be far more exalted than Christ. Christ was but a copy of the original, the high priest Melchizedek, who was the advocate of the heavenly powers before God. Epiphanius tells us that the "Theodotians" or "Mel -- chizedekians" offered their oblations in the name of Melchizedek – εἰς ὄνομα τοῦ Μελχισεδέκ, the true Son of God, the path to God, the prince of righteousness. That there was a theology of Melchizedek in the early Church cannot be denied. That Melchizedek replaced or was higher than Christ was in general quite contrary to the "orthodox" understanding of Melchizedek in the theology of the early Church. He was considered a type, a prototype of Christ, the eternal High Priest. The theology of the Theodotians was an innovation in many ways – they refused to recognize Christ as God, refused to use Θεός in any reference to Christ, rejected completely any type of Logos theology, and rejected the *Gospel of St. John*. Any objective evaluation of the teachings of the first Theodotus and the second Theodotus and their followers, based on the knowledge we possess of them, must conclude that they stood far outside the Church, that they in essence excom - municated themselves with their fanciful, unapostolic teachings.

ARTEMAS AND THE LINGERING OF DYNAMIC MODALISM IN ROME

Approximately thirty years later a certain Artemas, of whom we know exceedingly little, attempted to resuscitate the general thought of the Theodotians. All we know for certain is that Artemas also refused to call Christ "God." This Artemas was still living in 270 – we know this from the acts of the Council of Antioch which concerned Paul of Samosata. Indeed, Eusebius informs us that "Paul may write letters to Artemas and the followers of Artemas are said to hold communion with Paul." Novatian could very well be referring to the followers of Artemas in his *De Trinitate* when he mentions those who claimed that Jesus was *homo nudus et solitarius*. But in the decades and centuries to come Artemas found his name included in the common "Ebionites, Artemas, Photinus" – and later the name Nestorius will be added to this phrase. It became the standard phrase when referring to Adoptionists.

Adoptionist Christology – Dynamic Monarchianism – is essen - tially destroyed in Rome. But from time to time it raises its head in most unexpected places. St. Augustine tells us in his *De Confessione* (7, 19, 25) that he, before his ultimate conversion but while already under the influence of St. Ambrose in Milan, thought of Christ in a quite unorthodox way: "I conceived my Lord Christ only as a man of surpassing wisdom, whom no other could equal. Above all, because he was born in a wondrous manner of the Virgin, to give us an example of despising temporal things in order to win immortality, he seemed by the godlike care that he had for us, to have merited such great authority as a teacher. But what mystery was contained within those words, 'The Word was made flesh', I could not conceive . . . I accounted him a person to be preferred above all other men, not as the person of Truth, but because of some great excellence of his human nature and a more perfect participation in wisdom." But if St. Augustine ultimately rejected the tendencies of Dynamic Modalism in his Christology, his

Trinitarian doctrine will later reveal clear Modalism. St. Augustine's Christology will shed itself of Adoptionism but one can detect elements therein of Monophysitical tendencies. Whether St. Augustine's Adoptionist Christology at the time previous to his baptism was a lingering influence from his Manichean days or whether it was a result of his constant contact with Christians who may have had Adoptionist tendencies is unknown.

MODALISTIC MONARCHIANISM

It was not Adoptionism – Dynamic Monarchianism – that pre - sented the most serious challenge to Christ as the Divine Logos, to Logos Christology. Rather, it was the doctrine that viewed Christ as God in a human body, the Father become flesh. Against both forms of Monarchianism the battle was waged in the Latin West by Tertullian, Novatian, and Hippolytus and primarily by Origen in the Greek East. In the Latin West those who held this view were called *Monarchiani* and *Patripassiani*. In the Greek East they were called *Sabelliani* or Sabel - lians, though there too the term *Patripassiani* was used.

Just as St. Jerome will later say about Arianism – the Church woke up and found itself Arian, so also St. Hippolytus writes that the Monarchian controversy troubled, upset the entire Church μέγιστον τάραχον κατὰ πάντα τὸν κόσμον ἐν πᾶσιν τοῖς πιστοῖς ἐμ - βάλλουσιν Both Tertullian and Origen write that the majority of Christians were suspicious about the *oikonomic* Trinity and also about Christ as the Logos. Tertullian writes in his *Adversus Praxean* (3): "*Simplices quique, ne dixerim imprudentes et idiotae, quae maior semper pars credentium est, quoniam et ipsa regula fidei a pluribus diis saeculi ad unicum et verum deum transfert, non intelligentes unicum quidem, sed cum sua οἰκονομία esse credendum, expavescunt ad οἰ - κονομίαν . . . Itaque duos et tres iam iactitant a nobis praedicari, se vero unius dei cultores praesumunt . . . monarchiam inquiunt tenemus.*" And Origen in his *Commentary on St. John* writes (II, 3): ἕτεροι δὲ οἱ μηδὲν εἰδότες, εἰ μὴ Ἰησοῦν Χριστὸν καὶ τοῦτον ἐσταυρωμένον, τὸν γενόμενον σάρκα λόγον τὸ πᾶν νομίσ - αντες εἶναι τοῦ λόγου, Χριστὸν κατὰ σάρκα μόνον γιγνώσ - κουσι τοιοῦτον δὲ ἐστι τὸ πλῆθος τῶν πεπιστευκέναι νομιζομένων.

NOëTUS

According to the information provided by St. Hippolytus, Modalistic Modalism begins to make itself historically known in Noëtus of Smyrna, who taught from approximately 180 to 200. Hippolytus claims he was the originator – ἀρχηγόν – of the heresy of Modalism. However, it appears that Praxeas had come to Rome before the arrival of the disciples of Noëtus and that he was the "first to import into Rome from Asia this kind of heretical pravity" – *Iste primus ex Asia hoc genus perversitatis intulit Romam, homo et alias inquietus, insuper de iactatione martyrii inflatus ob solum et simplex et breve carceris taedium* (Tertullian, *Adversus Praxean* 1). Noëtus was not condemned at his first trial but at his second trial about the year 200. Our primary information on Noëtus comes from St. Hippolytus' *Philosophumena*, also known as *The Refutation of All Heresies* – Κατὰ πασῶν αἱρέσεων ἔλεγχος (9, 2-6; 10, 23) and from his shorter work known as the *Homily on the Heresy of Noëtus* – ὁμιλία εἰς τὴν αἵρεσιν Νοήτου τινός. This valuable document is not a homily but a short, anti-heretical doctrinal work, perhaps part of a larger work. Noëtus "alleged that Christ was the Father himself and that the Father himself was born, and suffered, and died. . . He alleged that he was himself Moses, and that Aaron [Elijah, according to Philastrius] was his brother. When the blessed presbyters heard this, they sum - moned him before the Church and examined him. But he denied at first that he held such opinions. Afterwards, however, taking shelter among some, and having gathered round him some others who had embraced the same error, he wished thereafter to uphold his dogma openly as correct. And the blessed presbyters called him again before them and examined him. But he stood out against them, saying 'What evil, then, am I doing in glorifying Christ' – τί οὖν κακὸν δοξάζων τὸν Χριστόν? Then, after examining him, they expelled him from the Church. And he was carried to such a pitch of pride that he established a school. . . They answer in this manner: 'If therefore I acknowledge Christ to be God, He is the Father himself, if he is indeed God. And Christ suffered, being himself God. Consequently, the Father suffered, for he was the Father himself." Noëtus appealed to the Scriptural texts of *Exodus* 3,6 and 20,3; *Isaiah* 45,14; and *Romans* 9,5. "In this way, then, they choose to set forth these things and they make use only of one set of passages, just in the same one-sided manner that Theodotus employed when he sought to prove that Christ was a mere man. But neither has the one party nor the other understood the matter rightly, for the Scriptures themselves confute their senselessness and attest to the truth." St. Hippolytus exclaims: "For who will not admit that there is One God? Yet he will not on that account deny the *oikonomia*." He then begins a devastating critique of Noetus' position.

Two disciples of Noëtus, Epigonus and Cleomenes, came to Rome and propagated this Modalism, ostensibly with the approval of Pope Zephyrinus (199-217). St. Hippolytus, depicting Pope Zephyrinus as a dull, corrupt, an uneducated man, writes: "Epigonus becomes the pupil [of Noëtus] and during his sojourn at Rome disseminated his godless opinion. But Cleomenes, who had become his disciple, an alien both in way of life and habits from the Church, corroborated this doctrine. At that time Zephyrinus imagines that he administers the affairs of the Church – an uninformed and shamefully corrupt man. And he, being persuaded by proffered gain, was accustomed to connive with those who were present for the purpose of becoming disciples of Cleomenes. But Zephyrinus himself, being in process of time enticed away, hurried headlong into the same opinions – and he had Callistus as his adviser and a fellow-champion of these wicked tenets. . . The school of these heretics during the succession [of these bishops] continued to acquire strength and augmentation from the fact that Zephyrinus and Callistus helped them to prevail" (*Philosophumena* 9,2). Epigonus and Cleomenes believed that "when the Father had not yet been born, he was rightly called Father. But when it had pleased him to submit to birth, having been born, he became the Son, he of himself and not of another. . . Christ is himself the Father and the Father himself was born and suffered and died." It was the belief in the full divinity of Christ which led these Modalists to this position: "For Christ was God and suffered for us, being the Father himself, in order that he might be able also to save us."

PRAXEAS

The essence of what we know about Praxeas comes from Ter-tullian's *Adversus Praxean*. He came to Rome towards the end of the second century from Asia where he is said to have suffered imprison-ment for his faith. Praxeas had come to Rome previous to the arrival of Epigonus and Cleomenes and probably before St. Hippolytus could have had any personal knowledge of him. It appears that he spent only a brief time in Rome, founded no school, and then moved on to North Africa where he was the first to raise the topic in Carthage. Praxeas was not only a Modalist but an anti-Montanist and exercised an influence on the Pope Victor and Pope Zephyrinus in turning them against the Mon-tanists. Tertullian writes that "after the Bishop of Rome had ac-knowledged the prophetic gifts of Montanus, Prisca, and Maximilla, and, in consequence of the acknowledgement, had bestowed his peace on the churches of Asia and Phrygia, he, by importunately urging false accusations against the prophets themselves and their churches, and insisting on the authority of the bishop's predecessors in the see, compelled him to recall the pacific letter which he had issued, as well as to desist from his purpose of acknowledging the gifts. By this Praxeas did a twofold service for the devil at Rome: he drove away prophecy and he brought in heresy." He proclaimed himself a leader of the Patri-passian Monarchians – those who protected the monarchy of God to the point that it meant that God suffered. Tertullian remarks that Praxeas "put to flight the Paraclete and crucified the Father" – *Patrem crucifixit*. Tertullian was already a Montanist when writing against Praxeas. He writes that Praxeas had renounced his error in writing but "had deliberately resumed his old . . . faith, teaching it after his renunciation of error." Thereafter "nothing was heard of him" but "the tares of Praxeas had then everywhere shaken out their seed, which having lain hidden for some while, with its vitality concealed under a mask, has now broken out with fresh life." Tertullian vows that "again it shall be rooted up." It appears that Tertullian in his *Adversus Praxean* is con - fronting not just Praxeas but the Modalism which had broken out in Rome from the influence of Noëtus. "The Father was born and the Father suffered. Jesus Christ is . . . the Father born, the Father suffering, God himself, the omnipotent Lord." The Father and the Son are therefore the same person (*Adversus Praxean* 5). Praxeas' appeal to Scripture includes *Isaiah* 45,5 and *John* 10,30; 14,9-10.

It must be emphasized that the Modalists were interested in both defending the monarchy of God, in protecting monotheism, and in defending the full divinity of Jesus. They believed that their opponents – those believing in the *oikonomic* Trinity – had injured the cause of monotheism – φάσκουσιν συνιστᾶν ἕνα θεόν. The likes of Tertul - lian and St. Hippolytus, the defenders of the Logos as the Son of God, the defenders of the three persons who are One God, were called ditheists – δίθεοι. St. Hippolytus feels compelled to defend himself on this – οὐ δύο θεοὺς λέγω . . . δημοσίᾳ ὁ Κάλλιστος ἡμῖν ὀνειδίζει εἰπεῖν· δίθεοί ἐστε. The Modalists attacked by Tertullian identify the Father and the Son – *ipsum dicit patrem descendisse in virginem, ipsum ex ea natum, ipsum passum ipsum denique esse Iesum Christum . . . post tempus pater natus et pater passus, ipse deus, dominus omnipotens, Iesus Christus praedicatur*. For them the Logos is not a substance but rather a sound – *quid est enim, dices, sermo nisi vox et sonus oris, et sicut grammatici tradunt, aër offensus, intellegibilis auditu, ceterum vanum nescio quid*. Tertullian's Modalists appeal to the same Scriptural texts that the opponents of St. Hippolytus use. They also despise Gnosticism. In any attempt they might make to take account of the Logos as the eternal Son of God they fail and fall into the "modes" or "aspects" of the One God. "For, confuted on all sides on the distinction between the Father and the Son, which we maintain without destroying their inseparable union . . . they endeavor to interpret this distinction in a way which shall nevertheless tally with their own opinions: so that, all in one Person, they distinguish two, Father and Son, understanding the Son to be flesh, that is man, that is Jesus; and the Father to be spirit, that is God, that is Christ" – *aeque in una persona utrumque distinguunt, patrem et filium, discentes filium carnem esse, id est hominem, id est Iesum, patrem autem spiritum, id est deum, id est Christum* (*Adversus Praxean* 27). "Thus they, while contending that the Father and the Son are one and the same, do in fact begin by dividing them rather than uniting them. For if Jesus is one, and Christ is another, then the Son will be different from the Father because the Son is Jesus and the Father is Christ. Such a monarchy as this they learned, I suppose, in the school of Valentinus, making two – Jesus and Christ " – *et qui unum eundemque contendunt patrem et filium, iam incipiunt dividere illos potius quam unare; talem monarchiam apud Valentinum fortasse didicerunt, duos facere Iesum et*

Christum (27). Tertullian's attack in this chapter and also in chapter 4 is powerful, and both exposes and shatters his opponents' position.

SABELLIUS

The most original form of Modalistic Monarchianism was that of Sabellius who may have come from Cyrenaica. Athanasius and Epiphanius inform us that it was Sabellius who gave Modalistic Monarchianism its metaphysical and philosophical basis. In the Greek East Modalistic Monarchianism became identified with "Sabellianism." St. Hippolytus writes that Sabellius was at first welcomed at Rome by Callistus but excommunicated after Callistus became Pope Callistus I in 217. It is not known whether Sabellius left Rome or remained there. In any event, his influence spread beyond Rome. It was in Pentapolis that a Trinitarian controversy erupted in 257 and the Modalists were referred to as "Sabellians," even though Sabellius was probably dead by that time – some bishops refused to identify Christ as the Son of God. Dionysius of Alexandria, their metropolitan and a disciple of Origen, challenged their teaching and excommunicated Sabellius at a council in Alexandria in 260 or 261. In challenging this Modalism Dionysius of Alexandria used language which some suspected of being tainted with subordinationism. In was in this context that Pope Dionysius (259-268) wrote against both the Sabellians and their "subordinationist" opponents. This exchange between the two bishops, Dionysius of Rome and Dionysius of Alexandria, foreshadows the coming Arian controversy.

Sabellius distinguished the monad from the triad in the divine nature. His essential thought is that the unity of God extends itself – ἡ μονὰς πλατυνθεῖσα γέγονε τριάς – in the course of the historical development of the world in three different modes and three different periods of revelation. The act of creation ostensibly begins this Modalistic Trinitarianism, for God begins to manifest himself in this three-fold way only with creation and then the giving of the law in the Old Testament – it is the Father who is modalistically revealed in the Old Testament, the Son in the Incarnation, and the Holy Spirit in "inspiration." The revelation of God in the mode of the Son terminates with the Ascension; the revelation of God in the mode of the Holy Spirit continues in regeneration and sanctification. Sabellius is said to have used the sun as an analogy of the Trinitarian modes of revelation. The Father as the form – τὸ σχῆμα, the Son as the light – τὸ φωτιστικόν, and the Holy Spirit as the heat or warmth – τὸ θάλπον. The Logos is "the monad in its transition to triad," the silent God – θεὸς σιωπῶν – as distinct from the "speaking God" – θεὸς λαλῶν. Each πρόσωπον is another διαλέγεσθαι and the three πρόσωπα are in reality successive evolutions of the Logos as God in relationship to the world – Πεμφθέντα τὸν υἱὸν καιρῷ ποτέ, ὥσπερ ἀκτῖνα καὶ ἐργασάμενον τὰ πάντα ἐν τῷ κόσμῳ τὰ τῆς οἰκονομίας τῆς εὐαγγελικῆς καὶ σωτηρίας τῶν ἀνθρώπων, ἀναληφθέντα δὲ αὖθις εἰς οὐρανόν, ὡς ὑπὸ ἡλίου πεμφθεῖσαν ἀκτῖνα, καὶ πάλιν εἰς τὸν ἥλιον ἀναδραμοῦσαν, τὸ δὲ ἅγιον πνεῦμα πέμπεσθαι εἰς τὸν κόσμον, καὶ καθεξῆς καὶ καθ᾿ ἕκαστα εἰς ἕκαστόν τῶν καταξιουμένων . . . οὐχ ὁ υἱὸς ἑαυτὸν ἐγέννησεν, οὐδὲ ὁ πατὴρ μεταβέβληται ἀπὸ τοῦ πατὴρ τοῦ εἶναι υἱός . . . πατὴρ ἀεὶ πατήρ, καὶ οὐκ ἦν καιρὸς ὅτε οὐκ ἦν πατήρ. Just as the Logos comes forth from God, so also the Logos will ultimately revert to God and the manifestation of the Trinitarian modes will cease.

According to Epiphanius the followers of Sabellius queried: "What shall we say? Do we have one God or three Gods?" – τί ἂν εἴπωμεν, ἕνα θεὸν ἔχομεν, ἢ τρεῖς θεούς. And they respond to their own question that they do not teach polytheism – οὐ πολυθεΐαν εἰσηγούμεθα. Both Athanasius and Hilary claim that Sabellius referred to the one being as υἱοπάτωρ, which simply referred to the one person of God. The level of sophistication allowed the Sabellians to assert that one should not speak of a suffering by the Father but rather that "the Father suffered with – συρπεπονθέναι – the Son." These formulae of *compassus est pater filio* may very well be formulae of compromise.

The supposition that the expression ὁμοούσιος was used by the Sabellians is quite possible, for they could use it within their theo - logical vision quite easily. Not only could they speak of the Son being *homoousios* with the Father but also of the Holy Spirit being *homoousios* with the Father and all these "modes" being *homoousios* with one another precisely because all these manifestations were the one essence manifesting itself in different forms or aspects. The Sabellian use of the term is decidedly different from the way that this important theological term will be used by St. Athanasius and the Council of Nicaea.

DYNAMIC MONARCHIANISM IN THE GREEK EAST

Origen informs us that many in the Greek East also rejected the Christology that united Christ with the Logos, and this was indeed among those who distinguished between the Father and the Son – καὶ τὸ πολλοὺς φιλοθέους εἶναι εὐχομένους ταράσσον, εὐλαβου - μένους δύο ἀναγορεῦσαι Θεούς, καὶ . . . τοῦτο περὶ πίπτοντας ψευδέσι καὶ ἀσεβέσι δόγμασιν, ἤτοι ἀρνουμένους ἰδιότητα υἱοῦ ἑτέραν παρὰ τὴν τοῦ πατρός, ὁμολογοῦντας θεὸν εἶναι τὸν μέχρι ὀνόματος παρ᾿αὐτοῖς υἱὸν προσαγορευόμενον, ἢ ἀρνουμένους τὴν θεότητα τοῦ υἱοῦ, τιθέντας δὲ αὐτοῦ τὴν ἰδιότητα καὶ τὴν οὐσίαν κατὰ περιγραφὴν τυγχάνουσαν ἑτέραν τοῦ πατρός, ἐντεῦθεν λύεσθαι δύναται. Origen in general considered these Adoptionists as ignorant or "simple" Christians. In fact, Origen had in his complete Christology laid such strong emphasis on the tenet of faith that Jesus was a true man that his opponents later linked him with Paul of Samosata and Artemas.

Pamphilus felt it necessary to come to the defense of Origen and pointed out that Origen "said that the Son of God was born of the very essence of God – ὁμοούσιος – which means, of the same essence with the Father but that he was not a creature who became a son by adoption but a true son by nature, generated by the Father himself" – *quod Origenes filium dei de ipsa dei substantia natum dixerit, id est, ὁμοούσιον, quod est, eiusdem cum patre substantiae, et non esse crea - turam per adoptionem sed natura filium verum, ex ipso patre generatum.* Origen attempted to reveal to the Adoptionists their error but in general ignored them.

A vehement reaction took place in Bostra, Arabia when the bishop Beryllus taught a form of Dynamic Monarchianism. The acts of the Council of Bostra have not survived but a few excerpts are found in Eusebius and Jerome and one excerpt in the *Apology* of Pamphilus. The council, according to the information we have, took place about 244 and Origen was called in to examine Beryllus. Eusebius tells us that Beryllus was convinced of his error by Origen and thanked him for correcting him. The important text from Eusebius lends itself to more than one interpretation – τὸν σωτῆρα καὶ κύριον ἡμῶν μὴ προϋφεστάναι κατ 'ἰδίαν οὐσίας περιγραφὴν πρὸ τῆς εἰς ἀνθρώπους ἐπιδημίας, μηδὲ θεότητα ἰδίαν ἔχειν, ἀλλ ἐμ - πολιτευομένην αὐτῷ μόνην τὴν πατρικήν. Based on the evidence, especially from a fragment of Origen's *Commentary on the Epistle of Titus*, it seems that Beryllus did in fact hold an Adoptionist view of Christ.

CHAPTER EIGHT

TERTULLIAN AND HIPPOLYTUS

Two of the champions in fighting both Dynamic Monarchianism and Modalistic Monarchianism were Tertullian and St. Hippolytus. Both theologians will have confrontations with the Church – indeed, Tertullian will leave that Catholic Church for which he battled so strenuously to join the Montanists and St. Hippolytus will become an anti-Pope finishing his life in exile.

TERTULLIAN

Quintus Septimius Florens Tertullianus is – with one qualification – the father of Latin theology and the most influential person in the Latin West in shaping the terminology of Latin Christianity. Tertullian is "father" of Latin theology in the sense that he was the first theologian of significance to write in Latin. In terms of influence on future generations, the title "father" of Latin theology indeed belongs to St. Augustine. Tertullian's influence on subsequent Latin Christian writers is clearly discernible. St. Cyprian would say, in reference to the works of Tertullian, "Hand me the master!"; Novatian's *De Trinitate* is based on Tertullian; St. Augustine enjoyed reading him; St. Vincent of Lérins' *Commonitorium* owes much to him; and Pope Leo's *Tome* draws heavily from him. He has been called "the real creator of the Latin of the Church" but that statement must also be qualified, for we do not have any way of evaluating the influence of the anonymous translators of the Latin Bible before St. Jerome's translation. Unfortunately little is known of Tertullian's life and what we know comes from his works or from St. Jerome. He was sharp, penetrating, intelligent. His personality comes through quite clearly from his writings.

Tertullian was born in Carthage, probably between the years 154 and 160. His father, St. Jerome tells us, was a "proconsular centurion" which could mean that he was a centurion of the city cohort stationed in Carthage or an official who bore that title out of traditional respect. Both parents were pagans and later he deplores his errors and his former sarcastic attitude towards Christian beliefs – "*Haec et nos risimus aliquando: de vestris sumus. Fiunt, non nascuntur Christiani.*" He specialized in law, gaining an enviable reputation as a lawyer in Rome. His legal background will contribute to the casting of certain Latin theological terms in a legalistic or juridical mode. It is now commonly accepted that he is the lawyer Tertullianus, excerpts of whose writings are quoted in the *Pandects*, the *Corpus Civilis*. It is apparent from his writings that he received an excellent Graeco-Roman education – he is acquainted with history, philosophy, poetry, ancient literature, medi -

cine, and of course law, and wrote with equal ease in both Greek and Latin. St. Jerome testifies to Tertullian's erudition – "*Quid Tertulliano eruditius, quid acutius. Apologeticus ejus et contra Gentes libri cunctam saeculi continent disciplinam*" [*Epistula* 70, 5]. St. Vincent of Lérins praises Tertullian's learning in his *Commonitorium* (24): "Who was more learned than this man? Who as competent as he in things divine and human? So much so that all philosophy, all the different sects of the philosophers, their founders, their adherents, and the systems defended by the latter, history and science under their multiple forms – all these were embraced by the great extent of his intellect." Eusebius tells us that Tertullian was "a man accurately acquainted with the Roman laws," a man was "especially distinguished among the eminent men of Rome." The statement by St. Jerome that Tertullian was a priest – *Tertullianus presbyterus* – is still debated – Tertullian queries in his *De exhortatione castitatis* [*Exhortation to Chastity*]: "*Nonne et Laici sacerdotes sumus?*" The prevailing opinion is that he was ordained priest about the year 200. That he was married is beyond doubt – he admits in his works that he frequently committed adultery and wrote a work *To His Wife – Ad uxorem* – which contains suggestions and instructions on how she should live when he dies. That his character was extremist is clear from what he himself tells us – as a young man, he writes, he "drained the cup of lust to the dregs" and was impassioned with a love and lust for immoral plays and the bloody spectacles in the arenas. In any case, he portrays himself as being overly licentious as a young man – "*ego me scio neque alia carne adulteria commisisse, neque nunc alia carne ad continentiam eniti* ." This in some way accounts for some of his extremism later in life. St. Jerome writes that Tertullian lived to an extreme old age – "*Fertur vixisse usque ad decrepitam aetatem.*"

Tertullian's conversion to Christianity took place between 193 and 195. In Carthage he devoted all his energies to the defense of Christianity, both by writing and by teaching in the catechetical school. A commonly used periodization of Tertullian's life as a Christian theologian is a division of that time into three periods: from 195 to 206 is considered his "Catholic" period; from 206 to 212 his "Semi-Montanist" period; and after 213 his "Montanist" period. He actually established his own party known as the "Tertullianists" and they possessed one of the basilicas in Carthage. The "Tertullianists" were only brought back into the Church almost two centuries later and the person who accomplished this and speaks of it is St. Augustine in his *De Haeresibus* (86).

Tertullian wrote prolifically. Thirty-one of his authentic works are extant. The content of his works is rich; the style unique, powerful, and vibrant. It is deplorable that the quality and uniqueness of his Latin is often overlooked or inaccurately judged as barbaric. Indeed the opinion of the eighteenth century German philologist, Ruhnken, influenced many subsequent scholars who merely quote his opinion, an opinion difficult to comprehend. He is perhaps the most quoted of all early Christian writers and perhaps the least read. Tertullian writes with enthusiasm – indeed, even with anger and outrage. He was quite aware of his fiery temper and made attempts to control it – "*miserrimus ego semper aeger caloribus impatientiae.*" He writes with pithy sarcasm, with bristling energy, with ardent conviction, and with a lucid and penetrating mind. He is often praised as a literary genius and rightly so. He created innumerable new words. It is true that at times his thought is obscure, but it is not that often. He combines both originality of style with penetrating insight into the truths of that faith once delivered. As a stylist he is unequalled in Latin Patristic literature. He combined puns, epigrams, paradoxical expressions, invective, and memorable phrases. It is no wonder that he is so often quoted. He is the author of such often quoted expressions as: *Credo quia absurdum est* or *credendum quia absurdum est* – the thought does indeed come from Tertullian, even if not in the words with which it has come down to us; it is from his *De carne Christi* (5): "And the Son of God died; it is by all means to be believed because it is absurd"; *Veritas non erubescit nisi solummodo abscondi*; *Quid ergo Athenis et Hierosolymis?*; *Christus veritas est, non consuetudo*; *Semen est sanguis Christianorum*; and *Testimonium animae naturaliter Christianae*. Indeed, the list is long.

Tertullian's *Ad nationes* [*To the Pagans*] is an attack on the unfairness of the Roman juridical process in relationship with Christians. Theologically the most interesting part of this work is Tertullian's discussion on the concept of God while the rest of the work is a rich defense of Christians on a legal basis by a brilliant, if impassioned, lawyer.

Some scholars consider his *Apologeticum* to be his most important work. Theologically it is not. It is a more refined and more unified work than his *Ad nationes* with a different audience in mind – it was addressed not to the pagan world in general but to the governors of Roman provinces. Still, the work contains some theologically important material. God is "invisible, though he is seen; incomprehensible, though manifested by grace; inconceivable, though conceived by human senses . . . It is God's infinity which gives us the conception of the inconceivable God, for his overwhelming majesty presents him to man as simultaneously known and unknown."

This work contains the famous statement that "the soul is naturally Christian." Tertullian presents a description of a Christian worship service (39), speaks of the "stupendous shock" of the "ending of the age" (32), of the coming resurrection and judgment (47), and the final restoration of the human race, a restoration where "there is no death nor repeated resurrection, but from now on we shall be the same and remain unchanged. The worshippers of God will be with God forever, clothed with the proper substance of eternity. But the profane and all who are not wholly devoted to God, in punishment of fire which is just as eternal" (48).

Tertullian briefly discusses Christology in this work: "He appeared among us, whose coming to renovate and illuminate man's nature was pre-announced by God – I mean Christ, the Son of God. And so the supreme Head and Master of this grace and discipline, the Enlightener and Trainer of the human race, God's own Son, was announced among us, born – but not so born as to make him ashamed of the name of Son or of his paternal origin. It was not his lot to have as his father, by incest with a sister, or by violation of a daughter or another's wife, a god in the shape of serpent or ox or bird or lover for his vile ends transmuting himself into the gold of Danaus. They are your divinities upon whom these base deeds of Jupiter were done. But the Son of God has no mother in any sense which involves impurity. She, whom men suppose to be his mother in the ordinary way, had never entered into the marriage bond. But, first, I shall discuss his essential nature so that the nature of his birth will be understood. We have already asserted that God made the world and all that it contains by his Word and Reason and Power. It is abundantly plain that your philosophers too regard the Logos – that is, the Word and Reason – as the Creator of the universe . . . And we, in like manner, hold that the Word and Reason and Power by which we have said God made everything . . . We have been taught that he comes forth from God and in that procession he is generated so that he is the Son of God, and is called God from unity of substance with God . . . Thus Christ is Spirit of Spirit and God of God, as light of light is kindled. So also that which has come forth out of God is at once God and the Son of God, and the two are one. In this way also, as he is Spirit of Spirit and God of God, he is made a second in manner of existence – in rank, not in nature. And he did not withdraw from the original source but came forth. This ray of God, then . . . descending into a certain virgin, and made flesh in her womb, is in his birth God and man united. the flesh formed by the Spirit is nourished, grows up to manhood, speaks, teaches, works, and is the Christ. . . in all the majesty of Deity unveiled . . . he was the Logos of God, that primordial First-Begotten Word, accompanied by power and reason, and based on Spirit – that he who was now doing all things by his word, and he who had done that of old, were one and the same. . . Surely Christ, then, had a right to reveal Deity, which was in fact his own essential possession" (21).

Tertullian in his *Apologeticum* argues that Christians are good citizens, especially stressing the point that Christians serve in the armed forces: "We sail with you, we serve in the army with you" (42). "We have filled every place of yours, cities, islands, villages, townships, market-places, the army camps" (37). He calls attention to Marcus Aurelius' testimony that the "prayers of Christians who happened to be in the army" dispelled a drought in Germany (5) – Tertullian refers to this also in *Ad Scapulam* (4). But in his *De Idololatria* Tertullian reveals his own view: "Now the question is raised whether a believer can serve in the military, and whether the military may be admitted to the faith, even private soldiers and all the lower ranks, who are not under the necessity of performing sacrifices or administering capital punishment. There is no congruity between the divine and the human sacramentum, between the standard of Christ and the standard of the devil, the camp of light and the camp of darkness . . . the Lord in disarming Peter unbelted every soldier from that time forth" (19). The two texts are not contradictory. In the first Tertullian is cleverly making the most of the fact that Christians are in reality in the armed services – he is arguing from fact, from the reality of the situation. In the second text he is proclaiming what he considers to be the ideal, the correct position. It is true that he conceals his own view in the *Apologeticum.*

Tertullian's work *Ad Scapulam* is a short masterpiece which contains some precious material on the ardent faith of Christians confronting persecution and matyrdom. It was written to Scapula, the Governor of Africa (211-213) and a persecutor of Christians. As elsewhere in his works, Tertullian here proclaims his belief in the freedom of conscience, the freedom of religion: "It is a fundamental human right, a privilege of nature, that every man should worship according to his own convictions: one man's religion neither harms nor helps another man. It is assuredly no part of religion to compel religion – to which freedom of will and not force should lead us – the sacrificial victims even being required of a willing mind. You will render no real service to your gods by compelling us to sacrifice. For they can have no desire of offerings from the unwilling, unless they are animated by a spirit of contention, which is a thing altogether undivine" (2). "A Christian is enemy to none, least of all to the Emperor of Rome, whom he knows to be appointed by his God" (2). Tertullian writes at length on the Emperor being "appointed by God," on the Emperor as "the human being next to God who from God has received all his power and is less than God alone" (2). He warns Scapula of punishment from God in the next world. He then presents a moving statement: "Your cruelty is our glory. Only see to it that, in having such things to endure, we do not feel ourselves constrained to rush forth to the combat, if only to prove that we have no dread of them but, on the contrary, even invite their infliction. . . We have no master but God. He is before you and cannot be hidden from you. But to him you can do no injury. But those whom you regard as masters are only men, and one day they themselves must die. Yet still this community will be undying, for be assured that just in the time of its seeming overthrow it is built up into greater power. For all who witness the noble patience of its martyrs, as struck with misgivings, are inflamed with desire to examine into the matter in question. And as soon as they come to know the truth, they at once enroll themselves its disciples" (5).

Tertullian's *Adversus Judaeos* contains some interesting material, draws at some points – especially chapter 8 – on St. Justin's *Dialogue with Trypho*, and contains an unauthentic section – chapters 9–14, which indeed are borrowed from the third book of Tertullian's *Adversus Marcionem* but are compiled hastily and in a sporadic and fragmentary way. One remarkable line of thought in this work is Tertullian's reasoning that the "Law" preceded Moses – indeed, that the Law was ontologically present from the beginning of mankind. "For why should God, the founder of the universe, the Governor of the entire world, the Fashioner of humanity, the Sower of universal nations be believed to have given a law through Moses to one people, and not be said to have assigned it to all nations? For unless he had given it to all by no means would he have habitually permitted even proselytes out of the nations to have access to it. But – as is consonant with the goodness of God and with his equity, as the Fashioner of mankind – he gave to all nations the selfsame Law, which at definite and stated times he enjoined should be observed . . . For in this Law given given to Adam we recognize in embryo all the precepts which afterwards sprouted forth when given through Moses . . . For the primordial law was given to Adam and Eve in paradise, as the womb of all the precepts of God. . . In this general and primordial Law of God, the observance of which . . . he had sanctioned, we recognize enclosed all the precepts especially of the posterior Law, which germinated when disclosed at their proper times. For the subsequent superinduction of a law is the work of the same Being who had before premised a precept. . . In short, before the Law of Moses, written in stone tables, I contend that there was a law unwritten, which was habitually understood naturally, and by the fathers was habitually kept. For why was Noah "found righteous," if in his case the righteousness of a natural law had not preceded? Why was Abraham accounted "a friend of God," if not on the ground of equity and righteousness in the observance of a natural law?" (2). Tertullian's line of reasoning based on the legal principle of equity and on natural law has fascinating ramifications theologically. This notion of all things being contained in embryo with Adam will have some influence later on St. Augustine as he develops his specific doctrine of original sin. In dealing with the Sabbath Tertullian distinguishes between the Hebrew Sabbath which was "temporary" and the Sabbath which is "eternal." Christians keep and participate in the "eternal" Sabbath. Tertullian handles the theme of the Christ, the Messiah, in a very specific manner. The Hebrew Scriptures predicted that the Messiah would come, that he would rule "the universal earth," in whom "all nations" would believe. It is the idea of universality that attracts the attention of Tertullian. "For upon whom else have the universal nations believed but upon the Christ who is already come? . . . For who could have reigned over all nations but Christ, God's Son, who was ever announced as destined to reign over all to eternity? For if Solomon "reigned," why, it was within the confines of Judea merely" (6). What distinguishes this work from other works of the same nature is the fact that Tertullian treats it as though it were a legal case, arguing each point the way he would in a Roman law court.

Tertullian's *De praescriptione haereticorum* [*On the Prescription of Heretics*] is interesting both in content and in the legal way it is presented. Legally it depends on the Roman legal term *praescriptio*, a juridical term which entails an objection that prevents the defendant from actually having a case. By using the legal device of the *praescriptio*, Tertullian deprives the heretics of the very basis of their position. He links the legal argument of the *praescriptio* with the appeal to apostolic tradition. One *praescriptio* is that Christ appointed the apostles to deliver his message. Therefore, no one except those appointed by Christ can be conveyors of this message. Linked to this *praescriptio* is a second. "From this, therefore, do we draw up our rule. Now, what that was which they preached – in other words, what it was which Christ revealed to them – can, as I must here likewise prescribe, properly be proved in no other way than by those very churches which the apostles founded in person, by declaring the gospel to them directly themselves, both *viva voce* . . . and subsequently by their epistles. If, then, these things are so, it is in the same degree manifest that all doctrine which agrees with the apostolic churches – the sources and origins of the faith – must be reckoned as truth because it maintains without doubt what the churches received from the Apostles, the Apostles from Christ, and Christ from God" (21). The entire work is a brilliant exposition of the ancient appeal to the apostolic deposit, to that which was delivered, to that which has been and still is preserved. And while he presents fully this doctrine of the apostolic deposit, Tertullian lashes out against specific heresies. The work is rich in idea and detail.

Tertullian's *Adversus Marcionem*, the longest of his works, is a devastating critique of Marcion and his thought. Even in recent times Marcion still has his supporters. Harnack essentially considers Marcion as the first to really understand the message of St. Paul – indeed, Harnack tends to glorify Marcion as a reformer, as one attempting to bring back the original truth of Christianity which was apparently quickly lost after St. Paul. Harnack writes: "Completely carried away with the novelty, uniqueness and grandeur of the Pauline Gospel of the grace of God in Christ, Marcion felt that all other conceptions of the Gospel, and especially its union with the Old Testament religion, was opposed to, and a backsliding from, the truth." Harnack calls Marcion's vision "evangelical." Marcion "had a capacity for appreciating the Pauline idea of faith; it is to him reliance on the unmerited grace of God which is revealed in Christ." "The twelve Apostles whom Christ chose did not understand him, but regarded him as the Messiah of the god of creation. And therefore Christ inspired Paul by a special revelation, lest the Gospel of the grace of God should be lost through falsifications. But even Paul had been understood only by few (by none?). His Gospel had also been misunderstood – nay, his Epistles had been falsified in many passages, in order to make them teach the identity of the god of creation and the God of redemption. A new reformation was therefore necessary. Marcion felt himself entrusted with this commission, and the church which he gathered recognized this vocation of his to be the reformer. Marcion's self-consciousness of being a reformer, and the recognition of this in his church is still not understood, although his undertaking itself and the facts speak loud enough. He did not appeal to a new revelation such as he presupposed for Paul. As the Pauline Epistles and an authentic εὐαγγέλιον κυρίου were in existence, it was only necessary to purify these from interpolations, and restore the genuine Paulinism which was just the Gospel itself. . . He was the first who laid the firm foundation for establishing what is Christian, because, in view of the absoluteness of his faith, he had no desire to appeal either to a secret evangelical tradition, or to prophecy, or to natural religion. . . In basing his own position and that of his church on Paulinism, as he conceived and remodelled it, Marcion connected himself with that part of the earliest tradition of Christianity which is best known to us, and has enabled us to understand his undertaking historically as we do no other. . . Marcion gives important testimony against the historical reliability of the notion that the common Christianity was really based on the tradition of the twelve Apostles. . . Marcion was the first, and for a long time the only Gentile Christian who took his stand on Paul. He was no moralist, no Greek mystic, no Apocalyptic enthusiast, but a religious character, nay, one of the few pronouncedly typical religious characters whom we know in the early Church before Augustine." In fairness to Harnack it must be stressed that he does approach Marcion critically, does distinguish his teachings from the Gnostics, and is very aware of how Marcion differed from the established Christianity. But Harnack's zeal for Marcion can only be understood when one realizes that he approaches the early Church from "without," that he is very unsympathetic to the inner life of the Christian faith as developed from the beginning, and that it is almost impossible for him to appreciate this inner life and thought of the Church. Harnack reads back into early Christian thought, reads into the life and thought of early Christianity from the perspective of the Reformation and from the perspective of the "higher criticism" then in vogue. His elevation of the Pauline Gospel comes directly from Luther. His enthusiasm for Marcion's critical approach to the Scriptures comes directly from the spirit of the then popular "higher criticism," many of the insights and conclusions of which have been proven totally incorrect by modern scholarship. Harnack is fair in presenting all the facts. He is, however, incapable of interpreting these facts from within, from the mind of the Church.

Marcion, according to Hippolytus and Epiphanius, a native of Sinope in Pontus and a wealthy shipowner, was the son of a bishop who excommunicated his own son on the grounds of immorality. He came to Rome about 140 and was excommunicated in 144. He appears to have been an excellent organizer and his "church" spread rapidly throughout the empire. His orthodox opponents testify to the fact of the spread of his "church" – Irenaeus in Lyons, Dionysius in Corinth, Theophilus in Antioch, Philip in Gortyna, Hippolytus and Rhodo in Rome, Bardesanes in Edessa, Melito in Sardis – according to Anastasius Sinaita – Tertullian in Carthage, and St. Justin. By the latter part of the third century most of the Marcionite churches had been absorbed by other groups, most significantly by the Manichees. Marcion rejected the Old Testament, accepted only ten of the epistles of St. Paul, and accepted his own edited version of the *Gospel of St. Luke*. His Christology was either emphatically Docetic or heavily tinged with Docetism. He rejected any allegorical interpretation of the Bible and his rejection of the Gospels, exclusive of his edited text of the *Gospel of St. Luke*, actually helped the Church – it expedited the Church's finalization of the canon of the New Testament.

Tertullian, as mentioned above, is not the first to oppose Marcion But Tertullian's *Adversus Marcionem* is the most exhaustive work in opposition to Marcion and his followers. In this work Tertullian not only attacks the thought of Marcion in general but criticizes in depth Marcion's own work, the *Antitheses*. Tertullian writes: "In the scheme of Marcion . . . the mystery of the Christian religion begins from the discipleship of Luke. Since, however, it was on its course previous to that point, it must have had its own authentic materials by means of which it found its own way down to St. Luke" (4, 3). "When Marcion complains that apostles are suspected (for their prevarication and dissimulation) of having even depraved the gospel, he thereby accuses Christ, by accusing those whom Christ chose. If, then, the apostles, who are censured simply for inconsistency of walk, composed the Gospel in a pure form, but false apostles interpolated their true record; and if our own copies have been made from these, where will that genuine text of the apostles' writings be found which has not suffered adulteration? Which was it that enlightened Paul, and through him Luke?" (4, 3).

Tertullian's *Adversus Marcionem* is a rich work – it covers numerous subjects. Indeed, it is not an exaggeration to claim that it is one of the more important works in patristic literature. Among the many topics Tertullian discusses is the nature of God. "Either God is one or he does not exist. For it is more fitting to ascribe non-existence than the wrong kind of existence." God is "eternal, unborn, uncreated, without beginning, without end." God "is the supreme being." We encounter in Tertullian's definition of God elements of Anselm's "ontological argument." "What, then, will be the postulate of this supreme being? Surely this, that nothing will be equal to it: and this is to say that there will not be another supreme being . . . the supreme being must be unique" (1, 3). He writes about time and creation: "That which created time had no time before time was, just as that which made the beginning had no beginning before the beginning." The cause of creation is in the goodness of God. And this principle of the goodness of God is also the cause of God's granting man freewill, "for good is to be performed voluntarily, that is, of free choice; a freedom which is in accordance with the purpose of man's creation but not in bondage to it. Thus man might be really good, being found good in accordance with his creation but at the same time of his own will, being good as it were of the proper quality of his own nature" (2, 5-6).

Tertullian foreshadows to some extent an element which would later become one of the components of St. Augustine's doctrine of original sin: "If the blessing of the fathers was destined to be transmitted to their posterity, before that posterity had done anything to deserve it, why should not the guilt of the fathers flow down to their sons, so that the transgression as well as the grace should spread through the whole human race?" (2, 15). But Tertullian's thought is not the same as St. Augustine's doctrine of original sin, even though there are some points of similarity – see also *Testimonium Animae* (3) and *De Resurrectione Carnis* (34 and 49).

Against the Docetic tendency in Marcion's thought Tertullian writes: "He who did not really suffer did not suffer at all; and a phantasm could not suffer. Thus the whole work of God is overthrown. The death of Christ, which is the whole essence and value of the Christian religion, is denied" (3, 8). Tertullian affirms the consub - stantiality of both the Son and the Spirit with the Father (3, 6).

Tertullian's most important work on Christology and the Trinity is his *Adversus Praxean*, written after Tertullian had become a Montanist. Praxeas was deeply anti-Montanist and hence Tertullian's rage is intensified in this work. "I derive the Son from no other source than from the substance of the Father. I describe him as doing nothing without the Father's will, as receiving all power from the Father. How then can I be abolishing from the faith that monarchy when I safeguard it in the Son, as handed down to the Son by the Father? Let this affirmation be taken as applying also to the third rank of the Godhead, since I regard the Spirit as proceeding from no other source than from the Father, through the Son – "*Spiritum non aliunde deduco quam a Patre per Filium*" . . . the monarchy remains unimpaired, despite the introduction of a Trinity" (4).

"Before all things existed God was alone. He was himself his own universe, his own place, everything. He was alone in the sense that there was nothing external to him, nothing outside his own being. Yet even then he was not alone, for he had with him something which was part of his own being, namely, his Reason. For God is rational and Reason existed first with him, and from him extended to all things. That Reason is his own consciousness of himself. The Greeks call it *Logos*, which is the term we use for discourse. And thus our people usually translate it literally as, 'Discourse was in the beginning with God', although it would be more correct to regard Reason as prior to Discourse because there was not Discourse with God from the beginning but there was Reason, even before the beginning, and because Discourse takes its origin from Reason and thus shows Reason to be prior to it, as the ground of its being" (5–7). The very "projection" – προβολή – of the Son is a "safeguard of unity." The same applies to the procession of the Holy Spirit. "But none of those is divorced from the origin from which it derives its own qualities. Thus the Trinity derives from the Father by continuous and connected steps and it in no way impugns the monarchy while it preserves the reality of the οἰκονομία" (8). "The Son is not other than the Father by separation from him but by difference of function, nor by division but by distinction: for the Father and the Son are not identical but distinct in rank. . . So the Father is other than the Son, as being greater, as he who begets is other than the begotten, the sender than the sent, the creator than the agent of creation" (9). Tertullian was, based on the preserved written documents, the first to use the term "*trinitas*." He was also the first to use the word "*persona*": the Logos is "another" than the Father – "*alium autem quomodo accipere debeas iam professus sum, personae non substantiae nomine, ad distinctionem non ad divisionem*" (12). In connection with the text in *Genesis* to which the early Christian writers so often refer – "Let us make man . . ." – Tertullian writes: If the number of the Trinity also offends you, as if it were not connected in the simple Unity, I ask you how it is possible for a Being who is merely and absolutely One and Singular to speak in plural phrase? . . . Or was it to the angels that he spoke as the Jews interpret the passage? . . . Or was it because he was at once the Father, the Son, and the Spirit that he spoke to himself in plural terms? . . . No, it was because he had already his Son close at his side, as a second Person, his own Word, and a third Person also, the Spirit in the Word." He spoke to "the Son who was one day to put on human nature and to the Spirit who was to sanctify man. With these did he the speak in the Unity of the Trinity" (12). Tertullian writes of a "*Trinitas unius Divinitatis, Pater et Filius et Spiritus Sanctus*" (21) and stresses the compatibility of unity and trinity: "*tres unius substantiae et unius status et unius potestatis*" (2). "Thus the connection of the Father in the Son, and of the Son in the Paraclete, produces three coherent Persons, who are yet distinct One from Another. These Three are one essence, not one Person" – "*Connexus Patris in Filio et Filii in Paracleto tres efficit cohaerentes, alterum e altero. Qui tres unum sunt, non unus*" (25).

The accusation, still often present today, that Tertullian – for all his brilliance in Trinitarian theology – succumbed to "sub - ordinationism," is more a misunderstanding of the theological perspec - tive from which he writes and as such the accusation is erroneous. Tertullian – and this is still difficult for Western theologians to grasp – writes about the *oikonomic* Trinity, not the eternal life within the Trinity. They still are unable to understand that inner theological vision inherited from the Apologists, they still have difficulty understanding the λόγος ἐνδιάθετος and the λόγος προφορικός in their *ad se* and *ad extra* Divine Life. The source of this inability to understand Tertullian and others when they write about the Trinity or the Logos is not difficult to discern – one is still reading the Church Fathers through the thought of St. Augustine's *De Trinitate*, and it is precisely St. Augustine who has difficulty with the distinctions within the Divine Life, with the Divine "persons," and it is St. Augustine who is ultimately the Modalist in his Trinitarian thought.

Two natures can exist in one person – "Jesus consisted of flesh and spirit; of flesh as man, of spirit as God. . . The Apostle confirms that he was composed of two substances when he designated him the 'mediator of God and man'." (27). There are numerous examples in the works of Tertullian which demonstrate his belief in two natures of the one person who was God. He at times uses language which clearly foreshadows the *communicatio idiomatum*. In his *De Carne Christi* [*On the Flesh of Christ*] Tertullian writes (5): "There are certainly other things also quite as foolish [as the birth of Christ] which have reference to the humiliations and sufferings of God. Or else let them call a crucified God 'wisdom'. . . For which is more unworthy of God, which is more likely to raise a blush of shame, that God should be born? Or that God should die? . . . Was not God really crucified? And, *having been really crucified, did he not really die?*" – "*Sunt plane et alia tam stulta quae pertinent ad contumelias et passiones dei. Aut prudentiam dic deum crucifixum aut aufer hoc quoque, Marcion, immo hoc potius. Quid enim indignius deo, quid magis erubescendum, nasci an mori? Carnem gestare an crucem? Circumcidi an suffigi? Educari an sepeliri? In praesepe deponi an in monimento recondi? Sapientior eris, si nec ista credideris . . . . Crucifixus est dei filius: non pudet quia pudendum est. Et mortuus est Dei filius; credibile est, quia ineptum est. Et sepultus resurrexit; certum est quia impossibile.*" The meaning that Tertullian ascribes to his Christological terminology becomes clear from an analysis of his numerous other expressions and their contexts. Too much is written about where a comma should be placed in one of his texts. In the totality of Tertullian's thought the meaning becomes clear without belaboring the position of a comma. When he is arguing against Marcion, Tertullian's main interest is the distinction of the natures. When he is arguing against Praxeas, his main interest is to stress the Son's own character as "person." The Chalcedonian formula is not precisely stated by Tertullian but he approaches it; it is foreshadowed in the very nature of his thought.

ST. HIPPOLYTUS

St. Hippolytus' life and works raise many questions. The sources allow no conclusive solutions. Still, patristic scholars have made much satisfactory progress in reconstructing at least the essentials of his life and writings.

He was the first anti-pope in history. He was probably born about 170 and it seems quite certain that he was from the Greek East. Daniélou maintains that Hippolytus was a Roman who knew Greek.

Most evidence, however, points to his Greek origin – he is familiar with Greek philosophy; he has a good knowledge of Greek mystery cults; his theology of the Logos is more similar to Greek rather than Latin thought; his language as well as his thought is Greek – indeed he is the last Christian writer living in Rome to write in Greek. St. Hippolytus has often been compared with Origen but such a comparison is overstated – he lacked Origen's depth of thought and his knowledge of both Greek philosophy and the Greek mystery cults is not as deep as Origen's. He is more preoccupied with questions of a practical nature than was Origen. But his breadth of interests was extensive: he wrote religious poetry, wrote anti-heretical works, a *Chronicle*, and an extremely valuable "Church Order." St. Photius makes the claim that Hippolytus – in a lost work – asserted that he was a disciple of St. Irenaeus (*Bibl. Cod.* 121).

Unlike St. Irenaeus, Hippolytus possessed a quite unirenic personality – he was passionate, vehement, and intransigent. When Pope Callistus (217-222) took a more moderate position concerning penitents guilty of mortal sin, Hippolytus accused him of departing from the tradition of the apostolic Church. In addition, he accused Pope Callistus of being a Sabellian and hence a heretic. Hippolytus, along with a small group of influential persons, separated from the Church in Rome and Hippolytus became the first anti-pope. This schism and his position as anti-pope lasted throughout Callistus' pontificate and extended into that of Pope Urban I (223-230) and Pope Pontianus (230-235). It was not until Emperor Maximinus Thrax (235-238) exiled both Pontianus and Hippolytus to Sardinia that the schism in Rome ceased. Some reconciliation took place, for Pontianus resigned in Sardinia to allow a new successor, Pope Anteros (235-236). Both Hippolytus and Pontianus died in exile. But Pope Fabianus (236-250) had their bodies brought back to Rome where they were interred sacredly – Pontianus in the papal crypt of San Callisto; Hippolytus in the cemetery of the Via Tiburtina. Hippolytus was buried on August 13 of 236 or 237 and it is on this date that he is commemorated as a martyr in the Roman Church. In 1551 a statue of St. Hippolytus was discovered on which a list of his works is engraved.

Hippolytus wrote in Greek but very little of the Greek originals remains. Most of his works have survived either in complete or fragmentary form in Latin, Syriac, Coptic, Ethiopic, Arabic, Armenian, Georgian and Slavonic. Not mentioned in the list on the statue is his important work entitled *Philosophumena* or *Refutation of All Heresies* which is also known as the *Labyrinth* – Κατὰ πασῶν αἱρέσεων ἔλεγχος. Hippolytus had written another work against heresies before writing the *Philosophumena* – his Πρὸς ἁπάσας τὰς αἱρέσεις, referred to by St. Photius (*Bibl. Cod.* 121) as the "*Syntagma against Thirty-Two Heresies* of Hippolytus, the Student of Irenaeus." St. Photius describes the work: "Beginning with the Dositheans, it extends to the heresies of Noëtus and the Noëtians, which he writes were refuted by Irenaeus in his lectures, of which his present work is a synopsis. His style is lucid, somewhat severe, and lacking in redundancies. . . " The original is lost but the extant fragments allow a reconstruction. Only one of Hippolytus' dogmatic works has survived – *The Antichrist, Περὶ τοῦ ἀντιχρίστου* – and it has survived in its complete Greek text in three manuscripts. An Old Slavonic and a Georgian version also exist, as do fragments in Armenian. Patristic literature has nothing comparable to this work on the question of the Antichrist.

In 234 he wrote his *Chronicle – Χρονικῶν βίβλοι* – of the history of the world, from creation to his time. His purpose was to expose the heretical view of the imminent end of the world, the Day of Judgment, and the millennium. In an attempt to disengage the Church from dependence on the Jewish calendrical cycle in its calculation of the date of Easter, Hippolytus wrote his *Calculation of the Date of Pascha – ἀπόδειξις χρόνων τοῦ πάσχα* – but his astronomical calculations were inaccurate.

His exegetical and homiletic works are difficult to distinguish. St. Jerome mentions in his *De viris illustribus* (61) that when Origen visited Rome about 212 he heard in a Roman church a sermon "On the Praise of Our Lord and Savior" and was much impressed. The deliverer of the sermon was Hippolytus. The sermon is lost.

Hippolytus' work entitled *The Apostolic Tradition – ἀποστολικὴ παράδοσις* – is, along with *The Didache*, one of the most important documents in early Church history. It contains a wealth of information on the liturgical life of the Church – the rubrics and forms for ordination, the duties of the various ranks of the hierarchy, the celebration of Pascha, the form of baptism. The title of this work is inscribed on the chair of the statue of Hippolytus but it was thought to be lost until 1910 when E. Schwartz was the first to associate the work with the *Egyptian Church Order,* known by this name only because it became known in the modern world in Ethiopic and Coptic translations. The importance of this discovery by E. Schwartz cannot be exaggerated – it provided a new basis for the study of the Roman liturgy. It is historically significant that Hippolytus' *Apostolic Tradition* had very little influence in the Latin West and appears to have been soon forgotten there – along with Hippolytus' other works. Rather, it was in the East where the work had its influence, especially in Egypt. The Coptic, Ethiopic, and Arabic translations influenced the very shape of the liturgy, canon law, and Christian life in these churches. Of all the Eastern versions it is only the Sahidic which is based directly on the Greek original – it was preserved in a collection of laws known as the *Egyptian Heptateuch.*

Works known to have been written by Hippolytus but now lost include *Against Marcion*; *Against Gaius*; *On the Resurrection*; *Against the Heresy of Artemon*; *On the Cosmos,* and *Against the Greeks and Plato,* about which St. Photius makes an interesting comment (*Bibl. Cod.* 48): "Of Christ the true God he speaks like ourselves, openly giving him the name of God and describing, in language to which no objection can be taken, his indescribable generation from the Father." He also wrote a work *On the Gospel of John and the Apocalypse* – ὑπέρ τοῦ κατά Ἰωάννην εὐαγγελίου καί ἀποκαλύψεως – apparently directed against the Alogi who rejected these two books.

Hippolytus has suffered a worse fate than most of the Apologists because of his Christology. Hippolytus has been constantly accused of ditheism. Great emphasis has been placed on Hippolytus' statement that the Logos only becomes the true and perfect Son in the Incarnation. Although Hippolytus, like all the Apologists, was groping for terminology, his expressions are understandably imprecise. Does he indeed believe as the critics charge? It must be remembered that not only is he writing without the necessary precision of theological terminology but also that he is writing against the Monarchians and hence he must distinguish, make distinct, the Son from the Father. It must also be remembered that we lack the complete body of the works of Hippolytus and thus can make no final judgment.

St. Hippolytus focuses the Incarnation in the *oikonomic* activity of God. He presents the Logos in two stages of his existence: the λόγος ἄσαρκος, which is the un-fleshed, pre-existent Logos; and the λόγος ἔνσαρκος, the en-fleshed or incarnate Logos – ὁ λόγος τοῦ θεοῦ, ἄσαρκος ὤν, ἐνεδύσατο τήν ἁγίαν σάρκα ἐκ τῆς ἁγίας παρθένου. Hippolytus has been sharply upbraided for using the term "perfect Son" – υἱός τέλειος – in reference to the Incarnation. But for Hippolytus the Logos reveals himself also in the Old Testament theophanies – he is here speaking of the historical revelation of the Logos and not the eternal life of the Logos. The revelation given through the theophanies in the Old Testament was "imperfect" and it is only in the Incarnation that revelation becomes "perfect." In this sense, the word perfect – τέλειος – takes on a different meaning. Hippolytus states that the Logos revealed himself only "in part" – μερικῶς – in the theophanies. He links his theology of the Incarnation with his theology of redemption, a theology of redemption akin to that of St. Irenaeus in which Christ experiences every aspect and age of the life of man. He distinguishes so much between the λόγος ἄσαρκος and the λόγος ἔνσαρκος that the principle of unity between these two "states" of being is difficult to discern but the distinction is clear, for there is the Logos and the Flesh. Hence there is an affirmation of the Divine and the human. The Logos wraps or clothes himself in flesh, he dwells in the body, his temple – ἐνδύομαι, ἐπενδύομαι . And for the first time in Christian literature – based on the written documents known to us – we encounter the word ὑφιστάναι as well as the meanings with which that word will later be associated. It is even closely positioned to another word of importance – σύστασις. The text comes from a fragment against Noëtus: "He has, by calling himself Son, taken for humanity the new name of love, for the Logos before the Incarnation and when by himself was not perfect Son, although he was perfect

Logos, the Only-Begotten. Neither could the flesh exist by itself apart
from the Logos, for it had its existence in the Logos. Then was thus
manifested one perfect Son of God – οὔτε γὰρ ἄσαρκος καὶ καθ
ἑαυτὸν ὁ λόγος τέλειος ἦν υἱός, καίτοι τέλειος λόγος ὢν
μονογενής, οὔθ 'ἡ σάρξ καθ 'ἑαυτὴν δίχα τοῦ λόγου ὑπο -
στᾶναι ἠδύνατο διὰ τὸ ἐν λόγῳ τὴν σύστασιν ἔχειν. οὔτως
οὖν εἷς υἱὸς τέλειος θεοῦ ἐφανερώθη. Hippolytus certainly lays
the basis for a unity in the God-Man, Jesus Christ, even if his
terminology is not completely precise. From this text the meaning of
Hippolytus' term "perfect Son" becomes clear.

CHAPTER NINE

ORIGENISM AND ARIANISM

Continuous theological debate, unending theological turmoil and controversy breaks out at the end of third century and continues for the next few centuries. In the fourth century this centers primarily around the struggle of the Church with Arianism. It is a mistake to oversim - plify the Arian problem. The Arian movement was complex. It was not homogeneous. The teaching of Arius received a positive response from a variety of different theological schools of thought. The crucial question is why? That question and its answer is determinative for the theological controversies which will shake the Christian world and cause sore division within Byzantium for the next few centuries. The outbreak of the Arian controversy begins in Alexandria with the deacon Arius. But the root cause lies under deeper strata.

It is not without foundation that a link has been seen between the teaching of Arius and Lucian of Antioch – moreover, even with Paul of Samosata. From the very inception of the controversy between Arius and Alexander, bishop of Alexandria, Alexander called attention to this. Arius' ideas, he said, "were fermented by the impious Lucian." There may be a link but that link does not necessarily imply a conscious dependence of Arius on Lucian. It does not mean that Arius simply borrowed his ideas from Lucian. It is historically difficult to deny Arius' independence as a theologian.

In his theological views Lucian was close to Origen. It is significant that many of his students were Origenists. And this is true of Arius himself. The Arians frequently refer to Origen and to Dion - ysius of Alexandria. Opposed to Origen in their exegesis, the Arians remained Origenists in their theology. Thus, the problems of Arian theology can only be understood in terms of the presuppositions and premises of Origen's theological system.

The same fear which Origen had for Modalism can be seen among the Arian theologians. Since the Arian movement was possible only on the basis and on the foundation of Origenist theology, the struggle against Arianism was precisely a struggle against certain tendencies in Origen's thought. It is significant, however, that Origen's name is seldom mentioned in this controversy. The reason for this silence was that the opponents of Arius, including Alexander of Alexandria, were themselves Origenists. Origen was not an Arian but it is not difficult to discern how the Arians reached their conclusions not merely from misunderstandings of Origen's teachings but precisely from Origen's actual premises. Historically, therefore, the defeat of Arianism proved at the same time to be a defeat of Origenism – at least in his trinitarian theology.

The basis of Arius' theology is the conception of God as a perfect unity and as a self-enclosed monad. For Arius this self-enclosed monad is God the Father. Everything else in existence is alien to God in its essence. The absolute nature of the Divine Being makes it impossible for God to give or to endow his essence to anyone else. Therefore, the Word, the *Logos*, the Son of God, as an hypostasis, as one who has actual existence, is unconditionally and completely alien and unlike the Father. He receives his Being from the Father and by the will of the Father, just as all other creatures do, and He comes into being as a mediator for the sake of the creation of the world. Thus there exists a certain "interval" between the Father and the Son. Hence, the Son is not coeternal with the Father. If the Son were coeternal with the Father, then there would be two "eternals" or two "ultimate principles." And this would abrogate, would destroy completely the truth of mono - theism. In a very accurate sense Arius was the upholder of strict monotheism and this in a still pervasively pagan society.

For Arius "there was a then, when the Son was not" – ἦν ποτέ ὅτε οὐκ ἦν. The Son did not exist but he came into being and had an origin. This means that the Son comes into being "out of things that do not exist" – ἐξ οὐκ ὄντων. The Son is a creature, something which is generated and therefore like all generated things the Son has a "mutable" nature. The Son is endowed with Divine Glory in advance, from without, "by grace" and by God's foreknowledge of the future. Judged from the fragments of Arius' compositions which have survived and from the evidence of his contemporaries, his theological system was in essence a rejection of the Holy Trinity. For Arius the Trinity is something derived and generated. It has a beginning, an origin. And the hypostases of the Holy Trinity are, for Arius, separated by "temporal intervals" – διάστημα. they are "eternally dissimilar." It is a kind of diminishing Trinity, a union, or – in the words of St. Gregory of Nazianzus, an "association" of three essences which are not alike. It is a union of three hypostases which are united by essence; it is three coexisting wills which are distinguished by essence.

Strict monotheism was the core of Arius' system. For Arius a Trinity cannot be a single God – Trinity, for him, philosophically precludes monotheism. Arius' thought approaches that of Judaism. Although there was a strong, vibrant Jewish community in Alexandria, it is not necessary to posit a direct Jewish influence on Arius. If there is a Jewish influence, then that influence comes not necessarily directly but internally, from within the very development of Christian reflection on the nature of God, from the confrontation of the Hebraic *Shema'* ["Hear, O Israel: the Lord our God is one Lord – *Deuteronomy* 6:4] with the revelation of God through, by and in Jesus Christ – "I and the Father are one" (*John* 10:30). It is not only the Old Testamental monotheism with which Arius struggled but also the philosophical problems inextricably connected with the concept of monotheism, of oneness. This is not the only problem which divided the Hebraic system of thought from that of the early Christianity of the Hellenic mind. Origen could not think in Hebraic terms when confronting the question of creation. For the Hebraic mind the world has a beginning but no end. For the Hellenic mind any beginning implies an end and any end implies a beginning – thus the Hellenic notion of the preexistence and eternality of the soul. Both the Christian teaching of creation and the Christian revelation of the Holy Trinity were to cause problems for the Hellenic mind. And the Christian revelation of Holy Trinity would cause grave problems for both the Hebraic and the Hellenic mind. Arius is a clear example of this.

For Arius there is a one and only God and that is God the Father. The Son and Spirit are the highest and first-born creatures who are mediators in the creation of the world. In this doctrine Arius approaches Paul of Samosata and the Dynamic Monarchians, but he is actually even closer to Philo. It is not difficult to understand why his arguments found supporters among the Alexandrians and Origenists.

The connection between Arius' dogma and the problems of time and the creation of the world are immediately apparent. Creation implies origination. That which is created is that which has a beginning, which exists not from itself or through itself, but from another. It is that which does not exist before it comes into being. In Arius' system creation is indistinguishable from generation because, for him, both entail origination. And in his understanding origination can take place only in time.

This difficulty arises because of the ambiguity of the conception of "origination." That which is generated has an origin, a reason for its being outside of and before itself. But "origin" can have two meanings: it can be the cause or source of being or it can be a moment in time. For Arius both meanings coincide. For him "eternity" or timelessness means ontological primacy. He therefore refuses to grant that the existence of the Son is "without beginning" or eternal. This would be a denial of his "generation" and the fact that he is begotten, and, if this were not true, then the *Logos* or Word would be a second and independent God. If the Logos is from the Father, then he must have been begotten. Otherwise, he is not from the Father. From tradition Arius knows that the Logos is the God of revelation and the most immediate cause of creation. But a creature is subject to change because it is temporal. This gives Arius another reason to connect the existence of the Logos with time.

Arius was, it appears, in sharp disagreement with Origen. In Origen's doctrine the generation of the Logos is eternal and this proves that the Divine Being is immutable. However, Origen inferred too much from this. Because he believed that origination is incompatible with the immutability of God, he posited that the creation of the wold is also eternal. In his system the generation of the Son and the creation of the world are united by the concept of origination. To protect the immutability of God Origen essentially denied that any origination ever takes place. There is nothing in existence about which he was willing to say "there was a then, when it did not exist."

Origen concluded that all existence is eternal and that everything coexists with God, a doctrine which is similar to Aristotle's doctrine of the eternity of the world. For Origen the world was not a created thing. This conclusion was unacceptable to his followers who, while rejecting his conclusions, did not deny his premises. Arius also reasoned this way. He denied that the world is eternal. The entire emphasis of Arius' system is in affirming the temporal character of everything which is generated or which has the "origin" of its being in another. From this he concluded that the Son also is generated in time. Arius differed from Origen in his conclusions but agreed with him in his premises. Within the bounds of Origen's system there was an inescapable dilemma: it was necessary either to admit the eternity of the world or to reject the eternal generation of the Son. This dilemma could be avoided only by denying Origen's premises. For this reason Arius' system attracted those disciples of Origin who did not accept his idea of an eternal world.

It is not an exaggeration to assert that the root cause of the Christological controversies in the fourth century centered on the *vital questions involved in the ideas of creation, generation, the nature of the One God and how God relates to the world.* Too often these issues, these vital theological concerns of the Christian faith are not addressed – even as background – for their direct bearing on the relation of the Logos of God to God the Father. Indeed, the Christian understanding of creation and generation are necessary for an understanding of the Christological controversies that will beset the Church in the fourth and fifth centuries – and later also.

The idea of creation was for the world outside of Judaism a stunning innovation. The problem itself was alien and even somewhat incomprehensible to the Greek mind. The Greek mind was strongly attached to the idea of an eternal cosmos, one that was permanent and immutable in its essential composition and structure. This cosmos was simply there; *it simply existed.* And moreover its existence was *necessary.* It was an ultimate assumption, a first principle of reality, a first *datum.* And beyond this neither thought nor imagination could penetrate. There was, of course, movement within this world – "the wheel of origin and decay" – but the cosmos as a whole was un - changeable. Its permanent structure was repeatedly and unfailingly exhibited in its rotation and self-iteration. The world was not static. In it there was an intense dynamism but this dynamism was one of inescapable circulation. The cosmos was both *necessary* and *immortal.* The "shape" of the world might be exposed to changes and it was in a perpetual flux but its very existence was *perennial.* One simply could not ask intelligently about the origin or beginning of the cosmic fabric in the order of existence. It was precisely at this point that the Greek mind was radically challenged by Biblical Revelation. This was a hard message for the Greeks. Indeed, it is still a hard message for philos - ophers today.

"In the beginning God created . . ." Thus begins the Biblical narrative. And this has become a credal statement in the Christian Church. The cosmos was no longer regarded as a "self-explanatory" being. Its ultimate and intrinsic dependence upon God's will and action has now been vigorously asserted. But much more than just this relation of "dependence" was implied in the Biblical concept: the world was created *ex nihilo*; that is, it did not exist "eternally." The narrative in *Genesis* may not explicitly state a doctrine of *ex nihilo* but that was certainly the belief of the Hebrews. Despite the common opinion of many contemporary scholars of the Old Testament, the Hebraic mind did not believe that God created from preexisting matter. The *Genesis* narrative ought to be interpreted within the framework of the entirety of Hebraic thought and literature, including the statement from *II Maccabees* 7:28 – οὐκ ἐξ ὄντων ἐποίησεν.

The tension between the two visions, Hellenic and Biblical, was sharp and obvious. Greeks and Christians were dwelling, as it were, in two different worlds. Accordingly, the categories of Greek philosophy were inadequate for the description of the world of Christian faith. The main emphasis of Christian faith was precisely on the radical con - tingency of the cosmos, on its contingency precisely in the order of existence. Indeed, the very existence of the world pointed, for Christians, to the Other, as its Lord and Creator. On the other hand, the creation of the world was conceived as a sovereign and "free" act of God, and not as something which was "necessarily" implied or inherent in God's own Being. Thus, there was actually a double contingency: on the side of the cosmos – which might not have existed at all; and on the side of the Creator – who could not have created anything at all. God would be God whether he created or not. The very existence of the world was regarded by the Christians as a mystery and as a miracle of Divine Freedom.

Christian thought matured gradually and slowly, by a way of trial and retraction. The early Christian writers would often describe their new vision of faith in the terms of old and current philosophy. They were not always aware of, and certainly did not always guard against, the ambiguity which was involved in such an enterprise. By using Greek categories Christian writers were forcing upon themselves, without being consciously aware of it, a world which was radically different from that in which they lived by faith. They were therefore often caught between the vision of their faith and the inadequacy of the language they were using. This predicament must be taken very seriously. Etienne Gilson once suggested that "*la pensée chrétienne apportait du vin nouveau, mais les vieilles outres étaient encore bonnes.*" ["Christian thought brought the new wine but the old skins were still good enough."]. It is an elegant phrase but is it not rather an optimistic overstatement? Indeed, the skins did not burst at once, but was it really to the benefit of nascent Christian thought? The skins were badly tainted with an old smell, and in those skins the wine acquired an alien flavor. In fact, the new vision required new terms and categories for its adequate and fair expression. This problem is apparent in the earliest Christian literature – if the Apologists are understood from within the mind of the Church, it is clear about which they are speaking. But as soon as one attempts to understand the Apologists "from without," from categories other than the apostolic deposit, one can read into their thought many things which they would have rejected. It was an urgent task for Christians "to coin new names, as St. Gregory of Nazianzus was to point out – τὸ καἰοτομεῖν τὰ ὀνόματα.

The radical contingency of the created world was faithfully ac - knowledged by Christian writers from the very beginning. The Lordship of God over all his creation was duly emphasized. God alone was mighty and eternal. All created things were brought into existence and sustained in existence solely by the grace and freedom of God, by his sovereign will. Existence was always a gift of God. From this point of view even the human soul was "mortal"; that is, mortal by nature. In the depth of Christian theology there is no immortality of the soul "by nature." The soul too was contingent because it too was created and was maintained only by the grace of God. In opposition to Platonic arguments for the immortality of the soul, St. Justin was quite explicit on this point – the soul is immortal, not by nature, but by grace. For St. Justin "immortal" meant "uncreated." [St. Justin, *Dialogue with Trypho*, c. 5 and 6]. But it was not then clear how this creative "will" of God was related to his own "being." And this was the crucial problem. In early Christian thinking the very idea of God was only gradually released out of that "cosmological setting" in which it used to be apprehended by Greek philosophical thought. The mystery of the Holy Trinity itself was often interpreted in an ambiguous cosmological context rather than primarily as a mystery of God's own Being. The mystery of the Holy Trinity was approached from the perspective of God's creative and redemptive action and self-revelation in the world. This was the main predicament of the *Logos-theology* in the Apolo - gists, in Hippolytus, and in Tertullian. All these writers did not dis - tinguish consistently between the categories of the Divine "Being" and those of Divine "Revelation" *ad extra*, in the world. It was no more than a lack of precision in language, an inadequacy of language rather than any obstinate doctrinal error. The Apologists were not pre-Arians or pro-Arians. Most would unhesitatingly have subscribed to the definitions of Nicaea and Chalcedon. The "innocent speculations of the Apologists," as G. L. Prestige has written, "came to provide support for the Arian school of thought."

The case of Origen is especially significant for its influence on the Christological controversies which erupt first with Arius and continue for centuries. Origen failed to distinguish between the ontological and cosmological dimensions. As Bolotov has aptly stated, "the logical link between the generation of the Son and the existence of the world was not yet broken in the speculation of Origen." It can even be contended that this very link has been rather reinforced in Origen's thinking. The ultimate question for Origen was precisely this: is it possible or per- missible to think of God without conceiving him at once as Creator? The negative answer to this question was for Origen the only devout option. An opposite assumption would be sheer blasphemy. God could never have become anything that he has not been always. There is nothing simply "potential" in God's Being, for everything is eternally actualized. This was Origen's basic assumption, his deepest conviction. God is always the Father of the Only-Begotten, and the Son is coeternal with the Father – any other assumption would have compromised the essential immutability of the Divine Being. But God also is always the Creator and the Lord. Indeed, if God is Creator at all – and it is an article of faith that he is Lord and Creator – we must necessarily assume that he had always been Creator and Lord. For God never "advances" toward what he had not been before. For Origen this implied inevitably also an eternal actualization of the world's existence, of all those things over which God's might and Lordship were exercised. Origen himself used the term παντοκράτωρ, which he borrowed from the Septuagint. Its use by Origen is characteristic. The Greek term is much more pointed than its Latin or English renderings: *Omnipotens* and "Al- mighty." These latter terms emphasize might and power. The Greek word stresses specifically the actual exercise of power. The edge of Origen's argument is taken off in Latin translation. As J. N. D. Kelly has correctly observed in his *Early Christian Creeds*, "παντοκράτωρ is in the first place an active word, conveying the idea not just of capacity but of the actualization of capacity." The Greek word παντοκράτωρ means κύριος, the ruling Lord. And God could not be παντοκράτωρ eternally unless τά πάντα also existed from all eternity. God's might must have been eternally actualized in the created cosmos. Therefore the cosmos appears to be an eternal concomitant, a companion, as it were, of the Divine Being. In this context any clear distinction between *generation* and *creation* was actually impossible – both were eternal relations, indeed "necessary" relations, as it were, intrinsic for the Divine Being.

Origen was unable and indeed reluctant and unwilling to admit anything "contingent" about the world itself, since, in his conception, this would have involved also a certain "change" on the Divine level. In Origen's system the eternal Being of the Holy Trinity and the eternal existence of the world are indivisibly and insolubly linked together – both stand and fall together. The Son is indeed eternal, and eternally "personal" and "hypostatic." But the Son is eternally begotten in relation to the eternally created world.

Origen's argument is straight and consistent within the thought structure of his basic assumptions. It would be flagrantly impious to admit that God could ever have existed without His Wisdom, even for a single moment – *ad punctum momenti alicujus*. God is always the Father of his Son, who is born of him but "without any beginning" – *sine ullo tamen initio*. And Origen specifies: "not only of that kind which can be distinguished by intervals of time – *aliquibus temporum spatiis*, but even of that other kind which the mind alone is wont to contemplate in itself and to perceive, if I may say so, with 'the bare intellect and reason" – *nudo intellectu*. In other words, Wisdom is begotten beyond the limit of any imaginable "beginning" – *extra omne ergo quod vel dici vel intelligi potest initium*. Moreover, as Origen explained elsewhere, the "generation" of Wisdom could not be inter - preted as an accomplished "event," but rather as a permanent and con - tinuous relationship, a relation of "being begotten," just as radiance is perpetually concomitant with the light itself, and Wisdom is, in the phrase of the *Wisdom of Solomon* (7:26), an ἀπαύγασμα φωτὸς ἀϊδίου – οὐχὶ ἐγέννησεν ὁ πατὴρ τὸν υἱόν – *Homily on Jere - miah*, 9,4. In the very subsistence of Wisdom, according to Origen, the whole design of creation is already implied. The whole creation – *universa creatura* – is prearranged in Wisdom – *De principiis* I, 2, 2:29-30. The text of this important passage might have been somewhat edited by the Latin translator – Rufinus – but surely the main argument was faithfully reproduced – see the fragment in Greek in Methodius, *De creatis*, quoted by St. Photius, *Bibl. Cod.* 235. Origen spoke of "pre - vision" – *virtute praoscientiae*. But, according to his own basic prin - ciple, there could be no temporal order or sequence. The world as "previewed" in Wisdom had to be also eternally actualized. It is in this direction that Origen continued his argument. And here the terms "*Father*" and "*Pantokrator*" are conspicuously bracketed together. "Now as one cannot be father apart from having a son, nor a lord apart from holding a possession or a slave, so we cannot even call God almighty if there are none over whom he can exercise his power. Accordingly, to prove that God is Almighty we must assume the existence of the world." But, obviously, God is Lord from all eternity. Consequently, the world, in its entirety, also existed from all eternity – *necessario existere oportet* – *De principiis* I, 2, 10: 41-42. (See the Greek quotation in Justinian, *Epistula ad Mennam* in *Mansi* IX, 528). In short, the world must be always coexistent with God and therefore coeternal. Origen, of course, meant the primordial world of spirits. Actually, in Origen's conception there was but one eternal hierarchical system of beings, a "chain of being." He could never escape the cosmological pattern of Middle Platonism.

Origen seems to have interpreted the generation of the Son as an act of the Father's will – ἐκ τοῦ θελήματος τοῦ πατρὸς ἐγεννήθη – quoted by Justinian in *Mansi* IX, 525. On the other hand, he was utterly suspicious of the phrase: ἐκ τῆς οὐσίας πατρός. He probably even formally repudiated it. For him it was a dangerous and misleading phrase, heavily overloaded with gross "materialistic" associations and suggesting division and separation in the Divine essence (*On John* 20,

18: 351; *De principiis* IV, 4, 1: 348; see the quotation by Marcellus given in Eusebius, *Contra Marcellum* I, 4: 21). The textual evidence is confused and inconclusive. It may be true that at this point Origen was opposing the Gnostics, especially the Valentinian conception of προβολή and only wanted to vindicate the strictly spiritual character of everything Divine. Yet there was a flagrant ambiguity. Both the gener - ation of the Son and the creation of the world are equally attributed to the will or counsel of the Father. "And my own opinion is that an act of the Father's will – *voluntas Patris* – ought to be sufficient to ensure the subsistence of that which is produced by the deliberation of his will – *nisi quae consilio voluntatis profertur*. Thus, it is in this way that the existence of the Son also is begotten of him – *ita ergo et filii ab eo subsistentia generatur*" (*De principiis* I, 2, 6: 35). The meaning of this passage is rather obscure, and we have no Greek text. But, in any case, once again the Son is explicitly bracketed together with creatures.

Arius himself contended that the *Logos* was a "creature," a priv - ileged creature indeed, not like others, but still no more than a κτίσμα originated by the will of God. Accordingly, God for him was primarily the Creator and, apart from that, little, if anything, could be said of the unfathomable and incomprehensible Being of God, unknown even to the Son. There was actually no room for "theology" in Arius' system. The only real problem was that of "cosmology" – a typically Hellenic approach. Arius had to define the notion of creation. Two major points were made. First, the total dissimilarity between God and all other realities which "had beginning," beginning of any kind. Second, the "beginning" itself. The Son had a "beginning" simply because he was a son; that is, originated from the Father as his ἀρχή. Only God (the Father) was ἄναρχος in the strict sense of the word. It seems that with Arius the main emphasis lay on the relation of dependence as such, and the element of time was comparatively irrelevant for his argument. Indeed, in his famous letter to Eusebius of Nicomedia Arius stated plainly that the Son came into existence "before all times and ages" – πρὸ κρόνων καὶ πρὸ αἰώνων (according to Epiphanius, *Haeres.* 69, 6; 156 and Theodoret, *Hist. eccl.* I, 4, 63: 25). St. Athanasius complained that the Arians evaded the term χρόνος (*Contra Arianos* I, 13). Yet they obviously contended that all things "created" did somehow "come into existence," so that the state of "being" has been preceded, at least logically, by a state of "non-being" out of which they have emerged, ἐξ οὐκ ὄντων. In this sense "they did not exist before they came into existence" – οὐκ ἦν πρὶν γεννηθῇ. Obviously, "creature - liness" meant for the Arians more than just "dependence": it implied also an "essential" dissimilarity with God and a finitude; that is, some limitation in retrospect. On the other hand, it was strongly stressed that all creation was grounded in the will and deliberation of God – θελήματι καὶ βουλῇ, as Arius himself wrote to Eusebius. The latter motive was Origenistic. Indeed, Arius went much further than Origen: Origen rejected only the Gnostic προβολή but Arius repudiated any "natural" affinity of the *Logos* with God. Arius simply had nothing to say about the life of God apart from his engagement in creation. At this point his thought was utterly archaic.

It is highly significant that the Council of Antioch in 324/325 – that is, before the Council of Nicaea – took up all these major points. The Son is begotten "not from that which is not but from the Father," in an ineffable and indescribable manner, "not as made but as properly offspring," and not "by volition." The Son existed eternally and "did not at one time not exist." The Son "is the express image, not of the will or anything else, but of his Father's very hypostasis." [Only a Syriac version of this important document is preserved. It was published for the first time and retranslated into Greek by Eduard Schwartz, "Zur Geschichte des Athanasius," VI in *Nachrichten von der Königlichen Gesellschaft der Wissenschaften zu Göttingen* (1905), pp. 272-273. It has since been published in his *Gesammelte Schriften*, Dritter Band (Berlin, 1959), pp. 136-143. The authenticity of the Council of Antioch has been vigorously contested by Harnack and others. But the best analysis of all the evidence and a convincing defense of the authenticity of the Council of Antioch is found in a series of articles by D. A. Lebedev: "The Council in Antioch of 324 and Its Epistle to Alexander, Bishop of Thessaloniki," in *Khristianskoje Chtenije* (1911, July/August, 831-858; September, 1008-1023); "On the Problem of the Council in Antioch of 324 and On the Great and Holy Council in Ancyra," in *Trudy Kievskoj Dukhovnoj Akademii* (1914, April; July/August; November; 1915, January); and continued in *Bogoslovskij Vestnik* (1915, July/August, p. 482-512). All these articles are in Russian; their evidence and conclusions have not been surpassed by any research on the subject since].

For all these reasons the Son could not be regarded as "creature." Nothing has been said about creation. But one can easily guess what "creation" and "creatureliness" meant for the Fathers of that Council. All elements, of which the later clear distinction between "begetting" and "creating" (or "making") has been construed, are already implied in the conciliar statement.

In his early writings before the outbreak of the Arian controversy St. Athanasius was already wrestling with the problem of creation. *For him it was intimately related to the crucial message of the Christian faith*: the redemptive Incarnation of the Divine Logos. Indeed, his interpretation of Redemption, as it was expounded in *De Incarnatione Verbi*, is grounded in a distinctive conception of the cosmos. There was, in the vision of St. Athanasius, an ultimate and radical cleavage or *hiatus* between the absolute Being of God and the contingent existence of the World. There were actually two modes of existence, radically different and totally dissimilar. On the one hand – the Being of God, eternal and immutable, "immortal" and "incorruptible." On the other – the flux of the cosmos, intrinsically mutable and "mortal," exposed to change and "corruption." The ultimate ontological tension was precisely between the Divine ἀφθαρσία and the φθορά of the cosmic flux. Since the whole creation had once begun by the will and pleasure of God, "out of nothing," an ultimate "meonic" tendency was inherent in the very *nature* of all creaturely things. By their own "nature" all created things were intrinsically unstable, fluid, impotent, mortal, liable to dis - solution – τῶν μὲν γὰρ γενητῶν ἡ φύσις, ἅτε δὲ ἐξ οὐκ ὄντων ὑποστᾶσα, ῥευστή τις καὶ ἀσθενὴς καὶ θνητὴ καθ᾽ἑαυτὴν συγκρινωμένη τυγχάνει. Their existence was precarious. If there was any order and stability in the cosmos, they were, as it were, super-imposed upon its own "nature" and imparted to created things by the Divine Logos. It was the Logos who ordered and bound together the whole creation – συνέχει καὶ συσφίγγει – counteracting thereby, as it were, its inherent leaning toward disintegration. Indeed, the creaturely "nature" itself is also God's creation. But it was inwardly limited by its creaturely condition: it was inescapably "mortal" and mutable. St. Athanasius formally disavowed the notion of seminal λόγοι, immanent and inherent in the things themselves. Creation stood only by the immediate impact of the Divine Logos. Not only was the cosmos brought into existence "out of nothing" by an initial and sovereign creative *fiat* of God but it was maintained in existence solely by the continuous action of the Creator. Man also shared in this "natural" instability of the cosmos, as a "composite" being and originated "out of the non-existing" – ἐκ τοῦ μὴ ὄντος γενόμενοι. By his very "nature" man also was "mortal" and "corruptible" – κατὰ φύσιν φθαρτός – and could escape this condition of mortality only by God's grace and by participation in the energies of the Logos – χάριτι δὲ τῆς τοῦ λόγου μετουσίας τοῦ κατὰ φύσιν ἐκφυγόντες. By himself man was unable "to continue forever" – οὐχ ἱκανὸν εἴη κατὰ τὸν τῆς ἰδίας γενέσεως λόγον διαμένειν ἀεί (*Contra gentes* 40 to 43; *De Incarnatione* 2, 3, 5). The pattern of this exposition is conspicuously Platonic. But St. Athanasius used it judiciously. The cosmic or "demiurgic" function of the Logos was strongly stressed in his conception. But his Divine transcendence was also vigorously stressed. Indeed, the Divine character of the Logos was the main presupposition of the whole argument. The Logos was, in the phrase of St. Athanasius, "the Only-Begotten God," originating eternally from the Father as from a spring, a πηγή. There was an absolute dissimilarity between the Logos and creatures. The Logos is present in the world, but only "dynamically," that is, by his "powers." In his own "essence" he is outside of the world – ἐκτὸς μέν ἐστι τοῦ παντὸς κατ᾽οὐσίαν, ἐν πᾶσι δὲ ἐστι ταῖς ἑαυτοῦ δυνάμεσι (*De Incarnatione* 17). This distinction between "essence" and "powers" can be traced back to Philo and Plotinus and, indeed, to the Apologists and Clement of Alexandria. But in St. Athanasius it has a totally new connotation. It is never applied to the relationship between God and Logos, as had been done even by Origen. It serves now a new purpose – to discriminate strictly between the inner Being of God and his creative and "providential" manifestation *ad extra*, in the creaturely world. The world owes its very existence to God's sovereign will and goodness and stands, over the abyss of its own nothingness and impotence, solely by his quickening "Grace" – as it were, *sola gratia*. But the Grace abides in the world.

In his struggle with the Arians St. Athanasius proceeded from the same presuppositions. The main demarcation line passes between the Creator and the Creation, and not between the Father and the Son, as the Arians contended. Indeed, the Logos is Creator. But he is Creator precisely because he is fully Divine, an "undistinguishable Image" of the Father, *ἀπαράλλακτος εἰκών*. In creation he is not just an "instru-ment," *ὄργανον*. He is its ultimate and immediate efficient cause. His own Being is totally independent of creation, and even of the creative design of the world. At this point St. Athanasius was quite formal. The crucial text is in *Contra Arianos* II, 31 – ὁ τοῦ θεοῦ γὰρ λόγος οὐ δι᾽ ἡμᾶς γέγονεν, ἀλλὰ μᾶλλον ἡμεῖς δι᾽ αὐτὸν γεγόναμεν, καὶ ἐν αὐτῷ ἐκτίσθη τὰ πάντα· οὐδὲ διὰ τὴν ἡμῶν ἀσθένειαν οὗτος, ὧν δυνατός, ὑπὸ μόνου τοῦ Πατρὸς γέγονεν, ἵν ἡμᾶς δι᾽ αυτοῦ ὡς δι᾽ ὀργάνου δημιουργήσῃ· μὴ γένοιτο. οὐκ ἔστιν οὕτως. Καὶ γὰρ καὶ εἰ δόξαν ἦν τῷ θεῷ μὴ ποιῆσαι τὰ γενητά, ἀλλ᾽ ἦν οὐδὲν ἧττον ὁ Λόγος πρὸς τὸν θεόν, καὶ ἐν αὐτῷ ἦν ὁ Πατήρ. Τὰ μέντοι γενητὰ ἀδύνατον ἦν χωρὶς τοῦ Λόγου γενέσθαι· οὕτω γὰρ καὶ γέγονε δι᾽ αὐτοῦ, καὶ εἰκότως. Ἐπειδὴ γὰρ Λόγος ἐστὶν ἴδιος φύσει τῆς οὐσίας τοῦ θεοῦ ὁ Υἱός, ἐξ αὐτοῦ τέ ἐστι, καὶ ἐν αὐτῷ ἐστιν, ὡς εἶπεν αὐτός οὐκ ἠδύνατο μὴ δι᾽ αὐτοῦ γενέσθαι τὰ δημιουργήματα. – Even supposing that the Father had never been disposed to create the world or a part of it, nevertheless the Logos would have been with God and the Father in him . . . This was the core of the argument. In fact, St. Athanasius carefully eliminates all references to the *οἰκονομία* of creation or salvation from his description of the inner relationship between the Father and the Son. This was his major and decisive contribution to Trinitarian theology in the critical situation of the Arian controversy. And this left him free to define the concept of creation properly. *Θεολογία*, in the ancient sense of the word, and *οἰκονομία* must be clearly and strictly distinguished and delimited, although they could not be separated from each other. But God's "Being" has an absolute ontological priority over God's action and will.

God is much more than just "Creator." When we call God "a Father," we mean something higher than his relation to creatures (*Contra Arianos* I, 33). "Before" God creates at all, *πολλῷ πρότερον*, he is Father, and he creates through his Son. For the Arians, actually, God was no more than a Creator and Shaper of creatures, argued St. Athanasius. The Arians did not admit in God anything that was "superior to his will," *τὸ ὑπερκείμενον τῆς βουλήσεως*. But, ob-viously, "being" precedes "will," and "generation," accordingly, surpasses the "will" also – *ὑπεραναβέβηκε δὲ τῆς βουλήσεως τὸ* πεφυκέναι (II, 2). Of course, it is but a logical order – there is no temporal sequence in Divine Being and Life. Yet, this logical order has an ontological significance. Trinitarian names denote the very character of God, his very Being. They are, as it were, ontological names. There are, in fact, two different sets of names which may be used of God. One set of names refers to God's deeds or acts – that is, to his will and counsel – the other to God's own essence and being. St. Athanasius insisted that these two sets of names had to be formally and con - sistently distinguished. And, again, it was more than just a logical or mental distinction. There was a distinction in the Divine reality itself. God is what he is – Father, Son, and Holy Spirit. It is an ultimate reality, declared and manifested in the Scriptures. But creation is a deed of the Divine will, and this will is common to and identical in all Three Persons of the One God. Thus, God's Fatherhood must necessarily precede his Creatorship. The Son's existence flows eternally from the very essence of the Father, or, rather, belongs to this "essence," οὐσία. The world's existence, on the contrary, is, as it were, "external" to this Divine essence and is grounded only in the Divine will. There is an element of contingency in the exercise and disclosure of the creative will, as much as his will reflects God's own essence and character. On the other hand, there is, as it were, an absolute necessity in the Trini - tarian Being of God. The word may seem strange and startling. In fact, St. Athanasius did not use it directly. It would have embarrassed Origen and many others, as offensive to God's perfection – does it not imply that God is subject to certain "constraint" or fatalistic determinism? But, in fact, "necessity" in this case is but another name for "being" or "essence." Indeed, God does not "choose" his own Being. He simply is. No further question can be intelligently asked. Indeed, it is proper for God "to create"; that is, to manifest himself *ad extra*. But this manifestation is an act of his will, and in no way an extension of his own Being. On the other hand, "will" and "deliberation" should not be invoked in the description of the eternal relationship between Father and Son. At this point St. Athanasius was definite and explicit. Indeed, his whole refutation of Arianism depended ultimately upon this basic distinction between "essence" and "will," which alone could establish clearly the real difference in kind between "generation" and "creation." *The Trinitarian vision and the concept of creation in the thought of St. Athanasius belonged closely and organically together.*

Some characteristic passages in the famous Athanasian *Discourses against the Arians* must be examined, for this is not merely an abstract theology but the very essence from which the Arian controversy springs and is fundamental for an understanding of all the Christological prob - lems that will confront the Church in the coming centuries. The ac - curate dating of these *Discourses* is irrelevant for our present purpose.

In I, 19 God is described in the Scripture as the Fountain of Wisdom and Life. The Son is his Wisdom. Now, if one admits with the Arians that "there was when he was not," this would imply that once the Fountain was dry, or rather, that it was not a fountain at all. The spring from which nothing flows is not a spring at all. The simile is characteristic of St. Athanasius. It reappears often in the *Discourses*. See, for example, II, 2: if the Logos was not the genuine Son of God, God himself would no longer be a Father but only a Shaper of creatures. The fecundity of the Divine Nature would have been quenched. The Nature of God would be sterile and not fertile – ἔρημος . . . μὴ καρπογόνος. It would be a barren thing, a light without shining, a dry font – ὡς φῶς μὴ φωτίζον καὶ πηγὴ ζηρα . See also I, 14 – ἄγονος ἦν ἡ πηγὴ καὶ ζηρά, φῶς χωρὶς αὐγῆς or II, 33 – ἥλιος χωρὶς τοῦ ἀπαυγάσματος. Both the argument and the imagery can be traced back to Origen. *Otiosam enim et immobilem dicere naturam Dei impium est simul et absurdum* (*De principiis* III, 5, 2; 272/Koetschau). But, as we have already seen, in Origen the argument was ambiguous and misleading. It was ambiguous because there was no room for any clear discrimination between "being" and "acting." It was misleading because it coupled "generation" and "creation" so closely and intimately together as not to allow any demarcation line. This ambiguity is avoided carefully by St. Athanasius. He never uses this argument – from the Divine "fertility" – in reference to the will of God. On the contrary, he formally refuses to follow Origen at this point – of course, without mentioning him.

In 1, 20 St. Athanasius asserts that God was never without anything that is his own – Πότε γοῦν τοῦ ἰδίου χωρὶς ἦν ὁ Θεός. On the other hand, created things have no affinity or similarity with the Creator – οὐδὲν ὅμοιον κατ 'οὐσίαν ἔχει πρὸς τὸν πεποιηκότα. They are outside God – ἔξωθεν αὐτοῦ. They have received their existence by the grace and appointment of the Logos – χάριτι καὶ βουλήσει αὐτοῦ τῷ λόγῳ γενόμενα . And St. Athanasius characteristically adds, "they could again cease to exist, if it pleased their Creator" – ὥστε πάλιν δύνασθαι καὶ παύεσθαί ποτε, εἰ θελήσειεν ὁ ποιήσας. For, he concludes, "such is the nature of created things" – ταύτης γάρ ἐστι φύσεως τὰ γενητα. See also II, 24 and 29 – πάντων ἐκ τοῦ μὴ ὄντος ἐχόντων τὴν σύστασιν. Now, at this very point St. Athanasius had to face an objection of his opponents. They said: is it not so that God must be Creator always, since the "power of creating" could not have come to God, as it were, subsequently? οὐκ ἐπιγέγονεν αὐτῷ τοῦ δημιουργεῖν ἡ δύναμις. Therefore, all creatures must be eternal. It is significant that this counterargument of the Arians was actually Origen's famous argument, based on the analysis of the term παντοκράτωρ. Only the conclusion was different. Origen's conclusion was that, indeed, creatures were eternal. For the Arians that was blasphemy. By the same argument they wanted to reduce *ad absurdum* the proof of the eternal generation. It was an attack both on Origen and on St. Athanasius. St. Athanasius meets the charge on his own ground. Is there really such a "similarity" between *generation* and *creation* – τί ὅμοιον – that what must be said of God as Father must also be said of him as Creator – ἵνα τὰ ἐπὶ τοῦ πατρὸς ταῦτα καὶ ἐπὶ τῶν δημιουργῶν εἴπωσι? This is the sting of the Athanasian rejoinder. In fact, there is total disparity. The Son is an offspring of the essence: ἴδιον τῆς οὐσίας γέννημα. Creatures are, on the contrary, "external" to the Creator. Accordingly, there is no "necessity" for them to exist eternally – οὐκ ἀνάγκη ἀεὶ εἶναι. But generation is not subject to will (or deliberation) τὸ δὲ γέννημα οὐ βουλήσει ὑπόκειται . It is, on the contrary, a property of the essence – ἀλλὰ τῆς οὐσίας ἐστὶν ἰδιότης. Moreover, a man can be called a "a maker," ποιητής, even before he has made anything. But nobody can be called "a father" before he has a son. This is to say that God could be described as Creator even "before" creation came into existence. It is a subtle but valid point in the argument. St. Athanasius argues that, although God could indeed have created things from all eternity, yet created things themselves could not have existed eternally, since they are "out of nothing," ἐξ οὐκ ὄντων, and consequently did not exist before they were brought into existence – οὐκ ἦν πρὶν γένηται. "How can things which did not exist before they originated be coeternal with God? – Πῶς ἠδύνατο συνυπάρχειν τῷ ἀεὶ ὄντι Θεῷ ?

This turn of the argument is highly significant. Indeed, if one starts, as Origen did, with the eternity and immutability of God, it is difficult to see how anything truly "temporal" could have existed at all. All acts of God must be eternal. God simply could not "have started." But in this case the proper "nature" of temporal things is ignored and disregarded. This is precisely what St. Athanasius wanted to say. "Beginning" belongs to the very "nature" of temporal things. Now, it is the beginning of temporal existence, of an existence in time and flux. For that reason creatures cannot "coexist" with the Eternal God. There are two incomparable modes of existence. Creatures have their own mode of subsistence – they are outside God. Thus creatures, by their very nature, cannot "coexist" with God. But this inherent limitation of their nature does not, in any sense, disparage the power of the Creator. *The main point of St. Athanasius was precisely this.* There is an identity of nature in generation and a disparity of natures in creation (see I, 26).

In I, 36 St. Athanasius asserts that since created beings arise "out of nothing," their existence is bound to be a state of flux – ἀλλοιουμένην ἔχει τὴν φύσιν. See I, 58: Their existence is precarious, they are perishable by nature – τὰ δυνάμενα ἀπολέσθαι. This does not imply that they will actually and necessarily perish. Yet, if they do not actually perish, it is only by the grace of the Creator. The Son alone, as an offspring of the essence, has an intrinsic power "to coexist" eternally with the Father – ἴδιον δὲ τὸ ἀεὶ εἶναι καὶ συνδιαμένειν σὺν τῷ Πατρί. See also II, 57 – the being of that which has existence "according to a beginning" can be traced back to a certain initial instant.

In the later part of his third *Discourse* St. Athanasius discusses at great length the Arian contention that the Son has been begotten by "the will and deliberation" of the Father – βουλήσει καὶ θελήσει γεγένῆσθαι τὸν Υἱὸν ὑπὸ τοῦ Πατρός (III, 59). These terms, pro - tests St. Athanasius, are quite out of place in this connection. The Arians simply attempt to hide their heresy under the cover of these ambiguous words. St. Athanasius suggests that they borrowed their ideas at this point from the Gnostics and mentions the name of Ptolemy. Ptolemy taught that God first thought, and then willed and acted. In a similar way, St. Athanasius contends, the Arians claim that the will and deliberation of the Father preceded the generation of the Logos. He quotes Asterius at this point. Asterius (d. after 341), student of Lucian of Antioch, was an Arian theologian, who wrote, in addition to his *Syntagmation* – fragments are contained in St. Athanasius and in Marcellus of Ancyra – commentaries and homilies on the *Psalms*. Substantial portions have been recovered by M. Richard and E. Skard and published for the first time in 1956. Asterius was also present at the Council of Antioch in 341.

The terms "will" and "deliberation" are in fact only applicable to the production of creaturely things. Now, the Arians claim that unless the Son's existence depended upon the "deliberation" of the Father, it would appear that God has a Son "by necessity" and, as it were, "unwil - lingly" – ἀνάγκῃ καὶ μὴ θέλων. This kind of reasoning, St. Athan - asius retorts, only shows their inability to grasp the basic difference between "being" and "acting." God does not deliberate with himself about his own Being and Existence. Indeed, it would be absurd to contend that God's goodness and mercy are just his voluntary habit and not a part of his Nature. But does it mean that God is good and merciful unwillingly? Now, what is "by Nature" is higher than that which is only "by deliberation" – ὑπέρκειται καὶ προηγεῖται τοῦ βουλεύ - εσθαι τὸ κατὰ φύσιν. As an offspring of the Father's own essence, the Father does not "deliberate" about the Son, since it would mean "deliberation" about his own Being – τὸν δὲ ἴδιον Λόγον ἐξ αὐτοῦ φύσει γεννώμενον οὐ προβουλεύεται. God is the Father of his Son "by nature and not by will" – οὐ βουλήσει ἀλλὰ φύσει τὸν ἴδιον ἔχει Λόγος. Whatever was "created" was indeed created by the good will and deliberation of God. But the Son is not a deed of will, like creatures, but by nature the Son is an offspring of God's own essence – οὐ θελήματός ἐστι δημιούργημα ἐπιγεγονώς, καθάπερ ἡ κτίσις, ἀλλὰ φύσει τῆς οὐσίας ἴδιον γέννημα. It is an insane and extravagant idea to put "will" and "counsel" between the Father and the Son (III, 60, 61, 62).

The theological writings of St. Athanasius were mainly occasional tracts, tracts for the time. He was always discussing certain particular points, the burning issues of the Arian controversy. He was interpreting controversial texts of Scripture, pondering and checking phraseology, answering charges, meeting objections. He never had time or oppor -

tunity for a dispassionate and systematic exposition. Moreover, the time for systems had probably not yet come. But there was a perfect consistency and coherence in his theological views. His theological vision was sharp and well focused. His grasp of the problems was un - usually sure and firm. In the turmoil of a heated debate he was able to discern clearly the real crux of the conflict. From tradition St. Athan - asius inherited the *catholic faith* in the Divinity of the Logos. This faith was the true pivot of his theological thought. It was not enough to correct exegesis, to improve terminology, to remove misunder - standings. What needed correction in the age of St. Athanasius was the total theological perspective. It was imperative to establish "Theology"; that is, the doctrine of God, on its proper ground. The mystery of God – "Three in One" – had to be apprehended in itself. This was the main preoccupation of St. Athanasius in his great *Discourses*. The contem - plation of the Divine Life in God himself – this was the concern of St. Athanasius. Only in this perspective can one see the radical difference between the Divine and the creaturely. One sees the absoluteness of the Divine transcendence – God does not need his creatures. His own Being is perfect and complete in itself. And it is this inner Being of God that is disclosed in the mystery of the Trinity. But the actual mystery is double. There is, indeed, the mystery of the Divine Being. But there is another concomitant mystery, the mystery of Creation, the mystery of the Divine οἰκονομία. No real advance can be achieved in the realm of "*Theology*" until the realm of "*Oikonomia*" had been properly ordered. This surely was the reason why St. Athanasius addressed himself to the problem of Creation even in his early treatises, which constituted, in a sense, his theological confession. On the other hand, the meaning of the redemptive Incarnation could be properly clarified only in the perspective of the original creative design of God. On the other hand, in order to demonstrate the absolute sovereignty of God it was necessary to show the ultimate contingency of the created cosmos, fully dependent upon the Will of God.

In the perspective of the Arian controversy two tasks were closely related to each other – to demonstrate the mystery of the Divine Gen - eration as an integral feature of the Divine Being itself and to emphasize the contingency of the created cosmos, which contingency can also be seen in the order of existence. It was precisely in the light of this basic distinction – between "Being" and "Will" – that the ultimate incom - mensurability of the two modes of existence could be clearly exhibited. The inner life of God is in no way conditioned by his revelatory self-disclosure in the world, including the design of Creation itself. The world is, as it were, a paradoxical "surplus" in the order of existence. The world is "outside" God – or, rather, it is precisely this "outside" itself. But it does exist, in its own mode and dimension. It arises and stands only by the will of God. It has a beginning precisely because it is contingent and moves toward an end for which it has been designed by God. The Will of God is manifested in the temporal process of the

Divine οἰκονομία. But God's own Being is immutable and eternal. The two modes of existence, the Divine and the creaturely, can be respec - tively described as "necessary" and "contingent" or as "absolute" and "conditional." The distinction between the Divine Being and the Divine Will was made and consistently elaborated, probably for the first time in the history of Christian thought, in the heat of the Arian controversy by St. Athanasius.

St. Athanasius' distinction between *Generation* and *Creation* – with all its vital implications – was already commonly accepted in the Church in his own time. How then Arianism? How then all the later Christological controversies? It is enough to point out the fact that, despite all the controversy, the vision of St. Athanasius ultimately prevailed and prevailed as the teaching of the Church. Hence, his theo - logical vision, his perception of the root cause of theological contro - versy in a proper distinction between Generation and Creation was in essence already a part of the living faith of the Church. And, moreover, there were various forms of Arianism, all of which differed in emphases and all of which had to be overcome, even if the process of triumph took decades and lingered in other aspects for centuries.

St. Athanasius' theological distinction between generation and creation was further developed in Byzantine theology. St. Cyril of Alexandria in general will repeat his great predecessor. Indeed, his *Thesaurus de sancta et consubstantiali Trinitate* will depend heavily upon St. Athanasius' *Discourses*. Only instead of "will" and "deliber - ation," St. Cyril will speak of Divine "energy" – τὸ μὲν ποιεῖν ἐνεργείας ἐστί, φύσεως δὲ τὸ γεννᾶν· φύσις δὲ καὶ ἐνέργεια οὐ ταὐτόν (*Thesaurus*, 18; *Patrologia Graeca* 75, 313). See also 15; *Patrologia Graeca* 75, 276 – τὸ γέννημα . . . ἐκ τῆς οὐσίας τοῦ γεννῶντος πρόεισι φυσικῶς (τὸ κτίσμα) . . . ἔξωθέν ἐστιν ὡς ἀλλότριον, see also *Patrologia Graeca* 75, 564-565. This antithesis – γονιμότης and θέλησις or βούλησις – will be one of the main dis - tinctive marks of Byzantine theology until the fourteenth century when St. Gregory Palamas (1296-1359) analyzes the problem. St. Gregory will contend that unless a clear distinction is made between the "essence" and "energy" in God, one will not be able to distinguish between *generation* and *creation*. This will also be emphasized by St. Mark of Ephesus. It was a definite Athanasian motive and his argu - ments will again come to the fore.

The questions arises: is the distinction between "Being" and "Acting" in God or, in other terms, between the Divine "Essence" and the Divine "Energy," a genuine and ontological distinction – *in re ipsa* ? Or is it merely a mental or logical distinction, as it were, κατ ἐπίνοιαν, which should not be interpreted objectively, lest the sim- plicity of the Divine Being is compromised? There cannot be the slightest doubt that for St. Athanasius it was a real and ontological difference. Otherwise his main argument against the Arians would have been invalidated and destroyed. The mystery will remain. The very

Being of God is "incomprehensible" for the human intellect – this will be the common conviction of the Greek and Byzantine Fathers. And yet there is always ample room for understanding. Not only is there a distinction between "Being" and "Will" but it is not the same thing, even for God, "to be" and "to act." This is the deepest conviction of St. Athanasius.

CHAPTER TEN

NICAEA AND THE ECUMENICAL COUNCIL

Any study of the ancient Church, especially of the period between 430 and 553 during the Nestorian, Monophysite, and later the Monothe - lite controversies, must confront the nature of authority and the nature of councils in the early Church. Moreover, any study of a particular council must be approached in its concrete historical setting, against its specific existential background, without any overarching pre-conceived definition. Each council, as each age, must be discussed on its own terms.

THE THEOLOGICAL NATURE OF A COUNCIL IN THE FIRST THREE CENTURIES

There was no "Conciliar Theory" in the early Church, no elaborate "theology of the Councils," and even no fixed canonical regulations. The councils of the early Church in the first three centuries were occasional meetings, convened for special purposes, usually in the situation of urgency, to discuss particular items of common concerns. They were *events*, rather than an institution. Or, to use the phrase of the late Dom Gregory Dix, "in the pre-Nicene times Councils were an occasional device, with no certain place in the scheme of Church government" ("Jurisdiction, Episcopal and Papal, in the Early Church," *Laudate* XVI (No. 62, June 1938), 108). It was, of course, commonly assumed and agreed already at that time that meeting and consultation of bishops, representing or rather personifying their respective local churches or "communities," was a proper and normal method to mani - fest and to achieve the unity and consent in matters of faith and discipline.

The sense of the "Unity of the Church" was strong in the early first three centuries, although it had not yet been reflected on the organ - izational level. The "collegiality" of the bishops was assumed in prin - ciple and the concept of the *Episcopatus unus* was already in the process of formation. Bishops of a particular area used to meet for the election and consecration of new bishops. Foundations had been laid for the future provincial or metropolitan system. But all this was rather a spontaneous movement. The precedent had been laid in *Acts* 15 and *Galatians* 2 by Council at Jerusalem. "When they came to Jerusalem, they were welcomed by the church and the apostles and the elders . . . the apostles and the elders were gathered together to consider this matter . . . then it seemed good to the apostles and the elders, with the whole church . . . it has seemed good to us in this assembly . . . for it has seemed good to the Holy Spirit and to us. This in a very real sense is the first Council of the Church; it is the precedent from which all coun - cils take their form, their existence.

It seems that councils came into existence first in Asia Minor by the end of the second century in that period of intensive defense against the spread of the "new prophecy" of the Montanist "enthusiastic explosion." Firmilian of Cappadocia (d. 268) in his letter to Cyprian (d. 258) first mentions that at that time – in the middle of the third century – the churches of Asia Minor held regular annual councils of bishops and priests (see among Cyprian's letter, *Epistola* 75). From that time an increasing number of councils are referred to in written documents, councils which take place in Egypt, Syria, Greece, North Africa, Italy, Spain, and Gaul.

It was in North Africa that a kind of "conciliar system" was established in the third century. It was found that councils were the best device, the best means, the best vehicle for witnessing, articulating, and proclaiming the common mind of the Church and the accord and unanimity of local churches. G. Kretschmar has correctly stated in his study on the councils of the ancient Church (see "Die Konzile der Alten Kirche" in *Die ökumenischen Konzile der Christenheit*, 1961) that the basic concern of the early councils was precisely with the "Unity of the Church." Yet this "Unity" was based on the identity of "Tradition" and the unanimity in faith, rather than on any institutional pattern.

CONSTANTINE AND THE ECUMENICAL COUNCIL

The situation changed with the conversion of the Empire. Since Constantine, or more precisely since the time of Theodosius I (emperor from 379 to 395), who continued the policy of Gratian and actually established the orthodox Christian state, it has been commonly assumed and acknowledged that the Church was co-extensive with the State; that is, with the "Universal Empire" which had been christened. The "con - version of the Empire" made the *universality* of the Church more *visible* than ever before. Of course it did not add anything to the essential and intrinsic universality of the Church. But the new oppor - tunity provided for its visible manifestation. It was in this situation that the First Ecumenical Council was convened, the Council of Nicaea in 325. It was to become the model for the later councils. As Dom Gregory Dix has written: "The new established position of the Church necessitated ecumenical action precisely because Christian life was now lived in the world which was no longer organized on a basis of localism but of the Empire as a whole. Because the Church has come out into the world the local churches had to learn to live no longer as self-contained units (as in practice, though not in theory, they had largely lived in the past."

In a certain sense the Ecumenical Councils as inaugurated at Nicaea may be described as "Imperial Councils," and this was probably the first and original meaning of the term "ecumenical" as applied to the Councils. The term "Ecumenical Council" – σύνοδος οἰκουμενικῄ – concilium *universale* – occurs first in the sixth canon of the Second Ecumenical Council, the Council of Constantinople in 381. This very name refers to the οἰκουμένη, the *orbis Romanus*, the Empire. As a result the Emperor will have a special significance in connection with the Ecumenical Councils. Emperor Constantine *convened* the First Ecumenical Council but the idea was probably suggested to him by friends among the bishops. Rufinus tells us that he summoned the council "*ex sacerdotum sententia.*"

THE ROLE OF BYZANTINE EMPERORS

The role of the Byzantine emperors in relationship to the Ecumenical Councils cannot be overlooked. The emperors *convened* or *called* the councils into being. They fixed the place and time of the council. They summoned the metropolitans and bishops of the empire by an edict. They provided the means of transit and they paid the cost of travel and other expenses from the public treasury. But, as becomes clear from any analysis of the Ecumenical Councils, the calling of an Ecumenical Council did not ensure its being "ecumenical." Moreover, the role of the emperors in the actual proceedings and in the theological results of the Ecumenical Councils was greatly *restricted*, as is clear in the controversies over Nestorianism, Monophysitism, and Monothel-itism.

The emperors not only *convened* the Ecumenical Councils but also, directly or indirectly, attempted to take an active part. Even if they were not physically present, the emperors were represented by imperial delegates or commissioners who were given full authority. These com-missioners opened the sessions by reading the imperial edict in both Latin and Greek, they presided to some extent in conjunction with the bishops, they in general conducted the transactions, preserved order and security, and closed the council by signing the Acts either at the head or at the foot of the signatures of the bishops. They attempted to exercise, especially if they had a theological interest in the topics on the agenda, their influence on the discussions and decisions. But, and this is the significance, *they had no vote*. And often they could not control the bishops, as is the case with St. Cyril and the Comes Candidian at the Third Ecumenical Council. Pope Stephen V, writing in 817, claims that Constantine *presided* at the First Ecumenical Council. But it must always be remembered that this presidency, when applied to the em-perors, was always *limited*, always *restricted*, always subject to the ulti-mate decision of the bishops and moreover always subject to the ultimate reception of any intended Ecumenical Council by the entire episcopate, by the entire Church. It was not unusual for an *intended* and *proclaimed* Ecumenical Council to be rejected at some later time by the Church, hence completely invalidating its claim of being "ecumenical."

CONSTANTINE AND THE DISTINCTION OF TWO AUTHORITIES

According to Eusebius Constantine introduced the main agenda with a solemn speech, constantly attended the sessions, and took the place of honor in the assembly. Many historians have been stunned by Eusebius' *Vita Constantini* – εἰς τὸν βίον τοῦ μακαρίου Κων- σταντίνου βασιλέως. Burckhardt, for example, condemns Eusebius as "the first completely dishonest and unfair historian of ancient times." But it is important to consider Eusebius' *Vita Constantini* in per - spective. First, Eusebius is employing the literary form of the "*Vita*," a form which is intrinsically exaggerated; it is not literary biography but rather praise, an encomium replete with eulogy. Second, Eusebius explicitly states that he does not intend to be objective. "This book will contain a description of those regal and noble acts which are pleasing to God. . . Would it not be disgraceful that the memory of Nero, and other impious and godless tyrants far worse than Nero, should meet with diligent writers to embellish the relation of their worthless deeds with elegant language, and record them in voluminous histories, and that I should be silent, to whom God himself has given such an emperor as is not recorded in all history, and has permitted me to come into his presence and enjoy his acquaintance and society? Therefore, if it is the duty of any one, it certainly is my duty, to make a sufficient proclamation of his virtues to all in whom the example of noble actions is capable of inspiring the love of God. . . My narrative, however unequal to the greatness of the deeds it describes, will yet derive luster even from the bare relation of noble actions. . . It is my intention, therefore, to pass over the greater part of the regal deeds of this thrice-blessed prince . . . The object of my present book is to speak and to write of those circumstances only which have reference to his religious character. And since these are themselves of almost infinite variety, I shall select from the facts which have come to my knowledge such as are most suitable and worthy of permanent record and attempt to narrate them as briefly as possible. . . Indeed, there is now a full and free opportunity for celebrating in every way the praises of this truly blessed prince." With such a warning, one can hardly expect objective biography. It is a fact, however, that Eusebius' work is replete with exaggeration. For example, he describes Constantine at the reception, which the emperor gave at the conclusion of the council, as a kind of Christ among his saints (see 3, 15: Χριστοῦ βασιλείας ἔδοξεν ἄν τις φαντασιοῦσθαι εἰκόνα, ὄναρ . . . εἶναι ἀλλ 'οὐχ ὕπαρ τὸ γινόμενον.

Although two traditions towards baptism existed simultaneously in the Church at that time; that is, infant baptism or baptism after a conversion to Christianity and the postponement of baptism until ap - proaching death precisely because of the significance and power of bap - tism, it is noteworthy that Constantine's prominence at the First Ecumenical Council is the prominence of an unbaptized emperor.

Neither must it be forgotten that Constantine claimed to be a divinely appointed bishop but a bishop in a figurative sense and, more - over, a bishop only over the external affairs of the Church. He always recognized that the internal and theological concerns of the Church belonged to the bishops. There is no reason not to take his words ser - iously. Addressing the bishops, he said: *ὑμεῖς μὲν τῶν εἴσω τῆς ἐκκλησίας, ἐγὼ δὲ τῶν ἐκτὸς ὑπὸ θεοῦ καθεσταμένος ἐπίσ - κοπος ἂν εἴην.* Constantine makes a distinction between two divin - ely authorized episcopates: one is secular or imperial and corresponds with the Roman concept of *Pontifex Maximus*; the other is spiritual or sacerdotal and resides in the episcopacy. After his opening address to the bishops at the First Ecumenical Council, Constantine turned the coun - cil over to the bishops: *ὁ μὲν δὲ ταῦτ᾽ εἰπὼν ῥωμαία γλώττῃ, ὑφερμηνεύοντος ἑτέρου, παρεδίδου τὸν λόγον τοῖς τῆς συν - όδου προέδροις.* This is the same distinction seen at the Third Ecu - menical Council between the imperial and ecclesiastical authorities or jurisdictions – one, external; the other, internal and doctrinally author - itative.

The *ratification* of an Ecumenical Council belonged to the emperor but that, too, was not actual fact. Partly by their signatures and partly by special edicts, the emperors gave the decrees of an Ecumenical Council legal status and legal validity. The emperors took the theo - logical decisions and elevated them to the status of imperial law. They were responsible for having them observed and they punished the recalcitrants with deposition and banishment. Constantine did this for the decisions of the First Ecumenical Council; Theodosius the Great did this for the decrees of the Second Ecumenical Council, the Council of Constantinople in 381; Marcian (emperor from 450 to 457) did this for the Fourth Ecumenical Council, the Council of Chalcedon in 451, even resorting to arms to enforce the council's theological decrees. But all this amounted to vain effort in the ultimate sense and final reality if the episcopacy; that is, the Church Universal, rejected those decisions. Bishops could be banished; decrees could be enforced by arms; depositions and exile could flourish. But everything that the imperial authority accomplished was of no avail in terms of the validity of the doctrine proclaimed by an Ecumenical Council *if that council was not ultimately accepted by the entire Church.* Often it took time for the Church to re-assert itself, to recover, to realize the mistakes of a council. Often the opposition resided in a minority. Often the op - position could reside in just one bishop, as was the case more than once with the Bishop of Rome. And most often, when the Church was torn asunder either by its own theological schools of thought or by imperial intrusion, the divided parties within the Church turned to Rome, to the Old Rome, and to the "primacy" – whether of honor only, as stated in the third canon of the Second Ecumenical Council and the famous twenty-eighth canon of the Fourth Ecumenical Council – τὰ πρεσ - βεῖα τῆς τιμῆς - ἴσα πρεσβεῖα – or a "primacy" of some type of authoritative appeal commonly known to exist in the Bishop of Rome. The reason for the "primacy" is primarily historical. The fact is that appeals were constantly and consistently being made to the Bishop of Rome.

THE FIFTH CANON OF THE COUNCIL OF NICAEA ECCLESIASTICAL ELITISM OR TRADITION?

Despite the predominance of the emperor and his commissioners, despite the external control over the council by the imperial authority, the fact remains that the essential character of the Ecumenical Councils was completely ecclesiastical, completely within the jurisdiction of the bishops. The fifth canon of The First Ecumenical Council makes it clear that bishops were the successors and heirs of the apostles. Some historians have seen in this canon the entry into the Church of an aristocratic spirit inspired by the imperial structure. But such a position on the status of a bishop is already clearly enunciated by St. Ignatius of Antioch (d. c. 107) in the early years of the Church. In his *Letter to the Ephesians* St. Ignatius writes: "for Jesus Christ, our inseparable life, is the Father's thought, and in the same way the bishops who are estab - lished in the farthest parts of the earth share in the thought of Jesus Christ . . . the presbytery, which is worthy of God, is tuned to the bishop, as strings to a lyre: and thus in your concord and harmonious love Jesus Christ is sung . . . if the prayer of 'one or two' has such power, how much more that of the bishop and all the Church . . . through our submission to the bishop we may belong to God." In his *Letter to the Magnesians* St. Ignatius writes: ". . . with the bishop presiding as the counterpart of God . . . you must do nothing without the bishop and the presbyters . . . Be submissive to the bishop and to one another, as Jesus Christ was to the Father."

If such was the language from one of the earliest of Christian doc - uments, it is hardly correct to claim that since bishops constituted the voting assembly at councils, it was a result of an aristocratic principle which entered the Church from the conversion of the Empire. The Ecumenical Councils used the same principle as that elaborated by St. Ignatius, as that which was in existence already before St. Ignatius wrote his letters. Yet it must not be overlooked that presbyters and deacons also participated in the councils. They may not have had a *votum decisivum* but they could participate and they could influence. It is enough to recall that St. Athanasius participated in the First

Ecumenical Council and at that time he was but a deacon. Despite the fact that he was a deacon, St. Athanasius probably exerted more in - fluence on the council than most of the bishops present. Yet there is one more fact. In those days bishops were usually elected by the voice of the people, the *vox populi*, by acclamation. In this sense the bishop truly represented the people and, hence, the precise opposite of an aristocratic episcopacy is the case. And what is more, the bishops were held accountable by the people for their actions, for their votes. Eusebius realized that he would have to justify his vote before his entire diocese in Caesarea. And the Egyptian bishops at the Fourth Ecu - menical Council feared an uproar, a popular outcry from their con - gregations.

What is true is that the Ecumenical Councils functioned in an age of absolute despotism more like a forerunner of representative govern - ment than like an elite, aristocratic group, cowed by and servile to the imperial and secular State. The procedures used in the meetings of the Ecumenical Councils in fact sanctioned the principle of discussion, the principle of common and open deliberation as the best means of arriving at an expression of the truth of the faith and settling con - troversies.

THE SILENT PRESENCE AT THE ECUMENICAL COUNCILS

With so much controversy over who presided at the Ecumenical Councils, with so much written on that subject, *one reality is often lost, neglected, or forgotten.* In the middle of the assembled clergy something special lay upon a desk or table. That something special held a special place and had a special significance at all councils. *On that desk or table lay an open copy of the Gospels.* It was there not only as a symbol but also as a reminder of the real presence of Christ in accordance with his promise that where two or three are gathered together in his name, he will be present. In a very real sense it was the *presence of the open Gospel* which presided. Christ is the Truth. The source and the criterion of the truth of Christianity is the Divine Revelation, in both the apostolic deposit and in the Holy Scriptures.

THE GUIDING HERMENEUTICAL PRINCIPLE AT THE ECUMENICAL COUNCILS

Yet, the presence of the open Gospel did not solve the problem. In fact, it meant that the problem was actually shifted a step further. A new question came to be asked – to resolve the problems which had arisen over the interpretation of the Gospel. *How was Revelation to be understood?* The early Church had no doubt about the "sufficiency" of the apostolic deposit and the "sufficiency" of the Scriptures and never tried to go beyond. But already in the Apostolic Age itself the problem of "interpretation" arose in all its challenging sharpness. What was the guiding *hermeneutical* principle? At this point there was no other answer than the appeal to the "faith of the Church," the *faith* and *kerygma* of the Apostles, the Apostolic tradition. The Scriptures could be understood only within the Church, as Origen had strongly insisted, and as St. Irenaeus and Tertullian had insisted before him. The appeal to Tradition was actually an appeal to the *mind of the Church*. It was a method of discovering and ascertaining the faith as it had been always held, from the very beginning – *semper creditum*. The *permanence* of Christian belief was the most conspicuous sign and token of its truth – *no innovations*. And this *permanence* of the Holy Church's faith could be appropriately demonstrated by the witnesses from the past. It was for this reason, and for that purpose, that "the ancients" – οἱ παλαιοι – were usually invoked and quoted in theological discussions.

This "argument from antiquity," however, had to be used with certain caution. Occasional references to old times and casual quotations from old authors could often be ambiguous and even misleading. This was well understood already at the time of the great Baptismal contro - versy in the third century. And the question about the validity or authority or "ancient customs" had been formally raised at that time. Already Tertullian contended that *consuetudines* [customs] in the Church had to be examined in the light of truth – *Dominus noster Christus veritatem se, non consuetudinem, cognominavit* [Our Lord Christ designated himself, not as custom but as truth – *De virginibus velandis* I, I]. The phrase was taken up by St. Cyprian and was adopted by the Council of Carthage in 256. *In* fact, "antiquity" as such might happen to be no more than an inveterate error – *nam antiquitas sine veritate vetustas erroris est* [for antiquity without truth is the age old error] – in the phrase of St. Cyprian's *Epistola* 74, 9. St. Augustine also used a similar phrase – *In Evangelio Dominus, Ego sum, inquit, veritas. Non dixit, Ego sum consuetudo* [In the Gospel the Lord says – I am the truth. He did not say – I am the custom (*De baptismo* III, 6, 9)]. "Antiquity" as such was not necessarily a truth, although the Christian truth was intrinsically an "ancient" truth and "innovations" in the Church had to be resisted.

On the other hand, the argument "from tradition" was first used by the heretics, by the Gnostics, and it was this usage of theirs that prompted St. Irenaeus to elaborate his own conception of Tradition – in opposition to the false "traditions" of the heretics which were alien to the mind of the Church. The appeal to "antiquity" or "traditions" had to be selective and discriminative. Certain alleged "traditions" were simply wrong and false. One had to detect and to identify the "true Tradition," the authentic Tradition which could be traced back to the authority of the Apostles and be attested and confirmed by a universal *consensio* of churches. In fact, however, this *consensio* could not be so easily discovered. Certain questions were still open. The main criterion of St.

Irenaeus was valid – Tradition – Apostolic and Catholic [Universal]. Origen, in the preface to his *De Principiis*, tried to describe the scope of the existing "agreement" which was to his mind binding and restrictive, and then he quotes a series of important topics which had to be further explored. There was, again, a considerable variety of local traditions, in language and discipline, even within the unbroken communion in faith and *in sacris*. It suffices to recall at this point the Paschal controversy between Rome and the East in which the whole question of the authority of ancient habits came to the fore. One should also recall the conflicts between Carthage and Rome, and also between Rome and Alexandria in the third century, and the increasing tension between Alexandria and Antioch.

Now, in this age of the intense theological controversy and context, all participating groups used to appeal to tradition and "antiquity." "Chains" or *catenae* of ancient testimonies were compiled on all sides in the dispute. These testimonies had to be carefully scru - tinized and examined on a basis more comprehensive than "antiquity" alone. Certain local traditions, liturgical and theological, were finally discarded and disavowed by the overarching authority of an "ecumenical" consensus. A sharp confrontation of diverse theological traditions takes place at the Council of Ephesus. The Council of Ephesus is actually split in twain – the "Ecumenical" Council of St. Cyril and Rome und the *conciliabulum* of the "Easterners." Indeed, the reconciliation will be achieved, and yet there will still be a tension. The most spectacular instance of condemnation of a theological tradition, of long standing and of considerable if rather local renown, is the dramatic affair of the *Three Chapters*.

At this point a question of principle is raised – to what extent is it fair and legitimate to disavow the faith of those who had died in peace and in communion with the Church? There is a violent debate on this matter, especially in the West, and strong arguments are produced against such retrospective discrimination. Nevertheless, the *Three Chap - ters* will be condemned by the Fifth Ecumenical Council. "Antiquity" was overruled by Ecumenical *consensio*, as strained as it probably was.

It has been rightly observed that appeal to "antiquity" was changing its function and character with the course of time. The Apostolic past was still at hand, and within the reach of human memory in the times of St. Irenaeus or Tertullian. Indeed, St. Irenaeus had heard in his youth the oral instruction of St. Polycarp, the immediate disciple of St. John. It was only the third generation since Christ! The memory of the Apostolic Age was still fresh. The scope of Christian history was brief and limited. The main concern in this early age was with the Apostolic foundations, with the initial *delivery of the kerygma*. Accordingly, Tradition meant at that time primarily the original "delivery" or "de - posit." The question of accurate transmission over a bit more than one century was comparatively simple, especially in the Churches founded by the Apostles themselves. Full attention was given, of course, to the lists of episcopal succession (see St. Irenaeus or Hegesippus), but it was not difficult to compile these lists. The question of "succession," however, appeared to be much more complicated for the subsequent generations more removed from the Apostolic Age. It was but natural under these new conditions that emphasis should shift from the question of initial "Apostolicity" to the problem of the preservation of the "de - posit." Tradition came to mean "transmission," rather than "delivery." The question of the intermediate links, of "succession" – in the wide and comprehensive sense of the word – became especially urgent. *It was the problem of faithful witnesses*. It was in this situation that the authority of the Fathers was *for the first time* formally invoked – they were witnesses of the *permanence* or identity of the *kerygma*, as trans - mitted from generation to generation. Apostles *and* Fathers – these two terms were generally and commonly coupled together in the argument from Tradition, as it was used in the third and fourth centuries. It was this double reference, both to the origin and to the unfailing and con - tinuous preservation that warranted the authenticity of belief. On the other hand, Scripture was formally acknowledged and recognized as the ground and foundation of faith, as the Word of God and the Scripture of the Spirit. Yet there was still the problem of right and adequate inter - pretation. Scripture *and* Fathers were usually quoted together, that is, *kerygma* and *exegesis* – ἡ γραφὴ καὶ οἱ πατέρες.

THE MEANING OF "THE FATHERS" AND "SCRIPTURE"

The reference or even a direct appeal "to the Fathers" was a distinctive and salient note of the theological research and discussion in the period of the Ecumenical Councils, beginning with the Council of Nicaea. The term has never been formally defined. It was used occa - sionally and sporadically already by early ecclesiastical writers. Often it simply denoted Christian teachers and leaders of previous generations. It was gradually becoming a title for the bishops, in so far as they were appointed teachers and witnesses of faith. Later the title was applied specifically to bishops who attended councils. The common element in all these cases is the teaching office or task. "Fathers" were those who transmitted and propagated the right doctrine, the teaching of the Apostles, who were guides and masters in Christian instruction and catechesis. In this sense it was emphatically applied to great Christian writers. It must be kept in mind that the main, if not also the only, written manual of faith and doctrine was, in the Ancient Church, *precisely Holy Scripture*. And for that reason the renowned interpreters of Scripture were regarded as "Fathers" in an eminent sense. "Fathers" were teachers, first of all – *doctores*, διδάσκαλοι. And they were teach - ers in so far as they were witnesses, *testes*. These two functions must be distinguished and yet they are most intimately intertwined.

"Teaching" was an Apostolic task – "teach all nations." And it was in this commission that their "authority" was rooted – it was, in fact, the authority to bear witness. Two major points must be made in this con - nection. First, the phrase "the Fathers of the Church" has actually an obvious restrictive accent. They were acting not just as individuals, but rather as *viri ecclesiastici* – the favorite expression of Origen – on behalf and in the name of the Church. They were spokesmen for the Church, expositors of her faith, keepers of her Tradition, witnesses of truth and faith – *magistri probabiles*, in the phrase of St. Vincent of Lérins. And in that was their "authority" grounded. It leads us back to the concept of "representation."

The late G. L. Prestige in his book entitled *Fathers and Heretics* has rightly observed that "the creeds of the Church grew out of the teaching of the Church: the general effect of heresy was rather to force old creeds to be tightened up than to cause fresh creeds to be constructed. Thus the most famous and most crucial of all creeds, that of Nicaea, was only a new edition of an existing Palestinian confession. And a further im - portant fact always ought to be remembered. *The real intellectual work, the vital interpretative thought, was not contributed by the Councils that promulgated the creeds, but by the theological teachers who supplied and explained the formulae which the Councils adopted. The teaching of Nicaea, which finally commended itself, represented the views of intellectual giants working for a hundred years before and for fifty years after the actual meeting of the Council."*

The Fathers were true inspirers of the Councils, while being present and *in absentia*. For that reason, and in this sense, the Councils used to emphasize that they were "following the Holy Fathers" – ἐπόμενοι τοῖς ἁγίοις πατράσιν, as the Council of Chalcedon puts it. It was precisely the *consensus patrum* which was authoritative and binding, and not their private opinions or views, although even they should not be hastily dismissed. Again, this *consensus* was much more than just an empirical agreement of individuals. The true and authentic *consensus* was that which reflected the *mind* of the Catholic and Uni - versal Church – τὸ ἐκκλησιαστικὸν φρόνημα. It was that kind of *consensus* to which St. Irenaeus was referring when he contended that neither a special "ability" nor a "deficiency" in speech of individual leaders in the Churches could affect the identity of their witnesses, since the "power of tradition" – *virtus traditionis* – was always and every - where the same. The preaching of the Church is always identical – *con - stans et aequaliter perseverans*, according to St. Irenaeus. The true *consensus* is that which manifests and discloses this perennial identity of the Church's faith – *aequaliter perseverans*.

The teaching authority of the Ecumenical Councils is grounded in the *infallibility of the Church*. The ultimate "authority" is vested in the Church which is forever the Pillar and the Foundation of Truth. It is not primarily a canonical authority, in the formal and specific sense of the term, although canonical strictures or sanctions may be appended to conciliar decisions on matters of faith. It is a charismatic authority, grounded in the assistance of the Holy Spirit – *for it seemed good to the Holy Spirit and to us.*

THE COUNCIL OF NICAEA

The city of Nicaea was selected as the city to host the First Ecumenical Council. Constantinople was to be officially inaugurated only in 330 and hence at the time of the convening of the Council of Nicaea the imperial residence was in Nicomedia, very close to Nicaea. Nicaea – its name comes from the Greek for "victory" – was easily accessible by sea and land from all parts of the empire. The imperial letter convening the council is no longer extant. Eusebius informs us that the emperor sent letters of invitation to the bishops of all countries and instructed them to come quickly – σπεύδειν ἀπανταχόθεν τοὺς ἐπισκόπους γράμμασι τιμητικοῖς προκαλούμενος. All expenses were to be paid from the imperial treasury. The number of bishops present has come down to us as 318 – so states Athanasius, Socrates, and Theodoret. An element of mystical symbolism became attached to this number of 318, some seeing in the Greek abbreviation a reference to the cross and a reference to the "holy name of Jesus." St. Ambrose in his De fide (i, 18) connected the number of 318 with the number of servants of Abraham in Genesis 14: 14. The number differs in other accounts. For example, Eusebius gives the number as two-hundred and fifty – πεντήκοντα καὶ διακοσίων ἀριθμόν. But Eusebius does not include the number of priests and deacons. Arabic accounts from a later period give the number of more than two-thousand bishops. The extant Latin lists of signatures contain no more than two-hundred and twenty-four bishops. There appears to be no reason why the number of 318 is not in fact accurate. If one includes the number of priests, deacons, and others, then the number may have reached two thousand.

The Eastern provinces were heavily represented. The Latin West, however, had only seven delegates, one of whom exercised considerable influence – Hosius of Cordova, Spain (c. 257-357), who was an ecclesiastical adviser to Constantine. In addition to Hosius, the Latin West was represented by Nicasius of Dijon, Caecilian of Carthage, Domnus of Pannonia, Eustorgius of Milan, Marcus of Calabria, and the two presbyters from Rome, Victor or Vitus and Vincentius, who represented the bishop of Rome, St. Sylvester (bishop from 314 to 335). A Persian bishop by the name of John was present and a Gothic bishop, Theophilus, who was apparently the teacher of Ulfilas (c. 311-383), the Arian translator of the Bible into Gothic – the influence of Ulfilas upon subsequent history, especially in the West, was great; known as the "Apostle to the Goths," Ulfilas, according to Philostorgius, translated the entire Bible except the books of Kings; in translating the Bible into Gothic and in converting the Goths to Arian

Christianity, Ulfilas' casts his shadow over the West for centuries to come.

The official opening of the Council of Nicaea took place with the arrival of Constantine, probably on the fourteenth of June. Eusebius describes in his usual style the entrance of the emperor: "When all the bishops had entered the main building of the imperial palace . . . each took his place . . . and in silence awaited the arrival of the emperor. The court officers entered one after another, though only those who professed faith in Christ. The moment the approach of the emperor was announced . . . all the bishops rose from their seats and the emperor appeared like a heavenly messenger of God – οἷα Θεοῦ τις οὐράνιος ἄγγελος – covered with gold and gems, a glorious presence, very tall and slender, full of beauty, strength, and majesty. With this external adornment he united the spiritual ornament of the fear of God, modesty, and humility, which could be seen in his downcast eyes, his blushing face, the motion of his body, and his walk. When he reached the golden throne prepared for him, he stopped, and he did not sit down until the bishops so indicated. After he sat, the bishops resumed their seats."

After a brief address from "the bishop on the right of the emperor," Constantine delivered "with a gentle voice" in the official Latin language the opening address, which was immediately translated into Greek. Although the accounts of this speech differ slightly in Eusebius, Sozomen, Socrates, and Rufinus, they agree on the essentials. "It was my greatest desire, my friends, that I might be permitted to enjoy your assembly. I must thank God that, in addition to all other blessings, he has shown me this highest one of all: to see you all gathered here in harmony and with one mind. May no malicious enemy rob us of this fortunateness . . . Discord in the Church I consider more fearful and painful than any other war. As soon as I, with God's help, had overcome my enemies, I believed that nothing more was now necessary than to give thanks to God in common joy with those whom I had liberated. But when I heard of your division, I was convinced that this matter should by no means be neglected. And in the desire to assist by my service, I have summoned you without delay. I shall, however, feel my desire fulfilled only when I see the minds of all united in that peaceful harmony which you, as the anointed of God, must preach to others. Do not delay, therefore, my friends. Do not delay, servants of God. Put away all causes of strife and loose all knots of discord by the laws of peace. Thus shall you accomplish the work most pleasing to God and confer upon me, your fellow servant – τῷ ὑμετέρῳ συνθε – ράποντι – an exceeding great joy."

After this opening speech the emperor, according to Eusebius, turned the council over to the bishops – παρεδίδου τὸν λόγον τοῖς συνόδου προέδροις. The bishops began their work but the emperor continued to take an active part in the proceedings.

According to Socrates' history (I, 8) Sabinus of Heraclea asserted that the majority of the bishops present at the Council of Nicaea were uneducated. Harnack writes that this "is confirmed by the astonishing results. The general acceptance of the resolution come to by the Council is intelligible only if we presuppose that the question in dispute was above most of the bishops." In general, this may be the case. But the fact cannot be overlooked that there were competent theologians present and quantity does not ensure the deliberation of truth. St. Athanasius, even though a deacon, was present with Alexander of Alexandria. Hosius, to whom St. Athanasius refers as "the Great" – ὁ μέγας, was apparently not a mediocrity. The most learned bishop was probably Eusebius of Caesarea. Others present, although they cannot be considered theologians in the strict sense of the word, are noteworthy for their lives as confessors and for their spirituality. Paphnutius of the Upper Thebaid was in attendance. Potamon of Heraclea, whose right eye had been blinded, was present. Paul of Neocaesarea had been tortured under Licinius – both hands had been crippled and he had been tortured with red hot iron. Jacob of Nisibis, the hermit, and Spiridon of Cyprus, the patron saint of the Ionian islands, were present.

Traditionally the Council of Nicaea is looked upon as having had two opposing theological parties. But closer analysis indicates that there were three parties. This becomes clear from the position of Eusebius of Caesarea, from the nature of his confession, and from the subsequent history of the controversy. St. Athanasius simply lumped the two opposing parties as one opposition. The "orthodox" party, at first a minority, was represented by Alexander of Alexandria, Eustathius of Antioch, Macarius of Jerusalem, Marcellus of Ancyra, Hosius of Cordova, and by the deacon, St. Athanasius.

The Arians came to the Council of Nicaea apparently confident of victory, for the bishop of Nicaea was their supporter and the Arians had substantial influence with the imperial court. The Arians – or the Eusebians, as they were called – numbered approximately twenty bishops, headed by the influential bishop Eusebius of Nicomedia. The presbyter Arius was present and was called upon frequently to put forth and explain his views – "*evocabatur frequenter Arius in concilium,*" as Rufinus puts it. Others in support of Arianism were Theognis of Nicaea, Maris of Chalcedon, and Menophantus of Ephesus.

The middle group, which represented the majority, was headed by Eusebius of Caesarea. This moderate, Eusebian party was composed of a variety of groups and hence could be swayed in various directions.

It was the Arians who produced the first confession of faith at the Council of Nicaea. This was a logistical error on their part. The creed they produced was conveyed to the council by their spokesman, Eusebius of Nicomedia, and it was a creed that made their theological position clear and unambiguous. Their creed met with manifest disapproval and was, reportedly, torn to pieces. Those who signed this confession of faith, with the exception of the Egyptians Theonas and Secundus who remained steadfast, regrouped in the hopes of presenting at least some -

thing that might be accepted. In essence, they had abandoned the cause of Arius.

The focus then turned to Eusebius of Caesarea and the moderates. Eusebius of Caesarea proposed an ancient Palestinian creed which was in general terms similar to the Nicene. It acknowledged the divine nature of Christ but avoided the term ὁμοούσιος, *consubstantialis, of the same essence*. It appears that Constantine had seen this creed and had approved it: πιστεύομεν εἰς ἕνα θεὸν πατέρα παντοκράτορα, τὸν τῶν ἁπάντων ὁρατῶν τε καὶ ἀοράτων ποιητήν, καὶ εἰς ἕνα κύριον Ἰησοῦν Χριστόν, τὸν τοῦ θεοῦ λόγον, θεὸν ἐκ θεοῦ, φῶς ἐκ φωτός, ζωὴν ἐκ ζωῆς, υἱὸν μονογενῆ πρωτότοκον πάσης κτίσεως, πρὸ πάντων τῶν αἰώνων ἐκ τοῦ πατρὸς γεγεννημένον, δι᾽ οὗ καὶ ἐγένετο τὰ πάντα, τὸν διὰ τὴν ἡμετέραν σωτηρίαν σαρκωθέντα καὶ ἐν ἀνθρώποις πολιτευσάμενον καὶ παθόντα καὶ ἀναστάντα τῇ τρίτῃ ἡμέρα καὶ ἀνελθόντα πρὸς τὸν πατέρα καὶ ἥξοντα πάλιν ἐν δόξῃ κρῖναι ζῶντας καὶ νεκρούς, καὶ εἰς ἓν πνεῦμα ἅγιον. Eusebius – for safe measure – added to this an anti-Sabellian section explicitly emphasizing that the Father is truly the Father, the Son truly the Son, and the Holy Spirit truly the Holy Spirit. According to Eusebius this confession of faith was unanimously proclaimed "orthodox" – ταύτης ὑφ᾽ ἡμῶν ἐκτεθείσης τῆς πίστεως οὐδεὶς παρῆν ἀντιλογίας τόπος, ἀλλ᾽ αὐτός τε πρῶτος ὁ θεοφιλέστατος ἡμῶν βασιλεὺς ὀρθότατα περιέχειν αὐτὴν ἐμαρτύρησεν. οὕτω τε καὶ ἑαυτόν φρονεῖν συνωμολόγησε καὶ ταύτῃ τοὺς πάντας συγκατατίθεσθαι, ὑπογράφειν τε τοῖς δόγμασι καὶ συμφωνεῖν τούτοις αὐτοῖς παρεκελεύετο.

The problem arose because of the suspicion of the "orthodox" party – it appears that the Arian minority was willing to accept this con- fession of faith; if so, then something was wrong with it. The "orthodox" party insisted on a confession of faith to which no Arian could honestly subscribe. They insisted on inserting the homoousios, a term hated by the Arians, a term they considered unscriptural, Sabellian, and materialistic. We know from Eusebius that the emperor sided with those demanding the *homoousios* and that Hosius was the one who suggested this to Constantine. Yet the insertion of the word *homo- ousios* did not settle the matter. It was thought that the Creed of Caesarea contained expressions which could be interpreted in an Arian sense.

Hosius of Cordova stepped forth to announce that a confession of faith would be read by Hermogenes of Caesarea, at that time a deacon but later a bishop, who was the secretary of the council. It was a very carefully constructed doctrinal formula which claimed to be a revision of the Creed of Caesarea. The input of the Alexandrians can be seen here, as well as that of Eustathius of Antioch and Macarius of Jerusalem. But the main person of influence was Hosius – it is St. Athanasius who writes of Hosius: οὗτος ἐν νικαίᾳ πίστιν ἐξέθετο. The first alter- ation was replacing ἁπάντων ὁρατῶν ("of all seen things whatsoever") by πάντων ὁρατῶν ("of all seen things"). The reason for this was to exclude the creation of the Son and Spirit. The second change was to substitute the word "Son" for "Logos" at the beginning of the second section so that everything that followed referred to the Son. The word "Logos" is completely absent from the Nicene Creed and neither St. Athanasius nor the Arians objected to its exclusion. The third change was the extension of θεὸν ἐκ θεοῦ ("God of God") to γεννη - θέντα ἐκ τοῦ πατρὸς μονογενῆ θεὸν ἐκ θεοῦ ("begotten of the Father, only begotten God of God"). It appears that in the final discussions the words τοῦτ 'ἐστὶν ἐκ τῆς οὐσίας τοῦ πατρός ("that is of the essence of the Father") were inserted between μονογενῆ and θεὸν to exclude any Arian interpretation. The fourth change ad - dressed several expressions which were considered unsatisfactory, ambiguous, and prone to misinterpretation. The expressions ζωὴν ἐκ ζωῆς ("life of life"), πρωτότοκον πάσης κτίσεως ("the first-born of every creature"), πρὸ πάντων αἰώνων ἐκ τοῦ πατρὸς γεγεννη - μένον ("begotten of the Father before all ages") were deleted. In their place was inserted: θεὸν ἀληθινὸν ἐκ θεοῦ ἀληθινοῦ, γεννηθέντα, οὐ ποιηθέντα, δι 'οὗ τὰ πάντα ἐγένετο ("true God of true God, begotten, not made, by whom all things became"). Here, however, another insertion was deemed necessary as the discussions continued – after ποιηθέντα ("made") the words ὁμοούσιον τῷ πατρί ("of the same essence with the Father") were added, again because without the addition the text could be interpreted in an Arian sense. The fifth change was to replace the evasive and indefinite ἐν ἀνθρώποις πολιτευσά - μενον ("having lived among men") with the definite ἐνανθρωπή - σαντα ("having become incarnate"). Finally, anything which ap- proached an Arian sense was condemned and excluded from the final creed.

The opposition parties did not simply die; they debated. The debates became so intensive that the emperor felt it necessary to participate – ἐρωτήσεις τοιγαροῦν καὶ ἀποκρίσεις ἐντεῦθεν ἀνεκινοῦντο, ἐβασανίζετο ὁ λόγος τῆς διανοίας τῶν εἰρη - μένων, according to Eusebius in Theodoret's history (I, 11). From the accounts of St. Athanasius it appears that the Eusebians continued to make proposals of a conciliatory nature and to attempt to include certain expressions that could be interpreted in an Arian sense. But the expressions ἐκ τῆς οὐσίας ("of the essence") and ὁμοούσιος ("of the same essence") prevailed in the Nicene Creed.

For the first time a new type of document enters into the history of the Church – the signatures of the bishops to the Acts and decisions of an Ecumenical Council. The State, the Empire, only a short time before so hostile to the Church, now supports the Church, now elevates the doctrinal decisions of the Church to the status of imperial law. Almost all the bishops signed. It is significant that the name heading the list is Hosius of Cordova. Next to his signature is that of the two Roman presbyters, signing in the name of their bishop, the bishop of

Rome. After a day's reflection Eusebius of Caesarea signed. Only the two Egyptian bishops, Theonas and Secundus, refused to signed. They, along with Arius, were banished to Illyria.

The bishops had deliberated. The emperor had interacted and participated. But it is clear that the theological decisions came from within the Church. Now with the signatures of the bishops the Acts of the First Ecumenical Council become imperial law. Now the power of the State is to be felt. The emperor ordered the books of Arius to be burned. In his history Socrates relates that anyone found with Arian books was to be punished by death (I, 9). Moreover, the emperor declared that henceforth those adhering to Arianism were to be called "Porphyrians" – that is, they were to be considered on the same level as the worst enemies of Christ. In his letter to the Alexandrian Church the emperor is convinced that the results of the council were the work of the Holy Spirit – ὃ τοῖς τριακοσίοις ἤρεσεν ἐπισκόποις οὐδὲν ἔστιν ἕτερον ἢ τοῦ θεοῦ γνώμη, μάλιστά γε ὅπου τὸ ἅγιον πνεῦμα τοιούτων καὶ τηλικούτων ἀνδρῶν ταῖς διανοίαις ἐγκείμενον τὴν θείαν βούλησιν ἐξεφώτισεν. And yet another form of persecution began, the persecution of those unwilling to subscribe to or accept the decisions of Ecumenical Councils. This is the first example of civil punishment of heresy. Before the conversion of the Empire the ultimate penalty for heresy was excommunication. Now exile and death were added, for any disobedience to the Church was regarded simultaneously as a crime against the State.

The Age of Constantine is a turning point in Christian history. But precisely what was the Church's view of the Empire before the Empire was christened? Once christened, what was the gain and what the loss for the Church? What, in essence, was the "Byzantinization" of the Church?

Among the early Christians there was nothing anarchical in the attitude toward the Roman Empire. The "divine" origin of the State and of its authority was formally acknowledged already by St. Paul, and he himself had no difficulty in appealing to the protection of Roman magistrates and of Roman law. The positive value and function of the State were commonly admitted in the Christian circles. Even the violent invective in the book of Revelation was no exception. What was denounced there was iniquity and injustice of the actual Rome but not the principle of political order. Christians could, in full sincerity and in good faith, protest their political innocence in the Roman courts and plead their loyalty to the Empire. In fact, early Christians were devoutly praying for the State, for peace and order, and even for Caesars themselves. One finds a high appraisal of the Roman Empire even in those Christian writers of that time who were notorious for their resistance, as Origen and Tertullian. The theological "justification" of the Empire originated already in the period of persecutions. Yet, Christian loyalty was, of necessity, a restricted loyalty. Of course, Christianity was in no sense a seditious plot, and Christians never intended to overthrow the existing order, although they did believe that it had ultimately to wither away.

From the Roman point of view, however, Christians could not fail to appear seditious, not because they were in any sense mixed in politics, but precisely because they were not. Their political "indifference" was irritating to the Romans. They kept themselves away from the concerns of the "commonwealth" at a critical time of its struggle for existence. Not only did they claim "religious freedom" for themselves. They also claimed supreme authority for the Church. Although the Kingdom of God was emphatically "not of this world," it seemed to be a threat to the omni-competent Kingdom of Man. The Church was, in a sense, a kind of "resistance movement" in the Empire. And Christians were "conscientious objectors." They were bound to resist any attempt at their "integration" into the fabric of the Empire. As Christopher Dawson has aptly said: "Christianity was the only remaining power in the world which could not be absorbed in the gigantic mechanism of the new servile state." Christians were not a political faction. Yet, their religious allegiance had an immediate "political" connotation. It has been well observed that monotheism itself was a "political problem" in the ancient world (Eric Peterson). Christians were bound to claim "autonomy" for themselves and for the Church. And this was precisely what the Empire could neither concede nor even understand. Thus the clash was inevitable, although it could be delayed. The Church was a challenge to the Empire, and the Empire was a stumbling block for the Christians.

After a protracted struggle with the Church, the Roman Empire at last capitulated. Constantine, the Caesar, converted and humbly applied for admission into the Church. The Christian response was a response that was by no means unanimous. There were many among Christian leaders who were quite prepared to welcome unreservedly the conversion of the Emperor, the Caesar, and the prospective conversion of the Empire. But there were not a few who were apprehensive of the imperial move. To be sure, one could but rejoice in the cessation of hostilities and in that freedom of public worship which now will be legally secured. But the major problem is not yet solved, and it is a problem of extreme complexity. Indeed, it was a highly paradoxical problem.

Already Tertullian had raised certain awkward questions, although in his own time they were no more than rhetorical questions. Could Caesars accept Christ and believe in Him? Caesars obviously belonged to "the world." They were an integral part of the "secular" fabric, *necessarii saeculo*. Could then a Christian be Caesar? Could then a Christian belong at once to two conflicting orders, the Church and the World? (*Apologeticum* 21, 24). In the time of Constantine this concept of the "Christian Caesar" was still a riddle and a puzzle, despite the eloquent effort of Eusebius of Caesarea to elaborate the idea of the "Christian Empire." For many Christians there was an inner contra -

diction in the concept itself. Caesars were necessarily committed to the cause of "this world." But the Church was not of this world. The office of Caesars was intrinsically "secular." Was there really any room for Emperors, as Emperors, in the structure of the Christian community? It has been recently suggested that probably Constantine himself was rather uneasy and uncertain precisely at this very point. It seems that one of the reasons for which he was delaying his own baptism was precisely his dim feeling that it was inconvenient to be "Christian" and "Caesar" at the same time. Constantine's personal conversion con - stituted no problem. But as Emperor he was committed. He had to carry the burden of his exalted position in the Empire. He was still a "Divine Caesar." As Emperor, he was heavily involved in the traditions of the Empire, as much as he actually endeavored to disentangle himself. The transfer of the Imperial Residence to a new City, away from the memories of the old pagan Rome, was a spectacular symbol of this noble effort. Yet, the Empire itself was still much the same as before, with its autocratic ethos and habits, with all its pagan practices, including the adoration and apotheosis of Caesars. We have good reasons to trust Constantine's personal sincerity. No doubt, he was deeply convinced that Christianity was the only power which could quicken the sick body of the Empire and supply a new principle of cohesion in the time of social disintegration. But obviously he was unable to abdicate his sovereign authority or to renounce the world. Indeed, Constantine was firmly convinced that, by Divine Providence, he was entrusted with a high and holy mission, that he was chosen to reestablish the Empire, and to reestablish it on a Christian foundation. This conviction, more than any particular political theory, was the decisive factor in his policy, and in his actual mode of ruling.

The situation was intensely ambiguous. Had the Church to accept the Imperial offer and to assume the new task? Was it a welcome opportunity or rather a dangerous compromise? In fact, the experience of close cooperation with the Empire has not been altogether happy and encouraging for Christians, even in the days of Constantine himself. The Empire did not appear to be an easy or comfortable ally and partner for the Church. Under Constantine's successors all the inconveniences of cooperation became quite evident, even if we ignore the abortive attempt of Julian to reinstate Paganism. The leaders of the Church were compelled, time and again, to challenge the persistent attempts of Caesars to exercise their supreme authority also in religious matters.

And the victory at the Council of Nicaea is to be short-lived – Nicaea in a very real sense was the beginning, not the end, of continuous theological controversy over the nature of the God-Man and hence over the nature of God and the nature of man.

CHAPTER ELEVEN

FROM NICAEA TO EPHESUS

The Council of Nicaea did not bring peace to the Church. Indeed, ecclesiastical and imperial war would soon be declared. The Church will have to fight a lengthy struggle to maintain the Nicene doctrine. What appeared to be a time of great and victorious triumph became a time of trial and sorrow for the Church. The new epoch resulting from the conversion of the emperor, the new epoch of the imperial throne supporting the Church contained a risk, for the imperial throne could support any faction within the Church – heterodox or orthodox – and those who were not aligned with the policy supported by the emperor had to be prepared even for death, death in the name of the Empire but in combination with the party the throne was supporting.

The first moments of exhilaration at the victory, at the thought of the Empire not only supporting but becoming Christianized soon gave way to the reality of political life. The "world" brought with it both a great longing to be satisfied by the Church and a great pride to be subdued by the Church. A spiritual excitement gripped not just ecclesiastical circles but all of society, all classes of society. It was too soon to speak of any definite victory. The "world" still remained "outside" the Church. Paganism continued to flourish – pagan temples are still open and pagan teachers are still arguing against Christianity. Culture and domestic life are still filled with survivals of heathenism. It is no surprise that the monastic movement and the attraction of fleeing to the desert become intense – the motivation is more than a desire for seclusion and solitude. The life of a Christian in that world is not easy. Indeed, pagan culture will experience a revival in the fourth and even in the fifth century – it culminates with Iamblichus and the Athenian school of Neoplatonism. And there is a strange dichotomy, for in the collision between the two worlds of Hellenism and Christianity the Church does not reject Hellenism but the Hellenes refuse to accept the Church. The significance of this struggle is not just in the external or political events of the time. The internal struggle is even more painful and more tragic because every Hellene must now experience and overcome this division within himself. The spiritual rebirth of classical society begins in the fourth century but will be transformed slowly and this process is not completed until much later when a new Byzantine culture is born.

THE DOGMATIC MEANING OF NICAEA

The entire dogmatic meaning of the Council of Nicaea is contained essentially in *ὁμοούσιος* and *ἐκ τῆς οὐσίας* – "of one essence" and "from one essence." These expressions were carefully scrutinized at the

Council of Nicaea – "the meaning of the words was thoroughly examined," Eusebius informs us. It is very probable that Hosius of Cordova suggested the term "of one essence" – ὁμοούσιος. Of Hosius St. Athanasius writes that he "set forth our faith at Nicaea." Philostorgius, if his account is accurate, tells us that Hosius and Alexander of Alexandria agreed to concentrate on the word ὁμοούσιος while journeying to Nicaea.

In the Latin West this term – or more precisely its Latin analogue – had been a common expression since Tertullian. Novatian wrote about "one substance" and "a common substance" – *communio sub - stantiae ad Patrem* – in the Trinity. In the significant controversy between Dionysius of Rome and Dionysius of Alexandria it was Dionysius of Rome who reproved the bishop of Alexandria for not using the term "of one substance." This controversy was well remembered in Alexandria, for St. Athanasius writes that "the ancient bishops, who lived almost 130 years ago, the bishop of great Rome and the bishop of our city, condemned in writing those who asserted that the Son is a creature and not of one essence or substance with the Father." St. Athanasius made it clear that, although these expressions are not found in Scripture, they were used by the Church – they were borrowed by the Nicene fathers "from ancient times, from their predecessors." One problem was that the Latin term did not fully coincide with the Greek term. Another problem was that those who used this term had also been accused of subordinationism. In fact, the Greek term had been condemned at previous councils. It appears that the term was also used by the Gnostics – in a usage which clearly entailed emanation. This explains the negative or at least cautious attitude that Origen had toward the expressions "from the essence of the Father" and "of one essence." Dionysius of Alexandria avoided the term probably for the same reason. The later defenders of the *homoiousia* consider the term *homoousia* unsuitable for theology precisely because of its associations with "material" or "matter." The Council of Antioch in 269, convened to deliberate the theology of Paul of Samosata, rejected and condemned the term *homoousia*. St. Hilary of Poitiers claims the council condemned the term because Paul of Samosata had given a Modalistic meaning to the expression by asserting the complete singleness of the Divinity and the purely nominal distinction of persons – in Paul's conception "consubstantiality" or "*homoousia*" designated the Modalistic unity of the Godhead. St. Hilary borrows his explanation from the defenders of the *homoiousia*, for that was their explanation of the condemnation of the term by the Council of Antioch.

The words "consubstantial" and "*homoousia*" allowed for a variety of interpretations. A contemporary letter reflects the state of mind at the time – does "consubstantial" designate a "common kind," of which the Father and the Son are "aspects," or does it designate the unity of a preexisting, "corporeal" substratum, from which both the Father and the Son are generated through separation? Hilary of Poitiers in his book on the councils points out the different meanings the term had been given. The fathers at the Council of Nicaea had to isolate, refute, and exclude all these inexact shades of meaning from the theological use of the term ὁμοούσιος as understood and defined by the council. The strict Arians at the council precisely called attention to these nuances – the strict Arians understood "consubstantiality" as "co-materiality."

The doctrine proclaimed at the Council of Nicaea had to be elucidated and interpreted. This was possible only within the structure of an integral system of religious instruction. Only then could its exact meaning be explained and protected from unorthodox interpretation. It was first necessary to define the concept of essence or substance – *ousia*. In classical philosophy this word had different meanings for different philosophical schools. For the Platonists and Neoplatonists "essence" meant that which is general or common. For the Stoics also the term "substance" – *substantia* – designated a common, unqualified substratum, or matter in general, in opposition to the forms which distinguish it. For Aristotle and the Aristotelians, on the other hand, *ousia* meant primarily individual and indivisible existence, an individual and single thing in the fulness of its immutable attributes – the "first essence," πρώτη οὐσία. Only in a secondary sense was a common kind, uniting and comprehending individual existences, called an "essence." This is what Aristotle called the "second essence" – δευτέρα οὐσία. But for Aristotle himself *ousia* did not have an exactly defined significance and occasionally in his usage it coincides with the concept of existence, "that which is underlying." For Aristotle essence was also connected with the idea of origin, of coming into being – γέννεσις. By the fourth century it was this narrow Aristotelian meaning which was widely in use. *In this sense οὐσία is not only essence but also being.*

Another term from the Council of Nicaea had to be explicated and interpreted – the term ὑπόστασις, hypostasis. This term came into use in philosophy comparatively late – in any event after the time of Aristotle. For a long time this word was used in its literal sense – "that which stands under." It was even then not without a particular sig - nificance because for Aristotle καθ ' ὑπόστασιν meant the reality and actuality of a thing, as opposed to its outward appearance. In the *Septuagint* ὑπόστασις was used in various meanings and designated, among other things, "foundation" – foundation of a house, foundation of hope – and composition. In the works of Philo ὑπόστασις meant at times independence and uniqueness. The word signified "essence" for St. Paul in *Hebrews* 1:3 – ὃς ὢν ἀπαύγασμα τῆς δόξης καὶ χαρακ - τὴρ τῆς ὑποστάσεως αὐτοῦ. Its significance elsewhere in St. Paul's writings is varied – for example, in *II Corinthians* 9:43 and *Hebrews* 11:1.

The Neoplatonists were the first to define *hypostasis* as a philosophical term. Plotinus designates the forms in which the One reveals itself as ὑπόστασις. Characteristically Plotinus considers the term inappropriate to describe the ultimate principle. So also was the term and the idea of *οὐσία* because the One "is higher than any essence." The term apparently implied, for Plotinus, the act of generation. At the same time Origen also refers to "three hypostases," as did Dionysius of Alexandria after him. But the term "hypostasis" remained indistinct from the concept of essence and this is precisely why the terminology of Dionysius of Alexandria's theology was so disturbing to the Roman theologians. In general, until the middle of the fourth century *οὐσία* and *ὑπόστασις* were interchangeable both as ideas and terms. St. Jerome bluntly writes that "the school of worldly science knew of no other meaning for the word 'hypostasis' than 'substance'." In the anathemas pronounced by the Council of Nicaea *οὐσία* and *ὑπόστασις* are clearly identical – "from one hypostasis *or* essence." St. Athanasius also identifies them. But it should be noted that both of the Greek terms could be expressed in Latin only by one word – both *οὐσία* and *ὑπόστασις* were translated as *substantia*.

There remained one major ambiguity in the Creed of the Council of Nicaea. The confession of consubstantiality entailed the complete "identity of essence" of the Father and the Son. Was it then possible to speak of the generation of the Son "from the essence of the Father"? This difficulty was later eliminated when "from the essence of the Father" was omitted from the Creed of the Council of Constantinople, the Second Ecumenical Council (381). Moreover, the works of St. Athanasius make it clear beyond doubt that in the minds of the Nicene fathers there was no contradiction or hesitation. For them the ex - pressions "from the essence" and "of one essence" affirmed from different viewpoints one and the same thing – the true, immutable, co-belonging of the Father and the Son in an identity of unchanging Life which was common to both of them. By opposing the Arian terms "from the desire" or "from the will" with their own definition "from the essence," the Nicene fathers tried to express the immanent and ontological character of the Divine generation as an internal, everlasting and essential condition, rather than an act, of the Divine Being.

For the Nicene fathers "from the essence" meant "in essence" or "by essence," and this excluded the idea of an act of the will from the concept of Divine generation. Generation and "being from the essence" coincide in the Nicene interpretation – they were opposed to the con - cepts of creation and being as a result of desire or will, which had frequently been linked together. The shortcoming of the Creed of the Council of Nicaea lay elsewhere – there was no common term to name the three which made up the unity of the Godhead. The unity and indivisibility of the Divine Being had been expressed more clearly than the distinctions of the Trinity. The Divine Being was one essence yet three – there was a number but no noun to follow it.

Shortly after the Council of Nicaea an intense theological debate flared up over the Creed promulgated by the council. The political, social and personal motivations which complicated and exacerbated the passionate argumentation are not of particular interest for the history of doctrine. There were enough purely theological reasons for the conflict without these, though they are interesting historically and in them - selves. The manner of expression used in the Creed was confusing to many because it was familiar and seemed to be inexact. By the standards of contemporary usage it appeared that the language of the Creed of the council did not express with sufficient strength and precision the hypostatic distinctions, especially in relation to the Son as Logos or Word. There was also the danger of the Marcellian heresy, which St. Athanasius and the Nicene fathers regarded with perhaps too much tolerance.

The anti-Nicene opposition held various doctrinal positions. Numerically predominant among them were the conservative bishops of the East. These bishops refrained from using Nicene terminology in favor of the older, more familiar expressions of Church tradition. They were united by their common fear of Sabellianism. The most active group of opponents were the "Eusebians," as St. Athanasius called them, who remained firm supporters of Origen and his doctrine of subordinationism. They openly rejected the language and Creed of the Council of Nicaea and they were joined by more extreme heretics who had not previously enunciated their views.

Socrates tells us that the bishops, after the term ὁμοούσιος was made the subject of examination, declared war on each other, a war "like a battle at night because neither side understood why it was abusing the other." Some rejected the expression ὁμοούσιος and claimed that those who accept it are guilty of the heresy of Sabellianism and are blasphemers who denied the personal being of the Son of God. Others, defending the ὁμοούσιος, considered that their opponents were polytheists and turned away from them "as from pagans." The anti-Nicene factions feared Sabellianism to such an extent that they became careless with regard to Arianism. They tried to protect themselves with sweeping anathemas that were stated in very general terms. And they attempted to replace the Creed of the Council of Nicaea with a new doctrine. Thus arose what Socrates calls "a maze of creeds."

It is enough to point out the basic features of these arguments without going into their finer points. In the first place, the deliberate rejection of Nicene terminology is immediately apparent in all the creeds written at this time. In the second place, their main purpose was to make clear the doctrine of the distinction and individuality of the different hypostases. The second creed of Antioch (341) contains the expression "three hypostases," which was qualified by the weaker definition "one by agreement." At the end of this long and confused struggle, complicated by deceit, duplicity, treachery, and the military intervention of various emperors, it turned out that no creed except the Nicene was capable of expressing and protecting the true and orthodox faith. It was in this sense that St. Athanasius called the Creed of Nicaea "the expression of the truth." He predicted that the dissent and confusion would not end until the "anti-Nicenes" came to their senses and said: "Let us arise and go to our fathers and say to them, 'We proclaim our anathema on the Arian heresy and recognize the Council of Nicaea'." St. Athanasius clearly saw the danger that was latent in the opposition to the Nicene doctrine. Given the prevalence of Arianism existing at that time, this opposition, in the form of Sabellianism, was a threat to orthodoxy. The older, traditional systems of theology now seemed ambiguous, and a sound, new system could be established only on the basis of the Nicene doctrine of ὁμοούσιος. The whole structure of theological reasoning had to be built and regulated by this concept – by ὁμοούσιος.

The first necessity was to present and clarify the premises and doctrines of the Creed of the Council of Nicaea, and this was the task of St. Athanasius. What was left incomplete by him is finished by the great Cappadocians. Their work also culminates in the creation of a new terminology. The differentiation of the concepts of οὐσία and ὑπόσ – τασις, and the exact definition of the attributes of the hypostases, gave both completeness and flexibility to the orthodox doctrine of the Trinity.

ST. ATHANASIUS

St. Athanasius writes that the Logos became man, similar to us in all respects. St. Athanasius uses the word "Incarnation" and by this he means that in assuming flesh the Logos became a full man, taking on an animate body with all the senses and sufferings that are proper to it. By virtue of its union with the Logos, "because of the Logos, which was in a body," the body was freed from its weakness and subjection to decay. The life-giving strength of the Logos freed the body of the Savior from natural weaknesses – "Christ thirsted, since that is an attribute of a body, but he did not perish from hunger." The body was subject to suffering but the impassible Logos was within it. The body experienced weakness by the permission and will of the Logos and not by necessity or against his will. The Lord tolerated everything proper to the body – he thirsted, wept, and even accepted death. But the death of the Lord took place because of his humility and love and not from necessity. He had the power to separate himself from the body, and his body was able to die. It could not, however, remain dead, for "it had become the temple of life." Therefore it immediately revived and arose from the dead "by virtue of the life that dwelled within it." The Logos was not bound by the body but freed the body from its limitedness and its inclination to sin. By the strength of the unchanging Logos, the mutable human nature in Christ became immutably good, and all delusions were powerless over it. "The works proper to the Logos were achieved through the body." The flesh was deified by serving the works of God, and the humanity in Christ was without sin. The Lord "became our brother through the likeness of the body," and his flesh "was saved and liberated before the others." Since we "share in his body," we also are saved and our life is renewed "because our flesh is no longer earthly but has been made identical with the Logos by the Divine Logos himself, who became flesh for our sakes."

St. Athanasius states that Holy Scripture tells us two truths about the Savior – he has always been God, Son, and Logos; and he became man. This occasionally leads to ambiguity in passages dealing with Christ because, although he is glorified, his human nature is underemphasized. The Logos did not simply "desire to become incarnate" or "manifest himself in a body." He did not descend to man but he *became* man – he made himself the Son of Man. In this respect St. Athanasius sometimes uses incomplete or inexact expressions – the Logos "clothes himself" or "dwells within," and he is a temple, dwelling-place, or agent. However, St. Athanasius carefully distin - guishes the appearance of the Logos in Christ from his appearance and presence in saints. Christ *became* man. The visible body of Christ was the body of God, not man. He made the body "his own," and the weakness of the flesh became "proper" to the Logos. Christ's works were not separated in such a way that one was accomplished by his divine nature and another by his human nature, but "everything was achieved in combination" and indivisibly. The very saliva of Christ was divine, healing, and life-giving because the Incarnate Logos "adopted" all the properties of the flesh and made them his own. It was he who both grieved for Lazarus and then resurrected him. God was born in the flesh from the Virgin, and Mary is the Θεοτόκος – the *Theotokos*, the Bearer of God. The flesh, which was born from Mary, did not become consubstantial with the Logos and the Logos was not joined to it. Mary was chosen so that the Lord could receive "from her" a body that would be "similar to ours" and not consubstantial with the Godhead. "From Mary the Logos received flesh, and a man was engendered whose nature and substance were the Logos of God and whose flesh was from the seed of David, a man from the flesh of Mary."

St. Athanasius clearly emphasizes both the unity of Christ the God-Man and his unmerging two natures. Christ has a divine nature by which he is consubstantial with the Father and also a human nature by which he is similar and related to us. For this reason he is the Savior, the Logos, and the Second Adam all at once. The Logos became man so that we could "become divine," "in order to deify us in himself." Deification is adoption by God, and "human sons have become the sons of God." We are "received by the Logos and are deified through his flesh" by virtue of the Incarnation. Born from the Virgin, the Logos was not united with only one man, but with the whole of human nature. Therefore everything that was achieved in the human nature of Christ is immediately extended to all men because they have a body in common with him. There is no coercion involved here. Men are more than similar to Christ – they are truly participants in the human nature of the Logos. Christ is a vine and we are the branches, "united with him by our humanity." In the same way that the tendrils which grow from a grapevine are consubstantial with it, so are our bodies consubstantial with the body of the Lord, and we receive what he has accomplished. His body is the "root of our resurrection and salvation." Everyone is renewed, anointed, healed, and exalted in Christ, for "he has taken everyone on himself." This is not merely similarity or sub - stitution but actual unity. Therefore all humanity is anointed by the Spirit in the Jordan, dies on the Cross, and is resurrected to immortality in Christ because "he himself bears our body."

St. Athanasius' explanation of the mystery of the Trinity was called forth by the Arian controversy also. The starting point of his trinitarian doctrine is the concept of God as the goodness and fulness of being. As a simple, holy, and incomprehensible Being, which is higher than any essence, God is beyond human understanding. The perfect simplicity and inner fulness of Divine Being and Life is the basis for St. Athanasius' teaching on the eternal generation and consubstantiality of the Only-Begotten, the Son and Logos. The Logos is generated by the Father and from his essence – he is the "proper generation of his essence." Everything which is generated is always consubstantial with that which engenders it. This is the basic feature of generation which distinguishes it from other modes of origination, and especially from creation. That which is created always originates either from some pre - existing matter or from nothingness – it always remains unlike and external to its creator, "of another essence."

The Son is generated. His being is a necessity of the Divine nature, which is fertile and fruitful in and of itself – the essence of the Father has never been incomplete, and that which is proper to it has never come to it at a later time." The denial of the Son's eternity and co-eternity with the Father is blasphemy not only against the Son but also against the Father. It diminishes the dignity of the Father and negates his immutability. It supposes that "he once was without his own Logos and Wisdom, that there was light which had no rays, that there was a spring which was dry and without water. God is eternal, the source is eternal, and therefore the Wisdom-Logos and his generation must also be eternal. If there was a time when the Son did not exist, then there was a time when God the Father and the Trinity did not exist. It would be as if "at one time the Trinity did not exist, but a Unity existed; as if there once was an incomplete Trinity, which at one time became complete." St. Athanasius uses this reasoning to show that the "mystery" of Arianism is a denial of the Divine Trinity. In fact, Arianism is a reversion to abstract monotheism – it rejects the knowl - edge of God as the Trinity, which is the highest truth of Christian revelation.

St. Athanasius stresses that the Father is immutable. He has always been the Father of "his own Son." There can be no question of succession in the relation of Father and Son, and there is not "interval" or "distance" between them. They are completely and perfectly coeternal. The possibility of a temporal relationship is excluded because it is impossible to designate the eternal and unchanging Father and the Son who always abides in him with temporal definitions. This eternity and co-eternity means that the Son is generated, not created. Since the Son is generated, he is "from the essence" – ἐκ τῆς οὐσίας . The Son is thus consubstantial with the Father – ὁμοούσιος. "That which proceeds from someone by essence is truly generated." Generation takes place "by nature," and not by will or desire. The "divinity of the Father unceasingly and permanently abides in the Son, and the divinity of the Son is never exhausted in the bosom of the Father." The Father and the Son are united in the unity of essence, in an identity of nature, and "in the indivisible identity of a single Divinity." The Son has the Father's nature without change, and the Divinity of the Son is the Divinity of the Father. St. Athanasius expresses this identity as a property or attribute – ἰδιότης. He considers that its most exact definition is the Nicene "consubstantial" – ὁμοούσιος.

St. Athanasius has no particular terms to describe the three which make up the Divine Unity. He never uses πρόσωπον. The meaning of "hypostases" coincides with the meaning of οὐσία for him, as it did for the fathers of the Council of Nicaea. St. Athanasius never distinguishes them as the Cappadocians were doing during his lifetime. He restricts himself to the proper names of Father, Son, and Spirit, and explains their mutual relation by such expressions as "the One who generates," and "the One who is generated," "One who is from someone," and "the One from whom he is." This leads to a certain lack of clarity in St. Athanasius' distinction of the three hypostases. He concentrates his attention on refuting attempts to divide or negate the consubstantiality of the indivisible Trinity. In his interpretation of the Nicene formulation "from the essence of the Father," he stresses the internal nature of the Divine generation and being. This expresses the "truth and immutability" of the Sonship, its "indivisibility and unity with the Father," and the "true eternity of essence from which the Logos is generated."

St. Athanasius decisively rejects and demonstrates the futility of the teaching of the Arians on the Logos as the mediator in creation. God does not need an assistant or helper because he can accomplish everything by a single movement of his will. God is not so conceited or fastidious that he would consider creation beneath his dignity and entrust it to another. God needs no instrument to create in the way that a carpenter needs a saw and axe. Furthermore, if it is not unsuitable for God to create, why should he create even one creature as an instrument for himself? The creation of one Mediator would entail the creation of another, and so on for eternity, and creation would thus be impossible. Since God can create, why should he need a mediator?

By approximately 360 the struggle against the terminology of the Council of Nicaea resulted in the reemergence and apparent victory of extreme Arianism. The symbol of this victory was the Second Formula of Sirmium of 357, referred to by Hilary as "the blasphemy of Hosius and Potamius." This was a daring attempt to end the discussion of the problem by declaring that it had in fact been decided. The purpose of this "Arian treachery," inspired not by sincere doctrinal motives but by tactical considerations, was to discredit the Nicene formulations on the grounds that they were not found in Scripture, that they were "incomprehensible to the people," and that the Nicene doctrines in general exceeded the measure of human knowledge and understanding. Catholic teaching was limited to the confession of "two persons" – not two Gods – of which the Father was greater in honor, dignity, and divinity by the very name of Father, while the Son was subordinate to him together with everything over which the Father had given him dominion.

ANOMOEANISM

This attempt to silence the dispute proved fruitless. The controversy soon burst out again with a new force. The propagation of "Anomoeanism" – "unlikeness– began in 356 in Alexandria, where Aëtius had established a circle of disciples. Soon he moved on to Antioch, where his preaching was very successful and was furthered by his pupil Eunomius. Sozomon informs us that Aëtius was "strong in the art of deduction and experienced in logomachy." Epiphanius writes that "from morning until night he sat over his studies in the attempt to define God by means of geometry and figures." Aëtius turned dogmatics into a dialectical game and he boasted that he "knew God better than he knew himself." Eunomius gave logical definition to the dialectics of Aëtius. His main doctrine is that the Father is an "eternally unique God," who "does not transform himself from one essence into three hypostases" and who "does not have a partner in his Divinity." His basic and "essential" positive definition of God is that he is unoriginate – $\dot{\alpha}\gamma\epsilon\nu\nu\eta\sigma\dot{\iota}\alpha$. Therefore the essence of God cannot be endowed to any - one else. The "consubstantial" generation of the Son – his generation "from the essence of the Father" – is impossible, since this would entail the division or breaking down of that which is simple and immutable. For this same reason a trinity of hypostases, which would abrogate the singleness and uniqueness of God, is inconceivable. Therefore, the Son is "of another essence" and is "not similar" to the Father because any comparison or compatibility is incommensurate with the absolute uniqueness of the Father, who is superior to everything. The Son is a creature and does not exist prior to his origination. For Eunomius the ideas of "generation" and "creation" are identical. The Son is distinct from all other creatures in that he is the immediate creation of the Father, while everything else, including the Holy Spirit, is created indirectly, *through* the Son. Therefore, the Son is similar to the Father with a "primary similarity" – in the same way that a completed work bears the reflection of the artist. He is the image or stamp of the energy and will of the Almighty.

ST. BASIL

When the opponents of the Creed of the Council of Nicaea were confronted with the resurgence of Arianism, the inadequacy of their irresolute pronouncements was immediately evident. The anti-Nicenes who had remained within orthodoxy became alarmed and their anxiety was expressed first by the movement of the *homoiousians*, a movement concentrated around St. Basil. The teaching of the *homoiousians* was first set forth at the Council of Ancyra in 358 when the fathers stated that they "wanted to express the Creed of the Catholic Church as thoroughly as possible," hoping at the same time to introduce into this explanation "something of their own." This new element "of their own" was the concept of the kinship or the unity by relation – γνησία – of the Only-Begotten Son and the Father. This was a milder form of consubstantiality. The main concern of the fathers of Ancyra was not to emphasize the separateness and distinction of the persons but to make clear their commonness and unity. By stressing the mystery of the Sonship, St. Basil – who was apparently the sole author of the doctrinal "Epistle of the Council" – distinguished the "generating energy" of the Father from his "creating energy." In the act of generation not only the will and power of the Father are revealed but his "essence" also is made manifest. What is essential in generation is likeness by essence. Being a father means being the father "of a like essence."

St. Basil also tried to define the concept of ὑπόστασις and the in - dividuality of the Divine Persons. He writes that it is necessary to consider the Son "as an independent 'hypostasis', different from the Father." As the *homoiousian* theologians later explain, in using the word "hypostasis" as well as the word "person," they wanted to express the "independently and actually existing properties" of the Father, Son, and Holy Spirit and they also wanted to avoid Sabellian Modalism in doing this. Although they were not always precise, they tried to main - tain a distinction between the concepts of *essence* and *hypostasis*, the latter term which was understood as the individual existence of an essence. The "individuality" of the Second Person is his Sonship and his generation from the Father. The unity of the Persons was designated by the common term "Spirit." This theological system on the whole was a successful refutation of Arianism, although the *homoiousians* weakened its impact by their anathema against the term ὁμοούσιος, a term which in their understanding implied the identity of Father and the Son.

St. Basil's main contribution to theology is his definition and explication of the Trinity. The Nicene teaching on the unity of the Divinity, expressed by the word ὁμοούσιος, was more clearly devel -

oped than the idea of the Divine Trinity, which had been given less emphasis. This was the reason that the Nicene fathers were accused, unjustly, of Sabellianism. Since the concepts *essence* and *hypostasis* were considered to be identical, there was no word sufficient to express the nature of the "three" which had been left undefined. The concept of "person" had not been clearly elaborated at this time. Indeed, the classical world did not know the mystery of personal being and in the classical languages there was no word which exactly designated individual personality. The Greek word πρόσωπον meant mask rather than person and, moreover, it was tainted through its association with Sabellianism. Therefore, St. Basil considered that it was inadequate and dangerous to speak of "three persons" and not of "three hypostases." "Person" was too weak, as was also the Latin *persona*. Indeed, St. Jerome experienced the controversy personally – he came under suspicion in Antioch for his refusal to confess "three hypostases." He avoided the new term of what was to him "three substances" and confessed instead one substance and three persons. It is only after the work of St. Gregory of Nazianzus, who identified the concepts of hypostasis and person, and after the Second Ecumenical Council in 381 that an agreement was finally reached between the Greek East and the Latin West on theological terminology. But by the fifth century St. Augustine was objecting to Cappadocian theology and searching for new paths in his *De Trinitate*.

For St. Basil the only way to overcome the indefiniteness of Trinitarian terminology was by distinguishing and opposing the terms οὐσία and ὑπόστασις. It had to be logically demonstrated that these were not just different words but distinct concepts. The term ὑπόστασις had been used in the past to distinguish the three in the Holy Trinity, especially by Origen and by Dionysius of Alexandria. For them, however, ὑπόστασις designated almost the same as οὐσία, and they considered that, as a definition, it was too strong and that it com - promised the unity of essence, honor, and glory. Bolotov has correctly remarked that "the teaching of three natures and three essences lies hidden behind the radiant concept of three hypostases." Therefore, when the fathers of the Council of Ancyra began to talk about three hypostases they were immediately accused of "tritheism." Under the direction of St. Athanasius the Council of Alexandria in 362 declared that both forms of expression had the same meaning. This, however, did not resolve the problem. Both terms had to be defined and established within an integral conceptual system. It was not possible to be satisfied with classical philosophical terminology because its vocabulary was insufficient for theology. Classical terms and concepts had to be reshaped. This task was undertaken by the Cappadocians, and first of all by St. Basil.

St. Basil speaks most frequently about the Three. What he calls *hypostasis* is really closer in meaning to *ousia* or Aristotle's "first es - sence" – πρώτη οὐσία. At the same time the term οὐσία – essence –

becomes identical to the Aristotelian term of "second essence" – δευτέρα οὐσία, which is used to signify common or generic being. It designates the qualitative characteristics of an object – "what it is" – in distinction to its concrete modes of existence – "how it is." St. Basil refers to this as μορφή. In this way the concept *ousia* becomes similar to the concept "nature" – φύσις. For St. Basil, however, *ousia* does not designate only common features which are secondary or derived, or which are differentiated and distinguishable by quality. Οὐσία primarily refers to the indivisible numeric unity of Divine Being and Life – οὐσία is being.

The formula "three consubstantial hypostases" was not entirely new. The innovation of the Cappadocians consisted in freeing familiar concepts from their previous ambiguity. Most importantly, a clear distinction was made between the concepts *ousia* and *hypostasis*. St. Basil sees these as opposites, as "that which is general" in distinction to "that which is particular" and belongs to an individual. "If I must state my views," he writes, "οὐσία – essence – is related to ὑπόσ – τασις – hypostasis – in the same way that the general is related to the particular." St. Basil clearly explains himself in a letter to his brother, St. Gregory of Nyssa. This letter's authenticity has been questioned. It may still prove authentic and, even if not, the thought here is identical to St. Basil's. This letter is an important document in the history of theology because it sets forth St. Basil's doctrinal beliefs. He begins by pointing out that there are different kinds of names and definitions. "Some names, which are used about objects which are multiple and can be counted, have a meaning which is common to many objects. An example of such a name is man. Whoever says this word designates by this name a common nature. This name is not used to specify or designate some one man. Peter is not more 'man' than Andrew or John or James. The common nature of the object being designated extends to everything that can be signified by the same name. Therefore it must be subdivided so that we can recognize Peter or John, and not man in general. Other names have a particular or individual meaning. They refer not to the common nature of the object which they designate but to the object's distinguishing properties, which are not shared by other objects which are similar to it. An example of such a name is Paul or Timothy. Such words do not refer to a common nature, but name certain specific objects and separate them from their collective sig - nificance. Therefore we can say that an 'hypostasis' is a proper name. The meaning of the word 'man' is not definite, and when we use this word we convey a general idea. Although this word indicates the nature of an object, it does not designate a real object by its proper name. In using the word Paul we point to the proper nature of the object we are naming. Thus, hypostasis is not a concept of indefinite essence, and it does not designate an object by the elements it has in common with other objects. Hypostasis is a concept which represents an object by its visual and distinctive properties, and gives form to that which is general and undefined in a given object." In other words, the noun οὐσία – essence – refers to a certain group of characteristics which are common or generic – *homogeneous.* Within this group of common elements the "hypostatic" names single out "that which is particular." They define something individual – "a certain man" – "by its particular features." By increasing the number of features they narrow the range of the concept. In doing this these names concentrate attention on that which actually exists.

Hypostasis – ὑπόστασις – is the "distinguishing sign of individ - ual existence." St. Basil takes this grammatical and logical idea and "transfers it to divine dogma." In the first place, "every idea about the Being of the Father" must be identically and immutably true for the Son and the Spirit. This is necessary because of the "consubstantiality" – ὁμοουσία – and because of the unity of essence and Divinity of the Godhead, because of the "very Being of God." This truth is contained "not only in some one individual thought," for "Divine Being is higher than any thought." It is also expressed in the many names of God, all of which are equally and identically applicable to the Three. In the second place, the Trinity is not only called "Three," but *is* Three. The names of the Trinity are "hypostatic," that is, they designate what is real and actual. "Therefore," writes St. Basil, "we confess that the Divinity has one essence, and we do not express differing concepts of Divine Being. We also confess individual hypostases so that our ideas about the Father, Son, and Holy Spirit are clear and unblurred. For if we do not recognize the distinguishing features of the Fatherhood, the Sonship, and the Sanctification, we confess only the general concept of Divine essence, and it is impossible for us to correctly set forth the teachings of our faith."

For St. Basil Scripture has revealed to us that One God has the names Father, Son, and Spirit. These names are distinguished not by general features, nor by degrees of divinity, glory, honor, or cognos - cibility – as was done by Arius and the subordinationists in general, especially by Origen. These names are distinguished by incom - mensurable and "unmerged" ontological characteristics. They maintain the completeness of "substantial" or "essential" definitions but also enrich them by adding new ontological features. Thus it is necessary to say "God the Father, God the Son, and God the Holy Spirit." "Until we reach a particularized conception of the individual qualities of Each, it is impossible for us to properly glorify the Father and the Son and the Holy Spirit."

St. Basil insists on the confession of three hypostases and is not satisfied by the acknowledgement of "three persons." The concept "person" lacks the definiteness which "hypostasis" has in its very etymology. St. Basil claims that whoever does not use the expression "three hypostases" is confessing only a distinction of persons. St. Basil tries to exclude the possibility of sequential transformation from the concept of hypostasis by insisting that Each of the Three has "its own Being."

St. Basil's teaching, despite its logical structure, is not entirely free from ambiguity. It is not without reason that his contemporaries accused him of splitting up the Trinity, and even of tritheism. St. Basil's trinitarian theology can in fact produce such an impression if it is limited to his opposition of the general to the particular, and if this is considered to be self-sufficient and definitive. However, St. Basil never states that this opposition exhausts the mystery of the Divine Trinity and Unity. Instead, he uses it as the basis for a clear theological terminology which strengthens ideas by giving them form. For St. Basil, this opposition is only formal and logical. It is true that the examples he uses to elucidate his thought seem to entail division, and not merely distinction, and it is questionable that the three Divine hypostases can be strictly compared to three men. The basis of the theological problem is not the fact that the three hypostases must be enumerated but the fact that these Three are united in One God. It is necessary not only to demonstrate the hypostatic nature and ontological stability of the distinctions within the Trinity, but first of all it must be shown that these are the forms of a single Divine Being. The concept hypostasis must be delimited not only from "mode" or "person" in the Sabellian sense but also from "individual."

One God is knowable in a Trinity of hypostases, not of modes – as in the teaching of Sabellius – and not of individuals. St. Basil understands that an hypostasis is not the same as an individuality, and he is not satisfied by general references to "distinguishing features." It is clear that not every distinguishing feature is hypostatic simply by virtue of its particular definiteness. While it is true that hypostases are differentiated by their distinguishing features, it is not easy to logically separate "hypostatic" features from other distinguishing features. There are no clear boundaries between distinctions that are "accidental" – κατά συμβεβηκός – and "hypostatic." The fact that there can be nothing "ac - cidental" in the Divine Being does not resolve the problem. These distinguishing features have been devised by man, and many of them define God in terms of his activity in creation and salvation. In a certain sense these are "accidental" with respect to Divine Life. It is these features which have led men into the error of subordinationism, in which the *oikonomic* distinctions of the manifestations or actions of the hypostases are considered proof of their ontological inequality.

Hypostatic distinctions, however, were established not by logic but by experience and Revelation. A logical structure has only been superimposed on the testimony of Revelation in order to give it form. For St. Basil "it is enough for us to contemplate the names which we have received from sacred Scripture and to avoid innovations. Salvation is not in devising names but in truly confessing the Divine Being in which we believe." The task of theology is therefore to explain the names of the Trinity as revealed in the Word of God. Logical systems are a means for achieving this.

God is single by nature and "unity is present in the very foundation of his essence." Such unity, wholeness, and concentration of Being and Life, such complete "simplicity," is proper only to God. Therefore it is necessary to enumerate the Divine Hypostases in an orthodox way, "not by addition, not by going from one to many by saying one, two, and three, or first, second, and third." When the Lord taught us about the Father, Son, and Holy Spirit "he did not name them by counting, for he did not say "I baptize you in the name of the first, second, and third, or in one, two, and three'. Instead he gave us the knowledge of the truth in the Holy Names." The abstract form of the number three does not account for the concrete truth of the Tri-Unity which is contained in the Names. In order to form a created unity many things are put together. A created unity is a derivative and a sum. It is not simple and it can be divided into many things. The components of this kind of "unity" and "plurality" are ontologically distinct and independent. This is connected with the logical abstractness of "limited number" as a formal device. In theology this problem is not a matter of the formal interrelationship of numbers. The Divine Unity is realized fully and integrally as an immutable and indivisible Trinity. The Trinity is a perfect unity of essence and being. It is not an abstract formula of triunity but a specific Triunity which is revealed to us in the doctrine of the Father, Son, and Holy Spirit. St. Basil therefore opposes "enumeration" – whether it is subordinate or consecutive – with the Names. The knowledge of these Names, which designate ontological relations or states, leads us to a knowledge of the perfect Unity.

St. Basil writes that "there is much which separates Christianity from the errors of paganism and Judaism but in the Gospel of our salvation there is no doctrine more important than faith in the Father and the Son." In Christianity God is revealed not only as a creator but also as a Father of the Only-Begotten Son. The name Father reveals the Divine generation and Sonship, and also reveals the Spirit, who proceeds from the Father. Thus the name Father reveals the mystery of the Trinity, which is not a formal Triunity but is three separate hypostases – the Father, the Son, and the Holy Spirit. St. Basil always designates the hypostatic features within the Divine Life by the names which have been received through Revelation – the Fatherhood, the Sonship, and the Sanctification. In this he differs from St. Gregory of Nazianzus, who defines the hypostatic attributes more formally as Ungeneratedness, Generation, and Procession. And he differs from his brother, St. Gregory of Nyssa, who uses the terms Ungeneratedness, Only-Begottenness, and Being through the Son. The names of the Trinity reveal the mystery of Divine Unity. "Unity," writes St. Basil, "is present in the very idea of their οὐσία – their 'essence'." Although there is a difference in the number and properties of each, Unity is contained in the very idea of the Divinity. This is because a single "principle," a single "source," a "single cause of Divine Being" is inherent in God. The Father is the principle and cause of the Son who is generated and the Spirit who proceeds. The Father is the central point of Divine Being and Life. The causality contained within Divine Life is eternal, for everything in the Divinity is unchanging and immutable. The opposition of "that which causes" to "that which is caused" and the distinction of "first" and "second" are meaningful only in the context of our process of reasoning. They designate the order in which we are able to comprehend the Divinity. In the Divine Hypostases "there is nothing which has been added, nothing which is independent from or differs from the Divine nature. This nature cannot be separated from itself by the insertion of something extraneous. There is no empty or unoccupied space to interrupt the Unity of Divine Essence or to split it apart with empty intervals." On the contrary, between the Divine Hypostases there is "a certain incomprehensible and ineffable relationship," "an uninter-rupted and indissoluble relationship," "a relationship of essence," and "a relationship of nature." The wholeness of Divine nature reveals the unity and identity of Divine Being. St. Basil expresses the relationship of the hypostases by saying that "by his essence God is consubstantial with God by his essence." Our conceptions about God must therefore also be integral and unbroken. "Whoever conceives of the Father at the same time conceives of the Son. Whoever thinks about the Son does not separate the Son from the Spirit."

St. Basil expresses the unbroken and undiminishing unity of Divine Life with the word "consubstantiality" – ὁμοούσια. For him this Nicene term signifies not only complete coincidence, not only the identity of the divine properties and attributes of the Three Hypostases, and not only "similarity in everything" or "similarity in essence." Most importantly it designates the "mutual relationship" of the Three and the ineffable Unity of the Trinity. This is later referred to as "inter-penetration" – περιχώρησις.

St. Basil is more concerned with the urgent issue of bringing the *homoiousians* to an understanding of the *homoousian* doctrine than he is with the concerns of the Christological problem of the two natures. In fact he does not address the issue of Christology from a polemical perspective. In general St. Basil's language about the Logos is tra-ditional. He uses such terms as ἐνσωμάτωσις, σάρκωσις, and ἐναν-θρώπησις. In one instance St. Basil comes quite close to Antiochene theology. In his *Homily on Psalm 45* St. Basil writes that "the flesh of Christ is the 'bearer of the Godhead', sanctified through union with God" – τάχα τὴν σάρκα λέγει τὴν θεοφόρον, ἁγιασθεῖσαν διὰ τῆς πρὸς τὸν θεὸν συναφείας. St. Basil concerns himself more with the distinctions of the human and divine in Christ rather than with the unity of Christ's person. For St. Basil there is no suffering in the Godhead itself – suffering is ascribed either to the flesh, to the soul, or to the flesh endowed with a soul. St. Basil emphasized the reality of Christ's human soul – it was the subject of grief, weariness, anxieties, cares. But the human soul in Christ did not experience things that could darken the "purity of our life." St. Basil also rejected the idea that Christ was unaware of the hour and day of the second coming and the judgment – Christ knew but his knowledge came from the Father.

The Anomoeans and the supporters of the *homoiousian* doctrine – the Third Formula of Sirmium in 358 – met with hostility and oppos - ition. The *homoiousians* were forced to replace the expression "of like essence" – ὁμοιούσιος – with the ambiguous "like in everything" – ὅμοις κατὰ πάντα. Although St. Basil signed the so-called "Dated Creed," he insisted on specifying what he understood by "like in every - thing" – "that is, not only by desire, but by hypostasis and essence." He anathematized those who limited this likeness "to any one thing." This "Dated Creed" – the Fourth Formula of Sirmium in 359 – was largely a repetition of previous doctrinal statements but it also con - tained a particular prohibition against the use of the term "essence" – οὐσία – in defining God. The authors of the creed justified themselves by claiming that this expression was not found in Scripture and that it could lead to error among the faithful. Later the explanatory κατὰ πάντα – "in everything" – was omitted from the new creed, and the generation of the Son was declared inaccessible to human understanding. The prohibition against the term οὐσία was repeated and a new prohib - ition against ὑπόστασις was added. Thus, from the testimony of un - orthodox groups we learn that those who were orthodox deviated from the *homoiousian* formulas. This was the opinion of the supporters of the Creed of the Council of Nicaea. St. Hilary of Poitiers, exiled to the East for his role in the struggle against Arianism in Gaul, saw in the Council of Ancyra and the *homoiousian* doctrine a light in the darkness and a ray of hope. In his interpretation "of like essence" meant the same as the Nicene term "of one essence" – ὁμοούσια – that is, unity of na - ture, but not person. In his writings about the councils St. Athanasius admitted that "it is not necessary to treat people like Basil (of Ancyra) as enemies. They should be considered as brothers who differ from us by one word alone but who think the same as we do." Although by itself the concept of "like essence" is vague and inadequate, when qualified by the affirmation of generation "from the essence," it is equal to "consubstantiality" – ὁμοούσια – in the Nicene sense. The expression "like in everything" is found in the writings of Alexander of Alexandria, and St. Athanasius himself had used it earlier to elucidate "consubstantiality" – ὁμοούσια.

ST. GREGORY OF NAZIANZUS

The Church has given St. Gregory of Nazianzus the title "Theo - logian of the Trinity." This is appropriate for him not only because he spent his whole life defending the orthodox doctrine of the Trinity against false and heretical teachings but also because for him the contemplation of the Trinity is the ultimate goal of all spiritual life.

Much of St. Gregory's doctrine of the Trinity is developed from the teaching of St. Basil, whom he recognized as his "teacher of dogma." St. Gregory uses St. Basil's terminology in his own theology but in a more exact and structured way. He does not hesitate to "devise new names" when it is necessary for him to be clear and orthodox. St. Gregory is also influenced by St. Athanasius, especially in his doctrine on the divinity of the Holy Spirit. St. Gregory's basic premise is that "the Trinity is in truth a Trinity." "In truth" means in reality. The name of the Trinity, he writes, "does not enumerate several unequal things, but designates a totality of things which are equal to each other," united by and in nature. St. Gregory constantly emphasizes the complete unity of the Divinity. "The perfect Trinity is composed of three perfect elements." "As soon as I think about One," he writes, "I am en - lightened by Three. As soon as I distinguish Three, my mind is elevated to One. When I conceive of One of the Three, I still consider It as a whole."

St. Gregory avoids trying to explain the mystery of the Trinity by drawing analogies to the created world. The source of the spring, the spring itself, and the flow of the spring are not separate in time, and even when these three properties are distinguished it is clear that they are all a single phenomenon. St. Gregory writes, however, that he does "not want to propose that the Divinity is a spring which never ceases (this is in distinction to Plotinus) because this comparison involves a numerical unity." The distinction among the waters of a stream exists "only in our way of thinking about it." St. Gregory is aware that analogies from the created world are not helpful in the sense that they always contain "the idea of motion" or deal with "imperfect and fluc - tuating natures."

Triunity is an interpenetration or motion within the Divinity. St. Gregory echoes Plotinus when he states that the Trinity is "over - flowing" but he qualifies this. "We do not dare to call this process an excessive effusion of good, as did one of the Hellenistic philosophers who, when speaking about the first and second causes, referred to an 'overflowing cup'." St. Gregory rejects this interpretation of Divine Being because it involves uncaused, independent motion. For St. Gregory the Triunity is a manifestation of Divine Love. God is love and the Triunity is a perfect example of "unity of thought and internal peace." The complete unity of the Trinity is primarily expressed by the fact that Its existence is unconditionally outside of time. God is eternal by nature and is beyond sequence and divisibility. It is not enough to say that God has always been, is, and will be. It is better to say that God is because he "contains within himself the whole of being, which has no beginning and will never end." "If there has been One from the beginning, there have also been Three."

The being of the Father and the generation of the Only-Begotten coincide exactly but also without confusion. "There should be no one so zealous in his love for the Father that he would deny him the at -

tribute of being a Father. For whose Father can he be if we consider that he is separated not only from creation but also from the nature of his own Son! One should not detract from his dignity as a Source, since this belongs to him as a Father and Generator." "When I call him a Source, do not imagine that I am referring to a source in time, or that I am presuming an interval between the Begettor and the Begotten. Do not separate their natures or falsely assume that there is something existing to separate these two co-eternities abiding within each other." The generation of the Son and the procession of the Holy Spirit should be considered to have taken place "before there was time." The Father never began to be a Father in time since his very being had no begin - ning. He "did not take being from anyone, not even from himself."

Although the hypostases are co-eternal and superior to time, they are not independent of each other. The Son and the Spirit "have no beginning in relation to time" but they are "not without an ultimate Source." The Father, however, does not exist before them because neither he nor they are subject to time. The Son and the Spirit are co-eternal but, unlike the Father, they are not without a Source, for they are "from the Father, although not after him." This mysterious causality does not entail succession or origination. Nothing within the Trinity ever comes into being or originates because the Divinity is completion, "an endless sea of being." St. Gregory is aware that this distinction is not easy to comprehend and that it can be confusing to "simple people." "It is true that that which has no beginning is eternal, but that which is eternal is not necessarily without a source, if this source is the Father."

For St. Gregory the complete and immutable unity of the Divinity determines the consubstantiality, the "identity of essence," of the hypostases of the Trinity. But the distinctions of each hypostasis do not disappear within the Divine Unity. The unity of the Divinity means an identity of essence and a monarchy that is from the Father and to the Father. The influence of Platonism is evident in the description of this "dynamic" unity. In St. Gregory's theology this dynamic aspect is dominant, and in this respect he is closer to St. Athanasius than to St. Basil.

Although St. Gregory conceives of the basic difference between "essence" and "hypostasis" as the difference between the general and the particular, he makes relatively little use of this concept. "What we hold in honor is monarchy," writes St. Gregory. "Not a monarchy which is limited to one person (this is in distinction to Sabellius), but one which is composed of an equality of nature, a unity of will, an identity of motion, and a convergence to a one, single Whole of those elements which are from this One. This is impossible in a created nature." Everything which the Father has belongs also to the Son, and every - thing which belongs to the Son belongs to the Father, so that "nothing is particular because everything is held in common. Their very being is common and equal, although the being of the Son is from the Father."

The individual properties of the Three are immutable. These "properties" – ἰδιότητες – "do not distinguish essence, but are distin - guished within one essence." In St. Gregory's understanding the concepts "hypostasis" and "property" are nearly the same. He also uses the expression "three Persons" – τρία πρόσωπα – which St. Basil avoids. St. Gregory is responsible for developing a theological terminology which is close to Western usage through his identity of hypostasis and person – τρεῖς ὑποστάσεις ἤ τρία πρόσωπα. St. Gregory also differs from St. Basil in his definition of the individual properties within the Trinity. He avoids the terms "Fatherhood" and "Sonship" and does not describe the personal attribute of the Spirit as "sanctity." He usually defines the properties of the hypostases as un - generatedness, generation, and procession – ἀγεννησία, γέννησις, and ἐκπόρευσις. Possibly he uses the term *procession* to designate an in- dividual property of the Father in order to put an end to the speculation of the Eunomians that "ungeneratedness" defines the essence of the Divinity. St. Gregory takes this word from Scripture, from *John* 15:26 – ὅ παρά τοῦ πατρὸς ἐκπορεύεται, in the hope of avoiding pointless arguments on the "fraternity of the Son and the Spirit." St. Gregory also attempts to forestall possible efforts to explain the exact meaning of these terms through analogics with the created world. Only the Trinity Itself knows "the order It has within Itself." How is the Son generated? How does the Spirit proceed? Divine generation is not the same as human generation. It is impossible to equate things which cannot be compared. "You have heard about generation. Do not attempt to determine how it occurs. You have heard that the Spirit proceeds from the Father. Do not try to find out how." "How? This is known by the Father who generates and the Son who is generated, but it is veiled by a cloud and inaccessible to you in your shortsightedness."

The hypostatic names express the mutual relationship of the persons – σχέσεις. The three persons are three modes of being, insep - arable and yet not confused, each "existing independently." They cannot be compared in such a way that one can be said to be greater or less than the others. Neither is one before or after the others. "The Sonship is not an imperfection" in comparison with the Fatherhood, and "procession" is not less than "generation." The Holy Trinity exists in complete equality. "All are worthy of worship, all have dominion, they all share a single throne and their glory is equal."

St. Gregory clearly distinguishes the "two natures" of Christ. One nature is "subject to suffering" and the other is "immutable and above suffering." This is the main thrust of his exegetical polemic against the Arians. "There was a time when he who is now despised by you was superior to you. Now he is a man, but once his nature was not compound. He remains that which he has always been, and he has assumed that which he previously did not have." St. Gregory examines the evidence of the two natures contained in the Gospel by considering the "mystery of the names," the mystery of the double names and the double symbols, the manger and the star. All names and all symbols, however, refer to one and the same," "One God from both."

St. Gregory is the first to use the word κρᾶσις to express the dual - ity of the two natures in the God-Man – "his natures and his names have been commingled and therefore they each are transformed into the other." St. Gregory writes: "He was a mortal, but also God; he was from the tribe of David, but he was also the Creator of Adam; he had a body, but was incorporeal; he was borne by the Virgin, but could not be contained; the cradle held him, but the Magi were led to him by the star. As a man he struggled, but he cannot be overcome and he defeated the tempter three times. As a mortal he was subject to sleep, but as God he tamed the seas. He was tired by his journeys, but he gave strength to the weak. He prayed, but who is it who hears the prayers of those who are perishing? He was a victim, but also the High Priest. He is the Priest, but he is God." He is One Person, One God-Man, One Christ, One Son, and "not two sons," which is the false teaching of Apollinarius. His two natures have been joined in essence and have penetrated each other. The Divinity remains immortal and humanity is "deified." The unity of the two natures in the person of Christ is based on the principle that "that which is strongest is victorious." By "deification" St. Gregory does not imply that human nature is transformed or that it undergoes transsubstantiation. What he means is that it is complete communion and interpenetration with the Divinity. In the God-Man human nature has been deified at its very source, for God himself has become human. By virtue of this "commingling" each name is now applicable to the other.

St. Gregory devotes a great deal of attention to the suffering and death of God, since through this he confesses the unity of natures in the Person of the God-Man. For this reason St. Gregory insists on the name Θεοτόκος – "Bearer of God." "Anyone who does not recognize that Mary is Θεοτόκος is estranged from the Divinity." This will be - come the very issue of the Nestorian controversy – is the Blessed Mother *Theotokos* or *Christotokos*? The reason for this is that deifica - tion is possible for mankind only through the humanity of the Logos and the Logos' consubstantiality with mankind. In the Logos humanity is deified through commingling with God.

The term "of like essence" was used in spite of the fact that as a philological device it was awkward, for, as Aristotle had demonstrated, "likeness" refers to the "qualities" or properties of objects, not to their "essence." In dealing with a unity of essence it is necessary to speak about identity and not likeness. This had been pointed out by St. Athanasius. But here the meaning of "like essence" was related to "one essence" in a way that a recognition of an "identical essence" is a recog - nition of "one essence." In the first case it is the separateness of the compared elements which is being emphasized. After the Council of Alexandria in 362, which was presided by St. Athanasius, the question was again raised as to the meaning of the concepts οὐσία and ὑπόσ -

τασις. After heated argument, it was recognized that the same orthodox truth is professed by those who speak about "one hypostasis" in the sense of a "single essence" and the "identity of nature," and those who teach "three hypostases" with "one ultimate principle," in order to express the knowledge of the Trinity "not only in name, but as truly existing and enduring."

After the Council of Alexandria the expressions "of one essence" and "from the essence of the Father" entered the theological usage of many of the eastern churches – for example, in Laodicea, Antioch, Cappadocia. At the same time, the distinction of the concepts and terms οὐσία and ὑπόστασις as something general and something individual was affirmed. The historical and doctrinal achievement of the great Cap - padocians consists in their justification and propagation of this new usage. They were "the trinity which glorified the Trinity." The formula "one essence and three hypostases – μία οὐσία, τρεῖς ὑποστάσεις – has been maintained in general Church usage since their time. Unex - pectedly, much time and labor was required to prove to the West the validity of this formula and its identity with the time-honored Latin expression *tres personae*. St. Gregory of Nazianzus writes that "because of the poverty of their language and its lack of designations, the Westerners cannot distinguish between *essence* and *hypostasis*." Both were expressed in Latin as *substantia*. In the confession of *three hypo - stases* Westerners seemed to detect tritheism, a recognition of three substances or three gods.

ST. GREGORY OF NYSSA

St. Basil's younger brother, St. Gregory of Nyssa, has no definite terminology to describe the unity of the God-Man. Sometimes he speaks about συνάφεια, a close union, and about μίξις, a mingling or a combination, or κρᾶσις, a blending. He calls Christ the "Bearer of God" and sometimes he simply refers to ἕνωσις, a union or unity. St. Gregory of Nyssa's usage is frequently careless. He occasionally uses the term "mixture" to describe the organic unity of the body and συνάφεια to describe the indivisible unity of the Trinity. The way in which the unification of natures takes place remains incomprehensible to us but it may be partially explained by the co-existence of the body and the soul.

St. Gregory of Nyssa develops his doctrine of the full humanity of Christ in his polemic with the Apollinarians. He stresses that Christ's assumption of human nature is complete. "No Christian will say that the man who was united with God was only half a man but that his whole nature entered union with the Divine." After all, "anyone who lacks something, without which his nature is incomplete, cannot be called a man." This is vital for St. Gregory of Nyssa's understanding of the redeeming work of Christ. The Lord came and was incarnate for the sake of salvation. "It is not a body which perished but a whole man who had a complete soul. In fact, it is right to say that the soul perished even before the body." For St. Gregory of Nyssa "man" is the name of an essential nature and he emphasizes the integrity of the composition of man – "a body without a soul is a corpse and a soul without reason is a beast." In order to oppose the teaching of the Apollinarians St. Gregory of Nyssa stresses the identity of the flesh of Christ "with the rest of humanity." "We know what his body was composed of when he lived among people as a man." St. Gregory of Nyssa realizes that the corporeal nature of Christ is disturbing to many – "his human birth, his growth from infancy to maturity, his need to eat and drink, his weariness and need for sleep, his sorrow, tears, calumniation, trial, cross, death, and removal to the tomb – all these things which make up the mystery weaken the faith of people whose minds are not elevated." St. Gregory of Nyssa answers these doubts by developing an apology for human nature. None of the actions of Christ's life is unworthy of him because it is only base passions which are shameful. "God is born not into anything flawed but into human nature." The composition of man contains nothing which makes virtue impossible and there is nothing impure about birth itself. Voluptuousness and lust are impure but the birth of man into the world is not. "What can be unseemly about this mystery? God was united with human life through the very means which nature uses to fight against death." It is only passion, in the narrow sense of the word, that was not assumed by the Lord. He speaks frequently and clearly about the true corporeality of Christ in order to expose the false doctrine of the Apollinarians about the "heavenly flesh of Christ," which was their explanation of the mystery of the Incarnation. St. Gregory of Nyssa considered this explanation false because in their system creation would be brought no closer to the Creator and also because the Divinity has no need of deified flesh.

For St. Gregory of Nyssa the human nature of the Savior develops according to the norm established for mankind before the fall. Further - more, his humanity becomes deified through its union with God. This is the source of the salvation of human nature – it is its salvation, revivification, and restoration to its original state. St. Gregory of Nyssa writes that God the Logos "becomes flesh because of his love for mankind and he assumes our nature so that by mingling with the Divine humanity can be deified. In this way all the elements of our nature are sanctified." Once it is united with God human nature can raise itself to God's level, and that which ascends is that which has been raised up from destruction. "By commingling with the Divine, every - thing that is weak and corrupt in our nature also become Divine."

St. Gregory of Nyssa teaches not only the two natures in the God-Man but also the two wills and the *communicatio idiomatum.* "Christ existed always, not just in the time of *oikonomia* but also afterwards. But the human nature did not exist before or after but only during the *oikonomia,* for the humanity did not exist before the birth from the

Virgin nor did the flesh remain with its own properties after the ascent to heaven . . . Human nature is subject to change but the divine nature is unchangeable. The Godhead therefore remains unmoved in face of every change . . . but the human nature in Christ undergoes a change for the better, from perishable to imperishable." "We affirm that the Godhead was in him who suffered. We deny that the impassible nature became capable of suffering. Human nature takes its subsistence from the conjunction of an intellectual soul with a body . . . We affirm that the body in which he accepted his suffering, being mingled with the divine nature, became through that intermixture identical with the nature which assumed it." In commenting on a text from Scripture, St. Gregory of Nyssa speaks of that reality described by the *communicatio idiomatum* – "it is not meant that one person suffered and another person was honored by exaltation." In commenting on the Scriptural text "Not my will, but Thine, be done," St. Gregory of Nyssa writes that "there is a distinction between the divine and the human will, and he who made our sufferings his own utters, as from his human nature, the words which suit the weakness of humanity, but he adds the second utterance because he wishes the exalted will, the will that is worthy of God, to prevail over the human, for man's salvation. In saying 'Not my will' he indicated his manhood. In adding 'but Thine' he displayed the conjunction of his Godhead with that of the Father, and in that Godhead there is no difference of will because of the communion of nature."

St. Gregory of Nyssa attempts to demonstrate the truth of the Trinity by examining the nature of God. God is not mute, not *ἄλογος*. He therefore must have a Logos, *λόγος*. Because God is eternal his hypostatic Logos must also be eternal. This Logos must be considered to be living, to be "in life," otherwise it would not be hypostatic and have independent being. There is no distinction in the properties of the Father and the Logos. The Logos "differs from the One whose Logos he is." The very name of Logos indicates a relationship, since it neces - sarily entails that there is a Father of this Logos – "if this Logos were not the Logos of Someone, it would not be a Logos." The Logos and the One from whom the Logos is have separate hypostases. St. Gregory usually refers to the second hypostasis as the Son in order to emphasize the parallelism and interrelationship of the Divine names and to express both the indivisibility and the distinctness of the hypostases. "The very name of Father is a recognition of the hypostasis of the Only-Begotten."

In his definition of the properties of the hypostases St. Gregory of Nyssa differs somewhat from the other Cappadocians, especially from St. Basil, his brother. St. Gregory of Nyssa primarily distinguishes the Father and the Son as the Unoriginate and the Only-Begotten, *ἀγέννητος* and *μονογενής*. These names indicate two modes of being. He is not satisfied with stating that the Son is begotten but stresses the name Only-Begotten in order to distinguish his ineffable mode of being from that of the Spirit. St. Gregory of Nyssa is also not content with calling the hypostasis of the Spirit the "Sanctifier," as does St. Basil, nor is he satisfied with the term "procession," ἐκπόρευσις, which is used by St. Gregory of Nazianzus. St. Gregory of Nyssa considers that the distinguishing property of the Third Hypostasis is exactly that he is the third. He is from the Father through the Son – δι υἱοῦ. This through – διά – indicates the ontological status of the Spirit, not just his position within the Godhead. "Through," however, does not imply causality, which is the attribute of the Father, "from whom – ἐκ – the Trinity has its being." In this way St. Gregory of Nyssa emphasizes the single source of the Trinity.

THE HOLY SPIRIT

The theological movement of the fourth century had a Christological character. The focus of Church thought was the dual image of Christ as the God-Man and the Logos or Word Incarnate. The consubstantiality of the Son-Logos with the Father meant the con - fession of the completeness of the Divine nature in Christ, which was necessary for the understanding of the Incarnation as the basis for the salvation of mankind. The correlation of these dogmas was fully and clearly developed in the theological system of St. Athanasius. The denial of consubstantiality would invalidate the Redemption, which is based on the true union between creation and God. It was from this point of view that the doctrine of the Pneumatomachi, who detracted from or denied the consubstantiality and complete Divinity of the Holy Spirit, was debated and rejected. Since the Spirit is the principle and power which sanctifies and deifies creation, the sanctification which he brings is of no avail if he is not truly God. This movement also had its root in Arianism.

The doctrine of the Holy Spirit became the subject of debate about 350. This dogma was first examined in the works of St. Athanasius and later in the resolutions of the Council of Alexandria in 362. It was set forth in its entirety in the writings of the Cappadocians, especially with St. Gregory of Nazianzus. The elaboration of the doctrine of the Divinity of the Logos made a clear understanding of the significance of the Incarnation indispensable, but the problem of the manner in which the divine and human were united in Christ was not immediately raised. This doctrine was not developed until the Council of Chalcedon in 451, and more than two centuries of theological activity were still necessary before it was completely accepted.

APOLLINARIANISM

The struggle against Arianism was followed by another struggle – the struggle against Apollinarianism. Apollinarius of Laodicea was in the first years of his activity a zealous defender of the Nicene position. But even before 362 he had begun to express his own Christological views, apparently in order to counteract the teaching of Diodore of Tarsus, who at that time was the leader of the Antiochene school. Apollinarius tried to define the conditions in which the Incarnate Logos could be recognized as a complete union of divine and human natures within the person of Christ. Since he did not distinguish between "nature" and "hypostasis," Apollinarius saw in Christ not only a single person and hypostasis but also a single nature. "God and flesh made up a single nature, complex and composite." Unity of person, for Apol- linarius, is possible only in conjunction with unity of nature. A "complete unity" cannot be formed "from two complete entities." If God was united with a complete man, who consists of a spirit or intel - lect, soul, and body, then an irreconcilable duality would be formed. In the conception of Apollinarius, if the Logos assumed a human intellect, which has the properties of freedom and self-determination, then no true union would take place, for there would remain two center points, two ultimate principles. Redemption, which is the goal of the Incarnation, would not be achieved because it would be a man who died and not God as man. Furthermore, a human intellect, in maintaining its freedom and self-direction, would not be able to overcome sin within the soul. This is possible only for the Divine Intellect.

Apollinarius denied the presence of the complete triad of human qualities in the Incarnate Logos. He asserted that Christ did not assume a human "intellect," but that this was replaced by the Logos, which was united with an animate body. The Logos became flesh, but he did not become man. Apollinarius held that the animate body of Christ "co-existed" and indivisibly "grew together with" the Logos, who became the principle of action in it, and thus took on a new manner of exis - tence "in the unity of a complex incarnate Divine nature" – μία φύσις τοῦ θεοῦ λόγου σεσαρκωμένη. Apollinarius does not understand how "two complete components" can commingle and form a new and complete whole. It seems to him that if God is "completely" united with human nature in Christ, then Christ has two natures and the person of the God-Man is a unity only externally. Such a union cannot bring salvation. Apollinarius' reasoning rests on the premise that everything which is real and "complete" is also hypostatic – hence, each nature can be fully realized only in an individual person. Therefore, if the human nature of Christ is complete, he must contain a human person or hypostasis, but the unity of the person of the God-Man presupposes a unity of nature – μίαν φύσιν. In order to defend the unity of the person of the God-Man Apollinarius is forced to deny the full "completeness" of Christ's human nature. "An incomplete com - ponent united with a complete component does not result in a double nature." The other possibility is to deny the completeness of the Divinity in Christ. This Apollinarius does not accept because it inval - idates the truth of salvation. It seems to him, and not without reason, that this extreme position was the doctrine of the Antiochene fathers.

Apollinarius also considers that two intellects cannot be united since two sources of thought and two wills must always be in conflict. For him this is especially true because of the inclination of the human will to sin, and therefore he denies that Christ has a free and mutable human intellect. Christ assumes animate flesh only, only a body and a soul, and not a human "spirit" or "mind." He becomes flesh, not man. Apollinarius is a trichotomist. He holds that the flesh and the soul of Christ are human but that his "mind" – νοῦς – is the Divine Logos. Thus the humanity of Christ is only similar to ours, and not consub - stantial with it. Furthermore, Christ's animate body necessarily "co-exists" with the Divinity. It is an abstraction which has no independent existence apart from the Logos which assumes it. In effect Apollinarius denies any independence of action to the human nature in Christ, which is merely a tool of the Logos. His explanation of the union of that which is moved and its mover shows the influence of Aristotle.

St. Gregory of Nazianzus sharply attacked the teaching of Apollinarius. St. Gregory does not try to deny the premises of Apol - linarius' reasoning, nor does he argue with his identification of nature and person – φύσις and ὑπόστασις. Instead, St. Gregory of Nazianzus attacks his doctrine of salvation. St. Gregory tries to show that salva - tion is impossible in the terms which Apollinarius proposes because according to Apollinarius' conception no true union of the two natures takes place. "If Christ has flesh but no intellect," he exclaims, "then I am deceived. His body is mine, but whose soul does he have?" St. Gregory demonstrates that human nature is a unity and cannot be divided into parts.

Essentially the Apollinarians deny the human nature in Christ. "They deny his human nature and internal similarity to us by introducing this new idea of a likeness that is merely visible. This would purify only the visible part of us . . . When they say that his flesh is only as semblance and not real, this means that his flesh does not experience any of the things that are proper to us, and that his flesh is free of sin." St. Gregory concludes that "with such flesh the Divinity is not human." "Assuming flesh" without "assuming human nature" cannot bring redemption. "That which has not been assumed has not been healed, but that which is truly united with God is saved. If only a part of Adam fell, then he is completely saved only by complete union with him who has been born man in completeness." "Do not believe that our Savior has only the bones and sinews of human forms," St. Gregory writes, "behold a whole man and recognize his Divinity."

To the objection of Apollinarius that "two complete components cannot both be contained in one body," St. Gregory answers that this "co-presence" must not be understood only in the physical sense. It is true that bodies are impenetrable and that "a vessel with one capacity cannot hold two such natures." However, this is not true for things that are "intellectual and incorporeal." "I contain in myself a soul, and an intellect, and the gift of speech, and the Holy Spirit. Even before I existed the Father contained in himself this world, this totality of visible and invisible things, and also the Son and the Holy Spirit. This is the nature of everything that is conceptual, since such things are not corporeal and can be indivisibly united to things which are similar to them, and also to bodies. Our hearing can encompass many sounds and our sight perceives a multitude of features in visible objects, and this is also true of our sense of smell. Our senses do not limit each other or crowd each other out, and a tangible object is not made less by the great number of other objects."

The union of God and man is a mystery. We can approach an understanding of it only by means of our intellectual perception, which is what Apollinarius had attacked. Man's intellect has been formed in the image of God, and it is through this intellect that he can be united with God, the Highest Intellect, since that is what is "nearest to it and most like it." When two intellects are united, they do not lose their individuality but neither are they necessarily in conflict. The type of combination which the Apollinarians suggest would result in a purely external unity. "Their likeness resembles a mask worn at a theatrical performance," and in their conception God is not the God-Man but merely wears a "curtain of flesh." Their argument that the intellect is inclined to sin is also invalid because the flesh too is sinful. Is it not to heal these weaknesses that God takes on human nature? "If the worse element is assumed so that it is sanctified by Christ's assumption of the flesh, why is not the better element also assumed so that it may be sanctified through Christ's assumption of human nature? If the old mixture is leavened and becomes new, why cannot we also be leavened and be commingled with God, so that we may be deified through the Divinity?" It seems to St. Gregory that the reasoning of the Apol - linarians implies that the intellect is the only property of man which is condemned and beyond salvation. He therefore accuses them of granting too much dignity to man's physical nature. "You worship the flesh, for the man you propose has no intellect." For St. Gregory, on the contrary, even if the intellect is in need of healing, it is the property of man which is most open to salvation because it has been created in the image of God. "The renewal of the image" is the goal of redemption and the Logos comes to man as an Archetype to its image.

The Church's victory over Apollinarianism was an affirmation of human thought, of the capability of reforming and sanctifying human thought, of the affirmation of dogma. Apollinarianism is, in the deepest sense, a false anthropology, it is a false teaching about man and there - fore it is also a false teaching about the God-Man Christ. Apollin - arianism is the negation of human reason, the fear of thought − "it is impossible that there be no sin in human thoughts" − ἀδύνατον δέ ἐστιν ἐν λογισμοῖς ἀνθρωπίνοις ἁμαρτίαν μὴ εἶναι . And that means that human reason is incurable − ἀθεράπευτόν ἐστι − that is it must be cut off. The rejection of Apollinarianism meant therefore the fundamental justification of reason and thought. Not in the sense, of course, that "natural reason" is sinless and right by itself but in the sense that it is open to transformation, that it can be healed, that it can be renewed. And not only can but must be healed and renewed. Reason is summoned to the knowledge of God.

Apollinarius had many followers and the struggle against his teaching began at the Council of Alexandria in 362. About 370 a two volume treatise against Apollinarius was written by an unknown author and included among the works of St. Athanasius. At this same time Apollinarius was denounced by St. Basil and St. Gregory of Nazianzus. After a series of condemnations by various Church councils, Apollin - arianism was officially rejected at the Second Ecumenical Council in 381. In order to oppose Apollinarius the fathers of the fourth century, especially St. Gregory of Nazianzus and St. Gregory of Nyssa, de - veloped the orthodox doctrine of the unity of two natures in one hypostasis – it is the completeness of the human nature in Christ that makes salvation possible, for Christ is "one from two."

THE SECOND ECUMENICAL COUNCIL

The work of the Second Ecumenical Council – the First Council of Constantinople in 381 – is often neglected or underestimated. The Creed of Christianity comes from this council, not from the Council ot Nicaea. That which is usually referred to in the West as the Nicene Creed is in fact the Nicene-Constantinopolitan Creed. It was the Creed of the Universal Church, the Creed to which nothing could be added or subtracted or altered. The Second Ecumenical Council continued the work of the Council of Nicaea – after so many decades of Arian dominance the work of the Council of Nicaea was about to be confirmed, the Creed was to be expanded and altered in part, and the heretical schools of thought which were in existence were to be condemned. The uniqueness of the Second Ecumenical Council has been widely written about. Cardinal Orsi has pointed out that it was "a council of saints" – "perhaps there has not been a council in which has been found a greater number of Confessors and of Saints." Some who attended include St. Gregory of Nazianzus, St. Gregory of Nyssa, St. Meletius – who died during the council and was proclaimed saint by the council – St. Peter of Sebaste, St. Amphilochius of Iconium, St. Pelagius of Laodicea, St. Eulogius of Edessa, St. Cyril of Jerusalem, Diodore of Tarsus, Helladius of Caesarea in Cappadocia, Antiochus of Samosata, and Dionysius of Diospolis. The Second Ecumenical Council was presided at first by St. Meletius, bishop of Antioch, who was precisely the bishop of Antioch *not* in communion with Rome. He died out of communion with the Church of Rome, was proclaimed saint by the council, and is considered a saint by the Roman Church. Whether the Council of Constantinople intended itself to be an ecumen - ical council from inception is arguable – it was a local gathering of Eastern bishops; in fact, no diocese of the West was represented. The acts of the council have been lost and we therefore must rely only on the information contained in citations of the council. The fathers of the council refer to it as ecumenical – it was St. Gregory of Nazianzus who was troubled by the term "ecumenical" – St. Gregory became the second president of the council after the death of Meletius.

St. Gregory of Nazianzus was summoned out of his solitude in Seleucia to come to Constantinople to take part in the struggle against the Arians. When he went to Constantinople, it was one more time in his life that he did something "not by my own will, but by the coercion of others." His work in Constantinople was difficult. "The Church is without pastors, good is perishing and evil is everywhere. It is necessary to sail at night and there are no fires to show the way. Christ is sleeping." The see of Constantinople had been in the hands of the Arians for some time. St. Gregory writes that what he found there was "not a flock but only small traces and pieces of a flock, without order or supervision." St. Gregory began his ministry in a private house which was later made into a church and given the name *Anastasis* to signify the "resurrection of orthodoxy." Here he delivered his famous *Five Theological Orations*. His struggle with the Arians was often violent. He was attacked by murderers, his church was stormed by mobs, he was pelted with stones, and his opponents accused him of brawling and disturbing the peace. His preaching, however, was not without effect. "At first the city rebelled," he writes. "They rose against me and claimed that I was preaching many gods and not one God, for they did not know the orthodox teaching in which the Unity is contemplated as three, and the Trinity as one." St. Gregory was forced to struggle not only against the Arians but also he had to oppose the supporters of Apollinarius. He encountered further resistance from orthodox prelates, especially from Peter of Alexandria and the Egyptian bishops. When St. Gregory was elevated to the episcopal throne of the see of Con-stantinople, the Egyptians at first accepted him. But they then illegitimately consecrated Maximus the Cynic as bishop of Con-stantinople. St. Gregory later recalled the "Egyptian storm cloud" and Peter's duplicity with bitterness. Maximus was driven out but found a temporary shelter in Rome with Pope Damasus, who had a poor understanding of Eastern affairs. St. Gregory wanted to withdraw but the people held him back, exclaiming: "You will take the Trinity away with you!"

St. Gregory was victorious through the strength of his oratory, and towards the end of 380 the new emperor Theodosius entered the city and returned all the churches to the orthodox believers. Theodosius the Great was a Spaniard by birth who was educated in the Nicene faith. His long reign – until 395 – completed externally the triumph of orthodoxy in the Roman empire. Soon after becoming emperor Theodosius issued his famous edict which required all subjects to accept the orthodox faith. After his entrance into Constantinople Theodosius raised St. Gregory of Nazianzus to the patriarchal throne. The Arians, who had controlled

Constantinople for forty years, were driven from their churches and from the city.

To consolidate this fresh victory over the Arians Theodosius convened the council in May of 381. After the walk-out of thirty-six Semi-Arian Macedonians or Pneumatomachi, the council counted one hundred and fifty bishops. The question of the schism at Antioch came up and St. Gregory disagreed with the majority of prelates – St. Gregory sided with the Roman choice of Paulinus and not with the Meletians. The dissatisfaction which had long been building up against him suddenly burst out. Some churchmen were dissatisfied with leniency, since he had not requested the aid of the civil authorities against the Arians. St. Gregory had always been guided by the rule that "the mystery of salvation is for those who desire it and not those who are coerced." Other prelates were disturbed by the inflexibility of his doctrinal beliefs, and especially his uncompromising confession of the divinity of the Holy Spirit. Still others thought that his conduct was unbecoming to the dignity of his rank. "I did not know," St. Gregory writes ironically, "that I would be expected to ride fine horses or to make a brilliant appearance perched on a carriage, or that those who met me would treat me with servility, or that everyone would make way for me as though I were a wild beast." The question of the legality of St. Gregory's transfer from Sasima to Constantinople was also raised at the council. It was obvious that this was a pretext for intrigue against him. In great chagrin St. Gregory decided to give up his see and to abandon the council. He was bitter about leaving the "place of our victory" and his flock, which he had won to the truth by his actions and words. This bitterness never left him. On leaving Constantinople, St. Gregory wrote to Bosporius, bishop of Caesarea, "I will withdraw myself to God, who alone is pure and without deceit. I will retire into myself. The proverb says that only fools stumble twice on the same stone." He returned home exhausted both physically and morally and filled with bitter memories – "Twice I have fallen into your snares and twice I have been deceived."

St. Gregory sought rest and isolation but once again he was forced to take over the administration of the widowed church in Nazianzus, "forced by circumstances and fearing the attack of enemies." He had to struggle against the Apollinarians who had illegitimately established their own bishop in Nazianzus, and intrigues and quarrels began again. In desperation St. Gregory asked Theodore, the metropolitan of Tyana, to replace him with a new bishop and to remove this burden which was beyond his strength. He refused to attend any councils – "it is my intention to avoid all gatherings of bishops because I have never yet seen a productive outcome of any council, or any council which resulted in deliverance from evils rather than addition to them." He wrote to Theodore, "I salute councils and conventions, but only from a distance because I have experienced much evil from them." St. Gregory did not attain his freedom immediately. He was overjoyed when his cousin

Eulalius was finally invested as bishop of Nazianzus, and he retired from the world to devote the rest of his life to writing. He traveled to desert monasteries in Lamis and other places. He became weaker and frequently sought relief by bathing in warm water springs. The lyrics he wrote as an old man are filled with sadness. St. Gregory died in 389 or 390.

The Second Ecumenical Council which St. Gregory felt compelled to abandon because of intrigue was a council of harvest, of consol - idation, of confirmation, of identifying the unorthodox parties and anathematizing them, and of confirming the Creed of Christianity which still obtains in the Orthodox Church and is still the Creed of the Roman Catholic Church with the addition of the *Filioque*, an addition to the one Creed which still divides the Orthodox and Catholic Church. The Council confirmed rather than produced the Creed, for the text of "Constantinopolitan Creed" was actually completed after the Council of Alexandria in 362

The Second Ecumenical Council deleted from the Nicene Creed the expression "the Only-Begotten of the essence of the Father" – μονογενῆ τοῦτ ' ἔστιν ἐκ τῆς οὐσίας τοῦ πατρός· θεὸν ἐκ θεοῦ καί – and changed it to read "the Only-Begotten Son of God, begotten of Father before all worlds" – τὸν υἱὸν τοῦ θεοῦ τὸν μονογενῆ· τὸν ἐκ τοῦ πατρὸς γεννηθέντα πρὸ πάντων τῶν αἰώνων. Deleted was the "in heaven and on earth" after "by whom all things were made" so that the new version was simply "by whom all things were made" – δι ' οὗ τὰ πάντα ἐγένετο. Added to the Nicene Creed were "from heaven" after "came down" so that the final text read "came down from heaven" – κατελθόντα ἐκ τῶν οὐρανῶν, "by the Holy Spirit of the Virgin Mary" so that the Nicene text of "and was incarnate and was made men" became "and was incarnate by the Holy Spirit of the Virgin Mary, and was made man" – καὶ σαρκωθέντα ἐκ πνεύματος ἁγίου καὶ Μαρίας τῆς παρθένου, καὶ ἐνανθρω- πήσαντα, the entire statement of "he was crucified for us under Pontius Pilate" was added – σταυρωθέντα τε ὑπὲρ ἡμῶν ἐπὶ Ποντίου Πιλάτου, "and was buried" was not in the original Nicene Creed – καὶ ταφέντα, as was not "according to the Scriptures" – κατὰ τὰς γραφάς. Also not in the original Nicene Creed were "and sitteth on the right hand of the Father – καὶ καθεζόμενον ἐκ δεξιῶν τοῦ πατ- ρός, "again with glory" – καὶ πάλιν . . . μετὰ δόξης, and "whose kingdom shall have no end" – οὗ τῆς βασιλείας οὐκ ἔσται τέλος . The Nicene Creed simply had "And in the Holy Spirit" – Καὶ εἰς τὸ ἅγιον πνεῦμα. To this the Second Ecumenical Council added: "And in the Holy Spirit, the Lord, the Giver of Life, who proceeds from the Father, who together with the Father and the Son is worshipped and glorified, who spoke by the prophets. In one holy, catholic and apostolic Church. We acknowledge one baptism for the remission of sins. We await the resurrection of the dead, and the life of the world to come" – Καὶ εἰς τὸ πνεῦμα τὸ ἅγιον, τὸ κύριον, τὸ ζωοποιόν,

τὸ ἐκ τοῦ πατρὸς ἐκπορευόμενον, τὸ σὺν πατρὶ καὶ υἱῷ
προσκυνούμενον καὶ συνδοξαζόμενον, τὸ λαλῆσαν διὰ τῶν
προφητῶν. Εἰς μίαν ἁγίαν καθολικὴν καὶ ἀποστολικὴν ἐκκλη -
σίαν· ὁμολογοῦμεν ἓν βάπτισμα εἰς ἄφεσιν ἁμαρτιῶν· προσ -
δοκῶμεν ἀνάστασιν νεκρῶν καὶ ζωὴν τοῦ μέλλοντος αἰῶνος.
The original Nicene Creed appended an anti-Arian statement, a confes -
sional statement which is not appended to the Constantinopolitan
Creed. "And those who say there was a time when he was not, and he
was not before he was made, and he was made out of nothing, or out of
another hypostasis or essence, or the Son of God is created, or change -
able, or alterable – they are condemned by the holy, catholic and
apostolic Church" – τοὺς δὲ λέγοντας, ὅτι ἦν ποτε ὅτε οὐκ ἦν·
καὶ πρὶν γεννηθῆναι οὐκ ἦν· καὶ ὅτε ἐξ οὐκ ὄντων ἐγένετο· ἢ
ἐξ ἑτέρας ὑποστάσεως ἢ οὐσίας φάσκοντας εἶναι· ἢ κτιστόν,
ἢ τρεπτόν, ἢ ἀλλοιωτὸν τὸν υἱὸν τοῦ θεοῦ· ἀναθεματίζει ἡ
ἁγία καθολικὴ καὶ ἀποστολικὴ ἐκκλησία.

This Creed is an improvement on the Nicene Creed – it has taken
out the negative anathema to make the Creed a positive confession, it
has clarified that the Only-Begotten Son is "begotten" from the Father
rather than "from the essence" – ἐκ τῆς οὐσίας τοῦ πατρὸς in the
Nicene Creed, it has historicized the Incarnation with the addition of the
Virgin Mary and Pontius Pilate, it has placed greater emphasis on the
fact of the death of Christ with the addition of "crucified" and "buried,"
and it has acknowledged the sacred written tradition as well as the oral
tradition of Christianity with the addition of "according to the
Scriptures." The addition of the articles on the Holy Spirit, the Church
and Baptism, and the expectation of the resurrection of the dead and the
life of the world to come gives the Creed a fuller definition of the
Christian faith.

In addition to confirming and promulgating the Creed of
Christianity, the Second Ecumenical Council promulgated four canons.
Three additional canons were added by the local council of Constan -
tinople in 382. The first canon anathematized the Eunomians, the
Eudoxians, the Semi-Arians, the Pneumatomachi, the Sabellians, the
Marcellians, the Photinians, and the Apollinarians. The third canon is
later to be the source of great acrimony towards Constantinople on the
part of Rome and Alexandria, for that canon elevated the bishop of
Constantinople – "The Bishop of Constantinople, however, shall have
the prerogative of honor after the Bishop of Rome because
Constantinople is New Rome." This canon will surface again at the
Fourth Ecumenical Council as the Twenty-Eighth Canon of the
Council of Chalcedon, a canon which the bishop of Rome will refuse
to recognize. Pope Leo, strenuously objecting to the Twenty-Eighth
Canon of the Council of Chalcedon, claimed that the third canon of
Constantinople had never been brought to the attention of Rome
(*Patrologia Latina* 54, 1007). This canon sheds interesting light on the
perspective of the Eastern bishops regarding the "primacy" of Rome – it

was a primacy "of honor" based, it appears, on historical rather than theological reasons. At the request of the bishops Emperor Theodosius promulgated the decrees of the Second Ecumenical Council.

THE ROAD TO EPHESUS

Such is the Christological thought in general of the fourth century. However, it remained unclear how one should conceive and describe the unity of the representation of God Incarnate. In other words, how Divinity and humanity are united in Christ. This question in all its fullness had been posed already by Apollinarius (d.c. 390). He did not succeed in answering it. One could define Apollinarianism as a distinctive anthropological minimalism – the self-abasement of man, the abhorrence of man. Human nature is incapable of "deification." In the unity of God and Man, human nature cannot remain unchanged, cannot remain itself; it "coexists" with the Divinity of the Logos. And the human mind is excluded from this unity. The basic point for Apollinarius' opponents was precisely this doctrine of "co-existence." Apollinarians were refuted primarily as "Synousiasts" – from συν - ουσίαις. The *Synousiasts* were followers of Apollinarius who inter - preted his teaching in all its rigor and taught the consubstantiality – συνουσίωσις – of the flesh of Christ and his Divinity. They formed a kind of sect and were the real forerunners of Monophysitism. A Syrian *florilegium* has preserved 33 excerpts of Diodore of Tarsus' (d. c. 390) work *Against the Synousiasts,* some of the excerpts of which have been interpolated by the Apollinarians. Overcoming Apollinarianism stood for the rehabilitation, the justification of man. In this lies the whole sense of the Cappadocian polemic with Apollinarius. However, in this anthropological self-defense one could lose one's perspective and lapse into a certain anthropological maximalism.

This is what happened with Apollinarius' opponents from the Antiochene school, partly with Diodore of Tarsus (d.c. 390) and especially with Theodore of Mopsuestia (c. 350-428). For them, the image of Christ started to disintegrate. They asserted quite insistently the independence of human nature in Christ, thereby bringing God Incarnate too close to simple people, to "mere people." This was aided by the spirit of "Eastern" asceticism, which is primarily strong-willed, and which often led to a purely human heroism. The ideological, if not genetic, ties of this "Eastern" theology with Western Pelagianism, which was also born of a spirit of strong-willed ascetic self-affirmation, turned into a distinctive humanism.

Ultimately, the entire Antiochene school was also tempted by this very humanism. This temptation breaks through in Nestorianism. In the struggle with Nestorianism one discerns all the vagueness and imprecision of the Christological language of that time; that is, the shakiness of the entire system of Christological concepts. Words get tangled and split into two, and carry their thought away – the words have their own magic and power. Once again, a great exertion of analytical thought is needed to forge and strike concepts and terms which would not hinder, but rather help, identify and profess the truths of faith, as the truths of reason, so that it would be possible to speak of Christ the God-Man without ambiguity and contradiction. This theological work drags on for two centuries. The critique of Nestor - ianism will be developed by St. Cyril of Alexandria (d. 444) but it will not convince the "Easterners." On the contrary, it troubles them, not because they have all lapsed into the extremes of Nestorianism but because they fear the opposite extreme.

One has to confess that St. Cyril will not know how to find indisputable words and will not give precise definitions. This does not mean that his theological experiment is confused and ambiguous but he will not unite his theological perspicacity with the great talent for speaking which so distinguished the great Cappadocians. St. Cyril will be clearly short of words and through a fatal historical misunderstanding he will connect his theological confession with the disturbing formula, μία φύσις Θεοῦ Λόγου σεσαρκωμένη – One nature, Incarnate, of the Divine Logos. He will consider it the words of the great Athan - asius, while in actual fact it was Apollinarius' formula. In other words, the means for overcoming the Antiochene temptations will not be discovered in Alexandrian theology. Also not to be found is the strength to defend one's self from one's own temptations. This will be revealed in Monophysitism, which to a certain extent will speak St. Cyril's language. It is characteristic that the fathers of the Council of Chalcedon (451) will translate "Cyril's belief" into the language of Antioch. Alexandrian theology is threatened by the danger of *anthropological minimalism* and the temptation to dissolve, to extin - guish man in Divinity since the time of Origen (c. 185-c. 254). This temptation also threatens Egyptian monasticism – not so much the strong-willed kind as the meditative; not so much that which was tempering the will as that which was cutting off the will entirely. Later Monophysitism will find itself a favorable soil in this ascetic quietism. That is putting it briefly.

The Christological disputes begin with a clash of two theological schools. In actuality, this is a clash of two religions' *anthropological ideals*. With the Council of Chalcedon (the Fourth Ecumenical Council, 451) the history of Alexandrian Orthodoxy and Antiochene Orthodoxy will end, and a new epoch, the epoch of Byzantine theology *per se*, commences. And in it the varied tradition of the past becomes an integral synthesis. As in the epoch of the Arian troubles, the Church's solution anticipates a theological synthesis. Just as the Nicene Council only opened the disputes on Trinity, so will the Council of Chalcedon now open the Christological period in theology but will not close it. People also debate the Chalcedonian definition of faith, just as they debated the Nicene definition. This is only a theme for theology and the principle of faith must be disclosed in a creative and speculative theological synthesis.

The Christological disputes of the fifth century begin by chance and with a personal issue over the name Θεοτόκος, the Bearer of God or, as one usually and incorrectly translates into English, Mother of God. However, wide theological perspectives will immediately open up, as will the general issue of the sense of "Eastern" Antiochene theology. It will be only natural to move from a denunciation of Nestorius to a critique and analysis of the Christological views of his precursors and teachers Theodore and Diodore. St. Cyril will do this immediately after the Council of Ephesus (Third Ecumenical Council, 431). And the condemnation of Theodore of Mopsuestia, Ibas of Edessa (d.c. 457), and the Blessed Theodoret of Cyrus (d.c. 466) at the Fifth Ecumenical Council (Constantinople, 553) will be an entirely logical, though tragic, theological epilogue to the condemnation of Nestorius (d.c. 451) at the Council of Ephesus.

Nestorius is neither an outstanding nor an independent thinker; he is not even a theologian, properly speaking. Only external historical circumstances will move him to the center of a theological movement, mainly the fact that he will be Archbishop of Constantinople. Because of this his words will resound with significant power and will be heard everywhere. The whole significance of his theological pronouncements will reside in the fact that he is a typical one-sided Antiochene. The Nestorian disputes will concern not so much Nestorius himself as Anti - ochene theology in general. That is how the "Easterners" will under - stand St. Cyril. Hence, the "tragedy" of the Council of Ephesus. Almost immediately the question will be paradoxically formulated – it must be decided whether or not St. Cyril is correct in his critique of "Eastern theology." Experience shows that he was right, however debatable his own theological theses were – these he defends with a quick temper and irritation. St. Cyril correctly foresees the immanent dangers of Antiochene theology and points out the limits beyond which not only dubious orthodoxy begins but also direct error and heresy.

DIODORE OF TARSUS

St. Cyril sees Diodore of Tarsus as the forerunner of Nestorius, and with good reason: "Nestorius was the disciple of this Diodore." When living, Diodore was not tainted with suspicion; in the struggle with Arianism – with the *homoiousians* and the *Anomoeans* – he was a zealous defender of the faith. He was close to the Cappadocians, es - pecially St. Basil the Great, and after the Second Ecumenical Council (Constantinople, 381) he was proclaimed a "witness of the faith" for the Eastern diocese. Only at the height of the Nestorian disputes do the questions of Diodore's orthodoxy come up. However, he was never condemned at orthodox councils. He was excommunicated only by the Monophysites. One has to form an opinion about Diodore's theology from fragments. Only meagre remnants of his enormous literary legacy have come down to us. Be that as it may, we can say with assurance that in his struggle with the Apollinarians Diodore went too far. Not only did he repeatedly emphasize the "perfection" – that is, the completeness – of humanity in Christ, but he also sharply discerned and isolated in Christ the Son of God and Son of David, in which the Son of God resided, as in a temple. Therefore, he felt it was impossible to speak of the "two births" of the Logos. "The God-Logos did not endure two births, one before the ages and the other at the end, but was born of the Father in essence, while he who was born of Mary he established in the 'temple'. The God-Logos was not born of Mary – of Mary was born only a man similar to us. And the man who was born of Mary through grace became the Son. The Son, perfected before the ages, took in him who was descended from David, the Son of God, the Son of David." "For the flesh, which is of us, adoption, glory, and immortality is enough, for it became the temple of God the Logos." Diodore denies that he is introducing a "duality of sons." The Son of God is One, and the flesh "or man" taken by him is his temple and abode. What is important here is not so much the individual words or individual phrases because it is the very style and the inner tendency of thought that is characteristic. And in Diodore's representation Jesus' face undoubtedly doubled. He recognized if not "two sons," then in any case two subjects. From Diodore's premises, it was natural to draw further conclusions. They were indeed drawn by Theodore of Mopsuestia, with the rational directness characteristic of him.

CHAPTER TWELVE

THEODORE OF MOPSUESTIA

I

LIFE

Theodore of Mopsuestia (c.350-428) was born in Antioch about 350. He studied under the pagan sophist and rhetorician Libanius of An - tioch (314-393), who had taught at Athens, Constantinople, and Anti - och Theodore became friends with his fellow student John Chrysostom. It was John Chrysostom who persuaded Theodore to lead the life of an ascetic and a monk (Socrates, *Church History*, 6,3). Theodore and John left Libanius and entered the monastic school, the *Asketerion*, headed by Diodore, later to become bishop of Tarsus.

It appears that Theodore had known a certain woman named Herm - ione in Antioch. Memories of her besieged him while at the *Asketerion* of Diodore, and with these memories his love for her intensified. He left the monastic life for the love of Hermione. According the the Church historians Sozomen (c.400-c.450) and Hesychius of Jerusalem (d. after 451), it was John Chrysostom who wrote one letter (probably two) to Theodore titled *Ad Theodorum lapsum* (Migne, *Patrologia Graeca* 47, 277-316) to persuade him to return to monastic life. Hesychius' *Church History* is lost but a chapter from it was read at the Fifth Ecumenical Council (553) and survives in a Latin translation in Mansi 9, 248 ff. That section read at the Fifth Ecumenical Council claims that Theodore called the Savior "*hominem per vitae provectionem et passionum per - fectionem coniunctum Deo Verbo*." In any case, John Chrysostom's letter to his friend Theodore is noteworthy.

ST. JOHN CHRYSOSTOM'S
LETTER TO THEODORE OF MOPSUESTIA

"Who will give water to my head and a fountain of tears to my eyes? I weep and grieve not over the loss of a temple of stone but over a lost temple of the Holy Spirit. It stands there, robbed of its treasures, its gates wide open and unguarded so that every hostile passion might enter it. But I will not cease to mourn for it until its earlier radiance is given back to it. One thing you must not do. Do not doubt the pos - sibility of a return. To fall is human, but to remain fallen is devilish. But true repentance will wipe out every sin. Then return! Give up the joys of the world, even though they endure a hundred years, for Hell is eternal. And also eternal is the ineffable splendor of Heaven. Think of the example of the rich young Phoenix. He was a monk and also a priest. But he let himself be led astray by his relatives into a worldly life and various affections. Only some monks who knew him were able, through patience and discretion, to bring him back to the right way. The Apostle John was able, through love and gentleness, to make a saint of a robber who once had been his pupil. Therefore, do not despair of yourself! Make another beginning. Return! I will repeat these exhor - tations until they are successful." "You have withdrawn yourself from the ranks of the brethren and have trampled on your bond with Christ. For this desertion severe punishment awaits you, if you persist in it. A merchant can suffer shipwreck, an athlete be defeated, a soldier may have to flee, but they can come back again. King David fell, but he rose up again. Of what profit to you is the good fortune, the power, the riches, and the esteem? All that is but temporary. Now your friends, Valerius, Florentius, Porphyrius and many others are praying for you. If they do not despair of your salvation, why should you? Also life in the world brings its cares, dangers, and disillusionments. He who lives for Christ alone enjoys real freedom. Therefore away with despondency and fear, the sharpest weapons of evil. I do not despair of you. At any rate I will try, with the lifeboat of this letter, to save you from ship - wreck. If you have not completely forgotten me, then rejoice me by answering it." An answer is extant but it is obviously spurious.

THEODORE'S REPUTATION DURING HIS LIFE AND HIS POSTHUMOUS CONDEMNATION

Theodore did return and continued his studies under Diodore until 378. In 381 Theodore was ordained a priest of the Church of Antioch by Flavian, the bishop of Antioch. Eleven years later in 392 Theodore was named bishop of Mopsuestia in Cilicia (modern Misis, east of Adana). Throughout his long episcopate he possessed an excellent reputation for learning, eloquence, and orthodoxy. It is noteworthy that toward the end of his life he gave refuge to some of the condemned Pelagians, the most important of whom was Julian of Eclanum. Theodore died in 428, in the very year that another representative of the Antiochene School be - came bishop of Constantinople – Nestorius. Theodore was condemned 125 years after his death, sharing the fate of his master Diodore of Tarsus. Theodore's writings were the first of *The Three Chapters* to be condemned. However, it should be pointed out that during the decade following the condemnation of Nestorius at the Council of Ephesus (431) charges begin to be raised about Theodore's teachings by several prominent theologians, the most important of whom was St. Cyril of Alexandria who wrote a work titled *Contra Diodorum et Theodorum* (of which only fragments remain). St. Cyril accused Theodore of teaching the same "impiety" for which Nestorius was condemned (Migne, *Patrologia Graeca* 77, 340)

That *both Theodore and his writings* were condemned post - humously by the Fifth Ecumenical Council in 553 is undeniable. It is not just his writings that were condemned. The language of the council is clear and the question of whether one could condemn someone post - humously had already been raised and debated. Moreover, it is not only the person and his Christology that is condemned. It is more. His entire exegetical system is also condemned. The language of the council, offensive to modern ears, is simply a part of the historical record. The language is so vivid, direct, and clear that selections deserve quotation in order to participate in the flavor of the atmosphere of that time.

The emperor's letter to the council, contained in the *Acts of the Council*, states that "the Nestorians want to impose their heresy upon the Church. But since they could not use Nestorius for that goal, they quickly introduced their errors through Theodore of Mopsuestia, the teacher of Nestorius, who taught still more grievous blasphemies than [Nestorius] . . . we exhort you to direct your attention to the impious writings of Theodore and especially to his Jewish creed . . . his name has long since been struck from the diptychs of the Church of Mop - suestia. Consider the absurd assertion that heretics should not be anathematized after deaths . . ."

The statement of the council is especially graphic. "When we, therefore, saw that the followers of Nestorius were attempting to introduce their impiety into the Church of God through the impious Theodore, who was bishop of Mopsuestia, *and* through his impious writings . . ." "first we brought under examination the matter of Theodore of Mopsuestia. When all the blasphemies contained in his writings were revealed, we were astonished at the patience of God – that the tongue and mind which had framed such blasphemies were not immediately consumed by the divine fire . . . each blasphemy surpassed its predecessor in the magnitude of its impiety and moved from its foundation the minds of the listeners . . . all of us, moved with indignation by these blasphemies against God, both during and after the reading, erupted with denunciations and anathemas against Theodore, as though he were alive and present. O intolerable tongue! O the depravity of the man! O that high hand he lifted up against his Creator! For the wretched man who had promised to know the Scriptures had no recollection of the words of the Prophet Hosea . . . To these curses [from Hosea] the impious Theodore is justly subject." "The prophecies concerning Christ he rejected . . . attempting to show in many ways the divine words to be nothing but fables. And why should we add anything more? For anyone can take in his hands the writings of the impious Theodore or the impious chapters which from his impious writings were inserted by us in our acts, and find the incredible foolishness and the detestable things which he said. We condemn and anathematize, together with all the other heretics who have been condemned and anathematized by the four holy councils and by the Holy Catholic and Apostolic Church, Theodore, who was bishop of Mopsuestia, *and* his impious writings."

From the *Capitula*, the Twelfth is directed against Theodore: "If anyone defends the impious Theodore of Mopsuestia . . . if then anyone shall defend this most impious Theodore *and* his impious writings . . . and if anyone does not anathematize *him or his impious writings*, as well as all those who protect or defend him or who assert that his *exegesis* is orthodox, or who write in favor of him and of his impious works, or those who share the same opinions, or those who have shared them and still continue until the end of this heresy, let him be anathema." Such was the tragic end of one who had lived and died in peace with the Church.

II

WORKS

Theodore of Mopsuestia is one of the most typical and important representatives of the Antiochene School of Biblical exegesis. One could consider him the most famous writer of that school. The later Nestorians, as we shall see, considered him *the exegete* of Scripture. He wrote commentaries on nearly all the books of the Bible, employing an inquisitive and critical investigation into such questions as dating and authorship. He is often considered the first to utilize "literary criticism" in the exegesis of the Bible.

KNOWLEDGE AND PRESERVATION OF THE WORKS OF THEODORE OF MOPSUESTIA

As with most heretics who were condemned by ecumenical councils, we should expect that most of his works perished. We are historically fortunate, however, because many of his works were preserved in Syriac by the Syrian Nestorians. In addition, mention must be made here of the significance of St. Photius, not only for Theodore's works but also in general for numerous works. St. Photius (c.810 - c.895) was one of the main figures in the Byzantine intellectual renaissance of the ninth century. His immense knowledge earned him the respect even of his most bitter enemies. In addition to St. Photius' historical importance in the Ignatian schism and in the great contro - versy with Rome over the *Filioque* and other matters, contained in his brilliant work titled *On the Mystagogy of the Holy Spirit* , St. Photius left the world of scholarship an enormous debt with his *Bibliotheca* or *Myriobiblion – μυριόβιβλον.* In his *Bibliotheca* St. Photius provides a mine of information on books, many of which are now lost. He describes 280 books, often giving exhaustive analyses and substantial excerpts. He was acquainted with works by Theodore of Mopsuestia in Greek. Mention should also be made of Facundus, bishop of Hermiane in the province of Byzacena in Africa in the sixth century. During the Monophysite controversy Facundus was one of the main supporters of *The Three Chapters*. Because of the dispute Facundus journeyed to

Constantinople and there in 547-548 he completed his work titled *Pro defensione trium capitulorum*. In this work he argued for the orthodoxy of Ibas of Edessa and Theodoret of Cyrus. He did the same for Theodore of Mopsuestia but with certain reservations in Theodore's case. As a result of his work, Facundus has preserved certain passages from the works of Theodore. Mention must also be made of the very council that condemned Theodore, for the Acts of the Fifth Ecumenical Council (553) have preserved a few fragments of Theodore's works.

More significant is the discovery in the twentieth century of Theo - dore's *Catechetical Homilies*. In 1932 Mingana discovered and published with an English translation the Syriac text of the important *Cate - chetical Homilies*. Not only was this intrinsically important but it served as the catalyst for the recent revival of interest in Theodore of Mopsuestia and his theological thought by such scholars as Mingana, R. A. Norris, F. A. Sullivan, P. Galtier, J. L. McKenzie, M. Richard, W. Laistner, L. Abramowski, R. Tonneau, J. M. Vosté, V. Bulhart, A. Vaccari, X. Ducros, W. L. Lorimer, E. Dekkers, U. Wickert, R. Abra - mowski, F. J. Dölger, E. Amann, W. de Vries, F. J. Reine, J. Quas - ten, G. Touton, J. Gross, P. Parente, K. McNamara, R. Arnou, M. Jugie, M. V. Anastos, I. Onatibia, J. Lécuyer, R. Greer, and *the monu - mental work* done by R. Devreesse.

The Nestorian writers of the thirteenth and fourteenth centuries give us the best lists of Theodore's writings, especially the list by Ebedjesu [in J. S. Assemani, *Bibl. or. Clem.-Vat.*, III, 1, 30 ff.] and the list con - tained in the *Chronicle of Seert* [in *Patrologia Orientalis* 5, 289 ff.]. Ebedjesu is from the early fourteenth century and the *Chronicle of Seert* comes from the first half of the thirteenth century.

THEODORE'S *COMMENTARIES* ON THE OLD TESTAMENT

The only complete work by Theodore that has come down to us in Greek is his *Commentary on The Twelve Minor Prophets* [Migne, *Patrologia Graeca* 66, 123-632]. The reason for this may not be difficult to discern – the work has nothing significant to say about Christology! This work is mentioned in the lists by Ebedjesu and the *Chronicle of Seert*. It is noteworthy that Theodore, in applying his Antiochene exegesis that considers a text in its literal and historical context, applies those texts which in general the Church held to be "Messianic," to Jewish history only. Texts which allegorical exegesis applied to Christ, Theodore applies to the restoration of the Jewish state or to the vic - tories of the Maccabees.

Theodore's *Commentary on the Psalms* , which was apparently his first work, has come down to us in substantial portions. Written when he was quite young, Theodore later in life looked back upon it with regret. In the only extant passage from his work titled *Contra alle - goricos*, preserved by Facundus (3,6; Migne, *Patrologia Latina* 67,

602), Theodore complains about the imperfections in his *Commentary on the Psalms* . Ebedjesu claimed that the *Commentary on the Psalms* comprised five volumes. Of the fragments printed in Migne, *Patrologia Graeca* 66, 648-696, Devreesse rejects approximately fifty percent as spurious. But Devreesse was successful in restoring much of the text from manuscript *catenae* and from an ancient Latin version. The result is the restoration of the entire commentary on *Psalms* 1-16:11 and large sections of 16:12-40:13. Theodore is one of the first to insist that the *Psalms* be read in their historical context. He accepts Davidic author - ship for all the *Psalms* but, aware that many do not fit into the context of David's time, he explains many of them as being prophecies by David. For Theodore there is no *direct* Messianic – in Christian terms – references in the *Psalms*. The allusions in the New Testament he explains by *oikonomia* or accommodation. He does allow an exception for four *Psalms*: 2; 8; 44; and 109. But even here he refuses to consider them as authentically Messianic, although he does explain them as descriptions of the Incarnation and the Church *but not as authentic prophecy*. Theodore was quite opposed to the Messianic interpretations of the Old Testament coming out of the allegorically inclined Alex - andrian School on the grounds that such an interpretation violates the principle that each *Psalm* must be interpreted as a literary whole and unity and within its own historical context. There can be, for Theodore, no change of person, time, or situation in the same *Psalm*. He con - sidered all titles to the *Psalms* to be latter additions.

Fragments of Theodore's *Commentary on Genesis* exist. No longer are we limited to just the fragments in the *Catena Nicephori* in Migne. Additional fragments have been recovered from the *catenae* published by Devreesse, from citations by John Philoponus and Procopius of Gaza, and from a Syriac fragment. Minimally there has been a restoration of his commentary on the first three chapters of *Genesis*. St. Photius was aware of Theodore's interpretation of *Genesis* [*Bibl. Cod.*, 38] and comments on it prejudicially. "Read the book of Theodore of Antioch titled *Commentary on Genesis* (the history of creation), the first book of which contains seven volumes. The style is neither brilliant nor very clear. The author avoids the use of allegory as much as possible, for he is only concerned with the interpretation of history. He frequently repeats himself and produces a negative impression upon the reader. Although he lived before Nestorius, he vomits up Nestorius' doctrines by anticipation. This is that Theodore of Mopsuestia, from whom on several occasions John Philoponus (as the latter himself claims) demanded a serious explanation of his method of interpretation in his own work on the creation."

It is known that Theodore wrote a *Commentary on Samuel*, com - pleted by Elisa of Nisibis, of which there are no remains. His *Com - mentary on Job* was dedicated to none other than Cyril of Alexandria. A few fragments were preserved in the Acts of the Fifth Ecumenical Council (553). A Syriac version of his *Commentary on Ecclesiastes* was discovered by Soden in Damascus before World War I but it vanished as a war casualty. Two fragments remain of Theodore's *Commentaries* on the four major prophets, works listed also by Ebedjesu: *"Isiam quoque et Ezechielem et Jeremiam et Danielem singulis tomis commentatus est.* The excerpts, which are on *Isaiah* 10: 22-23, are pre - served in the *Catena* of Nicolas Muzalon.

The Acts of the Fifth Ecumenical Council (553) quote a passage from one of Theodore's letters (Mansi 9, 225-227). In this letter Theo - dore considers the *Song of Songs* to be Solomon's reply to the op - ponents of his marriage to the Egyptian princess. He refuses to allow any possibility for allegorical interpretation.

THEODORE'S *COMMENTARIES* ON THE NEW TESTAMENT

There is a complete Syriac version of Theodore's *Commentary on St. John's Gospel* which was published in 1940 with a Latin translation by Vosté. In addition, there are Greek fragments collected by Migne – one-third of these Devreesse claims are spurious. Devreesse, using the Syriac version as a guide and base, was able to restore the extant Greek fragments of this commentary, fragments formerly attributed to other writers.

According to Ebedjesu Theodore wrote commentaries also on *Matthew* and *Luke*. Numerous fragments of the commentary on *Matthew* exist. Ebedjesu also mentions that Theodore wrote on *Acts* – *Actus apostolorum uno commentatus est tomo*, a work from which the Fifth Ecumenical Council (553) quotes briefly.

There is a complete Latin version of Theodore's *Commentary on the Ten Minor Epistles of St. Paul* . This comes from the fifth century and is attributed, falsely of course, to Ambrose. Greek *catenae* have yielded considerable fragments of his exegesis of the major Pauline epistles. Ebedjesu lists commentaries by Theodore on all of the epistles traditionally attributed to Paul. In fact, fragments of all of them exist, some of great length.

THEODORE'S *CATECHETICAL HOMILIES*

Mingana's discovery in 1932 of the Syriac text of Theodore's *Catechetical Homilies* and his publication of this along with an English translation was an invaluable service to scholarship. This work is identical to the two works listed by Ebedjesu first among the non-exegetical works written by Theodore – *De sacramentis* and *De fide*. Now for the first time the full text was available of a work in which Theodore presented his interpretation of the faith of the Church to his catechumens. These sixteen homilies are divided into two parts. The first ten deal with the Nicene Creed; the other six interpret the Lord's Prayer (11), the liturgy of baptism (12-14), and the Eucharist (15-16).

THEODORE'S *DE INCARNATIONE* AND HIS *DISPUTATIO CUM MACEDONIANIS*

Theodore's work *De incarnatione* exists in Greek, Latin, and Syriac fragments. The entire text in Syriac was discovered by Addai Scher in 1905 in Seert but the manuscript became a casualty of World War I and perished entirely.

Theodore's *Disputatio cum Macedonianis* has come down to us complete in a Syriac version. It appears to be the actual stenographic minutes of a disputation in which Theodore defended in 392 at Anazar - bos the Divinity of the Holy Spirit against the Macedonians. It is quite probably identical with the work *On the Holy Spirit* listed by Ebedjesu and by the *Chronicle of Seert*.

THEODORE'S ASCETICAL WORKS

Theodore's three ascetical works are listed by Ebedjesu and by the *Chronicle of Seert* as *De sacerdotio* , *Ad monachos*, and *De perfectione*. Mingana has published some Syriac fragments of *De sacerdotio* and *De perfectione*. *Ad monachos* at present seems completely lost.

THEODORE'S *CONTRA EUNOMIUM*

St. Photius refers [*Bibl. Cod.*, 4] to Theodore's *Contra Eunomium* and comments: "Read the twenty-five books of Theodore of Antioch against Eunomius in defense of Basil. His style is somewhat obscure but the work is full of ideas and sound reasoning and contains a wealth of evidence taken from the Scriptures. He refutes the arguments of Eunomius almost word for word and amply proves that he is very ignorant of outside knowledge and still more so of our religion. I believe he is the Theodore who was bishop of Mopsuestia." Some fragments of this work exist in Facundus' work.

THEODORE'S WORK AGAINST APOLLINARIUS

The work titled *De assumente et assumpto* is probably the same which Ebedjesu refers to as his work against Apollinarius and which Facundus titles *De Apollinario et eius haeresi* – Facundus translated the beginning of this work. It reportedly consisted of four books. Seventeen fragments survive of the third and fourth books in a letter of Justinian, in the *corpus* attributed to Leontius of Byzantium, in the *Constitutum* of Vigilius, in Facundus, and in the Acts of the Fifth Ecumenical Council (553).

THEODORE'S WORK AGAINST ST. AUGUSTINE

Of special interest is Theodore's work titled *Adversus defensores peccati originalis* [*Against the Defenders of Original Sin*]. Both Ebedjesu and the *Chronicle of Seert* confirm that Theodore refuted "those who maintained that sin is a part of our nature." St. Photius gives a detailed report [*Bibl. Cod.*, 177] about this work. It should also be mentioned that the *Collectio Palatina* (51, 1-9) has preserved a num - ber of extracts from a work Theodore wrote against St. Augustine's doctrine of original sin. As mentioned previously, Theodore welcomed the condemned Pelagians. Hence, he obviously had first-hand knowledge of the raging controversy over predestination and original sin. Marius Mercator, the Latin Christian writer who was a friend and defender of St. Augustine in the controversy, knew the Pelagian controversy extremely well. Born not in Africa as has been commonly thought but in Italy and probably close to where Julian of Eclanum's family lived, Marius was in Rome in 418 to denounce the Pelagians. He knew Celestius, the associate of Pelagius, personally. Marius wrote two works, now lost, against the Pelagians. We know this from St. Augustine"s *Epistle* 193; that is, at least of one of his works. The second he wrote after St. Augustine's death in 430. In 429 Marius was at a Latin monastery in Thrace writing *Commonitorium adversum haeresim Pelagii et Coelestii vel etiam scripta Iuliani*. Marius also served as an agent for Pope Celestine in Constantinople. A collection of his writings, compiled about 100 years after his death, has survived in a Vatican MS [*Cod. Vat. Pal.* 234]. This consists primarily of Marius' translations of and replies to Nestorius' writings. It was one of the more important sources of our knowledge of Nestorius' doctrines. *But Marius also wrote two books against Theodore of Mopsuestia* which have also not survived. It is noteworthy that Marius was in - terested in both the Nestorian and Pelagian controversies and that he referred to Theodore of Mopsuestia as a "*Father of Pelagianism*." He is present for the condemnation of Celestius and Pelagius at the Council of Ephesus (431). After that there is no mention of him.

Whether Theodore was aware of St. Augustine's confrontation with Leporius on Christology is not known. It is quite probable that Theo - dore's Latin friends conveyed this to him. Leporius, a monk from Gaul, has been referred to as "a forerunner of Nestorius in the West." Lepor - ius, condemned by bishops in Gaul, fled to North Africa and there encountered St. Augustine. He was both a Pelagian and somewhat close to a "Nestorian" in his Christology. St. John Cassian writes his *De Incarnatione* precisely against the Nestorians – he was commissioned by Rome to undertake this task. Hence, what St. John Cassian has to say about Leporius is said within the perspective of the Nestorian con - troversy. In his *De Incarnatione* (1, 2) St. John Cassian writes in reference to Leporius that "just lately, in our own days, we saw a most poisonous heresy spring up from the greatest city of the Belgae, and though there was no doubt about its error, yet there was a doubt about its name because it arose with a fresh head from the old stock of the Ebionites, and hence it is still questionable whether it should be called old or new. For it was new as far as its upholders were concerned but old in the nature of its errors. Indeed, it blasphemously taught that our Lord Jesus Christ was born as a mere man and maintained that the fact that he afterwards obtained the glory and power of the Godhead resulted from his human worth and not from his divine nature. And by this it taught that he had not always his divinity by the right of his very own divine nature which belonged to him but that he obtained it afterwards as a reward for his labors and sufferings. Whereas then it blasphemously taught that our Lord and Savior was not God at his birth, but subse-quently taken into the Godhead, it was indeed bordering on this heresy which has now sprung up and is, as it were, its first cousin and akin to it, and, harmonizing both with Ebionism and these new heresies, came in point of time between them, and was linked with them both in point of wickedness. . . For Leporius, then a monk, now a presbyter, who followed the teaching or rather the evil deeds of Pelagius, and was among the earliest and greatest champions of the aforesaid heresy in Gaul, was admonished by us and corrected by God, and so nobly con-demned his former erroneous persuasion that his amendment was almost as much a matter for congratulation as is the unimpaired faith of many. For it is the best thing never to fall into error. The second best thing to make a good repudiation of it. Leporius, then, coming to himself con-fessed his mistake with grief but without shame not only in Africa, where he was then and is now, but also gave to all the cities of Gaul penitent letters containing his confession and grief."

St. John Cassian quotes from Leporius' confession in his *De Incarnatione Domine contra Nestorium Libri VII* (1, 5), a confession behind which is St. Augustine and in which it is clear that the Incar-nation is a uniting of the flesh to the person of the Logos or Word and not to divine nature – *solum proprie, personaliter, non cum Patre aut cum Spiritu sancto naturaliter.* "And from Leporius' confession or rather lamentation we have thought it well to quote some part for two reasons: that the recantation might be a testimony to us and an example to those who are weak, and that they might not be ashamed to follow in their amendment . . . 'I scarcely know, O my most venerable lords and blessed priests what first to accuse myself of, and what first to excuse myself for. Clumsiness and pride and foolish ignorance together with wrong notions, zeal combined with indiscretion, and – to speak truly – a weak faith which was gradually failing, all these were admitted by me and flourished to such an extent that I am ashamed of having yielded to such and so many sins, while at the same time I am profoundly thank-ful for having been able to cast them out of my soul. If then, not understanding this power of God, and wise in our conceits and opinions, from fear lest God should seem to act a part that was beneath him, we suppose that a man was born in conjunction with God in such a way that we ascribe to God alone what belongs to God separately, and attribute to man alone what belongs to man separately, we clearly add a fourth person to the Trinity and out of the one God the Son begin to make not one but two Christs – from which may our Lord and God Jesus Christ himself preserve us. Therefore we confess that our Lord and God Jesus Christ the only Son of God, who for his own sake was begotten of the Father before all worlds but who in time was for our sakes made man of the Holy Spirit and the ever-Virgin Mary, was God at his birth. And while we confess the two natures of the flesh and the Word, we always acknowledge with pious belief and faith one and the same Person to be indivisibly God and Man. And we say that from the time when he took upon him flesh all that belonged to God was given to man, as all that belonged to man was joined to God. And in this sense 'the Word became flesh' – not that he began by any conversion or change to be what he was not but that by the divine *oikonomia* the Word of the Father never left the Father and yet vouchsafed to become truly man, and the Only Begotten was incarnate through that hidden mystery which he alone understands (for it is ours to believe, his to understand). And thus God 'the Word' himself receiving everything that belongs to God cannot but be God. But since he is said to be incarnate and unmixed, we must not hold that there is any diminution of his substance, for God knows how to communicate himself without suffering any corruption, and yet truly to communicate himself. He knows how to receive into himself without himself being increased thereby, just as he knows how to impart himself in such a way as to suffer no loss himself. We should not then in our feeble minds makes guesses, in accordance with visible proofs and experiments, from the case of creatures which are equal, and which mutually enter into each other, nor think that out of such a fusion of flesh and the Word some sort of body is produced. God forbid that we should imagine that the two natures being in a way molded together should become one substance, for a mixture of this sort is destructive of both parts. For God, who contains and is not himself contained, who enters into things and is not himself entered into, who fills things and is not himself filled, who is everywhere at once in his completeness and is diffused everywhere, communicates himself graciously to human nature by the infusion of his power. Therefore the God-Man, Jesus Christ, the Son of God, is truly born for us of the Holy Spirit and the ever-Virgin Mary. And so in the two natures the Word and Flesh become one, so that while each nature continues naturally perfect in itself, what is divine imparts without suffering any loss, to the humanity, and what is human participates in the divine. Nor is there one person God and another person man, but the same Person is God who is also man. And again the man who is also God is called and indeed is Jesus Christ the only Son of God. And thus we must always take care and believe so as not to deny that our Lord Jesus Christ, the Son of God, Very God –

whom we confess as existing ever with the Father and equal to the Father before all worlds – became from the moment when he took flesh the God-Man. Nor may we imagine that gradually as time went on he became God, and that he was in one condition before the resurrection and in another after it, but that he was always of the same fulness and poser. But because the Word of God vouchsafed to come down upon manhood by assuming manhood, and manhood was taken up into the Word by being assumed by God, God the Word in his completeness became complete man. For it was not God the Father who was made man, nor the Holy Spirit, but the Only-Begotten of the Father, and thus we must hold that there is one Person of the Flesh and the Word. We must faithfully and without any doubt believe that one and the same Son of God, who can never be divided, existing in two natures . . . in the days of his flesh truly took upon him all that belongs to man, and ever truly had as his own what belongs to God – since even though he was crucified in weakness, yet he lives by the power of God."

St. John Cassian who precisely wrote against St. Augustine on the matter of predestination and grace, quotes from St. Augustine's *Tractatus in Joannis evangelium* on Christology in opposition to Nestorius in his *De Incarnation* (7, 27). "Augustine the priest of Hippo Regius says: 'That men might be born of God, God was first born of them, for Christ is God. And Christ when born of men only required a mother on earth because he always had a Father in heaven, being born of God through whom we are made, and also born of a woman, through whom we might be re-created'."

In his *Epistle 219* St. Augustine writes about the situation with Leporius – the letter is written to Proculus and Cillenius, bishops of Gaul, and signed by St. Augustine and two other African bishops, Florentinus and Secundus. After explaining how they had handled Leporius, St. Augustine writes that when Leporius "refused to admit that God was born of a woman, that God was crucified, and that he suffered other human woes, what he feared was that divinity might be believed to have suffered change in becoming man, or to have been tainted by its admixture with man." His "fear arose from his filial love, but his mistake from his lack of advertence. His filial love saw that divinity can undergo no change, but in his inadvertence he assumed that the Son of Man could be separated from the Son of God, so that there would be a difference between the one and the other, and that either Christ was neither of them or that there were two Christs. But after he had recognized that the Word of God, that is, the Only-Begotten Son of God, became the Son of Man without either nature being changed into the other but both remaining with their own substance, so that God in man suffered human vicissitudes while his divinity remained unchanged in him, he confessed without any fear that Christ is God and man, having a greater fear of the addition of a fourth person to the Trinity than of any loss of substance in the divinity."

THEODORE'S WORKS AGAINST MAGIC

St. Photius mentions that Theodore wrote three books against magic; Ebedjesu mentions two; and the *Chronicle of Seert* mentions one. St. Photius writes [*Bibl. Cod.*, 81]: "Read the three brief books by Theodore *On Persian Magic and How It Differs From Christianity*, dedicated to Mastubius, an Armenian and suffragan bishop. In the first book the accursed doctrine of the Persians, introduced by Zarades [Zoro - aster], concerning Zuruam [Zervan], whom he makes the beginning of all things and calls Fortune, is expounded; how that, having offered a libation to beget Horsmidas, he begot both him and Satan; thus the mixing of blood. Having set forth this impious and disgraceful doctrine in plain words, he refutes it in the first book. In the other two books he discusses the Christian faith, beginning from the creation of the world and at the same time rapidly going down to the law of grace. This Theodore is believed to be Theodore of Mopsuestia, since he mentions with approval the heresy of Nestorius, especially in the third book. He also foolishly talks of the restoration of sinners to their former con - dition." There are to date no extant fragments of this work.

THEODORE'S *LIBER MARGARITARUM*

According to Ebedju and the *Chronicle of Seert*, the work titled *Liber margaritarum* [*Book of Pearls*] was a collection of Theodore's letters. A fragment of the second letter addressed to Artemius, a priest at Alexandria, has been preserved by Facundus and three excerpts of a letter to Domnus are found in the *Doctrina Patrum*. Nothing else has survived – or better, nothing else has yet been discovered.

THEODORE'S *ADVERSUS ALLEGORICOS, DE OBSCURA LOCUTIONE* AND *DE LEGISLATIONE*

Theodore's work titled *Adversus allegoricos* [*Against the Alle - gorists*], mentioned above, was directed against Origen. The only existing fragment has been preserved by Facundus (3,6). Nothing re - mains of *De obscura locutione* [*On Obscure Language*] which appar - ently was an explanation of difficult passages in Scripture. Nothing re - mains also of his *De legislatione* [*On Legislation*].

III

THEODORE'S THEOLOGICAL THOUGHT

CHRIST AS PERFECT MAN UNITED WITH GOD

Theodore of Mopsuestia saw in Christ first of all the "the perfect man" who was born of Mary and about him we know that he was united with God. How can we conceive of this union? As a rule Theodore defines it as the indwelling of the Logos – *ἐνοίκησις*, as a connection or conjunction – *συνάφεια*, or as a correlation or partici - pation – *σχέσις*. He feels that one must not understand literally the phrase "And the Logos became flesh," for this would be "alienation from his essence and a condescension of him to the level of lower beings. "*He became*," in Theodore's opinion, *can only mean* "he seemed" – *κατὰ τὸ δοκεῖν*. "In so far as it seemed or appeared, the Logos was made flesh." The Logos resided in Jesus, as in the Son – *ὡς ἐν υἱῷ*. Moreover, it is impossible to assume that it dwelt "mater - ially," for this would mean that the Infinite is contained within tight material limits, which is absurd and contradicts Divine omnipresence. For that very reason, it is impossible to assume indwelling through the efficacious force or "energy" of the Divinity. For it is also impossible to contain God's force in a closed space.

THE INDWELLING OF GOD IN CHRIST

In Theodore's opinion, it is possible to allow only a certain partial indwelling. The Scripture frequently testifies to such an indwelling, stating that God "lives" or "walks" within his chosen ones. This is an honor which God grants to those who strive towards him "through his goodwill to them" – *κατ᾽ εὐδοκίαν*. One may only speak of this in - dwelling as a "unity by or through goodwill" in relation to Christ as well. And Theodore does not hide the fact that in this way Christ moves into the ranks of righteous men, prophets, apostles, holy men, although into a special and incomparable place, the first and the highest place, for in Christ the totality of God's goodwill was revealed. *Therefore the unity of human nature with the Logos was complete, perfect, and indivisible.* "Dwelling in Jesus, the Logos joined to himself completely everything he embraced," wrote Theodore.

THEODORE'S CONCEPT OF UNITY OF PERSON

He calls this unity the unity of person – *ἡ τοῦ προσώπου ἕν - ωσις*. However, here he means only the indivisible unity of will, action, supremacy, dominion, virtue, and power. And there can be no tie stronger than this, Theodore observes. But this is unity through goodwill, through a unity of will – ταυτοβουλία – and a unity by vir - tue of and in view of Jesus' *merits.* True, this unity starts with the conception of Jesus but through the *foreknowledge of future merits.* Further, this unity is developing and growing. Christ, as the "perfect man," grew like all people, grew both in body and soul. He also grew in cognition and righteousness. And to the extent that he grew, he received new gifts of the Spirit. He struggled trying to overcome passion and even lust. And in this he was assisted by the Spirit with "its moral influences." The Spirit illuminated him and strengthened his will in order to "destroy sin in the flesh, to curb its lust with a light and noble force." This was inevitable, Theodore thought, since Christ was a real man. In baptism he is anointed through goodwill, but only in death does he attain "perfect purity" and "unalterability in thoughts."

We must note that Theodore supposed that the Divinity separated from Christ at his death "since Divinity could not experience death." It is perfectly clear that Theodore distinguishes "two distinct subjects." It is curious that he compares the duality of the natures in the unity of the God-Man with the conjugal union of husband and wife "into a united flesh." The Jesus of the Gospels is for Theodore only a man who is joined to the Logos in moral obedience and harmony, and joined by the Logos to himself. In other words, he is man adopted to God, ὁ λαμβανόμενος.

THEODORE'S OBJECTION TO THE TERM *THEOTOKOS*

From this it is understandable why Theodore denied with indig - nation that one could call Mary the Mother of God, or more accurately, *Theotokos.* "It is folly to say that God was born of the Virgin," he states. "He was born of the Virgin who has the nature of the Virgin, not God the Logos. He was born of Mary who was of David's seed. It was not God the Logos who was born of woman but he who was formed in her by the power of the Holy Spirit." One can call Mary the Mother of God, or more accurately, *Theotokos*, in the metaphorical, non-literal sense of the phrase, just as one can call her the *Bearer of Man* – ἀνθρωποτόκος. She naturally bore a man, but God was in the man she bore, as he never had been in anyone before. It is perfectly clear that under "unity of person" Theodore understood only the com - pleteness of deified and grace-impregnated humanity. One must not conceive of perfect nature as being impersonal – ἀπρόσωπον, he sup - posed. Consequently, in so far as humanity was complete in Christ, he was a human being. Moreover, the nature of the Logos is not im - personal. But in the Incarnation the "unity of harmony" and the "con - nection of honor" is established and in the sense of a certain new "unity of person."

THEODORE'S ANTHROPOLOGICAL DESIGN

It is not difficult to perceive the anthropological design of Theo -
dore. He believed that man was created in order to strive for impassivity
and immutability. In Christ he saw the first example of the human
calling realized. Man, in an heroic feat, achieved God-Man-hood with
the aid of God, through goodwill and grace. God joined him to himself
and gave him all manner of primacy. He gave him a name far above any
other name. He ascended and sits at the right hand of the Father, and is
far above everything. And God prefers to do everything through him –
the judgment and trial of the entire world and his own second coming.
In Theodore, all stress is focused on human achievement. God only
anoints and crowns human freedom.

It is very characteristic that when Theodore was alive no one in the
East, apparently, ever charged him with heresy. He died in peace and
was recalled with veneration. "His name was quite renowned in the
East, and people marvelled at his compositions," St. Cyril observes.
And Cyril's attack on Theodore was met in the East with violent
indignation. This testified to how much Theodore's type of theology
corresponded to the religious ideals of the "Easterners." Of course,
Theodore's individual, "imprecise" expressions are not of decisive sig -
nificance here. In no way were they slips of the tongue. Theodore had a
painstakingly thought-out system. He spent many years working on his
main book *On the Incarnation* . One must not think that Theodore was
seduced by the imprecision of his theological language. He proceeded
from a firm soteriological hope, from a definite religious ideal. This
was the *reductio ad absurdum* of *anthropological maximalism*, the self-
exposure of ascetic humanism. The tolerance of the "Easterners" testi -
fied to their biases and to the vagueness of the "Eastern" soteriological
consciousness. From the perspective of this *anthropological maxi -
malism* there is an inner logic between what became known as
"Nestorianism" and Pelagianism. It was probably more than simply an
act of favor to Rome that Pelagianism was condemned at the Council of
Ephesus because the inner logic uniting Nestorianism and Pelagianism
was probably not completely overlooked by some of the fathers of the
Council of Ephesus. This also explains why Theodore so readily ac -
cepted the condemned and exiled Pelagians – they shared a certain
anthropological vision.

CHAPTER THIRTEEN

NESTORIUS

I

LIFE

Nestorius (d.c.451) was born of Persian parents in the last quarter of the fourth century at Germanicia in Syria Euphratensis. Trained at Antioch, Nestorius entered the monastery of St. Euprepius where he was ordained. It is possible that he had the opportunity to study at some time under Theodore of Mopsuestia. He gained a wide reputation as a preacher. According to historical sources, Nestorius is reported to have been very eloquent, to have had very "fine eyes," and to have been of "red hair."

THE CONDEMNATION OF APOLLINARIUS AT THE SECOND ECUMENICAL COUNCIL (381)

To understand Nestorius' situation in life, it is necessary to recall the Second Ecumenical Council [381 in Constantinople]. In addition to its theological work, the council also enacted Canon III which conferred on the bishopric of Constantinople "the prerogative of honor after the bishop of Rome, because Constantinople is the New Rome." The political and ecclesiastical ramifications of this canon are vast and cannot be dealt with here except to call attention to one vital fact – *the canon was to prove divisive*. It caused great concern for the older bishoprics of Rome, Alexandria, Antioch, and Jerusalem. It was to bring Rome and Alexandria even closer in uniting to stop the ecclesiastical power of the upstart Constantinople, the *Nova Roma*. Hence, a political and ecclesiastical rivalry intensifies, adding a heavier burden to the serious theological issues. Thus the period from 381 to 431 is dominated by the efforts of the aggrieved bishoprics of Rome and Alexandria to undo the work of that canon. Even if Rome was not aware of the canon, Rome certainly realized that Constantinople had ecclesiastical assumptions and ambitions. Simultaneously, the theo - logical emphases and differences in approach between the Antiochene theologians and the Alexandrian theologians continue.

The condemnation of Apollinarianism is of concern here. Apol - linarius – often Apollinaris in English; the Greek fathers always write Aπολλινάριος and Jerome in his *De viris illustribus* uses Apol - linarius – was born about 310 in Laodicea, the Syrian port in the south of Antioch where his father, Apollinarius "the Elder" taught grammar before being ordained to the priesthood. Apollinarius received an outstanding education. In the time of emperor Constantius (337-361) the bishop of Laodicea, George, was Arian, as had been Theodotus, bishop of Laodicea while Apollinarius was a reader. Certain scholars have attempted to trace the origin of Apollinarius' later heresy to his early Arian roots, but such a position is highly doubtful. Apollinarius was a staunch defender of the Nicene faith and was excommunicated by bishop George of Laodicea in 342 precisely because of his anti-Arian thought. Under emperor Julian the Apostate (361-363) Apollinarius and his father re-wrote much of the Bible in classical forms – under Julian it was prohibited for Christians to use pagan classics. Apollinarius developed a reputation for erudition and intelligence. St. Jerome studied under him in the 370s and wrote that Apollinarius authored "innumerable volumes on the Scriptures. He wrote a work of thirty-one books against Porphyry (c.232-c.303), a work which Philostorgius (c.368-c.439), the Arian ecclesiastical historian, considered the most brilliant refutation of Porphyry. Apollinarius also wrote against the Arians, against Eunomius, against Marcellus of Ancyra, and against the subordinationism of Origen and Didymus.

Epiphanius writes about the beginning of the Apollinarian controversy: "Some of our brethren, who are in high position, and who are held in great esteem with us and all orthodox, have thought that the mind or intellect – $\acute{o}$ *νοῦς* – should be excluded from the manifestation of Christ in the flesh, and have preferred to hold that our Lord Christ assumed flesh and soul but not our mind or intellect and therefore not a perfect man. The aged and venerable Apollinarius of Laodicea, dear even to the blessed father Athanasius, and in fact to all the orthodox, has been the first to frame and promulgate this doctrine. At first, when some of his disciples communicated it to us, we were unwilling to believe that such a man would put this doctrine in circulation. We supposed that the disciples had not understood the deep thoughts of so learned and so discerning a man, and had themselves fabricated things which he did not teach."

Apollinarianism has been called "the first great Christological heresy," "the most subtle and thorough-going attempt to work out a theory of Christ's Person in the fourth century," "the carrying out of the long accepted tendencies in Alexandrian thought to their logical conclusions." At first Apollinarius circulated his doctrine anonymously, mainly through his followers. Hence, the first writings against his doctrine, St. Athanasius' *Letter to Epictetus* does not mention him by name. This could also have been polite diplomacy on the part of St. Athanasius, who was a personal friend of Apollinarius because Apollinarius' ideas are readily perceived in his *Letter to Jovianus* (363) and especially in his *Letter to Serapion* (351). As early as 362 his idea was condemned at the Council of Alexandria. About 375 he was finally compromised by his disciple Vitalis, a priest at Antioch. Vitalis was denounced by Rome and hence went to Rome to explain himself. At first he was successful with Pope Damasus (pope from 366 to 384). But after Pope Damasus had received more information, Pope Damasus demanded an explicit profession of faith from Vitalis. Vitalis refused. He was condemned by Pope Damasus at the Council of Rome in 377. It was the Vitalis case which brought Apollinarius into the open. He consecrated Vitalis bishop of Antioch and broke with the Church at this time. The Council of Alexandria in 378 condemned him and so did the Council of Antioch in 379. Shortly after 376 Apollinarius explained his teachings in an enormous work entitled *Demonstration of the Divine Incarnation in the Likeness of Man* – many extracts from this are found in St. Gregory of Nyssa's *Antirrhiticus*.

The Apollinarians began to spread. St. Gregory of Nazianzus took strong measures against them in Cappadocia and Theodosius issued a series of imperial edicts in 383, 384, and 388 forbidding their assemblies, deposing their bishops, and preventing them from ordaining others. Such measures were not completely successful.

The Second Ecumenical Council condemned "every heresy," specifically calling attention to "that of the Eunomians or Eudoxians and that of the Semi-Arians or Pneumatomachi, and that of the Sabellians, and that of the Marcellians, and that of the Photinians, *and that of the Apollinarians*." In its seventh canon the Second Ecumenical Council – this canon probably comes from 382 and not 381 – gives an interesting description of how heretics are reunited with the Church: "Those who turn from heresy to orthodoxy . . . we receive according to the following method and custom: Arians, Macedonians, Sabbatians, Novatians, who call themselves Cathari or Aristeri, Quartodecimans or Tetradites, *and Apollinarians*, we receive, upon their giving a written renunciation and upon their anathematizing every heresy which is not in accordance with the Holy, Catholic, and Apostolic Church of God. Then they are first sealed or anointed with the holy oil upon the forehead, eyes, nostrils, mouth, and ears. When we seal them, we say "The Seal of the gift of the Holy Spirit." But Eunomians, who are baptized with only one immersion, and Montanists, who are here called Phrygians, and Sabellians, who teach the identity of Father and Son, and various other incorrect things, and adherents to all other heresies – for there are many such persons here, particularly among those who come from the country of the Galatians – all these, when they desire to turn to orthodoxy, we receive as heathen. On the first day we make them Christians; on the second, catechumens; on the third, we exorcise them by breathing thrice in their face and ears; and thus we instruct them and oblige them to spend some time in the Church, and to hear the Scriptures; and then we baptize them."

In the summary of faith contained in the Council's letter the *Heresy of Apollinarianism* is mentioned: "We moreover preserve unperverted the doctrine of the Incarnation of the Lord, holding the tradition that the *oikonomia* of the flesh is neither soulless nor mindless nor imperfect, and knowing full well that God's *Logos* was perfect before the ages and became perfect man in the last days for our salvation."

Apollinarius, in his zeal to preserve the true and full Divinity of Christ and also because of his fear of creating theologically a double personality in Christ, fell into the error of a partial denial of Christ's true humanity. Relying on *I Thessalonians* 5:23 and *Galatians* 5:17 and utilizing the psychological trichotomy of Plato – σῶμα, ψυχή, πνεῦμα – Apollinarius conceded that Christ possessed a full human body – σῶμα – and a human soul – ψυχή ἄλογος, anima animans – but *denied that Christ had a rational soul – ψυχή λογική – anima rationalis.* The Antiochene theologians feared Apollinarianism and their theology was far from any tendency in that direction. The Antiochene theological tradition emphasized the historical, the concrete. In their exegetical work on the Bible they focused on the historical and literary context and, in general, tried to avoid exaggerated allegorical interpretations. In their Christological thought they emphasized the full humanity of Christ without denying that Christ was consubstantial with God the Father. Any tendency that might swallow up the humanity of Christ by his Divinity they abhorred. Theologically they stressed the separateness of the two natures – the Divine nature and the human nature. The danger for Antioch was that they might overstress the separateness of the two natures and undermine the unity of Christ.

The Alexandrian theologians emphasized the Divinity of Christ. Their starting point was the Eternal God who became man. Human nature, in union with the Divine Nature of the Divine Logos, could be divinized. The danger for Alexandria was that they might overstress the Divinity and undermine the human nature of Christ. The Alexandrian tendency was towards *anthropological minimalism*; the Antiochene tendency was towards *anthropological maximalism*. This anthro - pological *maximalism* of the Antiochene theologians had a soterio - logical consequence of practical importance – they emphasized the exertion of the moral will. Hence, it is not by chance that Theodore of Mopsuestia or Nestorius would feel comfortable with the Pelagians. And it is not by chance that Nestorius, coming from the Antiochene school of thought, would be extremely cautious not to use any ter - minology that might be considered Apollinarianism. It is precisely this tendency in the direction of Apollinarianism that Nestorius thinks he finds in the thought of St. Cyril.

THE SELECTION OF NESTORIUS AS PATRIARCH OF CONSTANTINOPLE

In 428 the see of Constantinople was vacant. There is an historical account of why Theodosius II (emperor from 408 to 450) selected Nestorius as the patriarch of Constantinople. The Council of Ephesus (431) sent its representative, the archimandrite Dalmatius, to Con - stantinople to request that Theodosius II execute the decision of the council and depose Nestorius. The emperor gives a brief sketch of the background of ecclesiastical politics which led him to cause the selection of Nestorius:

"I find no evil in this man nor any cause deserving of deposition. I testify to you and to all men that I am innocent. For I have no love for this man through any human inclination that I should act this way and be criticized and condemned as one who withstands God and arrogates to himself the rights of the priests. Never did I insist upon his ordination that punishment and vengeance should be exacted of me because of his election, but through the agreement of all of you I of necessity introduced this man, though he was much beloved in his own country and among his own people. You were the cause of this and not I. You yourself, Damatius, I begged to undertake this office, and I implored you with many words not to refuse the ministry of God. But you refused and begged of me in turn, saying: 'Compel me not for I am an ignorant man'. And another also of the monks, a man who was thought to be capable and was well esteemed for his religiousness, I entreated, and he also refused as not knowing how to conduct this ministry because he was unlearned. Then you said: 'Constantinople requires a bishop who for his words and his conduct shall be agreeable to all, who shall be a teacher in the Church and a mouth to every one in all things'. But when you refused for these reasons, did I do anything by my own authority/ Did I not again beg of you to choose one of this character? Did I not implore of the clergy of Constantinople to choose one who was fitting? Did I not speak these same things to the bishops, saying: 'It is yours to choose and to make a bishop'? And you also I implored in like manner. Did I not leave the matter in your hands all this time, being patient in order that you should choose quietly, lest through haste some mistake should be made as to him who should be chosen? But did you choose and I not receive your choice? Do you wish me to say something against you? Shall I speak of their violence and bribery and presents, and their promises and oaths, and how they sought to turn the whole affair into a sale. Which of these men did you wish to be bishop? But I continue. Which choice did you wish should be made? Was it to you or that other of whom I spoke, or yet another? For some chose one, some another. They did not choose according to fitness but rather according to who was unsuitable. Every one recommended his own choice and spoke ill of him whom others chose, bringing damaging charges against him. You could not agree upon one man. But whom the people agreed upon you would not accept. I read before you what the people said of each one that was selected. What then ought I to have done that I did not do? You, the monks, did not agree with the clergy. The clergy were not of one mind. The bishops were divided. And the people in like manner disagreed. Each was contending for a different man. Yet not even so did I assume to myself the authority but I left the choice to you. But when you were all at a loss you came to me and deputed me to choose whom I would. And even then I scarcely consented, though you all begged of me. Now I considered that it was not right to appoint any one from here, lest he should have to contend against enmity and opposition, for every one hated, and was hated by the others, as though each was covetous of the office. So I sought to find a foreigner who should be unknown to those here and should not know them, one who should be a clear speaker and of good morals. And I was told that Nestorius of Antioch was such a one. Him I sent for and took, thereby causing sorrow to his whole city, and I brought him hither for your advantage – since this I held to be of more importance than that of the others. But when he was appointed this was not your estimate of him'."

Thus the selection of Nestorius. Even though the source is from Nestorius' *Bazaar of Heraclides* and hence may not be accurate in all details, it is probably a rather reliable portrait of what took place.

NESTORIUS' CHARACTER

What was Nestorius' character like? It is not easy to determine the true character of Nestorius because most of the contemporary statements about him come from his opposition. According to one biased account, Nestorius did not turn the other cheek. A report from Basilieus to emperor Theodosius states that Nestorius struck with his own hand a presumptuous monk who tried to prohibit him from approaching the altar. Nestorius, according to this account, then turned the monk over to the civil authorities who flogged him through the streets and then threw him out of the city. Socrates in his *Historia ecclesiastica* (7, 32) writes that Nestorius was too fond of his own voice, proud of his ability, that he mistook fluency for learning and rhetoric for argument. Socrates claims he is giving an objective evaluation. He had, he writes, read the works of Nestorius. Nestorius, he asserts, did not hold the views of Paul of Samosata or of Photinus. But Nestorius was, he writes, puffed up by his own eloquence and gloried in applause. Nestorius was unwilling to study the ancient Christian teachers, was ill-informed and "ignorant, though he considered himself well-educated." Socrates describes him as superficial, impetuous, and vainglorious. St. Vincent of Lérins (d. before 450) in his *Commonitorium* (XI, 29-30 describes the situation of Nestorius: "to take a very recent and plain case: what sort of trial was it which the Church experienced the other day when that unhappy Nestorius all at once metamorphosed from a sheep into a wolf?" St. Vincent, again with perhaps a lack of objectivity, writes that "there was always more than men admired than that by which they could profit [in Nestorius], more of show than reality." It was, he continues, "natural ability rather than divine grace that magnified him for a time in the opinion of the common people." Writing many years later Gennadius of Marseilles in his *De viris illustribus* (53) writes that Nestorius "composed innumerable tracts on various subjects in which with subtle malice he distilled the poison of his heresy, which later revealed itself; it was only hidden for a time because of his high moral character.

In some respects he was much like St. John Chrysostom; in other respects, quite different. Both were monks, both educated in Antioch, both became bishops of Constantinople, both were deposed, both managed to outrage certain persons and groups, both were great orators, both were devout, earnest, able, and diligent. But St. John Chrysostom spoke out and enraged people because of issues of morality. Nestorius carried this into the realm of doctrine. Nestorius lacked that sound, practical judgment which St. John Chrysostom possessed. Nestorius was impetuous, somewhat vain, and imprudent.

NESTORIUS' AGENDA UPON BECOMING PATRIARCH

Nestorius wasted no time after becoming patriarch in making his policy known and implementing it almost immediately. He intended to sweep Constantinople clean. He requested a free hand from the emperor to execute his policy; in return, he would put the might of the Church to aid the emperor against temporal enemies. He at once took strong measures against heretics, schismatics, and Jews. In their policy towards Jews Nestorius and St. Cyril of Alexandria did not, unfor - tunately, differ – in this regard they both could have learned something positive from St. Augustine. Nestorius attacked Arians and Mace - donians, Novatians and Quartodecimans. He spared, ironically, only the Pelagians and this will not help his pending problems with Pope Celestine (d.432). Nestorius began to demolish a private chapel in which local Arians worshipped. The Arians in desperation, set it on fire and a serious conflagration broke out. Nestorius became known from that time on, both by friends and enemies, as "Firebrand" or "Incen - diary." It was an ominous beginning. This took place within the first week of his becoming patriarch.

NESTORIUS AND THE TERM "*THEOTOKOS*"

Toward the end of 428 either Nestorius or Anastasius, a presbyter whom Nestorius brought to Constantinople with him, preached a sermon in which the term *Theotokos* – Θεοτόκος – was criticized – rather, attacked. It is claimed that Anastasius proclaimed: "Let no one call Mary *Theotokos*, for Mary was but a woman and it was impossible that God should be born of a woman." (Socrates VII, 32). Whether this attack on the terminology and meaning of *Theotokos* began with the presbyter Anastasius or with Nestorius is not the issue. Nestorius supported this vigorously and preached on the subject, regardless of whether he preached the first sermon. Thus began what St. Cyril refers to as the "scandal" of the household of the Church – σκάνδαλον οἰκουμενικόν.

Nestorius writes that he found the controversy already existing in Constantinople upon his arrival. Some, he writes, were using the term *Theotokos* – θεοτόκος, others the term "*Bearer of Man* – ἀνθρωποτόκος, and others the term "*Bearer of Christ*" – Χριστοτόκος. His account in his *Bazaar of Heraclides* is noteworthy. "A number of people who were discussing this matter came with one accord to the bishop's house, seeking to have their dispute settled and seeking an agreement. Some called those who spoke of the Blessed Mary as *Theotokos* Manichaeans, while the others called those who spoke of Blessed Mary as *Anthropotokos* Paulites or Photinians. But when I questioned them, the one party did not deny the manhood nor the other party the Godhead. But they made confession of both in the same manner, differing only as to the terms. Those accused of being connected with Apollinarius accepted the title *Theotokos* and those connected with Photinus the title *Anthropotokos*. But when I learned that in their quarrel they were not heretically minded, I said: 'Neither these nor those are heretics – for the one party knew nothing of Apollinarius and his doctrine nor did the others know anything of Photinus or of Paul.' And I tried to bring them out of their controversy and quarrel, saying: 'If without separating or severing or denying either the Godhead or the manhood, they employ those expressions that are used by them, they do not sin. Otherwise, let us employ that expression which is more guarded, I mean the expression of the Gospel – "Christ was born," or "the book of the birth of Jesus Christ," or any expression like that. We confess Christ to be God and man, for of the two was born Christ in the flesh, who is God over all. Then call Mary *Christotokos* in the union; and do not say that this and that are rent asunder in the Sonship, but employ the unexceptionable expression of the Gospel, and put away this dissension from among you, using the title that makes for harmony." When they heard this they said: 'Before God our controversy is settled.' And exceedingly did they praise and glorify God." Nestorius continues in his *Bazaar of Heraclides* by claiming that what actually caused the outbreak of the controversy were various political and ecclesiastical jealousies. He places the blame on those who were disappointed with the result of the election of bishop, on Cyril's agents who wanted money which he refused them, and on a group of Alexandrians who had brought complaints to Constantinople about Cyril's evil deeds.

THE SIGNIFICANCE OF THE TERM "*THEOTOKOS*"

The term *Theotokos* – Θεοτόκος – does not mean the same as "*Mother of God*" in English or the common Latin translation. In English one must translate *Theotokos* as "Bearer of God." The correct Latin would be *deipara* or *dei genetrix*, not *Mater Dei*. Had Nestorius been more prudent he would have realized that the term *Theotokos* had a comparatively long usage – it had been used by Origen, by Alexander of Alexandria, by Eusebius of Caesarea, Cyril of Jerusalem, Athanasius, Gregory of Nazianzus, Gregory of Nyssa, and Cyril. In the Latin West Tertullian had used the term *Dei Mater* in *De patientia* 3 and Ambrose also used it in his *Hexaemeron* V, 65 (*Patrologia Latina* 14, 248A). More significant is that the Antiochene theologian Eustathius (bishop of Antioch from c.324 to 330), so often considered a forerunner of Nestorius, had some remarkably un-Antiochene tendencies in his Christology, one of which was the use of the term *Theotokos*.

If there is a theological difference, however slight, between *Theotokos* and *Mother of God*, then there is certainly serious theological implications between *Theotokos* and the term favored by Nestorius – Χριστοτόκος – *Christotokos*. But there is even a differ-ence between *Theotokos* and *Mother of God*. Why would one want to stress the difference between *Theotokos* and *Mother of God*? Is it not becoming overly minute, insignificant, something that in reality is the same thing? But the fact is that there is a grammatical and conceptual difference between the two terms. If the Greek theologians had intended the diminished meaning of *Mother of God* , then they easily could have completely avoided Θεοτόκος by employing always the term μητήρ θεοῦ, a term readily at their disposal and one which they did use at times. But the point is that for them there was a difference between Θεοτόκος and μητήρ θεοῦ. The term *Mother of God* has no speci-ficity – by and of itself but within the thought world of Christian Trinitarianism it could grammatically and conceptually mean that the Blessed Virgin is the Mother of God the Father or of God the Holy Spirit. But the term *Theotokos* has specificity because of the "*tokos*" – by and of itself it can only refer to *Bearing God the Son*. The English term is too abrupt, not precise enough, and does not have the internal integrity that *Theotokos* has. Further, the English term has a tendency to bring into prominence the glory of Mary's motherhood, whereas the Greek term focuses attention on the Godhead of him who was born. In addition, the Greek term *Theotokos* protects in and of itself the revealed fact that Christ was very God who became man and, in assuming manhood from the Virgin, lost nothing of the Godhead which was his eternally. Conversely, the term *Theotokos* protects the revealed fact that he who was born of the *Theotokos* must have been man as well as God. The point of the term *Theotokos* is not as abstruse as many historians of Christian thought assume.

ST. JOHN CHRYSOSTOM AND NESTORIUS

The implications of Nestorius' thoughts on the term *Theotokos* have often brought forth a comparison with St. John Chrysostom's comments on the Blessed Mother. Inherent in this line of thought is the assumption that Antiochene theology did not have a very exalted view of the Blessed Mother. Such was not the case. However, there is truth in the assertion that St. John Chrysostom has spoken strangely at times on the subject of the Blessed Mother. By implication some historians of Christian thought attempt to include St. John Chrysostom in the category of a Nestorian.

Did St. John Chrysostom teach distinctly and clearly "two natures in one person?" In Christology St. John Chrysostom knows of the *communicatio idiomatum* – ἀντίδοσις τῶν ἰδιωμάτων – and this presupposes two natures in one person. Indirectly he even teaches that there were two wills in Christ when he writes that the Father and the Son have not one will but two wills. (see *Homily* 7, 6 in Migne, *Patrologia Graeca* 48, 765-766). There is no trace of Arianism or Semi-Arianism in Chrysostom. He distinguishes precisely between *ousia* and *physis* and between *hypostasis* or *prosopon*. That the Son is completely identical with the Father he teaches clearly and consistently. The word *homoousios* is used at least five times in his writings. More often he uses equivalent expressions such as "equal to the Father," "equality," "one in all things with the Father," "of the same nature," "unchanged in nature and power." And the Son possesses an individual personhood, distinct from the Father. Only once does he use the expression "similar to the Father in all things," an expression which was completely orthodox in this context. St. Basil recognized this expression as completely orthodox if it is understood in the sense of ἀπαραλλάκτως – unchanged, and that is precisely how St. John uses it.

At times St. John Chrysostom's thought is more Alexandrian than Antiochene. He puts the following words into the mouth of Christ: "Never have I considered the assumed humanity unharmonized with the divine operation – οὐδαμοῦ τὴν ἀναληφθεῖσαν ἀνθρωπότητα τῆς θείας ἐνεργείας ἄμικτον ἀπολέλοιπα – that is, functioning now as man, now as God with both signifying the nature . . . I teach that the humbler things are referred to the humanity and the nobler things to the divinity. By this unequal mixing of activity, I interpret the unequal union of the natures – διὰ τῆς ἀνίσου ταύτης τῶν ἔργων κράσεως τὴν ἄνισον τῶν φύσεων ἔνωσιν ἑρμηνεύων – and by my power over sufferings, I declare that my own sufferings are voluntary. As God, I controlled nature, sustaining a fast for forty days. But after, as man, I was hungry and tired. As God, I calmed the raging water. As man, I was tempted by the devil. As God, I cast out demons. As man, I am about to suffer for men" [*Patrologia Graeca* 50, 642-643]. In a stunning text explaining Christ's prayer in Gethsemane, St. John Chrysostom teaches the distinction of two wills as well as two natures [*Patrologia Graeca* 48, 766]. As Grillmeier has correctly observed, "The Antiochene, so persecuted by the Alexandrians, is far more Alexandrine than Antiochene in his Christology – a new indication of the care with which we must use a word like 'school'. Only with Theodore of Mopsuestia does 'Antiochene' Christology properly begin."

But St. John Chrysostom did not really deal with the problem – *he was not a theologian in the strict sense of the word*. This statement, however, needs qualification, it requires an explanation. Chrysostom's very character did not incline him to philosophical speculation. Rather, he was inclined towards asceticism, ethics, homiletics, and pastoral theology. Moreover, the times in which he flourished were relatively quiet in terms of dogmatic controversy. The Second Ecumenical Council of 381 had essentially ended Arianism in the East and the next theological tempest – Nestorianism – will erupt only after Chrysos - tom's death. Hence the need for dogmatic works was simply not pressing. Most importantly, however, is the fact that Chrysostom spoke *mainly as a pastor* . In a certain sense the people were exhausted from all the theological upheavals of the fourth century. St. John Chrysostom comments specifically on this situation: "I know that many expressions of that kind – *logos, ousia, hypostasis, homoousios, homoiousios, anhomois*, etc. – cannot be understood. Therefore I avoid *as much as is possible the treatment of speculative questions*, for the people are usually not able to follow these things. And if able, they still do not understand them clearly and with certainty." (see *Homily 4, 2 On John* in Migne, *Patrologia Graeca* 59, 48). He devoted himself to preaching and teaching the spiritual aspect of the Christian message, to educating his people in the faith of the Church, on the moral teaching of Christianity. He was interested in building in his people a faith of love to express in practical life. He was *par excellence* the pastoral theologian. He was not a systematic, speculative, or dogmatic theo - logian; *but he was still a theologian*. His enormous works reflect in scattered form the theology of the Church but in the context of pastoral, homiletical theology. If we cull out his random theological comments on the two natures of Christ, his references to the Incarnation, we will see them expressed not speculatively but pastorally. Because of this context it would be inappropriate and unfair to claim to see in his Christology any serious type of foreshadowing of Nestorian Christol - ogy – he may use the language and expressions of Antioch *but not the meaning* which later becomes associated with Antiochene Christology. Rather he is *naturally* inclined to use Antiochene expressions. He describes the Incarnation as σαρκὸς περιβολή –"clothing with flesh" – and σαρκὸς ἀνάληψις – "the assumption of flesh." And once he uses the expression ὁ θεὸς τὸν ἄνθροπον ἀνέλαβεν – "God has assumed the form of man." [For σαρκὸς περιβολή see *Homily 44, 3 On Matthew* in Migne, *Patrologia Graeca*, abbreviated as *PG* hereafter in these references, 67, 467; *Homily 7, 5* in *Contra Anomoes* in *PG* 48, 762; *Homily 11, 1 and 2 On John* in *PG* 59, 79 and 80; and in *Pater si possibile est 3* in *PG* 51, 38; for his use of σαρκὸς ἀνάληψις see *Homily 8, 1 On Matthew* in *PG* 57, 83; *Homily 11, 1 On John; Homily 58, 3 On Genesis* in *PG* 54, 510; in *Pater si possibile est* 3; and *Homily de Philogonio 3* in *PG* 48, 753; for his use of ὁ θεὸς τὸν ἄνθροπον ἀνέλαβεν, *Homily 7, 6* in *Contra Anomoes* in *PG* 438,

765]. He is inclined to define the σαρξ, the human flesh or nature, as the *holy tabernacle* – σκηνή – or *the temple* – ναός – in which the Godhead takes up its dwelling. He also never uses the "formula" ἕνωσις καθ' ὑπόστασιν – "unity of person."

His entire Christology can be expressed in one of his passages, which, incidentally, was quoted by Council of Chalcedon, the Fourth Ecumenical Council in 451.: "Through union, God the Logos and the Flesh are one, without the occurrence of a mingling, without the disap - pearance of the natures, but because of an ineffable, indefinable union. How this union took place, ask not. God alone knows." (see *Homily* 26, 1; *On the Gospel of John* in Migne, *Patrologia Graeca* 59, 154).

St. John Chrysostom writes that the Virgin Birth was "a great miracle," for "the Holy Spirit produced him from the body of a Virgin. But how I am unable to explain." (see *Homily* 25, 3 *On Matthew* in Migne, *Patrologia Graeca* 57, 331 and *Homily* 26, 1 *On John* in Migne, *Patrologia Graeca* 59, 154). He taught explicitly the perpetual virginity of Mary: Τίκτει ἡ παρθένος καὶ μένει παρθένος – "A Virgin gave birth and remains a Virgin." (see *Homily* 4, 3 *On Matthew* in Migne, *Patrologia Graeca* 57, 43).

But some of his explanations are surprising. In his *Commentary on St. Matthew* 12: 47 he writes that the Mother of Jesus had only come before the people in the midst of Jesus' sermon because she had maternal authority over her Son, of whose actual greatness she could have had no foreknowledge. This clearly proves ambition and impru - dence in her and in the others, for they should have waited until Jesus was finished with his sermon! (see *Homily* 44, 1 *On Matthew* in Migne, *Patrologia Graeca* 57, 464-465). In the same manner St. John Chrysostom states that it was perhaps motherly ambition when Mary said to her Son at the wedding in Cana that "they have no wine." (see *Homily* 21, 2 *On John* in Migne, *Patrologia Graeca* 59, 130). It is interesting that St. John Chrysostom's language is always much milder when he is commenting on *John* than on *Matthew*. In his *Fourth Homily on St. Matthew* he questions why the angel appeared to Mary before her conception and to St. Joseph after the conception. It was necessary, he writes, because otherwise the "admirable Virgin" herself would not have been able to explain how she had become a mother so suddenly. And then, he continues, perhaps from shame "she might have had an unholy idea and might have grasped either a cord or a sword." (Migne, *Patrologia Graeca* 57, 45).

Such explanations, astonishing as they are, can only be understood as incorrect interpretations and the use of "excessively human lan - guage," the tendency of which lies in the approach of Antiochene exegesis. It is important to remember that St. John Chrysostom did teach the miraculous conception, did teach the Virgin Birth, and did teach the perpetual virginity of Mary.

To see in some of St. John Chrysostom's expression a foreshadowing of Nestorian thought is quite untenable. Although St.

John never used the term *Theotokos*, he also never objected to such a term, not even by implication. Other, quite non-Nestorian Christian writers also never employed the term *Theotokos*.

THE REACTION TO NESTORIUS

Nestorius had unleashed a new theological controversy by attacking the usage of Θεοτόκος. Word spread quickly. St. Cyril had his repre - sentatives in Constantinople, as did Pope Celestine (bishop of Rome from 422 to 432). The lay people in Constantinople were disturbed – St. Cyril writes that the faithful were scandalized, σκανδαλιζόμενοι – and confused by this new development. As we know from the famous comment by St. Gregory of Nazianzus, everyone in Constantinople discussed theological issues. It was no exception this time. However, in this case the controversy did not originate from books of theologians but from the very pulpit of Constantinople. Hence, the issue, coming from the pulpit and dealing with a topic that was a part of their worship, had a more direct impact on the lay people in the capital city. A layman named Eusebius, who at that time was a lawyer but would later become bishop of Dorylaeum, publicly protested Nestorius' teachings by placing a Διαμαρτυρία [*Contestatio*] on the doors of Hagia Sophia. It was addressed to the entire body of clergy in Con - stantinople and, among other things, accused Nestorius of reviving the heresy of Paul of Samosata (bishop of Antioch from c.260 to 268]. This time the "Firebrand" had set off a theological conflagration. Eusebius had been sending copies of Nestorius' sermons to Pope Celestine and Marius Mercator was sending in his reports to Rome.

In general, the sequence of events unfolds approximately in the following way. Nestorius, aware that Rome is concerned about the state of affairs in Constantinople, sends a letter to Pope Celestine to explain his position on *Christotokos*, a letter written in Greek with no accom - panying Latin translation. The letter reportedly remained untranslated for months. To my knowledge the first complete translation of this important letter into English was done by Edward R. Hardy and published in Volume III of *The Library of Christian Classics*, *Christology of the Later Fathers* . The translation that follows is based on the above-mentioned translation.

NESTORIUS' FIRST *LETTER TO POPE CELESTINE*

"Brotherly communication with each other should indeed be enjoyed in order that we might, in unity, harmony, and concord, fight against the devil, the enemy of peace. Why this preface? A certain Julian, and Orontius and Fabius, saying that they are bishops from the West, have often approached our most pious and glorious emperor and bewailed their case, as orthodox men who have suffered persecution in an orthodox age. They have often addressed their complaints to us and as often have been rejected. Still they do not cease to repeat the same. Rather, they continue day by day filling the ears of all with their expressions of woe. We have spoken to them as is proper, even though we do not know the precise truth of their situation. But since we need a fuller knowledge of their case, so that our most pious and most Christian emperor may not continue to be annoyed by them; and that we may not be uncertain about the proper measures to take in this matter, being ignorant of their complaints, please give us information about them so that people may not cause trouble by improper consideration through ignorance of the true justice in this case. Also so that they may not expect something else after canonical sentence of Your Blessedness, given against them, I assume, because of religious divisions. For the rise of divisions calls for serious measures from true pastors."

"We have also found no slight corruption of orthodoxy among some of those here, which we have treated with both sternness and gentleness, as the case required. It is no small error but is similar to the corruption of Apollinarius and Arius, blending together the Lord's appearance as man into a kind of confused combination – so much so that certain of our clergy, some because of inexperience, others because of heretical error long kept hidden, as often happened even in the times of the apostles, err like heretics, and openly blaspheme God the Logos consubstantial with the Father, as if he took his beginning from the Christ-Bearing Virgin and grew up with his temple and was buried with it in the flesh. They even say that his flesh after the resurrection did not remain flesh but was changed into the nature of the Godhead. To speak briefly, they refer the Godhead of the Only-Begotten to the same origin as the flesh joined with it, and kill it with the flesh, and blasphemously say that the flesh joined with the Godhead was turned into deity by the deifying Logos, which is nothing more nor less than to corrupt both. They even dare to treat of the Christ-Bearing Virgin in a way as along with God, for they boldly call her *Theotokos*, when the holy and beyond-all-praise Fathers at Nicaea said no more of the holy Virgin than that our Lord Jesus Christ was incarnate of the Holy Spirit and the Virgin Mary – not to mention the Scriptures, which everywhere, both by angels and apostles, speak of the Virgin as mother of Christ, not of God the Logos. I presume that rumor has already informed Your Blessedness what conflicts we have endured for these things, and you have also learned that we have not struggled in vain, because many of those who had gone astray have by the grace of the Lord repented, learning from us that what is born is properly consubstantial with the parent, and that it was to the creature of the Lord's humanity, joined with God, of the Virgin by the Spirit, that what was seen among men had taken place. If anyone wishes to use this word *Theotokos* with reference to the humanity which was born, joined to God the Logos, and not with reference to the parent, we say that this word is not appropriate for her who gave birth because a true mother should be of the same essence as what is born of her. But the term could be accepted in consideration of this – that the word is used of the Virgin only because of the inseparable temple of God the Logos, for no one gives birth to one older than herself."

"I assume that rumor has already told you of these things, but we explain what has been happening to us in order to show in fact that it is in a brotherly spirit that we wish to know about the affairs of those whom we mentioned before, not out of mere importunate curiosity – since we tell you of our affairs as among brothers, sharing with each other the facts of these divisions, so that the beginning of this letter of mine may be indeed correct – for I said as I began this letter that we ought to enjoy brotherly communication with each other."

"I and those who are with me greet all the brotherhood in Christ which is with you."

NESTORIUS' DIPLOMATIC BLUNDER

Nestorius committed *a serious diplomatic blunder* by beginning and ending his letter to Pope Celestine with his mention of his concern for Julian of Eclanum and other Pelagians. Few things could have irritated a bishop of Rome then more than such a request concerning Pelagians. The Latin West had expended almost a decade on the Pelagian "case" and the matter was considered final. Now Nestorius wants "a fuller knowl - edge of their case," presumably to reexamine the matter. Although it began and presumably ended in the Latin West, the Pelagian "case" essentially travelled around the Roman empire – Rome, Sicily, Africa, Palestine, Gaul, Mopsuestia, and Constantinople.

Pelagius, born in Roman Britain, came to Rome – he was there as early as 409 – where he lived an exemplary life of asceticism, wrote a commentary on the letters of St. Paul, and fought quietly and skillfully against the lax morality prevalent in Rome at the time. He converted many to his life of monastic self-asceticism, the most important con - vert of which was Celestius. It was to be Celestius, not Pelagius, who triggered the entire Pelagian "case." Celestius also was more radical in his theological thought than was Pelagius. In a word, the essence of "Pelagianism" is the belief that man can earn his salvation, that man can attain perfection by the constant exertion of the will. It was a moral, an ethical, an ascetic system which, when put into theological terminology, undermined the significance of the freedom of God, of God's free gift of creation and salvation through his free gift of grace. Moreover, the entire Pelagian "case" is complicated by different phases and different theological positions among the so-called "Pelagians" themselves. What is significant is that the balance between the grace of God and the freedom of man is upset. The synergistic theology of the earlier Church fathers – one might say an almost spontaneous synergistic theological perspective – which would be loathe to deny the initiative of God in salvation and just as loathe to deny that man participates spiritually in salvation by at least accepting or responding to the initiative of God, if pressed to put their spontaneous synergy into theological perspective – it is this that Pelagianism threatened.

About 410 or 411 Pelagius and Celestius leave Rome, probably because of the sack of Rome by Alaric. After a brief stay in Sicily, which would become a stronghold of Pelagianism and produce an indigenous Pelagian theologian known as the "Sicilian Britain," Pelag - ius and Celestius arrive in Hippo. At the time St. Augustine was in Carthage because of problems with Donatism. Pelagius left a very polite letter for St. Augustine, to which St. Augustine responded politely. Pelagius leaves Hippo but Celestius travels to Carthage and there requests ordination. Suspicion had already been created. In either 411 or 412 the Council of Carthage questioned Celestius on six or seven propositions found in his writings. Celestius answered evasively, refused to recant, and he was excluded from the communion of the Church. Celestius quickly left for Ephesus and was there ordained. Although St. Augustine was not present at the Council of Carthage and though he had taken no part in the controversy up to this point, he became concerned when he realized the number of converts Pelagianism had made in Sicily and Africa. He began to write directly on the matter, although it is clear that his position against Pelagius had been taken long before he ever heard of Pelagius; that is, in his own theological writings he had already developed his "Augustinian" theology on grace and original sin.

The controversy soon spreads to Palestine and erupts there in 414. Two Latin theologians happened to be in Palestine at the time – Jerome and Paul Orosius. Orosius had been sent by St. Augustine to study with Jerome and to keep St. Augustine informed of the activities of Pelagius and Celestius – he had brought letters with him concerning Pelagianism and also Origenism. Bishop John of Jerusalem convoked a council in 415. The Council of Jerusalem did not condemn Pelag - ianism. Soon a second council took place in Palestine, this time in Diospolis (Lydda) in 415. Eulogius, bishop of Caesarea presided. Written charges had been drawn up by two bishops from Gaul – Heros of Arles and Lazarus of Aix. Pelagius was present at this council and was able to circumvent most of the questions quite easily, even condemning some of the ideas of Celestius – this he could honestly do because Celestius was more extreme than Pelagius. All accused of heresy were acquitted. St. Jerome refers to the Council of Diospolis as a "*synodus miserabilis*" and St. Augustine was quick to write that "it was not heresy acquitted at that council but the man who denied the heresy." St. Augustine was deeply concerned with the result and with what he considered Pelagius' dishonesty. This prompted St. Augustine to write his *De gestis Pelagii*, to which he appends the actual proceedings of that council. After the Council of Jerusalem Orosius had demanded that since the controversy had arisen in the Latin West, then the Latin West should determine the matter. Deputies and letters were sent to Pope Innocent I (402-417).

This prompted St. Augustine to convoke two councils in Africa in 416 – the Council of Carthage and the Council of Milevis in Numidia. Both councils condemned Pelagianism. St. Augustine sent the decision to Pope Innocent I and asked him to excommunicate Pelagius and Celestius. On January 27, 417 Pope Innocent I condemned Pelagius and Celestius. On September 23 of the same year St. Augustine, during a sermon, announced that he had received an answer from Rome: "*Inde etiam rescripta venerunt. Causa finita est. Utinam aliquando finiatur error.*" (see *Sermon* 131, 10; it was this that give rise to the *fictional* statement: *Roma locuta est; causa finita est.*)

Meanwhile, Pelagius wrote a letter to Pope Innocent I and Celestius left for Rome to deal with the matter personally. But Pope Innocent I had died. His successor, Pope Zosimus (417-418), a Greek by birth, was deeply impressed by Celestius. Pope Zosimus wrote to the African bishops in September of 417 and accused them of a hasty condemnation, even declaring that opponents of Pelagius and Celestius were "wicked slanderers."

St. Augustine convoked another council quickly and issued nine canons against Pelagianism. He sent the decision of this Council of Carthage to Pope Zosimus and claimed that the Pope had been misled. He wrote that "he should hold to the decision pronounced by Innocent against Pelagius and Celestius until both of them distinctly acknowl - edged that for every single good action we need the help of the grace of God through Jesus Christ and this not only to perceive what is right but also to practice it because without it we cannot either possess, think, speak, or do anything really good or holy." Pope Zosimus' reply is interesting. He declared he had already fully considered the matter. Yet he sent the Roman dossier to St. Augustine so "there could be consultation and agreement." Meanwhile, St. Augustine had persuaded the Western emperor Honorius (395-423) to issue an imperial edict denouncing Pelagius and Celestius. Pope Zosimus then decided to re - examine the case. The result was the condemnation of the two and the issuance of his *Epistola tractoria* to which all Western bishops were to subscribe. Eighteen Italian bishops refused to sign and they were exiled. *One of these was Julian of Eclanum.*

This is the very same Julian whom Nestorius mentions in his letter to Pope Celestine. Neither Pelagianism – in any of its forms – nor the Augustinian doctrines of grace, predestination, and original sin would ever leave the Church entirely. Seldom was the balance of strict orthodoxy maintained by theologians or theological schools of thought. Perhaps the most interesting and most orthodox theologian involved in the controversy was St. John Cassian, whose position has often been inaccurately cast as that of a Semi-Pelagian.

Here, of course, what is of importance is *the diplomatic blunder committed by Nestorius*. To mention the Pelagians in a form of inter - cession in the first and last parts of his letter was not only undiplo - matic. More than that. It implies the possibility of a reexamination of the Pelagian "case" by Nestorius. By implying this, Nestorius implies also that Constantinople has the ecclesiastical right to reexamine decisions made by Rome. In the letter it is clear that Nestorius knows that Rome has made "canonical sentence" in the matter. Nestorius seems more concerned about the Pelagians than about the furor caused by his attack on the usage of the term *Theotokos*. It almost seems as though he brings up the subject casually, *en passant*. This is not an auspicious beginning with Pope Celestine.

POPE ST. CELESTINE I AND THE AUTHORITY OF THE ROMAN SEE

Perhaps one could call it a *second diplomatic blunder*. In any case, Nestorius underestimated the authority and power of the Roman See and the character of Pope Celestine in his vigor to assert this authority. He seems unaware of Rome's consciousness of herself and seems unaware that he is dealing with a strong Pope who will implement this very consciousness that Rome had of herself, of her position in the Church.

Pope St. Celestine (422 432) had been an archdeacon of the Roman Church before his papacy. He was therefore knowledgeable of the Pelagian "case." The history of the authority and primacy of the Roman See is a history that is seldom approached objectively. Too often scholars writing on the subject begin with a pre-conceived notion and attempt to prove their position. Some have attempted to show that there was no such thing as a primacy; some that it was merely a "primacy of honor," and some that papal infallibility was already a *sine qua non* in the early years of the Church. The fact of the history of the early Church reveals quite vividly that Rome had a consciousness of herself, that Rome understood that she occupied a special place among the bishops of the Church, that Rome was constantly intervening in the affairs of other churches, and that other churches and individuals were constantly appealing to Rome. This does not establish in any sense the later doctrine of papal infallibility nor does it imply that Rome was always correct. It does reveal that Rome believed she had the right to interfere, to make judgments, and to receive appeals. What is, more - over, interesting is the fact that others appeal to Rome on a consistent basis – bishops, councils, priests, despite canonical regulations that in certain cases would preclude an appeal to Rome.

In Pope St. Celestine I Nestorius is dealing with a Pope who is quite aware of the authority of Rome. Whether this authority was "given to Rome by the fathers because Rome was the capital city," as the third canon of the Second Ecumenical Council and the twenty-eighth canon of the Fourth Ecumenical Council state, or whether Rome's primacy rests on other grounds, is not the issue. The historical fact is that Rome did interfere throughout the Church and others, throughout the Church, appealed to Rome. The fact that Rome was not always correct, the fact that Rome often handled certain situations undiplomatically and with a certain arrogance – this is not the issue. It is merely a fact that from the very beginning – see Pope Clement's early letter to the Church at Corinth – there was a certain recognized primacy of the Roman Church.

The case of Pope St. Celestine I is noteworthy. It is sufficient to remember the famous *Letter to Pope Celestine* from St. Augustine (*Letter* 209) in which St. Augustine writes that he is ready to resign in his old age if Pope Celestine does not help him and confirm a decision, an incorrect one, which St. Augustine made. The popes of the sixth century, when mentioning the Council of Ephesus (431) which deposes Nestorius, state that the council had for its presidents "St. Celestine and St. Cyril." For example, Pope Vigilius (537-555) in his *Encyclical Letter* of February 5, 552 writes "and the Council of Ephesus, over which our predecessor, Pope Celestine of blessed memory, and Cyril, bishop of Alexandria, presided." (See Migne, *Patrologia Latina* 169, 56); this is repeated almost verbatim by Pope Pelagius II (579-590) in his *Letter to Elias of Aquileia* in *Patrologia Latina* 72, 708); see also the *Liber Diurnus* in *Patrologia Latina* 105, 46-48).

At the Council of Ephesus, although the papal legates arrived late, there is the famous exclamation of the papal legate Philip: "There is no doubt, and in fact it has been known in all ages, that the holy and most blessed Peter, prince and head of the Apostles, pillar of the faith and foundation of the Catholic Church, received the keys of the kingdom from our Lord Jesus Christ, the Savior and Redeemer of the human race, and that to him was given the power of loosing and binding sins: who, even to this time and forever, lives and judges in his successors." The record of the council contains no objection to this assertion.

Thus it is that Nestorius finds himself confronted by a strong bishop of Rome and by the strong and vindictive personality of St. Cyril from a jealous throne of rivalry. In Pope Celestine Nestorius encounters his ecclesiastical match; in St. Cyril Nestorius encounters his theological match. Combined, Nestorius' chances are not very favorable. Pope Celestine has been receiving copies of Nestorius' sermons from Cyril, from Marius Mercator, and from Eusebius.

ST. CYRIL'S SECOND *LETTER TO NESTORIUS*

The circulation of Nestorius's sermons had caused disturbance among the monks of Egypt. In 429 St. Cyril writes his first letter to Nestorius. In February of 430 St. Cyril writes his *second letter* to Nestorius (see Migne, *Patrologia Graeca* 77, 44-50):

"Certain persons, as I hear, are taking liberty with my reputation before your Holiness . . . They utter ill-advised speeches to my disadvantage, although they have suffered no wrong at my hands, except that they have been reprehended, and that deservedly – one for having defrauded the blind and the poor, another for having drawn his sword upon his mother, and a third for having stolen money with a maidservant as an accomplice. . ."

"But I make no great account of these matters lest I should stretch the measure of my littleness beyond my Lord and Master."

"But I turn to what specially concerns me and I admonish you as a brother in the Lord to use all possible circumspection in teaching the people and in setting forth the doctrine of faith, bearing in mind that to offend even one of these little ones who believe in Christ, subjects the person guilty of it to intolerable punishment. And if so great numbers of persons have been thus injured how do we not need all possible care and study that we may do away the offenses and rightly expound the doctrine of the faith to those who are seeking the truth! And in this we shall succeed, if, considering the statements of the holy fathers, we are careful to esteem them highly, and, proving ourselves whether we be in the faith, as it is written, thoroughly conform our own beliefs to their sound and unexceptionable doctrines."

"The holy and great council then affirmed that the very "Only-Begotten of the Father," "very God of very God," "Light of Light" by whom the Father made all things "came down, was incarnate, and became man, suffered, rose again on the third day, and ascended into heaven." These words and these formulae we must adhere to, con - sidering what is meant when it is said the Logos which is of God "became incarnate and became man."

"For we do not affirm that the nature of the Logos underwent a change and became flesh, or that it was transformed into a whole or perfect man consisting of soul and body. But we say that the Logos, having in an ineffable and inconceivable manner personally united to himself flesh and a living soul, became man and was called the Son of Man, yet not of mere will of favor, nor again by the simple taking to himself of a person (that is, of a human to his divine person), and that while the natures which were brought together into this true unity were diverse there was of both one Christ and one Son: not as though the diverseness of the natures were done away by this union but rather the Godhead and Manhood completed for us the one Lord and Christ and Son by their unutterable and unspeakable concurrence and unity. And thus, although he subsisted and was begotten of the Father before the worlds, he is spoken of as having been born also after the flesh of a woman: not that his divine nature had its beginning of existence in the holy Virgin or needed of necessity on its own account a second generation after its generation from the Father, for it is foolish and absurd to say that he who subsisted before all worlds, and was co-eternal with the Father, stood in need of a second beginning of existence, but inasmuch as the Logos having "for us and for our salvation," personally united to himself human nature, came forth of a woman, for this reason he is said to have been born after the flesh. For he was not first born an ordinary man of the holy Virgin and then the Logos descended upon him, but having been made one with the flesh from the very womb itself, he is said to have submitted to a birth according to the flesh, as appropriating and making his own the birth of his own flesh."

"In like manner we say that he "suffered" and "rose again." Not as though God the Logos suffered in his own divine nature either stripes or the piercing of nails or the other wounds inflicted on him, for the Godhead is impassible because it is incorporeal. But inasmuch as that which had become his own body suffered these things, therefore again he himself is said to have suffered them for us. For the Impassible was in the suffering body."

"So likewise of his death. For the Logos of God is by nature both incorruptible and Life and Life-giving, but inasmuch as his own body by the grace of God, as Paul says, tasted death for every man, therefore once more he himself is said to have suffered death for us. Not as though he experienced death as regards his own divine nature – to say or hold which is madness – but that, as I said just now, his flesh tasted death."

"So likewise when his flesh was raised, the resurrection again is spoken of as his resurrection, not as though he had seen corruption, God forbid, but because once more it was his own body that was raised."

"Thus we confess one Christ and Lord, not as worshipping a man conjointly with the Logos, that there may not through this phrase "conjointly" be insinuated the semblance of division (as though we were dividing the one Christ into two Persons) – but as worshipping one and the same Person because the body of the Lord is not alien from the Lord, with which body also he sits with the Father himself: not again as though two sons do sit with the Father but one united to his own flesh. But if we reject this hypostatic union either as impossible or unfit, we fall into the error of making two sons. For in that case we must needs distinguish and speak of the man severally (the human person) dignified with the appellation of Son, and again of the Logos which is of God severally (the divine Person) possessing naturally the Sonship, both name and thing (that is, if we reject a union of essences or natures in the one Person, we make two Sons, and must perforce distinguish – speaking of the One, as merely dignified with the title of Son, the other as Son in reality as well as in name)."

"We must not then divide the one Lord Jesus Christ into two sons. To hold this will nowise contribute to soundness of faith, even though some make a show of acknowledging a union of persons. For Scripture does not say that The Logos united to himself the person of a man but that "he became flesh." But this expression "the Logos became flesh" is nothing else than that he became partaker of flesh and blood, just as we do, and made our body his own, and was born a man of a woman, not casting aside the being of God, and having been begotten of God the Father, but even when taking to himself flesh still remaining what he was. This is the doctrine which strict orthodoxy everywhere gives the place of honor to. Thus shall we find the holy Fathers to have held. So did they make bold to call the holy Virgin "*Theotokos*." Not as though the nature of the Logos or his Godhead had its beginning from the holy Virgin but inasmuch as his holy Body, endowed with a rational soul, was born of her, to which Body also the Logos was personally united, on this account he is said to have been born after the flesh."

"Thus writing out of the love which I have in Christ, I entreat you as a brother and charge you before Christ and the elect angels, to hold and teach these things with us that the bond of harmony and love between the priests of God may remain unbroken."

ST. CYRIL AND POPE ST. CELESTINE

Based on the information coming to St. Cyril from his agents in Constantinople, including copies of Nestorius's sermons, St. Cyril takes decisive action by writing to Pope Celestine, enclosing a dossier on the case, and accompanying a Latin translation of his material. From his own sources and from the letter that Nestorius had sent him, Pope Celestine is also informed on the situation. Pope Celestine commissioned St.Cyril to investigate the orthodoxy of Nestorius and in August of 430, after reviewing St. Cyril's evidence and the evidence provided to him by the Roman archdeacon Leo (later to become Pope Leo the Great), who relied on St. John Cassian's work on the subject – *De Incarnatione Domini contra Nestorium Libri VII*, Pope Celestine I convoked a Roman Council and Nestorius was condemned for his "innovations." Pope Celestine gave Nestorius ten days to retract and he entrusted St. Cyril with the responsibility of executing the sentence.

In November St. Cyril convoked a Council at Alexandria which condemned Nestorius. St. Cyril drew up his famous Twelve Anathemas or Twelve Chapters which were to be a test of Nestorius' doctrine. Nestorius was to agree with the twelve positions and give his signature. St. Cyril sends Nestorius his third letter, to which he appends the Twelve Anathemas.

ST. CYRIL'S THIRD *LETTER TO NESTORIUS*
NOVEMBER 430

"To the most reverend and God-loving fellow-minister Nestorius, Cyril and the synod assembled in Alexandria, of the Egyptian Province, Greeting in the Lord."

"When our Savior says, clearly: 'He that loveth father or mother more than me is not worthy of me and he that loveth son or daughter more than me is not worthy of me,' what is to become of of us, from whom your Holiness requires that we love you more than Christ the Savior of us all? Who can help us in the day of judgment or what kind of excuse shall we find for thus keeping silence so long with regard to the blasphemies made by you against him? If you injured yourself alone, by teaching and holding such things, perhaps it would be less of a matter. But you have greatly scandalized the whole Church, and have cast among the people the leaven of a strange and new heresy. And not to those there [Constantinople] only but also to those wherever the books of your explanation were sent. How can we any longer, under these circumstances, make a defence for our silence, or how shall we not be forced to remember that Christ said: 'Think not that I am come to send peace on earth: I came not to send peace, but a sword. For I am come to set a man at variance against his father, and the daughter against her mother.' For if faith be injured, let there be lost the honor due to parents, as stale and tottering; let even the law of tender love towards children and brothers be silenced; let death be better to the pious than living, 'that they might obtain a better resurrection,' as it is written."

"Behold, therefore, how we, together with the holy synod which met in great Rome, presided over by the most holy and most reverend brother and fellow-minister, Celestine, the Bishop, also testify by this third letter to you, and counsel you to abstain from these mischievous and distorted dogmas, which you hold and teach, and to receive the right faith, handed down to the churches from the beginning through the holy Apostles and Evangelists, who 'were eye-witnesses, and ministers of the Logos.' And if your Holiness have not a mind to this according to the limits defined in the writings of our brother of blessed memory and most reverend fellow-minister Celestine, Bishop of the Church of Rome, be well assured then that you have no lot with us, nor place or standing among the priests and bishops of God. For it is not possible for us to overlook the churches thus troubled, and the people scan - dalized, and the right faith set aside, and the sheep scattered by you, who ought to save them, if indeed we are ourselves adherents of the right faith, and followers of the devotion of the holy fathers. And we are in communion with all those laymen and clergymen cast out or deposed by your Holiness on account of the faith, for it is not right that those, who resolved to believe rightly, should suffer by your Holiness on account of the faith. For it is not right that those, who resolved to believe rightly, should suffer by your choice, for they do well in opposing you. This very thing you have mentioned in your epistle written to our most holy and fellow-bishop Celestine of great Rome."

"But it would not be sufficient for your reverence to confess with us only the symbol of the faith set out some time ago by the Holy Spirit at the great and holy synod convened in Nicaea: for you have not held and interpreted it rightly, but rather perversely; even though you confess with your voice the form of words. But in addition, in writing and by oath, you must confess that you also anathematize those polluted and unholy dogmas of yours, and that you will hold and teach that which we all, bishops, teachers, and leaders of the people both East and West, hold. The holy synod of Rome and we all agreed on the epistle written to your Holiness from the Alexandrian Church as being right and blameless. We have added to these our own letters and that which it is necessary for you to hold and teach, and what you should be careful to avoid. Now this is the Faith of the Catholic and Apostolic Church to which all Orthodox Bishops, both East and West, agree:"

"We believe in one God, the Father Almighty, Maker of all things visible and invisible, and in one Lord Jesus Christ, the Only-Begotten Son of God, begotten of his Father, that is, of the essence of the Father; God of God, Light of Light, Very God of Very God, begotten, not made, being of one essence with the Father, by whom all things were made, both those in heaven and those in the earth. Who for us men and for our salvation, came down, and was incarnate, and became man. He suffered, and rose again the third day. He ascended into the heavens, from thence he shall come to judge both living and the dead. And in the Holy Spirit. But those that say, There was a time when he was not, and, before he was begotten he was not, and that he was made of that which previously was not, or that he was of some other essence; and that the Son of God was capable of change or alteration – those the Catholic and Apostolic Church anathematizes."

"Following in all points the confessions of the Holy Fathers which they made (the Holy Spirit speaking in them) and following the scope of their opinions, and going, as it were, in the royal way, we confess that the Only-Begotten Logos of God, begotten of the same essence of the Father, True God from True God, Light from Light, through whom all things were made, the things in heaven and the things in the earth, coming down for our salvation, making himself of no reputation, was incarnate and made man; that is, taking flesh of the holy Virgin, and having made it his own from the womb, he subjected himself to birth for us, and came forth man from a woman, without casting off that which he was; but although he assumed flesh and blood, he remained what he was, God in essence and in truth. Neither do we say that his flesh was changed into the nature of divinity, nor that the ineffable nature of the Logos of God was laid aside for the nature of flesh. For he is unchanged and absolutely unchangeable, being the same always, according to the Scriptures. For although visible and a child in swad - dling clothes, and even in the bosom of his Virgin Mother, he filled all creation as God, and was a co-ruler with him who begat him, for the Godhead is without quantity and dimension, and cannot have limits."

"Confessing the Logos to be made one with the flesh according to essence, we adore one Son and Lord Jesus Christ: we do not divide the God from the man, nor separate him into parts, as though the two natures were mutually united in him only through a sharing of dignity and authority (for that is a novelty and nothing else), neither do we give separately to the Logos of God the name Christ and the same name separately to a different one born of a woman. But we know only one Christ, the Logos from God the Father with his own Flesh. For as man he was anointed with us, although it is he himself who gives the Spirit to those who are worthy and not in measure, according to the saying of the blessed Evangelist John."

"But we do not say that the Logos of God dwelt in him as in a common man born of the holy Virgin, lest Christ be thought of as a God-bearing man. For although the Logos tabernacled among us, it is also said that in Christ 'dwelt all the fulness of the Godhead bodily.' But we understand that he became flesh, not just as he is said to dwell in the saints, but we define that that tabernacling in him was according to equality. But being made one according to nature, and not converted into flesh, he made his indwelling in such a way, as we may say that the soul of man does in his own body."

"One therefore is Christ both Son and Lord, not as if a man had attained only such a *conjunction* with God as consists in *a unity of dignity alone or of authority*. For it is not equality of honor which unites natures; for then Peter and John, who were of equal honor with each other, being both Apostles and holy disciples, would have been one, and, yet the two are not one. Neither do we understand the manner of *conjunction* to be apposition, for this does not suffice for natural oneness. Nor yet according to relative *participation*, as we are also joined to the Lord, as it is written, 'We are one Spirit in him.' Rather we deprecate the term of *'junction'* as not having sufficiently signified the oneness. But we do not call the Logos of God the Father, the God nor the Lord of Christ, lest we openly cut in two the one Christ, the Son and Lord, and fall under the charge of blasphemy, making him the God and Lord of himself. For the *Logos* of God, as we have said already, was made hypostatically one in flesh, yet he is God of all and he rules all. But he is not the slave of himself, nor his own Lord. For it is foolish, or rather impious, to think or teach thus. For he said that God was his Father, although he was God by nature, and of his essence. Yet we are not ignorant that while he remained God, he also became man and subject to God, according to the law suitable to the nature of the manhood. But how could he become the God or Lord of himself? Consequently as man, and with regard to the measure of his humiliation, it is said that he is equally with us subject to God. Thus he became under the Law, although as God he spoke the Law and was the Law-giver."

"We are careful also how we say about Christ: 'I worship the One clothed on account of the One clothing him, and on account of the Unseen, I worship the Seen.' It is horrible to say in this connection as follows: 'The assumed as well as the assuming have the name of God.' For the saying of this divides again Christ into two, and puts the man separately by himself and God also by himself. For this saying denies openly the Unity according to which one is not worshipped in the other; but Jesus Christ is considered as One, the Only-Begotten Son, to be honored with one adoration together with his own flesh."

"We confess that he is the Son, begotten of God the Father, and Only-Begotten God. And although according to his own nature he was not subject to suffering, yet he suffered for us in the flesh according to the Scriptures, and although impassible, yet in his Crucified Body he made his own the sufferings of his own flesh; and by the grace of God he tasted death for all: he gave his own Body thereto, although he was by nature himself the life and the resurrection, in order that, having trodden down death by his unspeakable power, first in his own flesh, he might become the first born from the dead, and the first-fruits of them that slept. And that he might make a way for the nature of man to attain incorruption by the grace of God (as we just now said), he tasted death for every man, and after three days rose again, having despoiled hell. So although it is said that the resurrection of the dead was through man, yet we understand that man to have been the Logos of God, and the power of death was loosed through him, and he shall come in the fulness of time as the One Son and Lord, in the glory of the Father, in order to judge the world in righteousness, as it is written."

"We will necessarily add this also. Proclaiming the death, according to the flesh, of the Only-Begotten Son of God, that is Jesus Christ, confessing his resurrection from the dead, and his ascension into heaven, we offer the Unbloody Sacrifice in the churches, and so go on to the mystical thanksgivings, and are sanctified, having received his Holy Flesh and the Precious Blood of Christ the Savior of us all. And *not* as common flesh do we receive it; God forbid; *nor* as of a man sanctified and *associated* with the Logos according to the *unity of worth*, or as having a divine indwelling, *but* as truly the Life-giving and very flesh of the Logos himself. For he is the Life according to his nature as God, and when he became united to his Flesh, he made it also to be Life-giving, as also he said to us: 'Verily, verily, I say unto you, Except ye eat the flesh of the Son of Man and drink his Blood.' For we must not think that it is flesh of a man like us (for how can the flesh of man be life-giving by its own nature?) but as having become truly the very own of him who for us both became and was called Son of Man. Besides, what the Gospels say our Savior said of himself, we do not divide between two hypostases or persons. For neither is he, the one and only Christ, to be thought of as double, although of two and they diverse, yet he has joined them in an indivisible union, just as everyone knows a man is not double although made up of soul and body, but is one of both. Wherefore when thinking rightly, we transfer the human and the divine to the same person."

"For when as God he speaks about himself: 'He who hath seen me hath seen the Father,' and 'I and my Father are one,' we consider his ineffable divine nature according to which he is One with his Father through the *identity of essence* – 'The image and impress and brightness of his glory.' But when not scorning the measure of his humanity, he said to the Jews: 'But now ye seek to kill me, a man that hath told you the truth.' Again no less than before we recognized that he is the Logos of God from his identity and likeness to the Father and from the circumstances of his humanity. For if it is necessary to believe that being by nature God, he became flesh, that is, *a man endowed with a reasonable soul*, what reason can certain ones have to be ashamed of this language about him, which is suitable to him as man? For if he should reject the words suitable to him as man, who compelled him to become man like us? And as he humbled himself to a voluntary abasement for us, for what cause can any one reject the words suitable to such abasement? Therefore, all the words which are read in the Gospels are to be applied to One Person, to One Hypostasis of the Logos Incarnate. For the Lord Jesus Christ is One, according to the Scriptures, although he is called 'the Apostle and High Priest of our profession' as offering to God and the Father the confession of faith which we make to him, and through him to God even the Father and also to the Holy Spirit. Yet we say he is, according to nature, the Only-Begotten of God. And not to any man different from him do we assign the name of priesthood, and the thing, for he became 'the Mediator between God and men,' and a Reconciler unto peace, having offered himself as a sweet smelling savor to God and the Father. Therefore also he said: 'Sacrifice and offering thou wouldest not; but a body hast thou prepared me: In burnt offerings and sacrifices for sin thou hast had no pleasure. Then said I, 'Lo, I come (in the volume of the book it is written of me) to do thy will, O God.' For on account of us he offered his body as a sweet smelling savor, and not for himself; for what offering or sacrifice was needed for himself, who as God existed above all sins? For 'all have sinned and come short of the glory of God,' so that we become prone to fall, and the nature of man has fallen into sin, yet not so he (and therefore we fall short of his glory). How then can there be further doubt that the true Lamb died for us and on our account? And to say that he offered himself for himself and us, could in no way escape the charge of impiety. For he never committed a fault at all, neither did he sin. What offering then did he need, not having sin for which sacrifices are rightly offered? But when he spoke about the Spirit, he said: 'He shall glorify me.' If we think rightly, we do not say that the One Christ and Son as needing glory from another received glory from the Holy Spirit; for neither greater than he nor above him is his Spirit, but because he used the Holy Spirit to show forth his own divinity in his mighty works, therefore he is said to have been glorified by him just as if any one of us should say concerning his inherent strength for example, or his knowledge of anything, 'They glorified me.' For although the Spirit is the same essence, yet we think of him by himself, as he is the Spirit and not the Son. But he is not different from him, for he is called the Spirit of truth and Christ is the Truth, and he is sent by him, just as, moreover, he is from God and the Father. When then the Spirit worked miracles through the hands of the holy apostles after the Ascension of Our Lord Jesus Christ into heaven, he glorified him. For it is believed that he who works through his own Spirit is God according to nature. Therefore he said: 'He shall receive of mine, and shall show it unto you.' but we do not say this as if the Spirit is wise and powerful through some sharing with another, for he is all perfect and in need of no good thing. Since, therefore, he is the Spirit of the Power and Wisdom of the Father (that is, of the Son), he is evidently Wisdom and Power."

"And since the holy Virgin brought forth corporally God made one with flesh according to nature, for this reason we also call her *Theo - tokos*, not as if the nature of the Logos had the beginning of its existence from the flesh."

"For 'In the beginning was the Logos, and the Logos was with God, and the Logos was God,' and he is the Maker of the ages, co-eternal with the Father, and Creator of all; but, as we have already said, since he united to himself hypostatically human nature from her womb, also he subjected himself to birth as man, not as needing necessarily in his own nature birth in time and in these last times of the world, but in order that he might bless the beginning of our existence, and that that which sent the earthly bodies of our whole race to death might lose its power for the future by his being born of a woman in the flesh. And this: 'In sorrow thou shalt bring forth children,' being removed through him, he showed the truth of that spoken by the prophet, 'Strong death swallowed them up, and again God hath wiped away every tear from off all faces.' For this cause also we say that he attended, having been called, and also blessed, the marriage in Cana of Galilee, with his holy Apostles in accordance with *oikonomia*. We have been taught to hold these things by the holy Apostles and Evangelists, and all the God-inspired Scriptures, and in the true confessions of the blessed Fathers."

"To all these your reverence also should agree, and give heed, without any guile. And what it is necessary that your reverence should anathematize, we have subjoined to our letter."

THE *TWELVE ANATHEMAS* OF ST. CYRIL AGAINST NESTORIUS

I." If anyone will not confess that the Emmanuel is very God, and that therefore the Holy Virgin is the *Theotokos*, inasmuch as in the flesh she bore the Logos of God made flesh (as it is written, 'The Logos became flesh'), let him be anathema."

II. "If anyone shall not confess that the Logos of God the Father is united hypostatically to flesh, and that with that flesh of his own, he is one only Christ both God and man at the same time, let him be anathema."

III. "If anyone shall after the (hypostatic) union divide the hypostases in the one Christ, joining them by that connection alone, which happens according to worthiness, or even authority and power, and not rather by a coming together, which is made by natural union, let him be anathema."

IV. "If anyone shall divide between two persons or subsistences those expressions which are contained in the Evangelical and Apostolic writings, or which have been said concerning Christ by the Saints, or by himself, and shall apply some to him as to a man separate from the Logos of God, and shall apply others to the only Logos of God the Father, on the ground that they are fit to be applied to God, let him be anathema."

V. "If anyone shall dare to say that the Christ is a *Theophorus* (that is, God-bearing) man and not rather that he is very God, as an only Son through nature, because 'the Logos became flesh,' and 'has a share in flesh and blood as we do,' let him be anathema."

VI. " If anyone shall dare say that the Logos of God the Father is the God of Christ or the Lord of Christ, and shall not rather confess him as at the same time both God and Man, since according to the Scriptures, 'The Logos became flesh,' let him be anathema."

VII. "If anyone shall say that Jesus as man is only energized by the Logos of God, and that the glory of the Only-Begotten is attributed to him as something not properly his, let him be anathema."

VIII. "If anyone shall dare to say that the assumed man ought to be worshipped together with God the Logos, and glorified together with him, and recognized together with him as God, and yet as two different things, the one with the other (for this "Together with" is added, that is, by the Nestorians, to convey this meaning) and shall not rather with one adoration worship the Emmanuel and pay to him one glorification, as (it is written) 'The Logos became flesh,' let him be anathema."

IX. "If any man shall say that the one Lord Jesus Christ was glorified by the Holy Spirit, so that he used through him a power not his own and from him received power against unclean spirits and power to work miracles before men and shall not rather confess that it was his own Spirit through which he worked these divine signs, let him be anathema."

X. "Whosoever shall say that it is not the divine Logos himself, when he was made flesh and had become man as we are, but another than he, a man born of a woman, yet different from him, who is become our Great High Priest and Apostle; or if any man shall say that he offered himself in sacrifice for himself and not rather for us, whereas, being without sin, he had no need of offering or sacrifice, let him be anathema."

XI. "Whosoever shall not confess that the flesh of the Lord gives life and that it pertains to the Logos of God the Father as his very own, but shall pretend that it belongs to another person who is united to him (that is, the Logos) only according to honor, and who has served as a dwelling for the divinity; and shall not rather confess, as we say, that that flesh gives life because it is that of the Logos who gives life to all, let him be anathema."

XII. "Whosoever shall not recognize that the Logos of God suffered in the flesh, that he was crucified in the flesh, and that likewise in that same flesh he tasted death and that he is become the first-begotten of the dead, for, as he is God, he is the life and it is he that gives life, let him be anathema."

NESTORIUS' REACTION TO THE DECISIONS
OF ROME AND ALEXANDRIA

It was long believed that Nestorius answered Cyril with *Twelve Counter-Anathemas* but one can no longer rely on these as being authentic. In 1922 E. Schwartz offered rather convincing proof that these were not written by Nestorius but long after his death. Even the Latin translation of these *Twelve Counter-Anathemas*, attributed to Marius Mercator, seem to have originated much later.

What is known is that Nestorius turns to emperor Theodosius II (408-450) to request his convocation of an ecumenical council. It was to be in that forum of an ecumenical council where Nestorius would answer the charges brought against him. The events of that council, the Third Ecumenical Council (Ephesus, 431), are given later in this book, especially under the chapter on St. Cyril. The outcome, in any case, is the condemnation of Nestorius. The emperor was finally forced to condemn Nestorius and depose him. As Nestorius writes about the Council of Ephesus in his *Book of Heraclides*: "Cyril presided; Cyril was accuser; Cyril was judge; Cyril was bishop of Rome. Cyril was everything." At the beginning of September 431 Nestorius was sent back to the monastery of St. Euprepius by imperial order, living there in peace and in excommunication for four years. In 435 he was banished to Oasis in Upper Egypt. It is known that he outlived emperor Theo - dosius who died in 450. The precise date of Nestorius' death is not known.

II

THE WORKS OF NESTORIUS

By imperial edict in 435 the works of Nestorius were to be destroyed. Hence, again we have the situation of dealing with the thought of a condemned heretic whose works were consigned to fire. Again we must turn to the list of writings drawn up by the fourteenth century Nestorian Ebedjesu (who may have died about 1218). Ebedjesu lists the following as works by Nestorius extant in Syriac at that time: the *Tragedy*; the *Book of Heraclides*, a *Letter to Cosmas*, a lengthy *Liturgy*, one book of letters, and one book of *Homilies and Sermons*. Evagrius Scholasticus (c.536-600), a native of Coele-Syria, in his *Ecclesiastica Historica* (which extends from the Council of Ephesus in 431 to 594) gives the following list of the works of Nestorius: the *Book of Heraclides*, the *Theopaschites*, the *Tragedy*, and a book entitled *Historica*. It is possible that this *Historica* was a comprehensive title for his *Homilies and Sermons*.

Very little remains. In 1905 F. Loofs collected and edited the fragments of Nestorius' sermons, letters, and books in his book entitled *Nestoriana. Die Fragmente des Nestorius, gesammelt, untersucht und herausgegeben, mit Beiträgen von S. A. Cook and G. Kampffmeyer* (Halle). Since that time a number of new Syriac fragments have been made available by Lebon's first edition of the works of Severus of Antioch (see J. Lebon, *Fragments syriaques de Nestorius dans le 'Contra Grammaticum' de Sévère d'Antioche* (1923). Other fragments were collected by W. Lüdtke in *Armenische Nestoriana* (1908) and by A. Sanda in *Severi Philalethes* (1928). Fortunately we do not have to rely on the excepts from Nestorius' opponents, although often these are very reliable. In 1895 a Syriac translation of the entire *Book* or *Bazaar of Heraclides* was discovered and first published in 1910 from the manuscript in the Patriarchal Library at Kotchanes. It was this work that led modern scholars to revise the traditional opinion of Nestorius. However, the *Book* or *Bazaar of Heraclides* confirms to a great extent – on the more sophisticated theological level – St. Cyril's position. It appears that those who now see Nestorius as only a victim of eccles - iastical politics are, for the most part, historians and not theologians, that, in any case, they seem to miss the underlying theological vision of Nestorius.

THE BAZAAR OF HERACLIDES OF DAMASCUS

As mentioned above, this is the only work by Nestorius that is extant in its entirety. It was composed in his last years and hence there can be no misunderstanding of his position. He is no longer engaged in the strained atmosphere which colored his first year as patriarch of Constantinople. This is a work written after many years of reflection. He writes it in the form of a dialogue with the Egyptian Sophronius – it is both a defense of his teaching and a summary of his life. He is severely critical of the decisions of the Council of Ephesus and the teaching of St. Cyril. The title, of course, was the only way he could circulate the work; that is, under the name of "Heraclides of Damascus." It was originally written in Greek and then translated into Syriac.

In this work Nestorius gives an interesting account of how he believes St. Cyril handled the situation and his doctrines. "But perhaps some one will say: You have only read us a letter. Read also the blasphemies that are in your writings. You have perhaps written a letter with reserve and caution, according to the views of him to whom it was written. But your doctrines, which have been stated authoritatively by you, clearly interpret your meaning. And so a letter is not enough for us. But we have examined your doctrines that we might accurately learn everything about you. And not even so did we dare to assume authority, but we have set the doctrines of the Fathers also before us, and have compared them with these. And so, having made our examination with all accuracy, we have also given sentence, adducing the Fathers against whom you have fought. Wherefore, whereas you were called and did not answer, we have done all things justly. We have condemned your letter, we have examined your teachings, and we seek also to set up the teaching of the Fathers as law. What then ought we to do that we have not done? This man [Cyril] was present and said the things that ought to be said, and taught also; but you withdrew at that time, and now you blame and slander us. Why do you not accuse yourself instead of us? For we did not judge you in secret, but openly. If we omitted anything, if we acted on insufficient knowledge, tell us now, if this be the case, how it is – though, if we were not justly roused against you, you ought to have said so then, no now."

"For my part, though I could accuse them of having done and omitted many things, I pass on now from this subject, lest any should say, "he treats immoderately of these matters.' But I will convict them of judging me unjustly from these very things that they did against me. For they spoke deceitfully and led many astray, though they did not keep this examination secret . . . For he wished the matters not to be duly examined lest he himself should stand condemned, for he persuaded them all, as one who should know the secrets of the heart, and they who were in collusion with him so presented the matter to the others as though he were the vindicator of Christ's Divinity, and was preventing me from maintaining the opposite. And so he carried them all away into opposition to me, insomuch that they would not listen to a word until I should utterly make an end of Christ's humanity – as though I were maintaining to him [Cyril] that Christ was man in *ousia*, but God by an equality of honor. And he employed prejudice against me, and was saying against me, making God a man, that Christ should not be considered to be anything at all save only God the Logos. And I of necessity aimed my arguments against him, maintaining that he is also man. And I proved it to him from the Divine Scriptures and from the Fathers. And this also he used against me, as though I had said that Christ was man only. For ... I was accusing him of refusing to say that Christ is perfect man in nature and operations, and that God the Logos did not become the nature of man but is in the nature and operations of man – so that God the Logos should be both by nature."

"And these things I will demonstrate from the things that were writtten when he took passages from my teaching and from his own, which latter – whether they were so from the first, or whether, out of enmity to me and through the machinations of heretics, he changed them to the opposite sense – are really like those of Arius, since, inconsistently with the *ousia* of God, he attributed all the human things to the nature of God the *Logos through a union of hypostasis*, as though the Logos should suffer all human passions by physical sensation."

"Wherefore in the Incarnation this man [Cyril] assigns nothing to the control of the man, but only to God the Logos – in such a way that he employs the human nature for his own operations. So Arius and Eunomius and Apollinarius taught: for in name they say that Christ is God, but in fact they deprive him of being God, for they assign his human things by nature to his [the Logos'] own *ousia*. And they make void the generations of the descent of the Messiah, and the promises to the Fathers that from their seed the Messiah should spring according to the flesh. For this reason it was that the Evangelists recorded all those things that truly show the human nature, lest perhaps, on account of his Divinity, it should not be believed that he is man also. And to show moreover that he it is that was affirmed by the promises. And for this cause he [the Evangelist] mentioned the Blessed Virgin as being a woman betrothed to a man, and wrote even his [Joseph's] name and race and craft and place: that there might be nothing to cause doubt and prevent her from being believed to be truly a woman. For the same reason he wrote also of his being despised, and the announcement of his conception, and his birth, and the manger, and the making known of him that was born with her that bare him, that it might be established that he was truly man: the cradle in a manger, the wrapping in swad - dling clothes, with those things that are natural to babes: the gifts offered for his sake, his gradual growth in stature and wisdom before God and men, his conduct in the world, his watchings, his subjection, the petition he made, and all his fulfilling of the Law, his baptism and the voice that was uttered concerning him that he is the Son – even he who is Son from the womb by the union – the witness from the marking of his conduct, the voice of the Father, the manifestation of the Holy Spirit, his earthly life full of care for us, and not in the phantom or the mere fashion of a man, but in human nature and body, and a reasonable soul which thought and reasoned in the nature of men.

That he might be all that he was by the nature of man without ceasing
from the union with God the Logos. But the union was not one of
natures into a single nature, nor a confusion, nor a change, nor a
changing of *ousia* – whether of God into man or of man into God – nor
a mingling of natures, nor a compounding into one nature, so that they
should be mingled and be affected by one another as being physically
united as to natural functions. *Now all these things they make void by
a union of nature and of hypostasis*, and they take away from him all
those things which he has by his human nature and assign them by
nature to God the Logos: his human fear, his betrayal, his trial, his
answering, the smiting on his cheek, the sentence of the cross, his
setting forth, the laying of the cross upon his shoulder, the bearing of
his cross and its being taken away from him and laid on others, the
crown of thorns, the crimson garments, the setting up of the cross, the
crucifixion, the driving of the nails, the gall that was offered to him,
the other acts of violence, the delivering up of his spirit to his Father,
the bowing of his head, the taking down of his body from the cross, the
embalming, the burial, the resurrection on the third day, his mani -
festation in the body, his speaking and teaching – (all of which things
were done) that men might not suppose that it was the phantom of a
body that he had, but truly a body of flesh. And indeed the body and
soul were no phantom and illusion, but true and natural. Nothing is
concealed: all the human things which men now blush to say of him
the Evangelists were not ashamed to say: though these persons do not
blush to attribute these things to the Divine nature by means of a union
of physical hypostasis – God suffering the passions of the body which
is physically united, thirsting and hungering and being needy and
anxious, thinking, and making petition that he may conquer these very
human things that he suffers, and fight against human nature to the
undoing of our glorying and the undoing of our redemption. *And these
men will make void the proper things of God the Logos also*, and make
them human. That he [the Logos] should act and suffer physically in
his own nature by physical sensation, receiving sufferings physically
by his own *ousia*, even as the body suffers by means of the soul and the
soul by the body – this it would be a frightful and horrible thing for us
to think literally or to say to men endowed with the least intelligence
concerning the Son [making him] a slave and a creature, [and asserting]
that he was changed from impassible to passible, or from immortal to
mortal, or from unchangeable to changeable. Even if one should make
him into the *ousia* of the angels, and impassible, and say that he does
not act by his own nature and operation and power, but by that which
he has become he would flee away from being of like passions even
with such a nature. But one that is physically united cannot flee, for
even if he did not physically suffer the passions of the body, yet
psychically he should suffer instead of the soul, for he would be instead
of a soul that did not think as an intelligence. And in matters of the
intelligence He would be instead of the intelligence; and he would be

man in outward fashion only, and would be a deluder in the fashion of a man: as though he possessed the proper things of soul and body and intelligence, while these were deprived of their natural operations."

"Such things are said by those who are the would-be orthodox – to wit, that he is of the impassible and indefectible and unchangeable and unalterable nature of the Father – and then, like the Jews who, setting him at naught while they called him the Messiah, actually crucified him, these persons give to him the title of an unchangeable and impas - sible and indefectible nature, and then attribute to him all the passions and defects of the body, and assign all the things of the soul and of the intelligence to God the Logos by means *of a hypostatic union.*"

"And they maintain two perfect natures, of the Godhead and the manhood, and then maintain a change of the natures by the union, assigning nothing either to the manhood or to the Godhead, making these the natural things of the manhood and those the natural things of the Godhead, and yet not keeping the Divine things in the [Divine] nature, since they make God the Logos to be in the nature of both *ousias*, hiding away the man and all his proper things – he for whose sake and in whom the Incarnation took place, and by whom we are freed from the captivity of death."

"In name, then, they pose as orthodox, but in fact they are Arians. And they undo the perfection of God the Logos by all the naturally human things they say about him: such as, that he should act from the union of a physical hypostasis and suffer naturally all human things. And, that he employed human nature, it was not so that the manhood itself should act and suffer for our sakes, but that God the Logos should so act: not that he should employ a person, but a nature – for a union as to person is impassible, and this is orthodox; but the other implies passibility, and is the invention of heretics who fight against the nature of the Only-Begotten."

"To which union a man inclines he is sure to claim the credit of orthodoxy and not the reproach of heresy. Now all his [Cyril's] contrary arguments *concerning the hypostatic union* he has written without reserve in his "Chapters" and much has been written by many about them. But it will not do for us to make our book interminable by treating of things that are obvious. We have rather to reveal to all the gradual growth of this species of impiety; the which having myself foreseen, I have not withdrawn from what is right and orthodox, nor will I unto death. And even though through ignorance all oppose me – and even some of the orthodox – and are unwilling to hear and learn of me: well, let them have time to learn from the heretics themselves by fighting against them, even as they have fought against him who fought on their behalf."

Such are the thoughts of Nestorius as contained in his Bazaar of Heraclides of Damascus, a work written in quietude, a work written after excommunication, a work written after he had time and tranquillity to learn the position of St. Cyril. He had not changed.

TRAGEDY

This work, of which only fragments remain, was probably written by Nestorius during his four years after his excommunication and deposition at the monastery (431-435). It appears to have been a presentation of his case. The fragments that remain are in Greek, Latin, and Syriac. The most important research on Nestorius in this century, at least from a literary and historical perspective, has been done by L. Abramowski. In her research on the Nestorian Church historian Barhad - besabba she discovered important usage of Nestorius' *Tragedy*. See her dissertation entitled *Untersuchungen zum literarischen Nachlaß des Nestorius* (1956) and her work entitled *Untersuchungen zum Liber Heraclidis des Nestorius* published in 1963. She considers the *Tragedy* to be the first of two defenses or attacks on the Council of Ephesus and Cyril, the second being the *Bazaar of Heraclides*.

THEOPASCHITES

Only a few Syriac fragments remain of this work. As its title indicates, Nestorius wrote it against the "Theopaschites." In Greek the word θεοπασχῖται means "those who believe that God suffered." Nestorius believed that St Cyril was a "Theopaschite" because of his stress that God the Logos by means of the *communicatio idiomatum* experienced suffering. The term itself was applied in the early sixth century to a group of Monophysite theologians in Constantinople. It was apparently John Maxentius and a group of Scythian monks who defended the formula "One of the Trinity was crucified." The orthodoxy of this statement was upheld by Justinian and Leontius of Byzantium. Finally, however, the formula was rejected by the patriarch of Con - stantinople and by Pope Hormisdas, the latter, however, only after hesitation. There is still some doubt on the part of some scholars that the book entitled *Theopaschites* was written by Nestorius. For example, F. Scheidweiler in an article published in 1952 entitled "Ein Glaubens - bekenntnis des Eustathius von Antiochien" asserts that the author is Eustathius.

SERMONS

St. Cyril and Pope Celestine not only had copies of Nestorius' sermons preached while he was patriarch of Constantinople but they also had copies of sermons by Nestorius preached while he was still in Antioch. Copies of his sermons seem to have circulated widely. Since he preached for approximately twenty-three years, one must presume that numerous sermons existed. The collection by F. Loofs contains thirty sermons, ten of which are essentially complete; nine have been preserved by Loofs from the Latin translation by Marius Mercator (five on Christology and four on the Pelagians). It appears that four sermons found in the works of St. John Chrysostom actually belong to Nestorius: Loofs and Haidacher claim that the sermon on Hebrews 3, 1 in Chrysostom's works is by Nestorius; and F. Nau claims that the three sermons on the temptation of Christ found in Chrysostom's works belong to Nestorius. It is possible that Chrysostom's *Homily on Easter* and his two Homilies on the Ascension belong to Nestorius. See F. Nau, *Le livre d'Héraclide de Damas, suivi du texte grec des trois homélies de Nestorius sur les tentations de Notre Seigneur* (Paris, 1910), pages 333-358.

THE LETTERS OF NESTORIUS

Ten of the fifteen letters listed by Loofs are either complete or essentially complete. Of the ten, three still exist in the original Greek (one to emperor Theodosius II and two to St. Cyril). The others have come down to us only in Latin or Syriac. Four of the surviving letters in Latin translation are to Pope Celestine, one to the Pelagian Celestius, and one to Theodoret of Cyrus. There exists an interesting letter in Syriac which Nestorius wrote to the people of Constantinople in his last years. The ever-present possibility of embarrassment facing historians of textual criticism struck again over this letter. F. Loofs had maintained that it was not authentic but the discovery of the *Bazaar of Heraclides* has rendered his opinion inaccurate. See E. W. Brooks and F. Nau, "La lettre de Nestorius aux habitants de Constantinople," in *Revue de l'Orient Chrétien* 15 (1910), 275-281.

III

THE THEOLOGICAL TENDENCY OF NESTORIUS

Before his condemnation for heresy Nestorius did not try to reduce his theological views to a system. He was a preacher and spoke frequently and said much. Without a doubt he had a talent for speaking. But as a preacher he was more of a demagogue than a teacher, and would misuse rhetorical effects. We have an opportunity to judge his early efforts as a preacher. In them Nestorius reveals a set theological world view which took shape in the Antiochene atmosphere – he is continuing Theodore's theological work. But only subsequently, during his years of exile, during those years of bitter, but unrepentant, outraged reflection on his "tragic" fate, did he attempt to express himself through principles, if not systematically. This is his famous *Bazaar of Hera - clides*, which was discovered in 1895 in a Syriac translation and first published in 1910. It is more an apologetic pamphlet than a theological creed. This late confession shows that Nestorius had not even changed under excommunication. He is still carrying on polemics against Cyril of Alexandria and the fathers of the Council of Ephesus.

Still, through this book it is easier to understand Nestorius, and to understand not only St. Cyril's dogmatic correctness but his historical correctness as well. What is essential here, of course, is not the dispute over the name *Theotokos*, but rather Nestorius' basic Christological premises. He continues Theodore and, one could say, completes Theo - dore's thoughts. Nestorius' basic idea is his notion of the person – πρόσωπον. First, the "natural person," the principle of individuality, πρόσωπον φυσικόν, is a term which evidently belongs to Nestorius himself. "Perfect nature" is always self-sufficient, has enough of a foundation within itself for existence and stability, and is an individual. In this Nestorius was a consistent Aristotelian: in his eyes, only the concrete and individual is real, and the general and generic (the Aristotelian "second nature") is for him only an abstract concept. From this Nestorius concludes that in Christ both Divinity and humanity existed, each in its own properties, its own hypostases, and its own essence; and humanity is so complete in Christ that it could live and develop on its own. Thus, for Nestorius, the term "two natures" sig - nified for all practical purposes "two persons." Secondly, the "person of union or unity" – πρόσωπον τῆς ἑνώσεως – is the unified Person of Christ, *una persona Unigeniti* The entire sense of Nestorius' teachings lay in how he defines the relationship between these concepts and the facts and realities they reveal.

Nestorius distinguishes two natures in Christ and combines them in "worship." "Worship unifies" because the natures are united in Christ, and Nestorius emphasizes the completeness and indivisibility of this unification. It is Nestorius' opinion that God has never acted in Christ unbeknown to humanity. However, the primary thing is this: free unification or free unity, unification in love, and not in the sense only that the Logos by his will, through mercy and love, descends and is incarnate, but in the fact that the whole meaning of the Incarnation begins and ends with the unity of will and action – χωρίζω τὰς φύσεις, ἀλλ ' ἑνῶ τὴν προσκύνησιν.

For Nestorius this unity is also "the unity of the *oikonomia* of person." Here it is as if he is restoring the archaic sense of the concept of "person" when it signified first of all "juridical person," "role," and even "mask." Nestorius himself defines the combination of the "natural persons" as a unity of *oikonomia*, as a certain interchange and set of in - terrelations, as a "reciprocal utilization of images." Here we may recall the phrases "in the name of," "on behalf of." For Nestorius what is characteristic here is the *element of reciprocity*, of "taking" and "giving." The Logos takes or receives the "person" of a man and im - parts its "person" to him. God was incarnate in man, writes Nestorius, and "made man's person his own Person," took upon himself the "person" of guilty nature. In this, too, lies the immensity of Divine leniency: that "man's person becomes God's own, and he gives man his own Person." God uses man's person, for he accepted it, and what is more, he accepted it in a servile form. The Divinity uses the person of humanity, and humanity uses the person of Divinity, and in this sense we speak of "the unity of person for both of them" (a certain *symmetry* of natures). The concept of "use" here means "assimilation."

In this sense one may speak of the indwelling of the Divinity, of the embracing of humanity. One may speak of human nature in Christ as a tool of the Divinity, as the Chosen, for *in Christ* we contemplate and confess God. For Nestorius this unity of *oikonomia* is a developing unity. Perfect unity is preceded by a time of feat and struggle, when the Anointed Sovereign still does not have the right to his legacy and supremacy, when passions have not yet been conquered. This struggle has not yet been resolved, and Christ is not yet performing miracles, has not yet the power to teach, but is only obeying and fulfilling the commandments. Only after his temptation does he enter the desert. Only after his temptation is he baptized by John. Only after raising his soul to God by coordinating his own will with God's, does Christ receive the power and the force of God. "Since he was victorious and triumphed in everything, he received as a reward for his victory the power to preach and proclaim the Gospel of the Heavenly Kingdom." In other words: "when he finished his feat of personal perfection among all sorts of temptations, he acts for our sake and labors to deliver us from the sway of the tyrant," for his personal victory was not enough for him.

There is indisputable truth in Nestorius' attention to human effec - tiveness in Christ, but it is distorted by his *one-sided maximalist emphasis*. Nestorius almost sees nothing but the human feat in Christ by which God's goodwill is attracted. Nestorius designates the unity of the *oikonomia* of person by the name of Christ, the Son, the Lord. These are names which indicate the unification, the "two natures," in contradistinction to the names of the individual natures. It is character - istic that Nestorius distinctly contrasts the names God, Christ, and the Logos. One must never lump them together, for this would mean lumping together their very natures as well. It is perfectly clear that more than anything else, Nestorius is striving to dismiss the thought of the Divine Being of the Logos as the beginning or focus of unity. Hence his decisive denial of the "interrelation of properties" – *commun - icatio idiomatum*, the ἀντίδοσις τῶν ἰδιωμάτων – "if you read through the whole New Testament, you will not find that death is ascribed to God the Logos, but to Christ, the Lord or Son."

Here Nestorius is asserting something more than merely the non-mixing of natures among which are correspondingly allocated attributes, actions, and qualities. He is emphasizing the difference of the subjects before and after the Incarnation. And he avoids calling Christ the Logos Incarnate, limiting himself to the name Emmanuel., "God with us." Denial of the name *Theotokos* was a necessary consequence of Nes -

torius' premises. To this name he contrasts the name Bearer of Christ, *Christotokos*, as one which indicates the "person of unity or the person of unification or union," and the name Bearer of Man, as one which indicates the nature according to which Mary is the Mother of Jesus. And more – *Theodoxos*, the Receptacle of God, since Mary bore him in whom God was; "God with us"; "the Temple of Unity." In this sense one may also call her the Mother of God "through a manifestation, since God appeared in the Son of Mary, "came down from Heaven" and "was incarnate" but was not born of Mary.

It would not be correct to ascribe all of these inaccuracies and mis - takes of Nestorius to the vagueness of his theological and exegetical language, to the indistinctness of his theological concepts; that is, to the confusion of general and concrete names. Nestorius' error, for the most part, sprang from his anthropological premises, from an erroneous vision and perception of the Person of Christ. With this he repeats Theodore of Mopsuestia.

His arguments have their own consistency. The Gospels tell of him who was born, dwelt among people, suffered at their hands. But, indeed, all of this can be said of a man only. It is as though Nestorius was enticed by the realism of the Gospels. He refused to see God the Logos in the historical Christ, although he makes the proviso of the Logos Incarnate. For him this meant ascribing to God birth, muta bility, the ability to suffer, mortality, and death itself. That is, it meant allowing a certain enclosure and boundedness for the Divinity. God cannot be an historical subject and he must not be considered God who was an infant, was crucified, and died. Nestorius attributed the Gospel history to Christ but with the proviso that the Logos is not a subject for human narration. Thus it turned out that only a human "person" can actually be such a subject, precisely a "person" or "personality," and not a "nature" because, for Nestorius, "impersonal" nature is something illusory, something imagined, something only thought, but not really existing. This means that for Nestorius the Gospel character is Emman - uel, "God with us," or Christ, a human person adopted by God, "a Son through crucifixion with the Son."

In other words, to Nestorius, the Savior is a man, or a man was the Savior, even though he was joined to God. The unity of the Gospel story breaks down into two parallel or symmetrical lines or rows, although these are indissolubly linked. Each line or row is a closed entity and self-sufficient. From this certain soteriological conclusions suggest themselves. For Nestorius salvation began and ended with a moral and volitional – but not ontological – unity or union of human - ity with God, a distinctive moral concordance of man with God. Nes - torius could not bring himself to speak of deification as a religious ideal. It is no accident that "juridical" motifs – substitutionary sacrifice – receive such emphasis in Nestorius' soteriology.

CHAPTER FOURTEEN

ST. CYRIL OF ALEXANDRIA

I

LIFE

CYRIL'S BACKGROUND

Very little is known for certain about St. Cyril's life before his appearance on the Alexandrian throne. He evidently came from a respected Alexandrian family and was the nephew of patriarch Theophilus (d.412). He was probably born in the late 70s of the fourth century. Judging from St. Cyril's works, he received a wide and complete education. In him one discerns a good knowledge of the Scriptures. He began his literary activity with experiments in allegor-ical exegesis in the area of the Old Testament. According to information that is not completely reliable, Cyril putatively spent several years in seclusion in the desert. In 403 he accompanied his uncle, Patriarch Theophilus, to Constantinople to participate in the famous Synod of the Oak, which had been convened against St. John Chrysostom. Cyril was at this time already a member of the clergy. In 412, after Theo-philus' death, Cyril, despite the fact that the authorities wanted a specific archdeacon named Timothy to become patriarch, succeeded his uncle as patriarch of Alexandria. This did not come to pass without "a commotion among the people" and the interference of armed forces was required.

CYRIL'S EARLY YEARS AS PATRIARCH

Neither is much known about the first years of St. Cyril's episco-pate. Stormy relations were immediately established between the archbishop and Orestes, the imperial city-prefect of Alexandria. Accord-ing to the testimony of the historian Socrates, "Orestes spurned the patriarch's friendship" – "he hated the dominion of the bishops because they took away much of the power from officials appointed by the emperor." Monks from the desert of Nitria intervened in the disagree-ments between the bishop and the prefect, and intervened very unsuc-cessfully. An attack was made on the prefect, and he barely escaped the scuffle. One of the monks who had taken part in the attack was subjected to a cruel punishment and died as a result. The patriarch com-mitted his body to a sanctified burial as a martyr to piety. "Humble people," relates Socrates, "did not approve of this zeal of Cyril's, for they knew that Ammonius was punished for his recklessness and died in torment not because he was being forced to renounce Christ."

By his temperament St. Cyril was a man of struggle and on the episcopal throne he immediately showed himself to be an impassioned and imperious man. He immediately entered into a fight with the Novatians, locked up all the Novatian cathedrals in Alexandria, seized all the sacred utensils from them, and deprived their bishop Theopem - ptus of everything he owned. In doing so he took advantage of the assistance of the secular authorities. St. Cyril's struggle with Alex - andria's Jews also dates back to the first years of his episcopate. The relations between the Christians and the Jews in Alexandria gradually grew worse and worse. Finally, the Jews attacked the Christians at night. "Exasperated by this," relates Socrates, "Cyril went with a great multitude of people to the Jewish synagogues, seized them, drove the Jews out of the city, and handed over their property to be plundered by the people." Orestes came to the defense of the Jews and tried to convince emperor Theodosius II of the disadvantages of evicting the Jews from Alexandria *en masse*, but his arguments had no success. In this same period there was a popular revolt during which the philos - opher Hypatia was killed by being torn to pieces. At the time many people put the blame for this murder on the patriarch. This latter situ - ation with Hypatia, however, lacks any substantial proof that connects St. Cyril directly to the incident. In any case, St. Cyril's episcopate passed under trying and troubled conditions.

In general, Alexandria was a restive city. St. Cyril tried to instill tranquillity through his pastoral sermons and letters. He called his sermons his usual and constant occupation. In his time his sermons enjoyed great success – according to Gennadius of Marseilles, people would learn his sermons by heart. Comparatively few sermons have been preserved for us. In his early sermons St. Cyril persistently com - bats the Alexandrians' rebellious spirit, denounces brigandage, pagan superstitions, and Christian duplicity. In his later sermons dogmatic issues crowd out issues connected with moral living. Especially inter - esting are St. Cyril's "Paschal Epistles," written between 414 and 442. Twenty-nine of them have been preserved.

THE STORM CLOUD IN CONSTANTINOPLE

Nestorius, who ascended the patriarchal throne in Constantinople in 428, soon provoked confusion and agitation over Christological doc - trine. The sedition which began in Constantinople soon spread beyond its boundaries. "Everywhere," wrote John of Antioch a little later, "in places close to us and far away, everything has been set in motion. Everywhere one hears talk about one and the same thing. The Church has suddenly been caught in some kind of violent storm: day to day the faithful everywhere are being separated from one another as a con - sequence of this controversy. The West, Egypt, and even Macedonia have decidedly been separated from the unity (that is, from the unity with Nestorius)." The news from Constantinople reached Alexandria

very quickly – through the apocrisiaries of the Alexandrian patriarch –
and already in the spring of 429 Cyril came out against Nestorius.
However, he did not call him by name. In view of the fact that "ideas
which are strangers to truth have started to spread throughout Egypt,
too," St. Cyril sent a special detailed "Epistle to the Monks" which
elucidated Christological truths. After that, St. Cyril addressed another
epistle to Nestorius himself, calling on him to cut short the "universal
temptation" which his views and writings were provoking. St. Cyril
expressed himself gently and with restraint but Nestorius received this
interference from the "Egyptian" in his affairs with irritation and
exasperation. The further development of the Nestorian dispute was
greatly complicated by the constant rivalry and the mutual distrust
between Alexandria and Constantinople. Many recalled Theophilus'
struggle with the blessed Chrysostom. At court St. Cyril's interference
was met with great displeasure – it seemed that the "Egyptian" was
again disrupting the peace of the Church which had been established
with such difficulty. Nestorius' supporters set the emperor against St.
Cyril, as in their time the Arians had slandered the great Athanasius. St.
Cyril realized this with chagrin and, despite his innate ardor, he
continued to behave peaceably and with restraint. In early 430 he
addressed a second dogmatic epistle to Nestorius in which he elucidated
the mystery of the Incarnation on the basis of tradition and the
inalterable faith of the Church. This epistle was subsequently approved
at the Council of Ephesus.

At the same time, St. Cyril was writing to various persons about
disputed issues. He wrote three epistolary works *On the True Faith* [*De
recta fide*]. The first was addressed to emperor Theodosius II and the two
others were addressed ταῖς βασιλίσσαις [*ad reginas*] without
mentioning any specific names. It is John of Caesarea, writing at the
beginning of the sixth century, who claims that the first of the two
others was addressed to the emperor's two younger sisters, Arcadia and
Marina, and that the second was addressed to the emperor's elder sister
Pulcheria and to the empress Eudocia. In these epistles St. Cyril eluci -
dates the dogma of the Incarnation in great detail and investigates mis -
taken opinions about it. He specifically addresses the issue of the
Nestorians' objection to the true representation of Christ's God-Man
hypostasis. In doing this, St. Cyril cites a large amount of testimony
from the fathers.

Finally, St. Cyril releases his *Five Tomes Against Nestorius*,
which he composed in the spring of 430. In these *Five Tomes* St. Cyril
presents a critical examination of a collection of sermons published by
Nestorius in the previous year. The first book challenges Nestorius'
attack on the term *Theotokos* and the four other books attack the duality
of persons in Christ.

All of these works became widely disseminated. The question about
Nestorius' views was thus posed clearly and harshly. Apparently St.
Cyril charged his apocrisiaries in Constantinople with demanding that

Nestorius formally subscribe to Cyril's dogmatic exposition of faith. St. Cyril contrasted his creed with a homily by Nestorius. Not everyone everywhere regarded the favorable and polemical sides of St. Cyril's work equally, and not all of Nestorius' opponents were ready to unite around St. Cyril. This greatly delayed and impeded the victory of truth. In addition, by no means did everyone immediately grasp the full gravity and importance of the approaching dogmatic dispute.

THE ALLIANCE OF CYRIL AND POPE CELESTINE

It was grasped first of all in Rome. Complete unanimity was immediately reached between Pope Celestine and St. Cyril, and the pope authorized the Alexandrian patriarch to act in his name as his *locum tenens* (*vices gerens*). Rome passed judgment not only on the basis of the materials St. Cyril had delivered – Nestorius himself sent the pope a collection of his sermons. It is noteworthy that St. Cyril sent his material to the pope with a Latin translation; Nestorius submitted his in Greek. All of this material was submitted to the famous St. John Cassian – then in Marseilles – by the future pope St. Leo the Great, then an archdeacon in Rome and a friend of St. John Cassian. St. John Cassian responded in 430 with his *De Incarnatione Domini contra Nestorium Libri VII*. His conclusion was very harsh.

In August of the year 430 the pope and a local council declared Nestorius' doctrine heretical and instructed St. Cyril to admonish Nestorius once more. If Nestorius did not repent and bring his renunciation in ten days, then the pope would declare him deposed and excommunicated. Through St. Cyril the pope sent his epistles to Nestorius himself, to the Constantinopolitan clergy, and to certain bishops of the East. The next local council convened in Alexandria in October of 430. It iterated the decisions of the Roman council and supplemented them with a detailed formula of renunciation for Nes - torius. These were the renowned "*Chapters*" – *κεφαλάια* – or *Ana - themas* of St. Cyril, twelve in number.

THE REACTION TO ST. CYRIL'S TWELVE ANATHEMAS IN THE EAST

At the same time, St Cyril sent letters to John of Antioch, Juvenal of Jerusalem, and Acacius, one of the most honored and respected bishops of the East. On the basis of these letters and on the basis of the decisions in Rome, John of Antioch sent Nestorius an epistle of warning. But St. Cyril's *Anathemas* were greeted in the East with perplexity and even anxiety. On behalf of John of Antioch they were analyzed by Andrew of Samosata and even more harshly by Theodoret of Cyrus. St. Cyril was forced to write a defense against these objections. The shadow of heterodoxy and Apollinarianism was cast on Cyril by his opponents. Meanwhile, Nestorius was inciting the people of Constantinople against the "Egyptian" and was reminding them of former enmity of Alexandria to Constantinople and about the persecution of St. John Chrysostom which was instigated by Theo-philus of Alexandria, the uncle of Cyril. In addition, Nestorius held up implementation of the decrees of the Roman and Alexandrian councils by convincing to emperor to convene an Ecumenical Council. Notification about the convocation of the council was published on November 19, 430 and the convocation was set for Pentecost of the following year. In Constantinople people were afraid that St. Cyril would avoid the Ecumenical Council, that he would not appear. But St. Cyril greeted the news of the convocation of an Ecumenical Council with joy – he expected it to settle the affair. He energetically prepared for the council, gathering materials for a dogmatic critique of the issues which had been raised.

BEHIND THE SCENES AT THE COUNCIL OF EPHESUS

The Council of Ephesus was operating in a difficult and awkward situation. The chief fighter for orthodoxy was St. Cyril, who was supported by the local bishop Memnon and the Roman legates – who arrived late. Nestorius enjoyed the support of the emperor and Can-didian, the Captain of the Imperial Guard. Candidian was the emperor's plenipotentiary responsible for opening and keeping order during the Ecumenical Council. He also openly impeded the activities of the orthodox delegation. Immediately upon arriving in Ephesus, St. Cyril gave speeches and sermons – both at the bishops' meetings and before the people – in which he discussed the dispute, denounced Nestorius, and defended himself against the suspicions and charges being brought against him. Memnon, the bishop of Ephesus, openly took St. Cyril's side and denied Nestorius and his retinue access to the city's cathedrals. He also avoided contact with him, as if he were a man of dubious faith. Relations immediately became strained.

The opening of the Ecumenical Council was held up because the "Easterners" were late. After waiting for two weeks, St. Cyril decided to begin the council despite the strident opposition of Candidian and Nestorius and the protests of his supporters. St. Cyril presided over the opened council. All dogmatic materials were considered. Nestorius did not show up at the council, and the council's deputation was not allowed in his house by the emperor's guard. As a result, Nestorius was declared deposed and excommunicated, and St. Cyril's second – and evidently his third – epistle against Nestorius was accepted and approved. This took place on June 22. The resolution of this first meeting contains 197 signatures. Nestorius' protest was signed by ten bishops and Nestorius. These resolutions provoked the indignation of Candidian – he considered the meeting of June 22 an illegal mob and hindered the efforts of its members to communicate with Constantinople and other cities. However, he did not succeed in isolating the council fathers. St. Cyril managed to dispatch letters and couriers both to Alexandria and to Constantinople. The emperor came out on the side of Nestorius, who was also supported by the "Easterners" who had finally arrived with John of Antioch. They did not recognize the council which had opened and were unfriendly and inconsiderate towards its fathers. Without fully discussing the essence of the question, they, along with Nestorius' adherents, formed their own council at which they condemned and deposed Cyril and Memnon for their "heretical chapters" – *propter haereticum praedictorum capitulorum sensum* – and for disrupting the peace of the Church. Thus the bishops who had gathered in Ephesus were sorely divided.

The original council continued to operate even after the arrival of the "Easterners," despite their protests and the strident opposition of the secular authorities. At this time the Roman legates arrived and estab - lished contact with Cyril and the council – the meeting of July 11. In one of his speeches at Ephesus St. Cyril graphically describes the council's activity as a struggle with a ferocious multi-headed serpent, and depicts John of Antioch as a treacherous observer who has suddenly and unexpectedly taken the side of the enemy and has begun to shoot with arrows of hatred the badly wounded and exhausted warriors whom he should have helped. One could say without exaggeration that St. Cyril bore the brunt of the struggle more than the others, and therefore had every right to say of himself: "I have bared my sword and am taking my stand against him. For Christ I am fighting a beast."

In Ephesus he fought alone, while in Constantinople he fought through his apocrisiaries and through his special ambassadors Potamon and Comarius, who had stayed in Constantinople after taking the acts of the Roman and Alexandrian councils of 430 to the imperial city. The emperor confirmed the deposition of Cyril and Memnon but also confirmed Nestorius' deposition, hoping to reconcile the dissenters. The Count – or Comes – and Imperial Guard John was sent to carry out these instructions. He arrived in Ephesus in early August. Cyril and Memnon were taken into custody, although they still managed to communicate with the outside world. Nestorius was taken into custody as well. The original council protested the emperor's actions, objecting to his interference in affairs of faith. Both councils sent their own representatives to Constantinople. These delegates met with the emp - eror in Chalcedon in mid-September and here Cyril's supporters proved victorious. Nestorius was removed from Ephesus. A successor for him was installed and ordained in the person of St. Maximianus. However, the "Easterners" did not agree with this. Memnon and St. Cyril were freed from confinement. On October 31, 431 Cyril returned to Alex - andria, exhausted by the struggle but with the halo of a confessor. The delegates of the original council remained in Constantinople as a kind of provisional council attached to the new Constantinopolitan archbishop.

ST. CYRIL AND THE AFTERMATH OF
THE COUNCIL OF EPHESUS

After the Ecumenical Council of Ephesus St. Cyril continued the dogmatic struggle. The victory over Nestorius was achieved at the cost of a schism within the Church, at the root of which was a theological misunderstanding between the "Egyptians" and the "Easterners." Next came the task of reconciliation and reunification. In addition, Nestor - ianism had not been totally vanquished and the council's condemnation of Nestorius was not accepted by everyone in the East. The falsehood of Nestorianism had not yet been exposed to the "Easterners." The theological struggle had to intensify even more – there arose with new poignancy the question of the meaning of all Antiochene theology, especially the theology of Theodore of Mopsuestia and Diodore of Tarsus as the generally recognized teachers of the East. In addition, questions were also raised about Alexandrian theology, the typical representative of which was now St. Cyril. Directly after the council St. Cyril summed up the struggle in his *"Defense Speech to the Emperor"* [*Apologeticus ad imperatorem*]. Thereafter he worked on a critique of Theodoret's objections to his XII Anathemas.

The reunification issue was a very pointed one for the "Easterners." They set as a condition for reconciliation Cyril's renunciation of every - thing he had written against Nestorius, "be it the epistles, or fragments, or entire books," but especially his *"Chapters."* Of course, this was impossible and would mean a renunciation of the Ecumenical Council of Ephesus. St. Cyril considered impossible that retreat into dogmatic vagueness that the "Easterners" were suggesting – to confine oneself to the Nicene Creed and elucidate it through St. Athanasius' epistle to Epictetus of Corinth. In addition, St. Cyril was diligently explaining the meaning of his own theological judgments.

The cause of reconciliation progressed slowly. It was also necessary to fight court intrigues and to fight not only with words but with a sword. Gradually a group of moderates broke away in the East. They agreed to speak with Cyril but were adamantly opposed to Nestorius' deposition, although a few did consent to this. There was also no small number of people stubbornly opposed to St. Cyril and directly supporting Nestorius. At the end of 432 Paul of Emesa of the moderate majority of "Easterners" was sent to Alexandria. He managed to make arrangements with St. Cyril and was given an audience on Christmas Day in 432. In early 433 total unity was reestablished in the Church. St. Cyril marked it with his famous epistle to John of Antioch: "Let the heavens rejoice!"

This letter is tangible evidence that St. Cyril was not just interested in stirring out trouble, that he was not just interested in the rivalry with the ecclesiastical power obtaining in Constantinople. Rather it reveals St. Cyril's serious concern over a vital issue of faith.

CYRIL'S LETTER TO JOHN OF ANTIOCH
April 23, 433

"Let the heavens rejoice and the earth be glad, for the mid-wall of partition is broken down, and the cause of sorrow is removed, and all manner of dissension taken away, Christ, our common Savior, awarding peace to his own Churches, to which peace, moreover, the most religious Princes, most dear to God, have called us, who, nobly emulating the piety of their ancestors, preserve in their own souls the orthodox faith firm and unshaken, while they take exceeding great care of the holy Churches, that they may win eternal renown, and may make their Empire most illustrious; on whom also the Lord of Hosts himself bestows good things with a liberal hand, and gives them to prevail over their enemies, and grants them victory, for he would not utterly belie his word: "As I live, saith the Lord, them that honor me, I will honor."

"On the arrival then at Alexandria of my lord Paul, my brother and fellow-minister, most dear to God, we were filled with joy; and with good reason, seeing that such a man was acting as mediator, and had voluntarily encountered excessive toils that he might vanquish the envy of the devil, and join together what had been sundered, and having cleared away the stumbling-blocks which had been cast between us, might crown both our Churches and yours with unanimity and peace. How they came to be sundered it is needless to say. It behooves us rather, I imagine, both to mind and speak what is in keeping with a time of peace."

"We were delighted then at the happy coming of the aforementioned most religious man, who possibly anticipated that it would cost him no small exertion to persuade us that we ought to make peace between the Churches, and do away with the ridicule of the heretics, and moreover blunt the sting of the devil's malice, but, on the contrary, found us so ready for this that he had absolutely no trouble at all. For we bear in mind the Savior's words: "My peace I give unto you, My peace I leave unto you," and we have been taught moreover to pray, "O Lord our God, give us peace, for Thou art the bountiful giver of all things." So that if one becomes a partaker of the peace which God liberally supplies, he will lack no good thing."

"But that the variance between the Churches was altogether ground - less and without any real cause, we are now most entirely convinced, my lord, the most religious bishop Paul, having *produced a paper con - taining an unexceptional confession of faith*, which, he affirms, was drawn up by thy Holiness and the most religious bishops there at Antioch. The writing is to this effect, *and it is inserted word for word in this our letter*:

THE CONFESSION OF JOHN OF ANTIOCH AND THE EASTERNERS

"Concerning the Virgin Mother of God, how we both hold and speak, and concerning the mode of the Incarnation of the Only-Begotten Son of God, we will perforce declare in few words – not as though we were supplying some deficiency, but as a matter about which there can be no doubt, as we have held from the first, having received it both from the divine Scriptures and from the tradition of the holy fathers – we will declare, I say, in few words, making no addition whatever to the faith put forth by the holy Fathers at Nicaea. For that Faith, as we have already said, suffices both for all knowledge of godliness and for the denunciation of all heretical heterodoxy. And we will make the declaration, not rashly venturing to intrude upon what is beyond our reach, but, while acknowledging our own weakness, barring the way against those who would fain dictate to us, where we are dealing with matters too high for man."

"We confess, therefore, our Lord Jesus Christ, the Only-Begotten Son of God, perfect God and a perfect Man, consisting of a rational soul and a body, begotten of the Father before the ages as concerning His Godhead, the same, in the last days, for us and for our salvation, born of the Virgin Mary, as concerning His Manhood: the same of one essence with the Father as concerning His Godhead and of one essence with us as concerning His Manhood. For of two natures there has been made a union, for which cause we confess one Christ, one Son, one Lord."

"In accordance with this sense of the unconfused union, we confess the holy Virgin to be "*Theotokos*" because God the Logos became incarnate and was made man, and from the very conception united to Himself the temple that was received from her. And as to the expres - sions concerning the Lord in the Gospels and Epistles, we are aware that theologians understand some as common, as relating to one Person, and others they distinguish, as relating to two natures, ex - plaining those that befit the divine nature according to the Godhead of Christ, and those of a humble sort according to His Manhood."

"Having been made acquainted then with these sacred words of yours, and finding that we ourselves are of the same mind, for there is "One Lord, One Faith, One Baptism," we gave thanks to God, the Savior of the world, rejoicing with one another that our Churches, both ours and yours, hold a faith in accordance with the divinely inspired Scriptures and with the tradition of our holy Fathers."

"But when I learned that some of those who take delight in finding fault were buzzing about like spiteful wasps and were spitting forth odious speeches against me, as though I said that the holy Body of Christ 'was brought down from heaven and was not of the holy Virgin,' I thought it necessary to say a few words to them about this: – O fools, who know only how to slander, how have you been mispersuaded to take up this perverse notion, how have you fallen sick of so great folly? For you ought by all means to be aware that almost the whole of our contention for the faith has grown out of our confident assertion that the holy Virgin is "*Theotokos*." but if we affirm that the holy Body of Christ, the Savior of us all, was from heaven, and was not born of her, how can she be conceived of as the "*Theotokos*"? For whom in the world did she bear, if it be not true that she bore Emmanuel, according to the flesh? Let them be treated with scorn then, who prate thus about me. For it is no falsehood which the blessed Prophet Isaiah speaks when he says: 'Behold the Virgin shall conceive and bring forth a Son and they shall call His name Emmanuel, which being interpreted, is God with us.' And it is altogether true which the holy Gabriel said to the blessed Virgin: 'Fear not, Mary, for thou hast found favor with God. And behold thou shall conceive in thy womb, and shall bring forth a Son, and shall call His name 'Jesus,' for He Himself shall save His people from their sins'."

"But when we say that our Lord Jesus Christ is 'from heaven and from above,' we say it – not as though his holy flesh was brought down from above and from heaven, but we follow rather the divinely-taught Paul, who cries distinctly: 'The first man is of the earth, earthly: the second man is from heaven.' And we remember moreover the Savior's words: 'No one hath ascended up to heaven but he who came down from heaven, the Son of Man,' notwithstanding that he was born as to the flesh, as I said just now, of the holy Virgin. But forasmuch as he that came down from above and from heaven, God the Logos, emptied himself, taking the form of a servant, and was called the Son of Man, remaining still what he was, that is, God – (for he is unchangeable and unalterable as to his nature) – therefore he is said to have 'come down from heaven,' being even now conceived of as one with his own flesh, and he is named also 'Man from heaven,' the same perfect in Manhood, and conceived of as in one Person: for the Lord Jesus Christ is one, although we do not forget the difference of the natures, from which we affirm the ineffable union to have been formed."

"But let thy Holiness vouchsafe to stop the mouths of those who say that there was a mixture of confusion or blending of God the Logos with the flesh, for it is likely that some are spreading the report that I hold or say this also. But so far am I from holding anything of the sort that I look upon those as mad who at all imagine that 'shadow of turning' can befall the divine nature of the Logos, and that he is capable of change: for he remains what he is always, and hath undergone no alteration. Nor could he ever undergo alteration. Moreover we all acknowledge that the Logos of God is naturally impassible, even though, in his all-wise administration of the mystery, he is seen to attribute to himself the sufferings which befell his own flesh. Thus also the all-wise Peter says, 'Christ then having suffered for us in the flesh,' and not in the nature of the ineffable Godhead. For in order that he may be believed the Savior of the world, he appropriates to himself, as I said, in view of his Incarnation, the sufferings of his own flesh – as did the Prophet before, who said, speaking in his person, 'I gave my back to the scourges, and my cheeks to blows, and my face I turned not away from the shame of spitting'."

"But that we follow everywhere the sentiments of the holy Fathers, and especially those of our blessed and all-renowned Father Athanasius, refusing to vary from them in the least possible degree, let thy Holiness be assured, and let no one else entertain a doubt. I would have set down many passages of theirs, confirming my own words from them, if I had not been afaid of making my letter too long and therefore tedious. And we in no wise suffer any to unsettle the faith – the Symbol of the Faith I mean – defined by our holy Fathers assembled at Nicaea. Nor assuredly do we suffer ourselves or others either to alter a phrase of what is contained therein, or to go beyond a single syllable, remem - bering who said, 'Remove not the eternal landmarks which thy Fathers set.' For it was not they who spoke, but the very Spirit of God the Father, *who proceeds indeed from him* but is not alien from the Son in respect of essence. And in this the words of the holy teachers confirm us. For in the *Acts of the Apostles* it is written: 'When they had gone throughout Mysia they attempted to go into Bithynia and the Spirit of Jesus suffered them not.' The blessed Paul, too, writes in his Epistle: 'They that are in the flesh cannot please God. And you are not in the flesh but in the spirit, if the Spirit of God dwell in you. But if any man have not the Spirit of Christ, he is none of his."

"But when any of those who are inclined to pervert the right meaning of my words to what they please, let not thy Holiness marvel, as thou knowest that heretics also of every sort collect arguments in support of their error from the divine Scripture, corrupting by their own evil-mindedness what has been rightly spoken by the Holy Spirit and drawing down in full measure upon their own heads the unquenchable flame."

"But since we have learned that some have published a garbled edition of our all-renowned Father Athanasius' orthodox Epistle to the blessed Epictetus, so that many are being injured by it, therefore with a view to what may be useful and necessary to the brethren, we send your Holiness a transcript taken from ancient and correct copies which we have here."

"The Lord preserve thee in good health, and interceding for us, most honored brother."

THE DIFFICULTIES OF REUNION WITH THE EASTERNERS

However, this "reunification" with the East did not take place without disputes – both stubborn Antiochians and extreme Alexandrians

objected. St. Cyril was forced to explain the meaning of the "reunifi -
cation" to the extreme Alexandrians, and it took a long time to reassure
the East as well. Suspicions directed against St. Cyril were not
extinguished, and in addition the disputes over Theodore of Mopsuestia
had begun. Rabbula, the bishop of Edessa, had anathematized Theodore
right after the Council of Ephesus and Rabbula was inducing St. Cyril
to do so as well. The resulting heated argument, which had spread to
Constantinople, was quashed by an imperial ban on "undertaking
anything against those who have died at peace with the Church." At the
time this was good for the Church, since the condemnation of
Antiochene theologians threatened to disrupt the tranquillity of the East,
which had not yet become entirely peaceful. St. Cyril refrained from
any harsh action, but meanwhile was working on a book against
Theodore and Diodore and did nothing to conceal his negative feelings
for their "abusive tongues and pens."

As far as we know, St. Cyril's life almost until the very end
dissolves into the history of his time. Almost the only thing we know
about him is his struggle with Nestorianism, and the fact that most of
his energy went into this struggle. From the sermons and letters which
have been preserved we can imagine him as a persistent and steadfast
pastor who attentively looked after the life of his flock and his diocese.
After a stormy life, he died in 444.

The image of him which was forever imprinted in the memory of
the Church is that of a profound theologian with a keen mind. This was
not hindered by the fact that his name, his authority, and his words were
abused for so long by the Monophysites. St. Cyril always remained the
"rule of faith" for the orthodox people who struggled with Mono -
physitism – for Pope Leo and Patriarch Flavian. The fathers of the
Ecumenical Council of Chalcedon defined their faith as "the faith of St.
Cyril." The Fifth Ecumenical Council relied on St. Cyril's judgment
when they condemned the *"Three Chapters."* St. Maximus the
Confessor relied on St. Cyril in his struggle with the Monothelites, as
did the venerable Anastasius of Sinai, known more commonly as
Anastasius Sinaita. St. Cyril had less influence in the West. Here it is
as if he has been suppressed. In any case he is little known or remem -
bered. In the East St. Cyril's feast occurs on June 9, and in conjunction
with St. Athanasius on January 18. In the West it occurs on June 27
and formerly on February 9.

II

WORKS

St. Cyril was one of most prolific writers in the history of early
Christian literature. His writings fill ten volumes in Migne's *Patrologia
Graeca* – volumes 68-77. And moreover this is only what has come

down to us, for many of his works have been lost. He was still alive when the first Latin translations of some of his works appeared. Translations of his works appeared in Latin, Syriac, Armenian, Ethiopian, and then Arabic. Marius Mercator was the translator of some of the Latin translations; Rabbula of Edessa of some of the Syriac. It is indeed strange that such an important figure in Church history has been not written about in the West to the extent that one would expect. Moreover, it is almost impossible to find an extensive or reliable work on his life and thought in English. When one compares St. Cyril's importance in the history of Christian thought with that of St. Augustine, when one compares the prodigious output of writings of both men, then it is stunning when one compares the works written about St. Augustine and the lack of works on St. Cyril.

THE EARLY EXEGETICAL WORKS

Among St. Cyril's writings the earliest were exegetical works on the Old Testament. Even before his episcopate he wrote the book titled *The Adoration and Worship of God in Spirit and in Truth* – Περὶ τῆς ἐν πνεύματι καὶ ἀληθείᾳ προσκυνήσεως καὶ λατρείας, *De adoratione et cultu in spiritu et veritate*. It is written in the form of a dialogue between Cyril and Palladius and is an allegorical and typological exegesis. His main point in this work is that the law was suspended or abrogated only in its letter and not in its spirit. For St. Cyril everything in the Old Testament is a prefiguration of the adoration in the spirit and must be understood that way. *The Adoration and Worship of God in Spirit and in Truth* consists of seventeen books. In books nine through thirteen St. Cyril attempts to reveal how the Church and the priesthood were prefigured in the Old Testament. In books fourteen through sixteen he attempts to reveal the foreshadowing of the spiritual worship of Christianity in the institutions of the Old Testament. In the earlier books of this work St. Cyril deals with the sin of Adam and goes on to discuss the deliverance of mankind from the slavery of sin and the devil. Such deliverance can come only through Christ. He discusses how this takes place and goes into detail in the fourth and fifth books on the importance of the determination of the human will in the perseverance and preservation of salvation.

Also written early is his *Elegant Comments* – Γλαφυρά. This work consists of thirteen books and complements his work on *The Adoration and Worship of God in Spirit and in Truth* . Both works refer to each other. It is not in dialogue form. Seven books are on *Genesis*, three on *Exodus*, and one book each on *Leviticus*, *Numbers* and *Deuteronomy*.

His *Commentary of Isaiah* belongs to this period. It is an extensive work which fills almost the entirety of volume 70 of Migne's edition. And his *Commentary on the Minor Prophets* belongs also to this early period.

In these interpretations St. Cyril adheres to the Alexandrian method, sometimes *in extremis*. "Cut off the uselessness of history and take off somehow the wood of the letter, and get to the very heart of the plant – that is, painstakingly examine the inner fruit of what has been commanded and use it for food." That is how St. Cyril defines *the rule of interpretation*. He seeks "spiritual meaning" under the letter of the Scriptures. When applied to the Old Testament, this rule was entirely justified, "for images are what are given in the law, and the picture of truth is outlined in shadows." Therefore, the Law is abrogated only in its letter and not in its spiritual content and meaning. In its spiritual sense the law retains its force even to this day. In his first interpretative work, St. Cyril uncovers this mysterious, allegorical, and immutable sense of Mosaic Law and adds a coherent sketch of Old Testament foundations of spiritual preparation. In particular he dwells on the Old Testament prototypes of the Church. In his books of *Elegant Comments* he elaborates the same theme and sets himself the task of showing that "the mystery of Christ is prefigured in all of the Mosaic books." The allegory is somewhat more weakly expressed in the interpretation of the prophets, for here historical surveys predominate. Cyril's interpretations of the book of *Kings*, the *Song of Songs*, and the prophets *Ezekiel, Jeremiah, Baruch,* and *Daniel* survive only in fragments. St. Cyril not infrequently addresses the Hebrew as well as the Greek *Septuagint* text. According to St. Photius (*Dibl. Cod.* 229) St. Cyril also wrote an exegesis on the *Psalms*. This is also confirmed by the *Doctrina Patrum de incarnatione Verbi*.

THE COMMENTARY ON *THE GOSPEL OF ST. JOHN*

To the pre-Nestorian period belongs the extensive interpretation of the *Gospel of John* in twelve volumes. Only fragments remain of the seventh and eighth books. The commentary is of a dogmatic nature. The introduction states that particular attention is to be given to the dogmatic meaning of the text and the refutation of heretical thought. He sharply criticizes the the thought of the Arians, the Eunomians, and the Christology of the School of Antioch. Neither the name of Nestorius is mentioned nor the term *Theotokos*. The terminology is not the same as found in the writings of St. Cyril after the Nestorian controversy broke out. There is unanimity among scholars that it was written in the pre-Nestorian period.

THE COMMENTARY ON *THE GOSPEL OF ST. LUKE*

St. Cyril's *Commentary on the Gospel of St. Luke* is of a different nature. It is in fact a collection of homilies on the text with practical rather than dogmatic purposes. Of the Greek original only three complete *Homilies* and some fragments of *catenae* remain. There is, however, a Syriac version which preserves 156 homilies. The content of the Syriac version may provide a clue to the date of com - position. There is at least one reference to St. Cyril's *Anathemas* in *Homily* 63 and, if authentic, then it would indicate that it was written after the end of 430.

FRAGMENTS OF OTHER WORKS ON THE NEW TESTAMENT

Insignificant fragments remain of his interpretations of the *Gospel of Matthew* and other books of the New Testament. Leontius of Byzantium, Ephraem of Antioch and others knew of the complete text of the *Commentary on the Gospel of St. Matthew*. It dealt with all twenty-eight chapters. The date of composition seems to be after 428. St. Cyril's exegetical works were translated into Syriac and were hence available to the Syrian Monophysites. Rabbula of Edessa was respon- sible for some of the translations into Syriac. In addition, Armenian, Ethiopian and Arabic translations exist, as well as Latin translations by Marius Mercator.

DOGMATIC WRITINGS BEFORE THE NESTORIAN CONTROVERSY

St. Cyril wrote quite extensively on dogmatic themes. To the pre- Nestorian period belong two enormous works devoted to revealing Trinitarian dogma – the *Thesaurus de sancta et consubstantiali Trinitate* and the books *On the Holy and Consubstantial Trinity* [*De sancta et consubstantiali Trinitate*]. In the former St. Cyril , relying particularly on St. Athanasius, plainly and succinctly summarizes the entire anti- Arian polemic. He primarily dwells on Biblical arguments. In the latter St. Cyril develops his thoughts in a freer way and, moreover, in a form of dialogue. Here he touches upon the Christological theme as well. Both books were written for a certain friend by the name of Nemesius.

WRITINGS DURING THE NESTORIAN CONTROVERSY

During the Nestorian struggles St. Cyril wrote extensively. First, we must mention his famous *Anathemas* or *"Chapters"* against Nes - torius and the related *"Explanations"* and *"Defenses"* against the "Easterners" and against Theodoret. The *Scholia de Incarnatione Unigeniti* [*The Scholia on the Incarnation of the Only-Begotten*]and the books *On the True Faith* [*De recta fide*] belong to this period. The *Scholia* was composed after 431 and defines the hypostatic union as opposed to a mixture or external association. The entire text of the *Scholia* exists in an old Latin, Syriac, and Armenian translation. Only small portions remain of the original Greek text. *On the True Faith* was written shortly after the outbreak of the Nestorian controversy, and was addressed as previously mentioned,to the emperor Theodosius II and the imperial ladies.

St. Cyril's *Adversus nolentes confiteri sanctam Virginem esse Deiparam* [*Against Those Who Do Not Acknowledge Mary to be the Theotokos*] was composed after the Council of Ephesus. The emperor Justinian I acknowledges in his *Tractatus contra Monophysitas* (13-14) in 542 that this work is a genuine work of St. Cyril.

Quod unus sit Christus is a dialogue on the unity of person in Christ and is a thorough refutation of the false doctrine that the Word or *Logos* of God did not become flesh but was united only to a man. The work reveals mature and deeply penetrating thought by St. Cyril.

All of these works directed against Nestorius were translated, as previously mentioned, into Syriac very early on, partly by Rabbula, the bishop of Edessa. St. Cyril's work *Contra Diodorum et Theodorum* was written against Diodore of Tarsus and Theodore of Mopsuestia. It consists of three books. Numerous fragments are extant in Greek and Syriac. It was composed about 438. His *Contra Synousiastas* – the extreme Apollinarians – also exists only in fragments.

THE *LETTERS* OF ST. CYRIL

St. Cyril's letters are extremely important not only for the history of Christian doctrine but also for the history of the relationship between the Church and the Empire. They shed much light on the life behind the scenes at that time. Moreover, the rivalry between the theological schools of Antioch and Alexandria and the rivalry among the episcopal sees is seen more graphically in the letters than anywhere else.

Numerous letters are still extant. In Migne's collection there are 88 letters, although some of these are not authentic and seventeen of them are letters addressed to St. Cyril by others (see Migne, *Patrologia Graeca* 77, 401-981]. In addition to those in the Migne collection, E. Schwartz published the Greek text of five other letters, four of which were entirely unknown previously and one which was known only in a Latin version.

St. Cyril wrote numerous letters, many of which are dogmatic tracts. Such are the letters to Nestorius, the letter to John of Antioch, letters to Acacius of Melitene and Valerian, and two letters to Suc - census. St. Cyril's second letter to Nestorius obtained an "ecumenical status." The Council of Ephesus, at its first meeting on June 22, 431, approved that letter by a unanimous vote. The bishops asserted that the letter was in full harmony with the Nicene Creed and that it was an authentic expression of orthodox doctrine. Pope St. Leo the Great, the Council of Chalcedon (451) and the the Council of Constantinople (553) also approved this letter for the same reason. St. Cyril's third letter to Nestorius, which contained the appended *Twelve Anathemas*, was added to the *Acts* of the Council of Ephesus. Although the third letter was not formally accepted by a vote, it was adopted by the

Council of Chalcedon. The letter to John of Antioch in the spring of 433 was recommended by the Council of Chalcedon.

Among St. Cyril's letters mention must be made of his *Paschal Letters*. It was the custom of the bishops of Alexandria to send each year a "Paschal Letter" which set the date for Easter and the Lenten fast. St. Cyril continued this custom. In the editions of his works twenty-nine *Paschal Letters* are listed, written between 414 and 442. As was the custom with Paschal Letters, there is emphasis on the importance of fasting, abstinence, prayer, almsgiving, and works of mercy and charity. St. Cyril's *Paschal Letters* contain all such exhortations but, in addition, some contain dogmatic themes. *Paschal Letter* 12 deals with the doctrine of the Holy Trinity; *Paschal Letters* 5, 8, 17, and 27 deal with the doctrine of the Incarnation, especially against those who deny the eternity of the Son. St. Cyril's harsh words against pagans and Jews are vividly conveyed in some of these letters. Again, this is another indication that paganism still had a certain life, still had enough strength to it to concern Christian leaders. In *Paschal Letters* 12 and 14 St. Cyril warns Christians against *dipsychia* – that is, against a divided soul of practicing both Christianity and paganism, of participating in the liturgical life of the Church and its sacraments and simultaneously participating in pagan rituals. St. Cyril's vehemence against and disdain for the Jews is most graphically revealed in *Paschal Letters* 1, 4, 10, 20, 21, and 29. In *Paschal Letter* 17 for the year 429 St. Cyril raises objections against Nestorius – this letter is also extant in a Latin translation which was long falsely attributed to Arnobius, known as "the Younger" to distinguish him from Arnobius of Sicca.

St. Cyril prepared a "Paschal Calendar" for emperor Theodosius II which covered the years 403 through 512. It is no longer extant but the cover letter survived in an old Armenian translation and was published for the first time in 1907. Dionysius Exiguus (c.500 - 550) refers to St. Cyril's "Paschal Calendar," although the version to which he refers extends through the year 531 and was probably a later revision of St. Cyril's original (see Dionysius' *Epistola ad Petronium* in Migne, *Patrologia Latina* 67, 19f).

FOR THE HOLY RELIGION OF THE CHRISTIANS AGAINST THE BOOKS OF THE IMPIOUS JULIAN

The first ten books of an extensive apologetical work titled *For the Holy Religion of the Christians Against the Books of the Impious Julian* have been preserved. Only insignificant fragments – in Greek and Syriac – remain of the eleventh through the twentieth books. It is possible that the complete work may have totalled thirty volumes rather than twenty but the subject is still controversial. Some scholars are adamant that St. Cyril wrote no more than twenty books against Julian the Apostate. We know from a letter of Theodoret of Cyrus (*Ep.* 83) that Cyril sent this work to the patriarch John of Antioch. Thus the date of composition should be previous to 441, the year in which John died. Here St. Cyril critiques Julian the Apostate's three books against the Gospels and against Christians known commonly as *Adversus Christianos* or *Against the Galilaeans* and written in 363. Julian's books apparently retained their popularity in the beginning of the fifth century. It is noteworthy that Julian the Apostate's books are known to us only because of the extensive quotations preserved in St. Cyril's work against him. St. Cyril gives the text of his opponent almost in full and then critiques it in detail. The books which have been preserved concern the relationship between paganism and Judaism and between the Old and New Testaments. In particular, St. Cyril has much to say about the agreement between the Gospels, between the *Synoptics* and the *Gospel of John*. St. Cyril's polemics have a rather harsh character. There is not much in them that is new. St. Cyril repeats the previous apologists, especially Eusebius of Caesarea. The work, as indicated above, was written after the Council of Ephesus.

In St. Cyril's dogmatic works references to the tradition of the fathers play a dominant role. Apparently he also compiled a special code of the testimony of the fathers, a "book of texts," which Leontius of Byzantium mentions. It also seems that St. Cyril might have written against the Pelagians.

III

ST. CYRIL'S THEOLOGY

THE LIMITS OF LOGICAL CONSCIOUSNESS

In his theological works St. Cyril always starts from the Scriptures and the teachings of the fathers. With great harshness he emphasizes the limitedness of our reason and the insufficiency of our literary means, and from this infers the need to rely on the direct evidence of the Logos of God. "And in actual fact," St. Cyril observes, "pondering the Highest Essence of all and Its mysteries turns out to be a dangerous enterprise and one not "unharmful for many." What is more, he does not attach any special significance to the logical enunciation of the concepts used to determine the Truth of the faith. This was his weakness, a weakness which hindered him a great deal in his struggle with Nestorianism.

St. Cyril persistently emphasized the limits of logical con - sciousness – not only the Divine Essence but also the secrets of God's will are incomprehensible and undiscoverable to man, and man should not look for reasons and foundations too inquisitively. In its uniqueness the Divine nature is inaccessible, mysterious and beyond human imagination – and not only for human eyes alone but for all creatures. Only through examining God's works is it possible to ascend in some degree to knowledge of God but when doing so one must firmly remember the boundless distance between God and his creatures, the incommensurability of the Trinity's limitless nature with the creatures' limitedness. The impression is never equal to the stamp itself and the reflection of truth in our imagination is not identical to truth itself. We always "meagerly think about God." Knowledge of God is available to us only in shadows and mysteries. "No one sees," observes St. Cyril, "that our nature has neither the concepts nor the words through which we could possibly express the traits of Divine and ineffable nature correctly and with total certainty. Therefore we are forced to use words which are in conformity with our nature, even though they have to elucidate subjects which exceed our intellect. In fact, it is hardly possible to express something like this, something which exceeds our very thought. As a result, in taking the coarseness of human ideas for a symbol or image, we must try to use the image accessible to us to move on to the traits of Divinity themselves."

THE IMPORTANCE OF FAITH AS A NECESSARY PREREQUISITE FOR UNDERSTANDING

In the mysterious contemplation of the prophets there was revealed not the nature of God "as it is in its very essence" but only "the vision of a likeness of God's glory." In the Scriptures themselves truth is revealed incompletely and only when applicable, and *therefore genuine understanding of the Scriptures is impossible without abundant help and illumination*. The meaning of the Word of God is revealed only in the experience of *faith*. Only *faith*, not investigation, leads us out of our created limitedness. *Faith must precede investigation* – sound knowledge can be confirmed only on the *basis of faith*. Without illumination by the Holy Spirit, one cannot arrive at cognition of the Truth and one cannot attain an exact understanding of the divine dogmas. Neither does the Father grant cognition of Christ to the impure, for it is not seemly to pour precious chrism into a pit. Knowledge of God is *speculation* and *contemplation* in contradistinction to external knowledge. Our present knowledge is imperfect knowledge, "partial knowledge." But, in addition, it is true and authentic knowledge, for even in the slightest knowledge the truth's beauty shines unbroken in its entirety. In the future life this incompleteness and partialness will be removed and then we will "clearly and completely behold the glory of God who will have imparted to us the clearest knowledge of himself." "Then, no longer having the need either for some kind of image or for riddles and tales, we will understand the beauty of the Divine nature of God the Father with an open face, so to speak, and with an unhindered mind, for we will have beheld the glory emanating from him." The shining beauty of the stars fades in the power of the sun's light. In the same way, our present dark knowledge will be abolished in the perfect light of Divine glory – St. Cyril does not limit himself to apophatic theology, although he prefers knowledge

–gnosis – in an experience of spiritual life with Christ and in Christ to knowledge gained through investigation and reasoning. Being a shrewd and intelligent theologian, he was not a philosopher in his spiritual make-up at all. In much he was close to the Cappadocians, especially to St. Gregory the Theologian.

THE MYSTERY OF THE KNOWLEDGE OF COMPLETE TRUTH

Complete knowledge of God consists not only of knowing that God exists but also of knowing "that he is the Father and of whom he is the Father, obviously indicating here the Holy Spirit," writes St. Cyril. This is also the highest knowledge of God which is revealed by Christ, namely that he showed the name of Father to people, and that he led them to an understanding of the mystery of the Trinity. The name Father is more appropriate to God than the name God. God's Trinitarian nature is faith's highest truth, and is revealed only in Christ and through Christ. *This is Christianity's essential newness.* St. Cyril emphasizes that the Trinitarian truth is at the same time a mystery which cannot be completely known, which is accepted in faith, and is elucidated only partially through the imperfect analogies of created nature. In his exposition of Trinitarian dogma St. Cyril starts from the Scripture and relies on the tradition of the fathers, primarily the works of St. Athanasius.

THE ONTOLOGICAL CHARACTER OF THE TRINITARIAN HYPOSTASES

Given the circumstances of the anti-Arian polemic, St. Cyril pays particular attention to uncovering and proving the *ontological character of the Trinitarian hypostases*. Following the Trinitarian theology of the Cappadocians, St. Cyril clearly distinguishes the concepts of "essence" – or "nature" – on the one hand, and "hypostasis" on the other. A single Divine nature is cognized "in the three independent hypostases." Of course, not only "is cognized" but also "exists." The Trinitarian names indicate real differences and the features of hypostatic existence. The Trinitarian hypostases differ in their objective reality. Each exists in its own way – *ίδίως* – and is what it is. In addition, they are consubstantial. This consubstantiality signifies not only an abstract unity or identity of nature but also a perfect interpenetration and inter-communication of the Divine Persons, *τήν είσάπαν άναπλοκήν*. Therefore Each Person is entirely cognized in Each Person, since for all the uniqueness of their existence they "essentially reside in one another," *έν άλλήλοις ένυπάρχοντες ούσιωδῶς*. The Trinitarian names are relative and indicate the interrelationship of the hypostases. And in the Holy Trinity there are no differences other than the hypostatic differences. In this description of the Blessed Trinity St.

Cyril remains within the bounds of Cappadocian theology. For him, Divine unity means a perfect identity of natures and an indissoluble bond between the hypostases. This unity of Divine nature and Divine life is manifested in the perfect unity of God's will and Divine acts, and the kingdom and power of the Holy Trinity is united over all, for everything is inseparable from the Father through the Son in the Holy Spirit.

THE CHURCH AS THE PERFECT REFLECTION OF THE UNKNOWABLE TRINITY

The unknowable Trinitarian unity of Divine reality and life finds – and must find – its perfect reflection and likeness in the Church. Christ leads those who believe in him to spiritual unity "so that the indivisible unanimity of unity, concordant in everything, reflects the traits of the natural and essential unity which is conceived in the Father and Son. Of course, the union of love and like-mindedness does not attain the same indivisibility which the Father and the Son have in the identity of essence. However, the unanimity and like-mindedness of those who believe reflects the essential identity and perfect interpen - etration of the persons of the Holy Trinity, for there is a certain "natural unity" with which we are bound to each other and to God in Christ and through Christ. Thus, since each of us in and of himself is "within his own limit and hypostasis" and "is distinguished from each other in body and soul as a special personality," we are essentially united in the unity of Christ's Body – through the Eucharist. We become "co-corporal" to one another and "co-corporal" to Christ, who abides in us through his flesh. "Is it not clear then that we all constitute one entity," concludes St. Cyril, "both in each other and in Christ?" Again we are indissolubly joined in a unity of the Spirit – "having perceived the extra-terrestrial representation of the Holy Spirit, who has been joined to us." And so "we are all one in the Father, the Son, and in the Holy Spirit: one through the identity of characteristics, through sameness of religion, through communion with Christ's holy flesh, and through communion with the one Holy Spirit." Even though the similarity is incomplete, the Church, as a union of unanimity and peace, is to some extent the best image of the Divine unity – an image indicated by Christ himself in his pontifical prayer: even as Thou Father, art in me, and I in Thee, that they also may be in us." (*John* 17:21).

THE REVELATION OF GOD AS FATHER AND ITS TRINITARIAN SIGNIFICANCE

The Triunity of the Godhead which was alluded to in the Old Testament was revealed by Christ in the New. The revelation that God is the Father is a revelation of the Trinity, for Fatherhood presupposes Sonship, and the Father is the Father of the Son. The name of the

Father is the name of the hypostasis and points to the relationship of the First Person to the Second and the Third Persons. The Father is also called the Beginning and the Source, for he is the root and source of Divinity, while the name of the Source here signifies only "whence comes objective reality." The concepts of time and change are in no way applicable to Divine Life. Therefore, all hypostatic traits and relationships have to be conceived as eternal and immutable. There is no space between the Divinity and Fatherhood of the First Hypostasis and the eternity of the Fatherhood signifies the eternity of the ineffable Divine birth; that is, the eternity of the Sonship.

The eternal Son is born of the eternal Father. He does not "come into being," does not arise, but throughout eternity "was" and abides in the Father as in a Source. He has always existed in him as his *Logos*, Wisdom, Force, Imprint, Reflection, and Image. To these last attributes, the apostolic favorite attributes of St. Athanasius, St. Cyril ascribes a special significance – in particular they clearly express the perfect consubstantiality and equal sanctity of Father and Son. As the Image, reflection and "outline" of the Father's Hypostasis, the Son is inseparable from him whose reflection he is, although he himself is to be found in him and has the Father in himself, through a perfect identity of nature and traits – "He himself is naturally to be found in the Father." Without the perfect identity of characteristics there would be no precision in the reflection and outline. The Son is from the Father and of the Father, not outside of him, and he did not receive his own existence with time. He rather is to be found in the essence and radiates from it like rays from the sun. The birth is an act of nature – $\tau\tilde{\eta}\varsigma$ $\phi\dot{\upsilon}\sigma\epsilon\omega\varsigma$ – and not an act of will. This is what distinguishes the birth from creation. The Son abides "in the Father's bosom" as something "indwelling in it by the immutable identity of essence," as someone "who exists in, and has always existed with, the Father," $\dot{\omega}\varsigma$ $\dot{\epsilon}\nu\upsilon\pi\dot{\alpha}\rho\chi\omega\nu$. Therefore the Father is contemplated and "manifested" in the Son as in some mirror as in His "essential and natural image," as in the image of his own essence. The Son is called the outline or sketch precisely because the outline or sketch is of the same nature as, and inseparable from that essence of which it is an outline or sketch. Thus, "consubstantiality" for St. Cyril means not only a generic similarity and community of characteristics but also a perfect and indivisible *unity of life*. The concepts of "birth" and "outline" or "sketch" mutually augment and explain one another. The outline or sketch points out the perfect similarity of characteristics, while the birth points out the origin "from the essence" and "the natural co-abiding with the Father. The unique hypostasis of the Persons is not effaced in the "hypostasis" or "natural unity": with the unity of essence the Father and the Son Each abide "in their own Person" – $\dot{\epsilon}\nu$ $\dot{\iota}\delta\dot{\iota}\omega$ $\pi\rho\sigma\sigma\dot{\omega}\pi\omega$ – and in a special existence – $\dot{\iota}\delta\iota\alpha\sigma\tau\dot{\alpha}\tau\omega\varsigma$ – but without separation – at once and separately and jointly.

THE *LOGOS* OR WORD OF THE FATHER

In St. Cyril we do not find perfect sameness in his Trinitarian terminology, and, though the latest Cappadocian usage frequently is utilized by St. Cyril, he also utilizes the earlier terms from St. Athanasius and the Nicene controversy. He uses the entire aggregate of concepts and attributes to substantiate and disclose the perfect consub - stantiality of the Son and the Logos.

The Son is the Creator and Builder of the world, inseparable from the Father and the Holy Spirit, the Beginning and Organizer of every - thing which has arisen and is created. There is nothing secondary or subordinate in the Son's creative activity. On the contrary, it proclaims his mastery over everything. "Since by nature he himself is life, he diversely gives beings existence, life and movement. Not that by means of some division or alteration he enters each from existences having different natures – the creature itself is diversified by the ineffable wisdom and power of the Creator. And one is the Life of all, which enters each being as much as is fitting and as much as it can perceive." That is why the Evangelist says "that which has been made was life in him." (*John* 1: 3,4). Such, apparently, was the most ancient reading of these evangelical lines. It was changed in the post-Arian epoch. Every - thing that exists has life in the Logos. A creature comes into being and is animated through contact and communion with Life, and created existence has its life and existence in the Logos. The Son not only calls the creature to existence but also maintains that which has come into being through himself," as if adding himself to that which by its nature does not have an eternal existence, and becoming Life for the being so that it abides and remains entirely within the limits of its nature."

Existing in the creature through communion – διά μετοχῆς – and giving it life, the Logos, as it were, transcends the weakness of created beings which have come into being and are therefore subject to destruction as well, and "artificially creates eternity for them." The Logos is by nature Life or Self-Life and therefore it is Life for all creation. Through the light of the Logos creatures come into being out of the darkness of non-existence. Created existence comes into being "and the Light shines in the darkness." The presence of the Logos in creation does not extinguish the boundary between it and the creatures. On the contrary, this boundary becomes all the more clear to us when it is revealed that creation exists and lives only through communion with something different from it – only through communion with Self-Existing Life.

Creation is an inscrutable act of God's will and the creative force is distinctive only of God himself. Creation is of a different nature than God's and, since it had a beginning, it has to have an end. Only God's goodness protects it from this natural instability. These meditations of St. Cyril very much remind one of St. Athanasius' teaching in his early work *On the Incarnation*. And, together with St. Athanasius, St. Cyril repudiates Philo's representation of the Logos as an "intermediary" between God and the world in the act of creation and in forming creatures. There is nothing intermediary between God and all creation, no "middle nature" or being. Only God alone is higher than creation, and everything else "submits to the yoke of slavery."

THE HOLY SPIRIT

St. Cyril developed his doctrine about the Holy Spirit in rather great detail. For polemical motives he dwells on evidence of the Spirit's Divine Nature. The Holy Spirit is of God and is God – consubstantial with the Father and the Son – and is not at all lower or less than them in Divine dignity. The Holy Spirit has "an essence which exceeds all," and "the purest and most perfect nature." He is God of God, "Self-Wisdom and Self-Power," *αὐτοχρῆμα σοφία καὶ δύναμις*. Therefore, the Holy Spirit joins us to Divine Nature and, moving into us, through communion makes us temples of God and gods through grace. Through the Holy Spirit God dwells in people. The Holy Spirit is a plenitude of all blessings and the source of all beauty, the Spirit of truth, life, wisdom, and power. *The Holy Spirit proceeds from the Father* and the image of this Divine procession is not revealed to us and is not capable of being known by us. *Proceeding from the Father*, the Holy Spirit abides in the Father in essence, for the Holy Spirit proceeds "indivisibly and indissolubly" and is the Father's "own" Spirit. By virtue of the perfect and indivisible consubstantiality of the Holy Trinity, the Holy Spirit is also a "property" of the Son, "joined to the Son in essence." By nature the Holy Spirit is "innate" and belongs to the Son, abiding in him naturally. The Holy Spirit is the "proper" Spirit of the Father and the Son." What is more, the Holy Spirit exists hypostatically on his own. By virtue of this identity of natures, the Spirit is inseparable from the Son and by nature *proceeds through Him* . St. Cyril tries to emphasize the perfect consubstantiality and indivisibility of the Son and the Spirit: "Sharing in essence the natural blessings of the Father, the Son has the Spirit in the same way as should be understood for the Father – *that is*, not as something alien or external to Him." Therefore, he sends the Spirit into the world, or pours forth the Spirit.

THE PROCESSION OF THE HOLY SPIRIT

In speaking of the *procession through the Son* , St. Cyril does not mean to investigate or define the image of the "ineffable procession" but tries, on the one hand, to confirm the truth of consubstantiality and, on the other hand, to define the relationship between the activities in the world of the Spirit and of the Incarnate Son. In other words, St. Cyril is trying to elucidate the sense of the sending down of the Holy Spirit from heaven and the descent of the Holy Spirit to the world in connection with the Son of God's redemptive mission. The Savior speaks of the Spirit as "another Comforter" in order to distinguish the Spirit from himself and to show the unique or special hypostasis of the Holy Spirit. In addition, the Son calls the Holy Spirit the "Spirit of Truth" and evidently "stresses this" in order to certify that the Spirit belongs to the Divine Essence or Nature. "So that the disciples would see that he promised to give them not the inspiration of an alien and heterogeneous force, but himself (only) in another manner. To accomplish this, the Son calls the Paraclete the Spirit of Truth; that is, his Own Spirit, for the Holy Spirit is not conceived as alien to the essence of the Only-Begotten but naturally proceeds from the Son, and *with regard to the identity of natures* the Holy Spirit is not something else in comparison with the Son, although the Holy Spirit is conceived as something with an independent existence. Thus the expression "the Spirit of Truth" should lead us to a complete knowledge of the truth. As he who precisely knows the truth (of which he is the Spirit), the Holy Spirit will not partially reveal truth to those who honor him but will impart the mystery of truth entirely. "And he will say nothing which contradicts me, and he will not preach an alien doctrine to you, for he will not introduce any laws of his own. Since he is my Spirit and my mind, as it were, he will say that which is in me." The Savior said this not so that we would consider the Holy Spirit secondary, as some ignorant people claim, but, on the contrary, the Savior said this out of a desire to prove to the disciples that since the Holy Spirit was nothing which differed from him, *as regards consubstantiality*, his Spirit certainly would speak and act and desire in the same way. After all, "the Holy Spirit would not foretell the future the same as I if he did not exist in me and did not originate through me, and was not of the same essence as I."

St. Cyril has in mind the "natural unity" of the Son and the Spirit and their unity of mission which results therefrom. By virtue of the Trinitarian consubstantiality, the Holy Spirit, being the "pure image" of the Father, is also the "natural likeness" of the Son. Therefore, in the Spirit, which was sent from the Father, the Son enlightens his disciples and teaches them, and he enters them through the Spirit.

THE DIFFERENCE BETWEEN ST. CYRIL AND ST. AUGUSTINE ON THE DOCTRINE OF THE PROCESSION OF THE HOLY SPIRIT

To see St. Cyril approaching St. Augustine's notion of the proces - sion of Spirit and to equate St. Cyril's δι ' υἱοῦ with St. Augustine's *filioque* would violate the logical progression of St. Cyril's thought, and this is directly corroborated by St. Cyril's own testimony. In the *Ninth Anathema* against Nestorius St. Cyril condemned those "who say that the single Lord Jesus Christ is glorified through the Spirit, using his own power as something alien – ἀλλοτρια – to himself, and through him taking the power to conquer evil spirits and to create in people Divine signs, and who do not say, on the contrary, that the Spirit, through whom he worked these Divine signs, is a Spirit *proper* – *ἴδιος* – to him, let him be anathema."

The Blessed Theodoret observed in opposition to this: "If Cyril calls the Spirit proper to the Son in the sense that he is co-natural with the Son and proceeds from the Father, then we agree with him and recognize his expression as orthodox. If Cyril (uses this name) in the sense that the Spirit has its existence from the Son or through the Son, then we repudiate this expression as blasphemous and impious." St. Cyril confirmed in his reply that he did not mean at all the "impious" opinion suggested by Theodoret but wanted to emphasize that the Spirit is "not alien to the Son *because* the Son shares everything with the Father." The *Ninth Anathema* has, of course, a Christological content and in it St. Cyril rejects the fallacious notion of Christ's relationship through his human nature to the Spirit as to something "alien" to this nature. As a counterpoise to this, St. Cyril advances the thought of the "possession" or "affinity" between the Spirit and the Logos Incarnate.

St. Cyril intends to say: Christ and the Holy Spirit have a relationship which differs from that which exists between the saints and the Holy Spirit. Christ not only receives the Spirit through his humanity but he himself gives the Spirit as God for our sake, to and for the consecration of his flesh, as the foundation of our nature. The Son receives the Holy Spirit from himself, "accepts his Own Spirit and gives him to himself as God." St. Cyril's views on this issue never changed, and he never set himself the task of investigating the notion of procession "*through the Son.*"

In his Trinitarian confession St. Cyril sums up his already com - pleted theological struggle and work. There is little in him that is new and original. The whole interest and all the significance of his Trinitarian theology lies precisely in this lack of originality. He shows us an example of an average theological world view from the early fifth century. His doctrine about the Logos in creation deserves special attention – this is the last chapter in the history of ancient Christian teaching about the Word, about the *Logos*.

THE INCARNATION

Even in his early works the Christological thought of St. Cyril proceeds from a living and concrete image of Christ, the image imprinted in the Gospels and maintained in the Church. This is the image of the God-Man, the *Logos* or Word Incarnate, who came down from heaven and became man. With perfect clarity St. Cyril defines and describes the meaning of the Incarnation even in his early works, particularly in his exegesis of the *Gospel of John*. "The *Logos* became flesh" – this means that he became a man and was called the Only-Begotten. *Became flesh*, St. Cyril explains, "lest someone think that he appeared in the same way as to the prophets or other holy men. But in truth the *Logos* became flesh; that is, became a man."

When this happened the *Logos* or Word did not leave His proper and immutable Divine nature and did not turn into flesh. The Logos' Divinity was in no way diminished by the Incarnation. With the Incarnation the Son of God did not lose his Divine dignity, did not quit heaven, did not part from the Father. To assume a diminution of the Logos' Divinity during the Incarnation would mean the whole sense of the Incarnation would be destroyed, for this would mean that the Incarnation did not succeed in actually combining Divine and human nature entirely. The Logos by nature is God both in flesh and with flesh, and the Logos possesses flesh as *its own* and as something which differs from it. And when the Son of God, in the form of a man, "taking the form of a slave," dwelt and mingled among people on earth, the glory of his Divinity filled the heavens as before and he co-abided with the Father – "and we saw his glory, the glory of the Father's Only-Begotten Son."

The Divine dignity of the Incarnate Logos remains inviolable. "For this reason," St. Cyril observes, "although the Evangelist says that the Logos became flesh, he does not claim that the Logos was conquered by the weakness of the flesh or that the Logos was deprived of his primordial power and glory, as it soon became clothed in our weak and inglorious body," when he humbled himself to brotherhood with creatures and slaves. On the contrary, in Christ the servile nature is liberated, ascending to a mysterious unity with him who accepted and bore the "form of a slave," and through kinship with him his Divine dignity extends to all of us, is transferred to all humanity. For "we are all in Christ, and the general person of humanity rises to his person and he enriches all with well-being and glory through the consubstantiality of his nature with people."

This was not some kind of "second son" but the One and Only Son of the Father, who took on human flesh for our sake – "perfect through the nature of Divinity and thus condescended in terms of humanity." "The whole mystery of the Incarnation is to be found in the con-descension and humility of the Son of God," writes St. Cyril. Through this *kenosis*, through this ineffable and voluntary condescension and humility, the Logos Incarnate occupies "a kind of middle place" between God and mankind, between higher Divinity and humanity. Through him, as through an Intermediary, we "come into contact with the Father." For he also has us in himself, since he assumes our nature, "transforming it into his Own Life through a certain ineffable com-bination. With this earthly body, which had become the body of the Logos, he was at once God and Man, and combined in himself what was by nature divided and separated. By nature the flesh; that is, the humanity of Christ, is something "else," something which differs from that which exists of the Father and in the Father of the Incarnate Logos of God. But at the same time "we understand the Logos as something united with his own flesh."

In this ineffable "descension" – συνδρομή – and "unity" – ἕνωσις – is "all of Christ's mystery – "one out of two" – ἕν τι τὸ ἐξ ἀμφοῖν. Christ, the Son of God, has One Person and One Hypostasis, and everything said in the Gospels refers to this *single hypostasis* of the Incarnate Logos. St. Cyril illustrates this unity with the example of the indivisible unification of body and soul in a living person – they differ from one another but do not allow for isolation. Body and soul are used to compose a single man. The divinely inspired Scriptures preach a single Son and Christ. "Insofar as he is God the Logos, he is conceived as something other than flesh; and insofar as he is flesh, he is conceived as something other than the Logos. Insofar as the Logos, who is one with God the Father, became a man, we must get rid entirely of these "something other than-s" in view of the ineffable unification and con-descension. There was one single Son both before he combined with flesh and after he combined with flesh." Christ is not to be divided into a "duality of Sons" and we must not split the "Logos' own humanity" from "true Sonship." Christ was an authentic and complete man – τέλειος ἄνθρωπος – a "whole man," composed of a body and a rational soul. He was a man not through outward appearance or through the representation of the mind, although he was not only a "simple man" – ψιλὸς ἄνθρωπος.

He was a man authentically and naturally and possessed everything human except sin. He assumed the "whole nature of man," and here lies the whole meaning of his redemptive mission, for as St. Cyril iterates from St. Gregory of Nazianzus "that which cannot be assumed cannot be saved." In Christ the flesh which he has assumed is transformed into the "proper quality" of the life-giving Logos; that is, into life and becomes life-giving. Therefore, it also revives us. "Ineffably and beyond human reason the Logos, by combining with his flesh and, as it were, moving everything into himself, through his power can revive all who need life. It has banished putrefaction from our nature and has cast away death, which had primordially received its power over us because of sin. Just as he who takes a spark and spreads much chaff on it to preserve the seed, so our Lord Jesus Christ through his flesh conceals life in us and inserts immortality like some seed which completely destroys putrefaction in us."

The indivisible union and "interpenetration" of Divinity and complete humanity in the Single Person and Hypostasis of Christ, which transformed human nature into holiness and imperishability, performs a similar transformation in all people as well, to the extent of their unification with Christ, for human nature is substantially con-secrated and transformed in Christ. In his description of the Person of Christ, the God-Man, as being two natures and at the same time indivisibly united, St. Cyril, like St. Athanasius, is guided *by soteriological motives*, and, in general, he is very close to St.

Athanasius in his Christology. Only the "single Christ," the Logos Incarnate, can be the true Savior and Redeemer, not a "man chosen by God," for salvation primarily lies in the giving of life to creatures and therefore Self-Existing Life has to be indivisibly revealed in that which is naturally liable to decay. St. Cyril calls Christ the New Adam and emphasizes the communality and brotherhood all persons have with him through their humanity. But he gives the main emphasis not to this innate unity but to that unity which is brought about in believers through the mysterious joining with Christ during Holy Communion with his Life-Giving Body.

THE INCARNATION AND THE EUCHARIST

In the sacrament of the Holy Eucharist we are joined to Christ, fusing with him like pieces of melted wax. We are not merely joined to him by inclination or by love but in essence, "physically," and even corporally, like branches of a life-giving vine. And just like a little ferment will leaven all the dough, the Sacred Eucharist leavens our whole body, kneads it in itself, and fills it with its power "so that Christ abides in us and we in him, for there is every justification for saying that the leaven is found throughout the dough and the dough is found in all the leaven in exactly the same way. Through Christ's Holy Flesh the property of the Only-Begotten; that is, Life, penetrates us," and every living human being is transformed into eternal life, and a humanity created for eternal life is beyond death and is liberated from the mortality which entered with sin.

THE SINGLE PERSON OR HYPOSTASIS OF CHRIST FROM FAITH AND EXPERIENCE

For St. Cyril the Single Person or Hypostasis of Christ as the Logos Incarnate is not some abstract or speculative truth which he arrives at through reasoning – this is a direct confession of faith, a description of experience and perception. First of all, St. Cyril perceives the Single Christ in the Scriptures. "Since the Only-Begotten, the Logos of God, became flesh, he became subjected to division and descriptions of him come from a dual perception. However, although descriptions of him have doubled, as it were, he himself has remained the same in all regards, and after his union with flesh he cannot be divided in two."

The Gospel image mysteriously combines the glory of the Only-Begotten and the commonness of human nature, which for the time being concealed the Divinity of the Logos. For believers, however, the Divine Glory shines through the vision of the slave from the very beginning. For St. Cyril direct perception reveals the "interpenetration of traits," and he does not go beyond the bounds of experience when he transfers names from one nature to the other, for the human nature accepted by the Logos is proper to it.

NESTORIUS AND THE DENIAL OF THE ONTOLOGICAL UNITY OF CHRIST

In Nestorius' heresy St. Cyril saw a denial of the most true and ontological combination of Divinity and human nature in Christ, a denial of the single Christ, and a rending of him into a "duality of Sons." This primarily is what he is railing against. He points out the destructive conclusions which such a rending predetermines and which are bound up in soteriology. Above all, he stresses "ineffable interpenetration" and union. Here he explains that God the Logos himself is the beginning and the focus of this unity: "We say that the Logos itself, the Only-Begotten Son, is ineffably born of the essence of God the Father, is the Creator of the ages, through whom comes everything and in whom is everything; at the end of these days, through the Father's goodwill, He accepted Abraham's seed according to the Scriptures, took on flesh and blood – that is, he became man, accepted flesh and made it his own, and as flesh was born of Mary, the Holy Mother of God." In other words, *the Incarnation is a phenomenon and action of God himself* and is his assumption and acceptance of humanity. God the *Logos* is *the only acting subject in the act of the Incarnation*; the *Logos* himself was born a man of woman.

St. Cyril saw a *distinctive Docetism* in Nestorius' interpretation, a Docetism regarding Divinity which implies that the Incarnation is merely illusion and that duality is united in Christ only in our synthesizing perception. "If," Cyril reasons, "God's Only-Begotten Son, after becoming man from the worthy David and Abraham, assisted his development (in the womb of) the Holy Virgin, joined him to himself, accompanied him to death, and, after resurrecting from the dead, lifted him up to heaven and seated him on the right hand of God, then the holy fathers taught in vain, as do we and the whole divinely inspired Scripture teach, that he became man. In that case the whole mystery of the Incarnation is certainly overthrown completely," for then it turns out that it was not a case of God coming down and humbling himself in the form of a slave, but a case of a man being elevated to Divine glory and supremacy – *that is motion downwards, not upwards*.

On the contrary, St. Cyril constantly insists that Christ is *not* a "*man chosen by God* " – ἄνθρωπος θεοφόρος – who carries or embraces God, *but rather God Incarnate*. "It is not the man who has acceded to the throne in us, but God, who has appeared in humanity." The Only-Begotten *became* man and did not merely *assume* man. The Logos *became* human and therefore *Christ is one*. This is the unity of his life and his deeds, and it is only for this reason that the Logos redeems. Christ loved, suffered, and died as "God in the flesh" – ὡς θεὸς ἐν σαρκί, not as a man. "We profess," Cyril wrote to Nes -

torius on behalf of the council, "that the Son himself who was born of God the Father and is the Only-Begotten God, even though by his Own nature he is impassive, suffered as flesh for us, according to the Scriptures, and in his crucified body impassively assimilated the sufferings of *his own* flesh. Through God's goodwill, he accepted death for all by giving it his own body, although by nature he is life and resurrection. This he did so that by tasting death in *his Own flesh* . . . he, through his ineffable power, would be the first-born of the dead and first fruits of those who died, and would open up the path towards achieving imperishability for human nature."

THE EN-HYPOSTASIS IN CHRIST

This does not mean that suffering was transferred to Divinity. The impassivity and immutability of Divine nature are self-evident to St. Cyril. In the Incarnation the inalterable Logos remained what he is , was, and ever shall be, and did not cease being God. But "in the sense of the Incarnation the Logos became flesh, and the sufferings belong to the Logos' "*own humanity*" which does not exist in isolation or by itself. *His humanity belongs not to itself but to the Logos.* For St. Cyril what is decisive is the concept of assumption – *ἰδιοποίησις*– which was noted already by St. Athanasius. Christ's body, which was received from the Virgin and is consubstantial with us, is proper to the Logos in the same way that we all speak of our own body – *ἴδιον σῶμα.* The concept of "assumption" anticipates St. Cyril's later doctrine of humanity's being "en-hypostasized" in Christ, which was subsequently developed by Leontius of Byzantium. God the Logos was born of the Virgin, he gave his Blood for us, and "assumed or experienced the death of his flesh." With such an understanding, calling the Holy Virgin the *Theotokos*, which was denied by Nestorius, *becomes not only admissible but necessary*, for he who was born of the Virgin was God Incarnate, not a man externally joined to God.

HIS EARLY REJECTION OF APOLLINARIANISM

St. Cyril always brusquely and decisively rejected Apollinarianism. He came out against Apollinarius early. As early as his exegesis of the *Gospel of John* St. Cyril emphasizes the "integrity" of humanity in Christ and the presence of a "rational soul and mind" in Christ, as a subject of grief and human weakness. Here, too, he rejects any con - fusing of flesh and Divinity and any transsubstantiation of flesh into Divine nature. St. Cyril always represents the combination of Divinity and humanity as "unmingled" and "unaltered" – *ἀσυγχύτως καὶ ἀτρέπτως.* The Logos became flesh – not through transposition or application, not through mixing or mingling of the essences, *οὐ κατὰ μετάστασιν ἤ τροπήν.*

In his famous "second letter" to Nestorius St. Cyril professes: "We do not say that the Logos' nature changes and becomes flesh. Nor do we say that it settled in a whole man who consists of body and soul. We say that the Logos, *hypostatically* joining itself to a body, animated by a rational soul, became a man ineffably and in a way beyond our understanding. He was made the Son of Man not through will and favor alone, and not by accepting the person – or "role" – alone. We do not suppose that differences between the natures were destroyed in this unification but that in this ineffable and inexplicable unification Divinity and humanity remained *perfect*; that is, *complete*, appearing to us as the Single Lord Jesus Christ and Son. Thus we say that he who existed and was born of the Father before the ages was also born in flesh of a woman – it is not that his Divine nature received the beginning of existence in the Holy Virgin or that after his birth from the Father he needed to be born of her. For it would be foolhardy and frivolous to say that he who before all the ages always abided with the Father still needed to be born in order to begin his existence. Since he was born of woman for our sake and for the sake of our salvation, joining human nature to himself *hypostatically*, we therefore say that he was born as flesh. It is not that first he was born a simple man of the Holy Virgin and then the Logos descended upon him but that by uniting with flesh in the very womb, he was born as flesh, having assumed the flesh with which he was born. That is how we profess him in suffering and in resurrection. We do not say that the Logos of God by his very nature subjected himself to blows and wounds and other injuries because Divine nature, being non-corporal, is not capable of suffering – we say that since his body was subjected to all these afflictions and that *this body belongs to him*, the Logos suffered for us because the Impassive was in a suffering body."

This confession is correctly considered the most remarkable of St. Cyril's works because of its clarity and lucidity of thought. What is characteristic here is the insistent stress on "assuming flesh," on the fact that the flesh *belonged* to the Logos, and everything that Christ experienced and suffered in humanity relates to the Logos' *own* human nature. The fulness of the humanity in Christ is in no way limited or weakened. But this is the *humanity of the Logos and* not a special human "person." In this sense the Incarnate Logos is "one with his own flesh," "one out of two," "of two essences," "of two different things," "of two complete things" – ὡς ἐξ ἀμφοτέρων τῶν οὐσιῶν ἕνα ὄντα. Through this affirmation of unity St. Cyril explains and defends the ontological reality or "trueness" of the Incarnation. Here he is guided primarily *by soteriological motives*.

St. Cyril is always guided by the old patristic soteriological doctrine that "whatever is not assumed cannot be redeemed," whatever is not ontologically penetrated by the Divine nature and person cannot be transformed, transfigured, cannot be deified.

THE BASIS AND ESSENCE OF HIS ATTACK ON ANTIOCHENE CHRISTOLOGY

St. Cyril is elucidating and defending the truth of experience and faith, not a logical scheme or a theological theory. He is also not arguing so much against individual theological formulas. He was wrongly accused of carping at words and not wanting to understand that Nestorius and other "Easterners" thought correctly but expressed their faith in a different theological language. What he claimed was that they thought incorrectly, or in any event inaccurately, and that the "Eastern" way of perceiving things prevented an exact perception of the unity of the Person and Life of the God-Man. Most of all, the "Eastern" tendency towards "differentiation" struck him as dangerous, and the stubbornness of the "Easterners" only tended to justify his suspicions. He himself did not always look for or choose the clearest words, and he did not always express himself cautiously and precisely. This shows that he was not so much carrying on a theological dispute as much as holding a debate on beliefs. He starts from contemplation and not from ideas. Here is where his power lies. Soteriological motives completely determine the content of his famous "*Chapters*" or "*Anathemas*." He conducts his defence against the "Easterners" on soteriological soil, and in this he is the faithful successor of St. Athanasius.

In his soteriological arguments St. Cyril most frequently relies on two basic texts. The first is from *Hebrews* 2:14: "Since therefore the children share in flesh and blood, he himself likewise partook of the same nature, that through death he might destroy him who has the power of death, that is, the devil. . ." The second is from *Romans* 8:3: "For God has done what the law, weakened by the flesh, could not do: sending his own Son in the likeness of sinful flesh and for sin, he condemned sin in the flesh." In addition to these two texts, St.Cyril often quotes *II Corinthians* 5:15: "Christ died for all, that those who live might live no longer for themselves but for him who for their sake died and was raised." In other words, for St. Cyril, the Savior is first of all the High Priest. St. Cyril's soteriology is mostly the soteriology of the *Epistle to the Hebrews*.

Once again, this shows the influence of St. Athanasius. Like St. Athanasius, St. Cyril assumes that the Incarnation and life among humanity would not have been enough if the Savior had only been a teacher to give an example. But it was necessary to destroy death and therefore the death and suffering on the Cross was necessary – death for our sake, for the sake of the world. The angels themselves are sanctified by the redemptive work of the Logos Incarnate, for Christ is the source of all holiness and life, the great Intercessor as well as the New Adam, the source and root of reborn humanity, which is brought back to its primordial state. The redemption is authenticated by the resurrection which bears witness to Christ's Divinity and confirms the hope of our resurrection. With the Incarnation the historical foundation of the *oikonomia* of faith begins, which fulfills Divine prophesies and purposes. But it is fulfilled in death and St. Cyril stresses that Christ's death is redemption precisely because this is the death of the God-Man or, as he puts it, "the death of God in the flesh." Only the Logos Incarnate can be authentic "apostle and high priest of our confession." (*Hebrews* 3:1). "The Son of God, having graciously consented to descend to humility, accepts from the Father the calling of the priesthood, which befits not Divine nature but human nature, through which he, after becoming like us, experienced everything which is characteristic of our humanity, *without undergoing anything through Divinity but by assuming everything experienced through humanity through the assuming of flesh.*"

The Logos performs his ritual "through the human nature he has received," and it is not that the Logos is "applied to religious rites and rituals and to things pertaining to humanity before the Incarnation." It is the Logos himself which performs these rites. "If someone says that our high priest and intercessor is not God the Logos himself, when he was Incarnate and became a man like us, but says that he was a man born of woman who was somewhat different from the actual Incarnate Logos; or if someone says that he brought himself as an offering for himself and for us alone – after all, not knowing sin he had no need for an offering – this is anathema." This is Cyril's *Tenth Anathema* and this makes up one of the focuses of his anti-Nestorian polemic. The *Twelfth Anathema* is connected with this: "Whoever does not confess that God the Logos suffered as flesh, was crucified in the flesh, tasted death in that same flesh and that he has become the first-begotten of the dead, for, as he is God, he is the life and it is he who gives life, let him be anathema." The cutting edge of these denials is directed *against the idea of human performance of rites and sacrifice.* A human death cannot be enough and human sacrifice does not have redemptive power – this is what St. Cyril was trying to say. Salvation comes not from people, not from human deeds, but only from God. It is ontologically impossible for the brokenness of human nature to be redeemed, to be restored, to be made whole again by anything within human nature. Only God can ontologically create this newness, this total redemption of the fallen, weakened, imperfect human nature.

Here lies the basis of *kenosis*, the descent, condescension, self-emptying of the Logos. Together with this, there had to be a purification of human nature through sacrifice. "Suffering had to bring salvation to the world," writes St. Cyril, "but the Logos, being born of the Father, could not suffer in his own nature and hence he performs the act of salvation with great skill by assuming a body which is capable of suffering. That is why it is called Suffering Flesh, flesh subjected to suffering while abiding in Divinity which is outside of suffering. After all, the Scriptures call him who created everything the Savior – through him everything is reconciled with the Father and is "appeased by the blood of his Cross." "In whose death are we baptized? Through belief, in whose resurrection are we involved?" St. Cyril asks: "Have we really been baptized in the death of a common man? And through belief in him we receive redemption?" And St. Cyril answers: of course not, "but we proclaim the death of God Incarnate." This means in the redemptive passion, death, and sacrifice God's descent is revealed to us, not the heroism or the self-elevation of a man. This condescension or *kenosis* certainly does not consist of Divinity diminishing and submitting to suffering. St. Cyril resolutely rejects such a *kenosis* and the "Easterners" wrongly suspected him of and reproached him with transferring the sufferings to Divinity. On the contrary, he always emphasizes that suffering refers to the flesh – only the flesh suffers and is capable of passion; consequently, only sufferings "in the flesh" can be "real." But here St. Cyril affirms the inseparability – certainly not the indistinguishability – of the "flesh" from the Divinity. The suf - fering is performed through humanity and in human nature but it was not the suffering of a "man," an independent human personality.

St. Cyril is speaking precisely about this in all of his anathemas. With special bluntness he says in his *Fourth Anathema:* "If anyone shall divide between two persons or hypostases those expressions which are contained in the Evangelical and Apostolic writings, or which have been said concerning Christ by the saints, or by himself, and shall apply some to him as to a man separate from the Logos of God, and shall apply others to the only Logos of God the Father, on the ground that they are fit to be applied to God, let him be anathema." Primarily such a division denies the reality of the *kenosis* – " for where has the Logos condescended if he is ashamed of human aspects?" Again, this does not mean that what is proclaimed about humanity is transferred to Divinity, nor does it signify the mixing up of natures, rather "these words and others refer to Jesus Christ alone," for, St. Cyril observes, "we know that the Logos of God the Father is not incorporeal after the ineffable union." And one ought not to speak of the Logos before the Incarnation, although the Incarnation does not rearrange or alter the Divinity of the Logos. Through the Incarnation, says St. Cyril, "every - thing, Divine and human, belongs to him." And along with this he writes that "the grandeur or majesty of the glory" is not diminished "in proportion to the condescension." In other words, the difference between the natures does not signify a separation of "persons" or "hypostases." The two natures indivisibly proclaim the One but precisely *the One and Only.* "We do not dismiss the differences between the phrases," St. Cyril writes, "*but neither do we divide them up between two persons* ." The Single Christ is the Logos Incarnate, not a "chosen man" (*Anathema* V). He is "united with his flesh," that is, both God and Man together (*Anathema* II); and this is an "essential" or "natural" unity – ἕνωσις φυσική – not only a connection in honor, power, and strength (*Anathema* III). "We say," explains St. Cyril, "that one must not call Christ the chosen man lest one represent him as one of the saints but rather the true God, the Logos of God Incarnate.

The Logos became flesh. And if the Logos became flesh; that is, a man, then this is not a chosen man but God who through his will submitted himself to condescension and received flesh taken from a woman." Therefore the Logos is called Christ; that is, the Anointed One, to the extent and by virtue of his union with anointed humanity – and nothing else. In glorifying his humanity, the Logos is glorifying himself and not anyone else. St. Cyril expresses this idea in two anathemas: "If anyone shall dare to say that the Logos of God the Father is the God of Christ or the Lord of Christ, and shall not rather confess him as simultaneously both God and Man, since according to the Scriptures "the Logos became flesh," let him be anathema." (*Anathema* VI). "If anyone shall say that Jesus as man is only energized by the Logos of God, and that the glory of the Only-Begotten is attributed to him as something not properly his, let him be anathema." (*Anathema* VII). This idea is reinforced even more in the *Ninth Anathema*: "If any man shall say that the One Lord Jesus Christ was glorified by the Holy Spirit so that he used through him a power alien from him and from him received power against unclean spirits and power to work miracles before men and shall not rather confess that it was his own Spirit through which he worked these divine signs, let him be anathema." The stress here is on the juxtaposition between "alien" and "his own Spirit": "For people, the Holy Spirit is "alien" because he comes to us from God. There is no way one can say this about Christ, "for the Holy Spirit is as much a part of him; that is, God the Logos, as of God the Father" because of the identity of essence. The Logos acts through the Spirit, just like the Father. He himself performs Divine signs with the Spirit because he is the possessor of the Spirit: it is not as though the power of the Holy Spirit acts in him as something higher than him. This is what decisively distinguishes Christ from holy people. St. Cyril draws conclusions from this.

First, it is necessary to confess the Holy Virgin as the *Theotokos* (*Anathema* I) because she gave birth to the Logos Incarnate in flesh, gave birth "not for the beginning of existence but so that he, having become like us, could deliver us from death and corruption." And of the Virgin was born the Logos and nothing else – "not through a change of essence but through union with visible flesh." Secondly, one must not speak of a co-worship of humanity in Christ but rather of a "single worship" of the Logos Incarnate. (*Anathema* VIII). And thirdly, Christ's flesh was life-giving flesh (*Anathema* XI). This also refers to the Holy Eucharist where we glorify the flesh and blood not of a common man who is like us but the actual Body and Blood of the Logos which gives life to all. The consubstantiality of Christ's flesh with ours does not weaken this but since the Logos is by nature Life, he makes his own flesh life-giving as well. Through its union with and assumption by the Logos, the Body becomes the "Body of Life" and in this regard it becomes unique. Here one understands "flesh animated and rational." Here is the whole sense of the Eucharist in which we are joined to God the Logos who has become active for our sake as the Son of Man. Through all of St. Cyril's *Anathemas* there weaves a single lively dogmatic thread – he confesses *the single Christ, unity of person, and unity of life.*

IMPRECISION AND UNCLARITY IN HIS THEOLOGICAL TERMINOLOGY

St. Cyril's terminology was not distinguished by clarity and con-sistency. Not infrequently, he was willing to speak an imprecise language. For him, words are always only a means to an end and he demands and expects his listeners and readers to rise to contemplation through words. This does not mean that he is confusing concepts or that his idea is wavering or becoming ambiguous. On the contrary, St. Cyril is always steadfast in his profession of faith, as well as direct, and almost obstinate. Tied to this is his well-known verbosity, his over-indulgence in terminology. He amasses synonyms and uses too many images and similes. One should in no way try to systematize and stylize his theological language too much.

In his use of Christological expressions St. Cyril usually does not distinguish the terms φύσις, ὑπόστασις, πρόσωπον and he uses them one along side of the other, or together with another, as if they were obvious synonyms. In St. Cyril's thought all these terms mean one thing – concrete individuality, a living, concrete unity, a "person." This does not prevent him from using them differently in other cases, from speaking of "human nature" in Christ, from distinguishing "hypostasis" from "person," and from using the term "hypostasis" in a direct, broad, non-terminological sense. He uses it in this broad sense in the famous and controversial expression from the *Anathemas*: ἕνωσις καθ᾽ ὑπόστασιν. He also uses it for designating that fact which he defines as "the natural unity" and to which he applies the pseudo-Athanasian Apollinarian formula – μία φύσις τοῦ θεοῦ Λόγου σεσαρκωμένη. St. Cyril frequently does not notice that his words sound stronger and say more than he wants to say.

In this regard he really did lay himself open to imprecise, incorrect "Monophysite" interpretations. "Natural" or "hypostatic" unity to him means only a "complete union" and a "true unity," as opposed to the merely moral or conceivable "relative contiguity" – συνάφεια σχετική – of Nestorius and other "Easterners." This is how Cyril himself in his reply to Theodoret explained the expression: καθ᾽ ὑπόστασιν – it means "nothing other than the nature or hypostasis of the Logos – which denotes the Logos himself, which *in truth* – in actuality; κατ᾽ ἀλήθειαν – joined with human nature without any transformation or alteration . . . and is perceived as, and is, the Single Christ, God and Man"; "the Only-Begotten Son himself through acceptance of flesh . . . became a true man in such a way that he remains the true God." "Natural union" is a "true" unity; that is, one that does not mix or fuse the natures in such a way that they would have to "exist other than outside of union." For St. Cyril the basic task is always to exclude any isolation of humanity in Christ as something with an independent existence. He strives to confirm the truth of the unity. In his mouth μία φύσις means the unity of the existence of the God-Man or the life of the God-Man. In its fulness this unity and the form of union are unknowable and ineffable – one can only partially define it. The first thing that must be emphasized here is that the union begins *with the very moment of conception* in the Holy Virgin. It was not that the man was conceived first and then the Logos descended upon him; but what was conceived was the flesh of the descended Logos with which the latter was joined and which did not exist on its own – ἰδικῶς – for even the briefest instant. This union is not a combination of two pre-existing entities – this was "acceptance" as property and the joining to the Logos of a newly arisen human "quality" – ποιότης φυσική. One can imagine Christ's humanity *before* the union only logically. What is more, Christ's unity, as St. Cyril understands it, is not the *consequence* of the Incarnation or union. The Incarnation *is* acceptance and St. Cyril strives to explain that the acceptance of humanity does not violate the unity of the hypostasis of the Logos Incarnate. The hypostasis or person of the Logos remains unaltered and whole both within the Incarnation – Λόγος ἔνσαρκος – and without the Incarnation – Λόγος ἄσαρκος. In this sense the union is "hypo-stasized," for humanity is accepted into the Logos' eternal hypostasis. The union is "natural," for humanity is ineffably joined to the very nature and person of the Logos.

When he talks of the single "nature" of the Incarnate Logos, St. Cyril does not decrease humanity's fulness at all. He only denies its independence. Human nature in Christ is not something which "con-cerns itself" – καθ ' ἑαυτήν. However, the humanity received by the Logos is complete humanity and we can discern in Christ two "natural qualities" or two "perfect" or "complete" existences, each "with its own characteristic" – ὁ τοῦ πῶς εἶναι λόγος. The completeness of the humanity is not damaged by the union, not swallowed up by Divinity, or generally speaking not changed in any way. In his unity Christ has actual consubstantiality – he is consubstantial with both mother and Father. True, St. Cyril in general avoids speaking of the humanity in Christ as a nature or of two natures and prefers to speak of the "charac-teristics of the nature." The reason for this is that he understands φύσις as ὑπόστασις; that is, as a self-sufficient individuality not because he somehow diminishes or limits human nature itself. Therefore he can without hesitation add a formula of union which speaks of "two natures," since through its connection to the text the inadmissible understanding of this expression is excluded here. There he can speak of the union of "two natures" in two cases. The distinction between the "natures" – ἰδιότης ἤ κατά φύσιν – always remained very sharp for St. Cyril and therefore he always emphasized that the union was ineffable and inscrutable. As the invisible mystery of the Divine con-descension to humanity, the union appeared in the historical Person of Christ, and this is clearly engraved in the Gospels.

St. Cyril makes a clear distinction between the concepts of "distin-guishing" and "separating" or "dividing." One must not divide that which is dual in Christ but only distinguish it – that is, distinguish it mentally or logically. This is because the unity of the "heterogeneous" in Christ is indissoluble and incapable of decomposition, ἕνωσις ἀναγκαιοτάτη. "For this reason," explains St. Cyril, "if after the ineffable union we call Emmanuel God, we will mean the Logos of God the Father who has become Incarnate. If we also call him a man, we will nonetheless mean him who has, through Divine *oikonomia*, become one with humanity. We say that the Intangible became tangible, the Invisible became visible, for the body which we call tangible and visible and which was joined to him was not alien to him." St. Cyril emphasizes in every possible way the unity of Christ, the character in the Gospels. We must relate that which is said through Divinity with that which is said through humanity to one Subject – the Single Hypostasis of the Logos Incarnate. St. Cyril even relates the suffering to the Logos – of course with the explanation that this is determined by the union. It is not the Logos himself who suffers but the flesh. However, it is the Logos' own flesh – St. Cyril had no tendency toward "Theopaschism."

St. Cyril's theological idea is always perfectly clear but he could not find a finished expression for it. Here lies the basic cause of his long disputes and misunderstandings with the East. The formula of union is composed in Antiochene expressions. St. Cyril's favorite expressions did not enter into it. Instead of a "single nature," the formula of union speaks of a "single person" with two natures and within two natures. Furthermore, the future development of orthodox Christology was accomplished in the spirit and style of St. Cyril, despite the fact that what was now needed was not so much to defend the truth of the unity as much as to elucidate its non-fusion and to uncover somehow its measures and limits. However, the fathers of the Council of Chalcedon will claim emphatically that they embraced "Cyril's faith." And the same was repeated later. This was not hindered – indeed, it was facilitated – by the fact that genuine Monophysites persistently contended with the orthodox for the right to Cyril's legacy and succession. Cyril's formulas were abandoned but his power lay not in formulas but in his lively contemplation which he reveals in a complete Christological system. St. Cyril was a creative theologian with a great style. And he was the last of the great Alexandrians.

CHAPTER FIFTEEN

THE ROAD TO CHALCEDON

The Church answered Nestorius' heresy through the mouth of St. Cyril of Alexandria and it answered, for the most part, with a striking and ardent soteriological creed in which humility combined with the audacity of hope. The Council of Ephesus, the Third Ecumenical Council in 431 did not ratify any synonymous definition of faith. It limited itself to a reference to tradition and to the Nicene Creed. True, the council accepted and approved St. Cyril's polemical epistles and *Chapters* but more with the prohibitory "agonistical" sense than in the dogmatic or faith-defining sense. This is corrected, for the most part, with the very form of St. Cyril's *Chapters*. These were anathemas; that is, the definition of faith by contraries or negation. Besides this these *Chapters* of Cyril's immediately proved to be a cause for division, a subject for dispute. The fathers who had gathered at Ephesus split. True, only the council of Cyril and Memnon was an ecumenical council in the strict sense of the term, while the council or "councillette" of the "Easterners" was merely a "council of apostates." However, the dog - matic acts of the Council of Ephesus ended only with the reunification of the "Easterners" and the famous Formula of Reunion of 433, the dogmatic result and, strictly speaking, the epilogue of the Council of Ephesus.

THE FORMULA OF REUNION OF 433

This Formula of Reunion is composed in the theological language of Antioch, as will be the Chalcedonian definition of faith later at Council of Chalcedon, the Fourth Ecumenical Council in 451. The boundary between Orthodoxy and Nestorianism is thus more clearly visible here. Here is the test of this confession: "We confess that our Lord Jesus Christ, God's Only-Begotten Son, is perfect God and perfect man – Θεὸν τέλειον καὶ ἄνθρωπον τέλειον – with rational soul and body , that he was born before the ages of the Father through Divinity, and in the last days for our sake and for our salvation became man of the Virgin Mary; that he is consubstantial with the Father through Divinity and consubstantial with us through humanity, for the union of two natures has been completed – δύο γὰρ φύσεων ἕνωσις γέγονε. Therefore, we confess one Christ, one Son, one Lord. In view of such an unmerged union, we profess the Holy Virgin to be *Theo - tokos*, for God the Logos was Incarnate and became man, and at his very conception joined to himself the temple which was received from her – τὸν ἐξ αὐτῆς ληφθέντα ναόν. We know that theologians consider some of the Gospel and apostolic phrases to be general – κοινοποιοῦντες, referring to a single person – ὡς ἐφ' ἑνὸς προσώπου, others they differentiate as referring to two natures – ὡς ἐπὶ δύο φύσεων. They relate those that are pleasing to God to the Divinity of Christ and those that are disparaging, to his humanity." Incidentally, this *formula* was proposed by the "Easterners" as early as 431 at their "councillette" at Ephesus. Now St. Cyril accepts it. It was precisely this formula which was later reworked into the Chalcedonian definition.

In form it recalls Nestorius' definition. This, however, is but a philological similarity. One feels in the construction of this exposition of faith a different idea than we find in Theodore and Nestorius. First and foremost, this is the recognition of a single, unified subject, a single Person who is God-Man. The Lord is born of the Father and he himself – τὸν αὐτόν – is born of the Virgin in these last days. This is what Nestorius did not want to recognize nor say. He deviated from tradition and the rules of faith not when he spoke of "two natures" but when he separated two subjects and distinguished two ontological centers of reference or subjects in Christ. And then the Divine Logos is directly confessed as the principle of unity in the Formula of Reunion, as the single center of unity. It is true that this merely reproduces the logical scheme of the Nicene Creed which did not exclude different interpretations. It is necessary to add that by itself the Formula of Reunion does not settle the question: it proposes a definition of terms and demands a theological commentary.

To a certain extent this will be true also for the Chalcedonian *oros*, the definition of the Council of Chalcedon (451). In general, formulas of definitions of faith become finally persuasive only in a living and coherent theological interpretation. Thus the Nicene Creed was revealed in the theology of Athanasius and even more in the theology of the Cappadocian fathers. It is for this very reason that theological systems obtain great dogmatic authority. Hence, the councils' constant references to the testimony of the fathers, to the "faith of the fathers." And here, more than anything else, St. Cyril remained a "Christological teacher" forever and that which "Blessed" Theodoret wrote against him and his *Chapters* were condemned and repudiated at the Fifth Ecumenical Council at Constantinople in 553. It is characteristic that when he was reunited with the "Easterners," St. Cyril did not renounce his *Chapters*, as those in the East had been demanding of him before anything else, and the "Easterners" did not insist on this any longer. Therefore one could say that from the very beginning Cyril's *Chapters* turned out to be the theological explanation of a conciliatory creed.

In the East the Formula of Reunion of 433 was not accepted immediately, and then not by everyone. Many were reconciled only under the threat of force by the secular authorities. The recalcitrants were deposed. However, the confusion did not cease. The "Easterners" glimpsed a rejection of Cyril in the Formula of Reunion of 433. St. Cyril, however, understood it differently, and not only did he not recant his *Chapters*; he, on the contrary, extended his sharp criticism to the entire theology of the East. In the East there was a stronger temptation towards St. Cyril than there was direct sympathy for Nestorius. It was not so much Nestorius whom the "Easterners" defended against St. Cyril's theological criticism but it was more a defense of Theodore of Mopsuestia and Diodore of Tarsus.

EGYPT AFTER 433 AND THE RISE OF MONOPHYSITISM

In Egypt, too, by no means all people considered the Formula of Reunion with the "Easterners" to be final or even just obligatory. After St. Cyril's death there was an immediate attempt to abrogate the agreement of 433. Thus began the Monophysite movement. This was not a rebirth of Apollinarianism. The Monophysite formula comes from Apollinarius, but recognition of "one" or a "single" nature was not at all basic or essential in Apollinarius' doctrine. Apollinarianism is a doctrine about human incompleteness in Christ – God the Logos does not assume everything human. Monophysites spoke not of this incom - pleteness, but of the "change" of everything human in its hypostatic unity with God the Logos, during which the commensurability or the "consubstantiality" of the human in Christ with common human nature is lost. The question now was not about the human composition, but precisely about the form of the union and the unity. However, there is a certain psychological intimacy between Apollinarianism and Mono - physitism. What they have in common is *anthropological minimalism* . These basic traits of the Monophysitical movement are clearly pro - claimed in the work of Eutyches.

EUTYCHES

Eutyches (c.378-454) was an archimandrite of a large monastery at Constantinople and he had considerable influence at court through the eunuch Chrysaphius. His sharp opposition to Nestorianism led him to be accused in 448 by Eusebius of Dorylaeum of the opposite heresy; that is, of confounding the two natures in Christ.

Eutyches was not a theologian at all, and he did not have his own doctrine. He spoke of "one nature" because that is what St. Athanasius and St. Cyril had taught. Therefore he considered it impossible to talk of "two natures" after the union; that is, after the very union of God and Man. But this is not the point of his idea. For the fathers of 448 the decisive factor was Eutyches' refusal to confess that Christ is consub - stantial with us in his humanity. Eutyches wondered "how could the body of the Lord our God be consubstantial with us." He discerned "the body of man" and "the human body." He agreed that Christ's body is "something human" and that Christ was incarnate through the Virgin. But Christ's body is not the "body of man." Eutyches is afraid to equate Christ with, or bring him close to, "simple people" through recog - nizing human "consubstantiality" – after all, he is God. One senses, however, something more in his stubbornness – one senses a suppressed idea about Christ's incommensurability with people, even in his humanity. Eutyches' contemporaries called this "Docetism." The line of thought was in essence this – one can speak about the "human" in Christ only in a special sense, not directly. However, this was more a vagueness of vision –in the literal sense – than a vagueness of thought. Eutyches saw everything in Christ as too "transfigured," altered, different. This vision contains the source of genuine Mono - physitism.

The condemnation of Eutyches at the "permanent council" of 448 by the "Home Synod" – σύνοδος ἐνδημοῦσα – [see Mansi, *Collectio* VII, col. 92 on the establishment of this permanent "Home Synod": "A custom has long prevailed that bishops who are staying – ἐνδη - μοῦντας – in Constantinople should assemble when occasion requires for such ecclesiastical affairs as may by chance occur] produced a strong impression throughout the entire Christian world. Eutyches appealed to Rome and to Ravenna, and probably also to Alexandria. In any case, Dioscorus, patriarch of Alexandria, accepted him and rescinded the verdict of the council held at Constantinople. The emperor was on Eutyches' side and convened a great council at the latter's insistence. The council opened on August 1, 449 in Ephesus with Dioscorus presiding. It proved to be "a council of brigands," known historically as the "Robber Council" from Pope Leo's description of it – *in illo Ephesino non iudicio sed latrocinio*, from which comes its Latin name of *Latrocinium*. Dioscorus behaved like an eastern despot, like a "pharaoh." Fanatical eastern monks ranted and raved. The council did not work on dogmatic issues. It was nothing but a settling of personal accounts. Eutyches was rehabilitated. All who adhered to the Formula of Reunion of 433 and who spoke of "two natures" were condemned. Many were also deposed. Foremost among those deposed were Flavian of Constantinople and Theodoret of Cyrus. This was "mass murder" party reprisal. However, this was not a resolution to the dispute. The "Council of Robbers" submitted no dogmatic definitions and had no moral authority. The only way it could render any influence was through external violence. And when the external circumstances changed, the need for a new council became obvious. It was convened at Nicaea in the reign of the new emperor Marcian but it opened in Chalcedon on October 8, 451. This was the new – and the Fourth – Ecumenical Council. This Fourth Ecumenical Council consolidated the dogmatic results of the anti-Nestorian council in its famous definition of faith, known as the"*oros*." Besides this, this definition was pro - tection against the Monophysite ambiguities, for it turned out that the root of Monophysitism and its danger lay in the frivolousness of its thought and the vagueness of its theological vision. It was more heresy of the imagination than error of thought. For this reason it was possible to overcome it only in theological sobriety and in the clarity of the definition of faith.

CHAPTER SIXTEEN

THE COUNCIL OF CHALCEDON

THE PROBLEM OF THE TOME OF POPE LEO THE GREAT

Pope Leo I (d.461) sent his famous epistle – the *Tome* of 449 – to the council of 449, addressed to Flavian (d.449), the patriarch of Constantinople. It was suppressed at the "Council of Robbers." At the Council of Chalcedon in 451 it was accepted with consolation and ecstasy, and *as a confession of Cyril's faith* – Λεών εἶπε τά Κυρίλλου. This was not a dogmatic definition – it was a solemn confession of faith. Here lies its force and here lies its narrowness. Pope Leo spoke a liturgical, not a theological, language. Hence the artistic plasticity of his exposition. He always spoke and wrote in an original rhythmical style. He draws a vivid image of the God-Man. In addition, he almost hushes up the disputed issue: not only does he not define his theological terms; he simply avoids them and does not use them. He did not like to "philosophize" about faith and was not a theologian at all. Pope Leo wrote in the language of the Western theological tradition and did not even pose the question about how one should translate his confession into Greek and how one should express orthodox truth in the categories of the Greek tradition. This weakness of the papal "scroll" was immediately observed. Nestorius saw in it a confession of his own faith. The Chalcedonian fathers saw in it the "faith of Cyril." However, others of them – and, curiously, the Illyrian bishops – vacillated over accepting the *Tome* until they were assuaged by direct references to St. Cyril. All depended on how the Roman epistle was to be read, how it was to be "translated" and which theological categories were to be used.

Pope Leo proceeds from soteriological motives. Only the accep - tance and assimilation of our own nature by him, whom neither sin could ensnare nor death could imprison, could open up the possibility of victory over sin and death – *nisi naturam nostram Ille susciperet et suam faceret.* "And it is equally dangerous to confess the Lord Jesus Christ only as God without humanity and only as man without Divinity" – *et aequalis erat periculi, Dominum Jesum Christum aut Deum tantummodo sine homine, aut sine Deo solum hominem credidisse.* The denial of human consubstantiality between us and Christ overturns the whole "sacrament of faith." A genuine connection with Christ does not appear, is not established "unless we recognize in him the flesh of our race." If he has only the "form of a man" – *formam hominis* – but does not take from his Mother the "truth of the body" – *et non materni corporis veritatem*, then redemption is vain. The miracle of the Virgin Birth does not violate the consubstantiality of Mother and Son – the Holy Spirit provided the power of the birth but the "reality of

the body is from the body" – *veritas corporis sumpta de corpore est.*
Through this new – because it is pure – birth, the Son of God enters
this earthly world. But this birth in time does not weaken his eternal
birth from the Father. The Only-Begotten Son of the Eternal Father is
born of the Holy Spirit through the Virgin Mary. In his incarnation He
is truly united and "there is no deception in this unity." He who is true
God is also true man – *qui enim verus est Deus, verus est homo. Two
natures are united in a unity of person* – *in unam coeunte personam* –
and the "properties" of the natures remain "unchanged" – *salva
proprietate.* Grandeur accepts nothingness, might accepts weakness,
eternity unites with mortality, an "inviolable" nature unites with a
suffering one. God is born in the perfect nature of a true man, uniting
in this the completeness and integrity of both natures – *in integra ergo
veri hominis perfectaque natura verus natus est Deus, totus in suis,
totus in nostris.* He acquired the human without losing the Divine –
humana augens, divina non minuens. And this occurrence of the In -
visible was an impulse of goodness, not a belittling of might. The
acceptance of human nature by the Logos was to extol human nature; it
was not the diminution of Divinity.

Pope Leo achieves a greater expressiveness in this game of contrasts and antitheses. He defines the completeness of union as the unity
of Person. *However, he never defines directly and precisely what he
means by "person."* This was not an accidental oversight. It would be
inappropriate to pass this over in silence in a dogmatic *Tome.*

But Pope Leo *did not know how to define "person."* In his early
sermons Pope Leo spoke of the union of God and man sometimes as a
"mixture," sometimes as a "co-dwelling." Once again he could not find
the words. He achieves great clarity in his *Tome,* but in his descriptive
synthesis rather than in his individual definitions. An ineffable union
has been completed, but in the union each nature – each *"forma"* –
retains its properties – "features" or *proprietas.* Each form retains the
feature of its activity and the duality of activities does not destroy the
unity of person. A duality of activities and operations in the completed
union of an indivisible person – such is the Gospel image of Christ.
One Person. But one side shines with miracles while the other suc -
cumbs to suffering. One is a source of weakness common to both while
the other is a source of common glory. By virtue of the unity of person
in two natures – *in duabus naturis,* both weakness and glory are
reciprocal. Therefore one may say that the Son of Man descended from
Heaven, although in actual fact the Son of God received a body from the
Virgin. And from the other perspective, one may say that the Son of
God was crucified and buried, although the Only-Begotten Son suffered
this not in his Divinity which is ever-eternal and consubstantial with
the Father, but in the weakness of human nature. In the sequence of
events in the Gospels one feels a certain growth of mysterious mani -
festations – the human becomes clearer and clearer, and Divinity
becomes more and more radiant. A baby's swaddling clothes and the

words of angels, the baptism by John and the Father's evidence on the Jordan – these are the outward signs. Hungry and thirsty, wandering without shelter, and the great Miracle-Worker. Mourning a dead friend, and then resurrecting him with a single word of command. Something more is revealed here. Tears and the admission "My Father is *greater* than I" bear witness to the completeness and authenticity of human self-awareness. And the affirmation "the Father and I are one" discloses Divinity. *Not two, but One; but not one, but two (natures).* After the resurrection the Lord holds discourse with the disciples, eats with them, but passes through closed doors. He lets them feel him, but imparts the Spirit to them through his breath. This is done simultaneously and immediately so that they may recognize in him the indivisible union of two natures and understand that the Logos and the flesh form a single Son without merging the two.

In Pope Leo's portrayal a unified Christ can really be seen. He clearly and confidently reproduces the Gospel image of the God-Man. This was evidence of a strong and lucid faith which was bold and tranquil in its comprehension. Of course, Pope Leo was indeed ex - pounding "Cyril's faith," although not at all in Cyril's language. They are united not by formulas but by a community of vision, and the same almost naïve method of perceiving or observing the unity of God and Man. However, Pope Leo was even less able than Cyril to suggest or anticipate a monosemantic dogmatic definition. His words are very vivid, but as if shrouded by a radiant fog. It was not an easy or a simple matter to secure his words in the terms of dogmatic theology. It still remained unclear whether Pope Leo's *persona* corresponded to Cyril's ὑπόστασις or φύσις or to Nestorius' πρόσωπον τῆς ἐνώσεως. Does the Latin word *natura* correspond to the Hellenic φύσις? How exactly is this "unity of person in two natures," this "meeting" of two natures "in one person" to be understood? Finally, what is most unclear in Pope Leo is this concept of "form," which he took from a distant but still Tertullian tradition. In any case Pope Leo's *Tome* was not clear enough to take the place of the disputed "covenant" of 433. A genuine catholic definition was heard not from the West, but from the East, at Chalcedon in 451.

THE CHALCEDONIAN OROS

The Chalcedonian *oros* or definition was a revision of the expos - ition of faith of 433. The fathers of 451 did not immediately consent to the composition of a new definition of faith. It seemed possible to once more make do with a general reference to tradition and with prohibitions against heresy. Others were prepared to be content with Pope Leo's *Tome*. Apparently many were stopped here by fear of antagonizing the blind followers of St. Cyril through a premature dogmatic definition. These people were clinging to an inert stubbornness; not so much to his teachings as to his words. This fear was justified – the Chalcedonian *oros* or definition proved to be a stumbling block and a temptation for the "Egyptians" through its language and terminology alone. However, given the circumstances which had taken shape, to have stayed with the unreliable, ambiguous and debatable formulas would have been no less dangerous. We are unable to follow the history of the compositions of the Chalcedonian definition in all its details. From the council "acts" we can only guess at the disputes which took place. They quarrelled more outside of the general gathering, at private meetings and during the breaks. The text which was accepted reads thus:

"Following the holy fathers, we all agree to teach the confession of the Son, Our Lord Jesus Christ, who was perfect both in Divinity and perfect in humanity; who is both truly God and truly man, from the soul of reason and the body, consubstantial with us in his humanity, similar to us in everything except sin, born before the ages of the Father in his Divinity, and in recent days (born) of Mary the Virgin *Theotokos* in his humanity, for us and for our salvation; at one and the same time Christ, Son, Lord, the Only-Begotten; acknowledged in two natures without confusion, without change, without division, without separation, so that the difference between the natures is in no way violated by the union but rather the distinctive character of each nature is preserved and is united in a single person and a single hypostasis, not divided or separated into two persons but at one and the same time the Only-Begotten Son, God the Logos, Our Lord Jesus Christ; as the prophets of old taught of him and the Lord Jesus Christ himself taught us, and as the symbol of our fathers has come down to us."

The closeness to the Formula of Reunion of 433 is at once evident, but they have made a very characteristic addition to it. First, instead of "for the union of two natures was completed – δύο γὰρ φύσεων ἕνωσις γέγονε – it states "acknowledged in two natures" – ἐν δύο φύσεσιν. There was a debate at the council over this expression. In the original sentence, which has been lost, it read "of two natures" – ἐκ δύο φύσεων. And, apparently, the majority liked this. An objection was raised from the "Eastern" side. The formula seemed evasive. This was not a "Nestorian" suspicion. In actual fact, "of two" sounded weaker than simply "two." After all, even Eutyches agreed to speak of "two natures" *before union* – which is precisely what "of two" corresponds to – *but not in the union itself*. And Dioscorus declared flatly at the council that he would accept "of two" but not "two." Pope Leo had "in two natures" – *in duabus naturis*. After the new drafting conference, his formulation "in two" was accepted. This was sharper and more definite than the former "union of two" and more importantly it shifted attention away from the moment of union to the single Person himself. One can ponder the Incarnation in one of two ways – either in contemplation of God's logical *oikonomia* to arrive at the event of the Incarnation – "and the union was completed" – or to proceed from con - templation of the Person of God and Man, in which the two-ness is identified and which is revealed in this duality. St. Cyril usually thought in the first way. However, all the emotional content of his assertion is connected with the second – one ought not to speak of the Logos Incarnate in the same way as before the Incarnation, for the union *was completed*. And in this regard the Chalcedonian formula is very close to Cyril's spirit. Secondly, in the Chalcedonian definition the expressions "one person" and "one hypostasis – ἓν πρόσωπον καί μία ὑπόστασις – are concretely and resolutely put on the same basis. The first is strengthened and at the same time intensified through the second. This identification of the one concept with the other is perhaps the very cutting edge of the oros. Some of the words are taken from Leo – *in unam coeunte personam* becomes in the *oros*: εἰς ἓν πρόσωπον καί μίαν ὑπόστασιν συντρεχούσης. But added to that is the most significant "*and in a single hypostasis.*" It is here where the pointed and burning question of Christological terminology comes up.

The descriptive "Person" – not "personality" – is shifted onto the ontological plane – *hypostasis*. With this, the Chalcedonian *oros* clearly distinguishes two metaphysical concepts – "nature" and "hypo - stasis." This is not a simple contrast of the "common" and the "particular" – as was established by St. Basil the Great. In the Chalce - donian definition "nature" is not an abstract and general concept – it is not "the general as distinct from the particular," allowing for the "isolated" traits. Unity of hypostasis signifies unity of subject, while the two-ness of natures signifies the completeness of the concrete definitions (traits, features) through two natures, on two actual planes – "perfection" which is precisely this completeness of traits both "in Divinity" and "in humanity."

There is a paradoxical unspokenness in the Chalcedonian definition. Through the sequence of the discourse it is readily apparent that what is recognized as the hypostatic center of the unity of God and Man is the Divinity of the Logos – "at one and the same time Christ, the Son, the Logos, the Only-Begotten, acknowledged in two natures." Both the Son and the Only-Begotten. This is not said directly, however. The unity of the hypostasis is not defined directly as the hypostasis of the Logos.

Hence, the further vagueness about the human "nature." What does it mean to recognize "nature" but not "hypostasis"? Can there really be a "hypostasis-less nature"? Historically speaking, such was the main objection to the Chalcedonian definition. It clearly professes the absence of human hypostasis and to a certain extent precisely the "hypostasis-lessness" of the human nature in Christ. *But it does not explain how this is possible.* Here lies the intimacy of the definition and St. Cyril's theology. Admitting human "hypostasis-lessness" is admitting an asymmetry in the unity of the God-Man. In this the definition moves away from the "Eastern" way of thinking. In addition, two parallel ranks of "traits" and definition stretch out – "in two natures," "in Divinity" and "in humanity." This is precisely what is in Leo's *Tome*. But they close not only in unity of person but in unity of hypostasis. Unspokenness harks back to unspeakability. The paradox of the Chalcedonian *oros* lies in the fact that it immediately professes the "perfection" of Christ "in humanity" – "*consubstantial with us in his humanity, similar to us in everything except sin*, which means that everything that can and should be said about a man as a man, except for sin, can and should be said about Christ. And this denies that Christ was an ordinary man – he is God Incarnate. He did not "receive a man," but "became a man." Everything human can be said about him. He can be taken for a man but he is not a "man" but God. This is the paradox of the Truth about Christ which is expressed in the paradoxical nature of the Chalcedonian definition.

The Chalcedonian fathers were faced with a two-sided problem – removing the possibility of "Nestorian" thought on the one hand – that is why identicality ("both"; "at one and the same time") is so clearly ex - pressed in the *oros*, and why the unity of person is defined as the unity of *hypostasis*. On the other hand is the assertion of perfect "consub - stantiality" or "likeness" (that is, the coincidence of all qualitative attributes) of Christ through his humanity with the entire human race whose Savior he was, precisely because he became its Head and was born of the Virgin Mary. This is what is emphasized by the profession of two natures; that is, strictly speaking, by defining the "human" in Christ as a "nature" which is perfect, complete, and consubstantial. There obtains a sort of formal discrepancy – "completeness of humanity" but not "a man." All the expressiveness of the Chalcedonian *oros* is in this so-called "discrepancy."

But in it there is also a real unspokenness and a certain incom - pleteness. The *oros* makes obligatory its fixed "dyophysite" termin - ology, thereby prohibiting any other terminology. This ban applies, first of all, to St. Cyril's terminology, to his "literary" "Mono - physitism." This was necessary, first of all, because acknowledging a single nature would cover up a real Apollinarianism or Eutychianism – that is, a denial of Christ's human "consubstantiality." But secondly, this was also necessary for precision in the concepts. St. Cyril spoke of "a single nature" and spoke only of Divinity in Christ in the strict sense of the term as a "nature" – precisely in order to emphasize the "hypostasis-lessness" of humanity in Christ, in order to express Christ's non-commensurability with (ordinary) people because of the "form of existence" of humanity in him and certainly not because of the traits or qualities of his human composition. For him, the concept of "nature" signified precisely the concreteness of existence – existence itself, not only the "form" of existence; that is, in the sense of Aristotle's "first essence." Therefore he inevitably did not have enough words for a more exact definition of both the composition and the form of the existence of the human attributes in Christ.

Thus arose the vagueness which disturbed the "Easterners." It was necessary to clearly differentiate these two elements: the composition and "form of existence." This was achieved through a kind of sub - traction of "hypostasis-ness" from the concept of "nature," but without letting this concept change from the concrete ("particular") to the "general" or "abstract." Strictly speaking, a new concept of "nature" was developed. However, this was neither stipulated nor explained with sufficient clarity, neither in the *oros* itself nor in the council's "acts." And the "single hypostasis" was not directly defined as the *Hypostasis of the Logos*. Therefore, the impression could be created that the "completeness of humanity" in Christ is being asserted too abruptly, while the "form" of its existence remains unclear. This was not a flaw in the definition of faith, but it did demand a theological commentary. The council itself did not provide one.

This commentary was given much later – almost one hundred years after the Chalcedonian Council during Justinian's time by Leontius of Byzantium. The Chalcedonian *oros*, as it were, anticipated events – even more than the Nicene Creed had in its time. Perhaps its hidden meaning remained unclear to some at the council until the very end, just as at Nicaea not all understood the whole significance and resoluteness of professing the Logos as consubstantial with the Father. One should be reminded that in the Nicene Creed, too, there was a certain formal awkwardness and discrepancy – and almost the same one, for it makes no distinction between the concepts of "essence" and "hypostasis" and between "consubstantiality" and "from the essence of the Father." This created the need for further discussion and debate. The only thing that was immediately clear was the polemical or "agonistical" sense of the new definition – the line of demarcation and circumscription was confidently drawn. A positive confession still has to be revealed in the theological synthesis. A new theme was given for it. It still needs to be mentioned – the "union of natures" (or "the unity of hypostasis") is defined in the Chalcedonian *oros* as *non-continuous, inalterable, indivisible, and inseparable – ἀσυγχύτως, ἀτρέπτως, ἀδιαιρέτως, ἀχωρίστως*. All these are negative attributes. "Inseparability" and "indivisibility" define the unity, the form of the union. "Non-continuous" and "inalterability" refer to the "natures" – their traits ("features") are not removed or changed by the union but remain "immutable." They are even somehow strengthened by the union. The cutting edge of these negations is directed against all kinds of Apollinarianism and against any idea about the union as a transubstantiating synthesis. The *oros* flatly rules out any thought of "fusion" – *σύγχυσις* – or "mixing" – *κρᾶσις*. This signified a repudiation of the old language. In the fourth century the unity of the God-Man was usually defined as a "mixing" – *κρᾶσις* or *μίξις* – just to protect against Apollinarius. Now this seemed dangerous. And once again they did not utilize a precise word to express the form of the ineffable union in some simile or analogy.

CHAPTER SEVENTEEN

THEODORET OF CYRUS

I

LIFE

Theodoret was probably born in 393 in Antioch into a Christian family. He received a good, well-rounded education, Christian and Hellenic, although it is hard to say definitely with whom he studied. He probably was not a disciple of St. John Chrysostom and he could hardly have been the student of Theodore of Mopsuestia. As a child, Theodoret comes into close contact with the monastic milieu, although he could hardly have lived in some monastery himself. We know nothing of Theodoret's life before his election to the throne of Cyrus in 423. We know that he was a "reader" in Antioch, that he gave away his inher-itance after his mother's death, and that he then apparently withdrew to the monastery of Nicerte about 416, a "school of wisdom," as he terms it. One must think that he somehow proved his worth and attracted some attention. Only this can explain his election as bishop of the city of Cyrus in 423.

Cyrus was a small and nearly empty town not far from Antioch but Theodoret fell in love with it and called it "better than any other famous city." He cared for his flock both spiritually and in their worldly concerns – by his own confession he was "engaged in innumerable concerns, urban and rural, military and civilian, ecclesiastical and social." It is known that he sponsored the building of an aqueduct and a canal to give the city a supply of water not previously available. He repaired baths and buildings in general, built bridges and public buildings, and in general gave the city a new aesthetic atmosphere.

At the same time he did not break his ties with the hermits and ascetics and led an abstemious and non-materialistic life himself. "I have acquired nothing except the rags in which I am dressed," he said about himself as he approached old age. In his region, and in other cities of the East, he had to clash with pagans, Jews, and heretics of various kinds, and the struggle against them was not always without danger – "my blood would frequently flow and I was prematurely brought to the very gates of hell." Apparently, he was forced to do no small amount of travelling around the East, and wherever he went he would give a resounding and edifying address. He acquired respect and renown which went far beyond his own out-of-the-way province. We are able to reconstruct his brilliant and attractive manner from letters he wrote at this time.

Theodoret's quiet and productive life as the bishop of Cyrus, the city he loved so deeply, his life of serving that city in both its spiritual and environmental needs, was soon to be cut short. The storm cloud hanging over the situation in Constantinople with its patriarch Nestorius was about to burst forth on the ecclesiastical scene and no one would feel the results of this controversy as seriously as Theodoret it will have an effect not only on his life but also after his death. It is almost as though the restless that was characteristic of his life in his many travels would carry over into his death. He will never be able to fully convince the Church of his complete Orthodoxy. The final result will be his posthumous condemnation at the Fifth Ecumenical Council. There is a great tragic aspect to the life of Theodoret.

THEODORET AND THE OUTBREAK OF THE NESTORIAN CONTROVERSY

Theodoret moves into the front ranks of Church figures with the opening of the Nestorian controversy and he remains in the forefront a long time. There is reason to think that he took part in the composition of the Antiochene epistle to Nestorius which admonished Nestorius not to oppose naming the Holy Virgin as the *Theotokos*. He responded to St. Cyril's *Anathemas* harshly and severely – more harshly than Andrew of Samosata. He doubted they belonged to St. Cyril and saw in them the "empty and also impious doctrine of Apollinarius." Other "Easterners" received them no differently. Before John of Antioch was sent to Ephesus, John responded to Cyril's *Anathemas* as "the doctrine of Apollinarius." In any event, the spectre of Apollinarius disturbed the "Easterners" more than Nestorius' personality. And in Ephesus they wanted first of all to call Cyril to account.

Their suspicions were intensified by the haste and harshness of St. Cyril's actions at the Council of Ephesus. In the schism which occurred at Ephesus, Theodoret was one of the main figures on the "Eastern" side. "Once again Egypt is raving against God and warring against Moses and Aaron and his servants," he wrote to Andrew of Samosata from Ephesus. At Chalcedon, at the meeting of representatives from both sides convened by the emperor, Theodoret harshly responded to his opponents, equating them with pagans. He bitterly observed that even the pagans considered the sun and the sky, which they worshipped, impassive, and the stars immortal, while the Egyptians considered Christ to be passive. He applied Old Testament texts about transgressors and apostates to them.

THEODORET'S FEAR OF APOLLINARIANISM IN ST. CYRIL'S THOUGHT

Theodoret did not understand St. Cyril, was frightened by an imaginary danger, and in his enthusiasm inevitably gave in too much to Nestorius, calling him a "sweet-voiced pipe," representing him and defending him against "the injustice done to him by impious people."

A decisive factor in Theodoret's sympathy for Nestorius was the act of "homicide"; that is, the deposition of Nestorius which occurred "without a trial and illegally," as the "Easterners" felt. Theodoret did not enter into discussion of Nestorius' views and mostly argued with St. Cyril. After the council Theodoret returned to Syria with bad feelings – it seemed to him that "the most gloomy darkness of the Egyptian execution" was thickening, that the true faith had been disgraced, and that "wicked dogmatists" had triumphed. He passionately wanted peace but the "*impious Anathemas*" continued to frighten him and cause him alarm. At the same time, he steadfastly and precisely summarizes the dogmatic results of the dispute – more the dispute with St. Cyril than the one with Nestorius. In St. Cyril and his anti-Nestorian writings Theodoret saw the main obstacle and threat to peace. Reconciliation seemed possible to him only with the condition that Cyril renounce all that he had written against Nestorius, and this made a review of the entire case of Nestorius necessary. "To anathematize vaguely, without any restrictions means to anathematize piety itself," thought Theodoret. He decided "not to agree to the unjust and illegal censure of the holy and God-loving Nestorius by hand, by tongue, or by mind." This is what defines Theodoret's position in the history of the East's reunification with Egypt. He was soon convinced of Cyril's dogmatic orthodoxy but saw in the new and indisputable confessions of the Alexandrian archbishop a renunciation of the "false verbosity" of the impious *Anathemas*, and a repentance and conversion "from the false to the true," from "impious philosophizing" to the truth.

Therefore, Cyril's insistence in the question of Nestorius' con-demnation remained for him incomprehensible and suspicious. Nestor-ianism's danger remained obscure to Theodoret. The spectre of Apollinarius still stands before him. The most he was ready to agree to was to keep silent about the issue of Nestorius. He ultimately agreed to the cautious formulation of the condemnation "of all that he said or thought which differs from what is in the apostolic doctrine." He did not want to mention Nestorius' name at all in the conciliatory agreement. And St. Cyril was hardly right when he said of Theodoret, while defending his controversial *Anathemas*, that Theodoret "subtly contemplates the mystery – in a barely awake state, as if through a dream and intoxicated." In any event, fear of Cyril's imagined Apol-linarianism hindered the triumph of orthodoxy as much as fear of the imagined Sabellianism of the strict adherents to the Nicene Council hindered the triumph of orthodoxy during the struggle over the Nicene Council. As the spectre of Sabellius had hidden the true form of Arius, so now did the ominous shadow of Apollinarius obscure the whole dogmatic horizon for the "Easterners," including Theodoret. They preferred to retreat into dogmatic vagueness and obscurity. Peace finally comes to the East only in the late 430s, and concord with Egypt is restored only to be almost disrupted again by the question of the faith of Theodore of Mopsuestia and Diodore of Tarsus, a question raised in

Edessa and Alexandria. The restraint of St. Cyril and Proclus of Constantinople prevented a new break. Theodoret has a prominent place in the history of these troubles. He was the soul, if not the head, of the orthodox, though suspicious, East.

DIOSCORUS' CONTROVERSY WITH THEODORET

The earlier struggle continued under the cover of outward agree - ment. After St. Cyril's death in 444, the controversy erupted with new vigor under his stern and arrogant successor Dioscorus. The dispute over faith was complicated by personal and regional enmity and rivalry. Many people, not only in Egypt but in the East as well, were dis - satisfied with the dogmatic situation which had been established. The spectre of Apollinarianism began to be taken seriously. Actual Mono - physitism appears and, backed by the imperial palace, immediately goes on the offensive. Relying on the slander of offended fugitives from Antioch, Dioscorus, on the pretext of defending St. Cyril's memory and faith against the "shameful" objections of the "Easterners," directly raises the question of the orthodoxy of the entire East – and Theodoret in particular – in an epistle to Domnus of Antioch in 448. Even earlier that same year an imperial Edict appeared which forbade anyone to write, read, or keep books written against St. Cyril's opinions, under threat of death. The Edict clearly indicated "some ambiguous doctrines."

In addition to this, the emperor ordered Irenaeus, the metropolitan of Tyre, to be dismissed and deposed not long after he had been installed through Theodoret's council and participation. Irenaeus had an extremely dubious past – at the Council of Ephesus he was a zealous defender of Nestorius and after the Council of Ephesus he wrote in his defense a book titled *Tragoedia*, long lost but recently rediscovered and in which many fragments from Nestorius' *Tragoedia* are found. Irenaeus of Tyre was exiled to Petra in Arabia along with Nestorius. After his instal - lation he expressed himself incautiously and suggestively and this forced Theodoret to warn him not to argue about the name *Theotokos*. In addition, he was born from a second marriage. The occasion for the attack was therefore well-chosen but in the East they did not fulfill the imperial Edict and asked it to be rescinded. This time Theodoret correctly divined an enemy of the faith in Dioscorus. He suspected that a storm was approaching and started to prepare himself and others for it. He answered Dioscorus' suspicions with a clear and lucid confession in the spirit and sense of the Formula of Reunion of 433. But agitation increased in Alexandria. Dissatisfied monks from the East wandered everywhere, from Egyptian monastery to Egyptian monastery, repeating their warning about the danger to the "faith of Cyril." A special embassy was sent from Alexandria to Constantinople. The first thing the envoys did was level a charge of heresy and "they kept droning on to everyone about how Theodoret was preaching two Sons instead of One Son." However, it was not this accusation which drew the emperor over to the side of the "Pharaoh," as Theodoret called Dioscorus, but rather the allusions to Theodoret's restless soul and to the danger he presented for social order and authority. The struggle was being conducted primarily against Theodoret.

THE IMPERIAL EDICT AGAINST THEODORET

The Alexandrians managed to get an imperial Edict to retain Theodoret in Cyrus without the right to leave there. The reasoning behind this was the problem created by the fact that Theodoret "fre - quently convenes synods and thus angers orthodox people." In his honorary exile Theodoret did not break off his contacts either with his Eastern brethren or his friends in Alexandria and at the court. At that time, in November of 448, Eusebius, the bishop of Dorylaeum, lodged an accusatory complaint against Eutyches with Flavian of Constan - tinople at the so-called σύνοδος ἐδημοῦσα which was the Synod of Bishops who were in Constantinople, or the "Permanent Standing Synod." The complaint came from the metropolis of Sinai and Eutyches was condemned and excommunicated. For Theodoret this was, in his words, a ray of light in the dead of night. Soon after this decision by the σύνοδος ἐδημοῦσα, an "Eastern" embassy was sent to the capital to defend the orthodoxy of the suspicious East. This embassy did not enjoy lasting success but, at the behest of the synodal court, Theodoret met with his accusers. On March 30, 449 the imperial Edict regarding the calling of an Ecumenical Council at Ephesus scheduled for August 1 – it turned out to be the infamous "Robber Council" – was issued at their suggestion.

THE "ROBBER COUNCIL" AND THEODORET

Dioscorus was granted primacy at this council, while Theodoret, as someone under suspicion, was removed from participation, at least until the council saw fit. In answer to a request to rescind this prohibition the emperor repeated his decision: "because he dared to speak out against that which Cyril of blessed memory wrote." One could have foreseen what the impending council was going to be like. Theodoret clearly saw "the beginning of a total defection," and *he expected nothing good from this council*. The council had been convened in order to judge some of the eastern bishops who had been "infected by Nestorius' impiety," as the emperor put it in official documents addressed to Dioscorus. The council was already prepared to "expel them from the holy churches and wrench out the whole diabolical root." The council really did turn out to be a "Robber Council," and it has gone down in history with that epithet. Theodoret was condemned here *in absentia* as an inveterate Nestorian "deprived of any service, any honor, and any degree of priesthood." The sentence was based on a complaint of the Antiochene presbyter Pelagius. They based the sentence on excerpts from

Theodoret's book *In Defense of Diodore of Tarsus and Theodore of Mopsuestia* , which excerpts were presented by Pelagius of Antioch, and on Theodoret's letter against Cyril to the monks. The very fact that Theodoret "dared think and write against the works of our blessed father Cyril" proved his impiety before the council. What is more, he came to the defense of Nestorius' teachers. The sentence met with no objections from the "Easterners" who were present – they recognized Theodoret's deposition. Domnus of Antioch was among them, even though he himself was deposed along with Theodoret. Flavian of Constantinople, Eusebius of Dorylaeum – the first accuser of the now rehabilitated Eutyches – and Ibas of Edessa were deposed in addition. The sentence was secured by imperial decree. All communication with the condemned men was forbidden, " both in town and in field," under threat of the customary banishment. Theodoret's writings were to be publicly burned, just like those of Nestorius and Porphyry's anti-Christian books. It was forbidden to keep or to read them. All bishops had to voice their agreement with the council's decisions in writing. A special imperial functionary – one of Dioscorus' accomplices – was assigned to supervise the collection of signatures.

THEODORET'S APPEAL TO ROME

The Roman legates did not sign the council decisions and were forced to flee Ephesus. Before their departure they received an appeal to the Roman episcopal throne from Flavian and Eusebius. Theodoret also appealed to Rome. He expected the pope to conduct a formal review of the whole affair. He appealed to the pope as to the representative of a local church which had not yet expressed its opinion, and which was moreover not particularly dependent on Constantinopolitan pressure. Except for Rome, there was nowhere to turn. The East was powerless and weakened. Alexandria and Constantinople were under the enemies' sway. Theodoret expected the pope to intervene as an arbitrator. His counting on Rome proved to be justified – the pope did not recognize the acts of the Dioscorian "council." The Roman synod apparently received Theodoret into communion and restored him to his rank of bishop.

Theodoret himself was at this time living in his far-removed monastery in Apamea, evidently living in great want. In his letters he continued to complain of his unjust "murder," and he stressed the dogmatic meaning of his persecution. He was particularly disturbed and alarmed by the pusillanimity of the majority, which was cowed and dispirited by Dioscorus' drastic behavior. "What polyps change their color in conformity with the reef, or chameleon in conformity with the leaves, like these people change their opinion in conformity with the time?" Theodoret asked dolefully. He also called upon everyone to worry about "*akrivia*." He is writing a great deal at this time, and he elucidates Christological truths in his letters while repudiating the false exegesis and slanders being spread by his enemies. He points out Pope Leo's *Tome* to Flavian as a model of precise dogmatic exegesis – the *Tome* of Pope Leo was not accepted at the "Robber Council" but was subsequently approved at the Council of Chalcedon. "As soon as I read it," wrote Theodoret, "I lauded the all-merciful Lord, praising him for not abandoning the Church entirely, but preserving a spark of orthodoxy – nay, more than a spark – a great fire capable of igniting and illuminating the universe."

THE ACCESSION OF EMPEROR MARCIAN AND THE CHANGE OF POLICY

With the accession of emperor Marcian the situation in the empire changed. Those banished were permitted to return, and Theodoret returned to Cyrus. On May 17, 451 the imperial announcement of the convocation of an Ecumenical Council was published. It was to convene on September 1. This answered the wishes of Theodoret, who had asked flatly that there be "a council not of rebellious people and vagrants but of the people to whom God's work is entrusted." Theodoret met with a stormy reception at the Council. The Egyptians refused to recognize him as a bishop, and refused to meet with him. But the senate and the imperial officials, who were supported by the "Easterners," came to the defense of Theodoret as the plaintiff and prosecutor against the council of 449.

THEODORET AND THE COUNCIL OF CHALCEDON

At the very beginning Theodoret took part in the council votes and discussions as a full-fledged member. At the eighth session he was restored to his bishopric in Cyrus: "all doubt regarding the most Godly Theodoret was resolved." They demanded only a direct anathema on Nestorius from him. It is evident from the acts of the council that Theodoret attempted to evade this by offering to read his own exposition of faith so as to establish what he believed and taught. "I was slandered," he said, "and I have come to prove that I am orthodox. I curse Nestorius and Eutyches, but I will not speak of this until I expound what I believe." He was obviously afraid that a simple condemnation of Nestorius would turn out to be ambiguous, for both orthodox and Monophysites, who were hardly like-minded, would be able to agree with it. The excommunication of Nestorius still does not resolve the issue of the excommunicator's orthodoxy. Therefore, when the council did not wish to listen to his detailed confession of faith, Theodoret added references to the council's already existing decision –*oros* – and Pope Leo's *Tome* to his anathemas on Nestorius. In any event Theodoret was rehabilitated and returned to the episcopacy.

Almost nothing is known of Theodoret's life after the Council of Chalcedon. He apparently shunned Church events in his latter years, although Pope Leo summoned him to this in a special letter in 453. He probably died in 466.

THE DISPUTE OVER THEODORET CONTINUES
AFTER HIS DEATH

The dispute over Theodoret did not end with his death. Already after the Council of Chalcedon, Marius Mercator, who was well-known for his struggle with the Pelagians, came out against Theodoret in the West. He accused Theodoret of Nestorianism and substantiated his charge by comparing excerpts from Theodoret with the works of Theodore of Mopsuestia and Nestorius on the one hand, and with the writings of St. Cyril, Pope Celestine, and the decisions of the Council of Ephesus on the other hand. Such an assortment and comparison proved to be very unfavorable for Theodoret. Marius Mercator *did not attempt a critique of the essence of Theodoret's views*. This polemical performance had no practical consequences. The situation was exacerbated later. It is perfectly understandable that uncompromising hostility towards Theodoret was harbored in Monophysite circles. For the Monophysites, Theodoret's censure was naturally connected with a denial of the Council of Chalcedon, where he was received into com - munion and his orthodoxy was recognized. At the end of the fifth century the emperor Anastasius bluntly raised the issue of anathe - matizing Theodoret. Philoxenus of Hierapolis also came out against him at this time. Philoxenus selected many incriminating passages from Theodoret's works.

The excitement grew over the course of time, and in 520 emperor Justinian testified that "Theodoret is everywhere being accused of being deluded in his faith." As a counterweight to this gossip, the people of Cyrus organized solemn gatherings in honor and in memory of their blessed bishop. Under Justinian the Monophysites' offensive became particularly violent. At the Constantinopolitan discussions between the followers of Severus and the orthodox in 531, the issue of Theodoret was again bluntly raised. The Monophysites called into question the sincerity of his renunciation of Nestorius at the Council of Chalcedon. Once again questions about the meaning of the disagreement between Theodoret and Cyril came up.

Thus the question about the *Three Chapters* , about Theodoret, Ibas of Edessa, and Theodore of Mopsuestia, came gradually to the fore. This question was sharply posed by Justinian in his Edict of 544 (the probable date – it is known only in the retelling and in references). Evidently, this had a bit to say about Theodoret. They accused him of objecting to St. Cyril and brought up the censure of the Council of Ephesus. Justinian tried to separate the issue of Theodoret and the issue of the Council of Chalcedon, and claimed that neither Theodoret nor Ibas of Edessa took part in the dogmatic acts of the council and that they were called to the council only after Eutyches and Dioscorus had been condemned and the exposition of faith had been composed. Justinian managed to get the patriarch of Constantinople, Menas (also Mennas), and other patriarchs to consent to the condemnation of the *Three Chapters* under the threat of banishment.

POPE VIGILIUS' ATTITUDE TOWARD THEODORET AND THE "THREE CHAPTERS"

Pope Vigilius had given his consent even earlier. But the West, especially the African clerics, voiced their resolute protest. Then Vigilius changed his attitude and, summoned to Constantinople by the emperor, he there started his opposition – he excommunicated the patriarch Menas (Mennas). However, he soon had to give in to the emperor again. Then he was once again pressured from the West: Facundus, bishop of Hermiane in the province of Byzacena in Africa, produced a voluminous work *Pro Defensione Trium Capitulorum [In Defense of the Three Chapters]*. Facundus did not say much about Theodoret but tried hard to elucidate the meaning of his disagreements with St. Cyril and to generally justify the behavior of the "Easterners" at the Council of Ephesus. In addition, Facundus reveals the conclusions which could be drawn from condemnation of the *Three Chapters* to the detriment of the significance of the Council of Chalcedon. His point was that to condemn the *Three Chapters* was to reject the Christology of the Council of Chalcedon. He refutes Justinian's contention that Ibas of Edessa and Theodoret did not participate in the acts of the council. He concludes: "Theodoret's writings against the blessed Cyril cannot be condemned unless the Council of Chalcedon is also shown to be blameworthy because Theodoret took part in its discussions and decisions, defended Pope Leo's *Tome* which refuted Eutyches' mindlessness, and proved his case for those who misunderstood."

But even without the influence of Facundus' defense, Pope Vigilius speaks very mildly of the *Three Chapters* in his new opinion of April 11, 548 issued in his *Judicatum*, whereupon the bishops of Africa, Illyria, and Dalmatia, along with two of Pope Vigilius' deacons, separated themselves from his communion. He includes a proviso about the inviolability and worthiness of the former councils and limits his censuring of Theodoret to the latter's objections to Cyril's *Anathemas*. But even this opinion of the pope provoked protests throughout the West, and Vigilius again renounced it in 549. In 550 the African bishops not only rejected his *Judicatum* but anathematized Pope Vigilius and excommunicated him. In 551 Justinian revives the question of the *Three Chapters* in his confession of faith. Here questions about Theodoret come down to his struggles against the Council of Ephesus and St. Cyril, and to his individual objections. In addition, Justinian stresses recognition of the Council of Chalcedon.

THEODORET AND THE FIFTH ECUMENICAL COUNCIL

During these wavering decisions and opinions, the issue is freed little by little from Monophysite illumination. It received its final resolution at the Fifth Ecumenical Council. The details of its progress at the council are not entirely clear to us but the general sense of the decision of the council is completely certain. Theodoret's personality as man and teacher, as well as the rightness of his faith, are admitted to be above suspicion. However, among his works some have been discovered which for various reasons – because their exposition and language are incautious and not carefully considered – have to be viewed as corrupting. The council decided to repudiate "that which Theodoret impiously wrote against the true faith and the *Twelve Anathemas* of St. Cyril, against the first Council of Ephesus, and that which he wrote in defense of Theodore of Mopsuestia and Nestorius." This was not an excommunication of Theodoret but it signified a denial of his dogmatic authority on account of his unfortunate polemic with St. Cyril. This, however, does not give anybody the right to doubt the general correctness of his thinking. The pope then gave the exact same interpretation to the resolutions of the Fifth Ecumenical Council. In his *Constitutum* Pope Vigilius condemned certain propositions of Theodore of Mopsuestia "we condemn and anathematize Theodore [of Mopsuestia] and his impious writings." About Theodoret he wrote: "also [condemned and anathematized are] *the writings of Theodoret which are opposed to the right faith and are against the Twelve Chapters of St. Cyril and against the first Council of Ephesus*, which were written by him in defense of Theodore and Nestorius." Pope Vigilius died on his way back to Rome after the Council. In his *Constitutum* he left his final decision clear "and further we annul and abrogate by this present written definition of ours whatever has been said by me *a me* or by others in the defense of the above-mentioned *Three Chapters*." A careful reading of the acts of the Fifth Ecumenical Council and the *Constitutum* of Pope Vigilius makes clear that the person and the writings of Theodore of Mopsuestia were condemned and anathematized but that only certain writings of Theodoret of Cyrus were condemned and not his person. "We therefore anathematize the afore-mentioned *Three Chapters*; that is, the impious Theodore of Mopsuestia, with his execrable writings, and those things which Theodoret impiously wrote." In the case of Ibas only his "impious letter" to Maris was condemned.

THEODORET'S STATUS IN THE CHURCH'S CONSCIOUSNESS AS "BLESSED"

That is how Church consciousness perceived them as well. Theodoret is revered in the Church as a blessed man among the fathers of the Council of Chalcedon and as a teacher of piety, although his theological opinions are accepted with reservations, considering the imprecision and incautiousness of their exposition and language.

II

WORKS

Theodoret belongs among the most remarkable exegetes of antiquity. In approximately 450 Theodoret in his *Epistola* 145 (see also *Epistola* 116) claims that he had written about thirty-five books. Only a comparatively small number have come down to us. His writings reveal that he had read – at least in summary form – Plato, Aristotle, Homer, Isocrates, Demosthenes, Herodotus, Thucydides, Hes - iod, Apollodorus, Plotinus, Plutarch, and Porphyry. His own language was Syriac but he wrote in Greek and St. Photius praises the purity of his "Attic Greek" (*Bibl. Cod.* 203).

EXEGETICAL WORKS AND HIS PHILOSOPHY OF INTERPRETATION

He wrote a number of exegetical works on certain books – all the prophets, the *Song of Songs*, and all of the epistles of St. Paul. In addition, he composed explanations of selected difficult passages from the *Pentateuch* with an appendix on the books of *Joshua*, *Judges* and *Ruth*. The work, known by its Latin title as *Quaestiones in Octa - teuchum*, was composed most probably in 453 and was widely used by Anastasius Sinaita in the seventh century and by St. Photius in the ninth century. It was composed in question and answer form.

In his exegesis Theodoret relies upon an historical-grammatical analysis of the text, dwelling primarily on its literal meaning. In doing this, he takes into account variant readings of the Greek text and not in - frequently turns to the Hebrew text as well. However, his knowledge of Hebrew can hardly be called sound. He treats extreme allegorism harshly – he sees allegorical explanations as "fables of the foolish," "the ranting of intoxicated old women," and "the fabrications of babbles." He be - lieves that the interpreter's task is to "penetrate the mystery of the all-holy Spirit," and that to do this the interpreter needs illumination from on high. A restless imagination is utterly useless here. But Theodoret does not stop at "the simple letter" and he does not refuse to plunge into the depths and seize "the hidden pearl of understanding" when necessary. There is a lot in a Biblical text which is said metaphorically, and the exegesis has to uncover the meaning of these images and tropes. One has to explain the meaning of Old Testament ceremonial legis - lation "through the laws of allegory."

In his exegesis of the *Song of Songs* Theodoret opposes those who deny its spirituality, who do not know how to investigate meaning thoroughly and "discover the secret of the word." In his day they knew that Theodoret had Theodore of Mopsuestia in mind – "although he has hidden his name, he has revealed his mindlessness." In cutting himself off from Theodore in his commentary, Theodoret uses Origen instead. Besides allegorical and moral meaning, Theodoret finds in many Old Testament texts hidden allusions to Christian truths. Thus he recog -nizes "plurality" in the story of the creation of man as the prototype of the mystery of the Trinity; in the burning bush he sees an image of the Virgin birth. Thus in Theodoret there is a poignant connection between the two Testaments. To Theodoret, as to St. John Chrysostom, the Old Testament is the image of the new. And the fact that one can be seen as an impression of the other does not diminish historical realism – the facts have a prototypical meaning, and the persons are prototypes. Everything in Old Testament law is full of foreshadows of the kingdom of Grace. One must distinguish prophesies from images. All the prophets foresaw what has been realized in the Church but they saw from afar, and therefore they saw unclearly, and one must not seek the same clarity in the prophets' discourse as one sees in the apostolic works.

When explaining prophesies, Theodoret tries to avoid excessive allegory and he censures those who "applied the prophesies to some previous events, thus making their exegesis more beneficial for Jews than for pupils of the faith." Prophesy always exceeds the borders of its own time and points beyond its limits. Prophesy receives its full realization only in the kingdom of Grace. Not all of the prophesies have a direct Messianic meaning – many directly point to Old Testament events, events which themselves are prototypes of New Testament events; they are prototypes, not merely signs. In his exegesis Theodoret relied on previous exegetes, and he is very much indebted to them. At the same time, he remained independent and skillfully combined the truth of the Alexandrian and Antiochene schools of exegesis. In this respect he is close to St. John Chrysostom, whom he follows directly in his exegeses of the apostle Paul's letters. It must be added that even in antiquity people knew how to appreciate the language and style of Theodoret's exegeses – which are lucid, concise, and skillfully written.

THE CURE OF PAGAN MALADIES OR THE TRUTH OF THE GOSPELS PROVED FROM GREEK PHILOSOPHY

One of Theodoret's successful works is his book against the pagans entitled *The Cure of Pagan Maladies or The Truth of the Gospels Proved from Greek Philosophy* – Ἑλληνικῶν θεραπευτικὴ παθη - μάτων. This is the last in a series of ancient "apologies." Paganism had not yet died out by the middle of the fifth century and it had to be seriously reckoned with in pastoral practice. Theodoret often refers to his encounters and clashes with "adherents of pagan mythology," who ridiculed Christianity, and whose gibes did not pass harmlessly with weak people. In the objects of the struggle, particularly in issues which are difficult for the pagan consciousness, Theodoret begins with a positive disclosure of the Gospel truth so as to remove enmity from ignorance. When contrasted with Christianity, paganism is strikingly revealed in all its emptiness and feebleness. Theodoret emphasizes the helpless contradictions, fruitlessness, and instability of pagan thought.

The picture which obtains in his work is gloomy and not without bias. The entire history of Hellenism is found to be a history of the uninterrupted growth of evil, "for such is the insidiousness of the lie that those who withdraw from one path move over to another which is even worse." However, Theodoret adds the reservation that "those who lived before the arrival of the Lord have some slight excuse because the sun of truth had not yet started to shine, and they were walking as if in the gloom of night, guided by nature alone." Her "letters inscribed by God long ago" have been wiped of sin. But the sun has risen now, and it will not do "to go around blinded in the middle of the day."

Repeating earlier Apologists, primarily Clement of Alexandria and Eusebius, Theodoret tries to find strong points and starting points from which to turn to the true faith in pagan wisdom itself. He speaks of the ways of natural cognition of God – "Abraham's clan received the law and delighted in prophetic grace. The Ruler led all other nations to piety through nature and all of creation." Pagans, too, could rise to cognition of the Creator "through induction." Theodoret also repeats the old idea about the Hellene wisemen borrowing from Moses. Theodoret is not very original in his exposition. He hardly studied all of the pagan authors to whom he refers directly. It is more likely that he used summaries and collections – surely Aëtius (his Συναγωγή τῶν Ἀρεσκόντων written about A.D. 100); probably Plutarch or Pseudo-Plutarch's *Placita philosophorum* (written about A.D. 150); and probably Porphyry – his Πρὸς ἀνεβώ. For all of that, Theodoret succeeded in arranging this second-hand material into an orderly system, which is something his predecessors could not do.

HIS APOLOGETICAL WORK
TEN DISCOURSES ON PROVIDENCE

Among his apologetical works is his *Ten Discourses on Providence* [*De providentia orationes decem*]. This is one of his best specimens of eloquence and style. The first five discourses attempt to prove Divine Providence from a natural perspective. The remaining five discourses deal with Divine Providence from the moral and social perspective. He concludes with the Incarnation of the Logos as the best and most powerful evidence of God's "Providence," that is, God's loving concern and care for all of humanity. Scholars differ on the date of this work – some claim it was written before the Council of Ephesus;

others, basing their opinion on what they see as a "development of his doctrine," date the work from at least 435.

AD QUAESITA MAGORUM

Theodoret's works *Ad quaesita magorum* has not come down to us. Excerpts have survived only in Theodoret's own occasional quotations from it. From what fragments or excerpts we possess it is clear that Theodoret answers and refutes the objections of the Persian magi against the Christian faith, attacks their deification of the elements of nature, and censures them for the severe and long persecutions of the Christians during the reign of the Persian kings Bahram V and Jezdegerd II.

CONTRA JUDAEOS

Theodoret's work *Contra Judaeos* [*Against the Jews*] has also not come down to us. The purpose, it appears, was to show that the prophets foretold Christ," at least this is the indication from his *Epistola* 145. Most scholars who have been deeply involved with the study of Theodoret are certain that he is the author. Others have doubts, such as M. Brok (see "Un soi-disant fragment du traité Contre les Juifs de Théodoret de Cyr" in *Revue d'Histoire Ecclésiastique* 45 (1950), 490-494). Among the more reliable scholars who have defended Theodoret's authorship are Bardenhewer, Schulte, and Glubokovsky in his two volume study in Russian. M. Richard is of the opinion that it preceded the Council of Ephesus. Based on Theodoret's letters 113, 116, and 145 it, in any case, appears to have been written prior to 449.

THE HISTORICAL SIGNIFICANCE OF HIS HISTORIA ECCLESIASTICA

Theodoret's historical works, especially his *Historia ecclesiastica* [*Ecclesiastical History*], are extremely valuable. The *Ecclesiastical History* begins with "Arius' madness" and ends "with the demise of those praiseworthy men Theodore of Mopsuestia and Theodotus, the bishop of Antioch." Theodoret begins where Eusebius' *Ecclesiastical History* ends and extends to 428 or 429. Theodoret wrote it in 449 to 450 during his exile in Apamea. But one has to think that he started to gather materials and work on it much earlier. Theodoret sets himself the task of "describing what was omitted" in Eusebius' *Ecclesiastical History*." The question of Theodoret's sources for this work remains controversial. Without a doubt he used Eusebius; he also makes abundant use of Rufinus; and probably used Philostorgius as well. He hardly used the books of Socrates and Sozomen.

It is more difficult to determine the sources of his individual reports. There is no doubt that he used Athanasius' historical writings and selected factual data out of St. John Chrysostom and St. Gregory of Nazianzus. He greatly relied on oral tradition and stories. He treats the material he has gathered with sufficient fastidiousness, although his general ideas about the meaning and nature of what the Church has gone through during the one-hundred years of historical process he relates suffer perhaps from excessive simplicity. He misuses providence and too often neglects to give either a pragmatic or psychological analysis. However, given historiographic practice at that time, this is something we should have expected. Despite this, Theodoret skillfully gets into the meaning of the events he describes, the meaning for the Church, and in this respect he surpasses Socrates. With Theodoret history ceases to be merely a chronicle – he perceives the general meaning in the rhythm of events, and depicts the past as the Church's struggle with heresy, especially the heresy of Arianism. For us, *the main value of Theodoret's history is the fact that it preserves documents not known from anywhere* else, including Alexander of Alexandria's famous epistle to Alexander of Thessaloniki. Theodoret also preserved many details of the life of the East, and he always speaks warmly of the life of his own Church.

HISTORIA RELIGIOSA SEU ASCETICA VIVENDI RATIO

Theodoret composed his *Historia religiosa seu ascetica vivendi ratio* about 444. He adds as an appendix an *Oratio de divina et sancta caritate* to show that only the love of God enabled these heroes to gain victory over all the temptations of the world. This work is a series of images of ascetics who made their journey in the East, in Syria. Three of the "lives" are devoted to God-loving women – to Mara, Cyrina, and Domnina. Theodoret knew some of these people personally and he speaks of others from the accounts of eye-witnesses, whom he some - times names. He also had some records from which to work. Theo - doret's lives are completely authentic but one must remember that he is writing not history but biography, and he is striving not for com - pleteness and precision but for vividness or portrayal. He himself compares his characters with the memorable images which were erected by Olympic victors. "We will not depict corporeal traits," he writes, "but we will outline the thoughts of the invisible soul and show the invisible struggle and hidden exploits." Therefore he does not strive for completeness but tries to sort out "various images of life" in order to give examples suitable for different situations. Theodoret concentrates all of his attention on the inner life of the ascetics he portrays. He reports few details of their external life and is stingy with chronological indications. This does not violate the historical nature of his stories. He depicts living people, not typical images.

Theodoret's *Historia religiosa seu ascetica vivendi ratio* received much attention in subsequent hagiographic literature. Simeon Meta -

phrastes – also known as Simeon Logothetes, born probably in Constantinople about 900 and died sometime after 984 – recopies Theodoret almost verbatim. Theodore's appendix, *Oratio de divina et sancta caritate*, is in its own way a philosophical conclusion. Theodoret wants to uncover the driving principle behind the ascetic life and he finds it in love. "Love for God makes the ascetics capable of extending beyond nature's limit," and attaining passionlessness. "They receive the wounds of Divine love from every quarter; they impress their Beloved on their mind, scorning everything, and they make their body spiritual before the expected imperishability of the resurrection." This love draws them to Wisdom, and for Theodoret the ascetics are first of all "wor - shippers of true wisdom."

HAERETICARUM FABULARUM COMPENDIUM

Finally, to Theodoret's historical writings belongs his *Haereti - carum fabularum compendium* – αἱρετικῆς κακομυθίας ἐπιτομή, known in English as his *History of Heresies*. This work was composed after the Council of Chalcedon, probably around 453. Here Theodoret makes abundant use of previous literature on heresies. Theodoret men - tions among his sources Justin Martyr, Irenaeus, Clement of Alex - andria, Origen, Eusebius of Caesarea and Eusebius of Emesa. He relies heavily of Irenaeus, Eusebius' history, the *Philosophumena* – which he ascribes not to Hippolytus but to Origen, and the *Syntagma* or *Against All Heresies* – Πρός ἁπάσας τάς αἱρέσεις – by Hippolytus. Sometimes he uses heretical books also – thus, he read the works of Bardesanes, or more correctly, Bar-Daisan (154-222).Theodoret speaks of certain heresies from personal experience, since he had to encounter the remnants of ancient heresies – for example, the Marcionites in Syria. Theodoret regards the legendary stories about heretics with some mistrust and consciously avoids giving corrupting details. In this regard he is quite different from Epiphanius, whose work he evidently used, although he may not have known or used Epiphanius' *Panarion*. Theodoret brings his review of heresies up to to Eutyches but the chapter on Nestorius, of course, represents a later interpolation, although some scholars consider it authentic. There is not much new material in Theodoret, and the development of the heresies is nowhere to be seen, since he is striving to give complete and fixed types of delusion. *From him one obtains not a history but a system of heresies* – a composite image of the dark kingdom of lies which has risen up against the kingdom of God. As a source, the historical value of Theodoret's work is not great.

ON THE COUNCIL OF CHALCEDON

Zacharias Scholasticus (d. after 536); also known as "Zacharias of Mitylene" and "Zacharias Rhetor"), a Monophysite theologian, wrote a history of the Church which is especially valuable for the years 450 through 491. In his *Historia Ecclesiastica* Zacharias states that Theo - doret wrote a book on the Council of Chalcedon. Theodoret's work was allegedly used by Macedonius, the bishop of Constantinople in the early sixth century, for a *florilegium* of Antiochene theologians. Unfortunately this work, if it existed, has not come down to us in any form at all.

THEODORET'S DOGMATIC WORKS

DE SANCTA ET VIVIFICA TRINITATE AND *DE INCARNATIONE DOMINE*

Theodoret argued about faith his entire life and all of his dogmatic works have a polemical purpose and nature. He evidently wrote a great amount against the Arians, the Apollinarians, and the Marcionites in his early years. There is no shortage of polemical excursions in the writings of Theodoret which have been preserved. Two works, *De sancta et vivifica Trinitate* and *De incarnatione Domini [On the Holy and Vivifying Trinity* and *On the Incarnation of the Lord]*, long attributed to St. Cyril, belong to Theodoret. Cardinal A. Mai published them among St. Cyril's work but A. Ehrhard rightfully restored them to Theodoret. They were definitely not St. Cyril's, as any close reading could have discerned. In content and in their theological language they are very close to the compositions which are incontrovertibly Theo - doret's, and they are known and quoted by the famous Severus of Antioch under Theodoret's name. They should be dated earlier than 430.

REFUTATION OF THE TWELVE ANATHEMAS OF CYRIL OF ALEXANDRIA AGAINST NESTORIUS

To the era of the Nestorian controversy belong primarily Theo - doret's "Objections" to St. Cyril's *Chapters, Reprehensio duodecim capitum seu anathematismorum Cyrilli [Refutation of the Twelve Anathemas of Cyril of Alexandria Against Nestorius]*. The Fifth Ecumenical Council in 553 condemned this work and therefore the original is lost. But the entire text appears to be preserved in St. Cyril's answer, *Epistola ad Euoptium adversus impugnationem duodecim capitum a Theodoreto editam*. This work was reportedly written at the request of John of Antioch. In it Theodoret explains the Antiochene view, defends the orthodoxy of Nestorius, and accuses St. Cyril of "Monophysitism."

PENTALOGOS

After the Council of Ephesus Theodoret again wrote a lengthy work of "Objections," referred to as the *Pentalogos*. This work was also condemned at the Fifth Ecumenical Council and hence only excerpts have come down to us, mostly from Marius Mercator. (Sometime prior to 550 the writings of Marius Mercator were inserted together with other works of a Scythian monk into the collection known as the *Collectio Palatina*). Greek quotations are preserved in the *Catena* on *Luke* by Nicetas of Heraclea. St. Photius describes the work without mentioning its title (*Bibl. Cod.* 46). In 1922 E. Schwartz published a collection of Greek fragments; in 1934 M. Richard added to Schwartz's collection of Greek fragments in his *Les citations de Thédoret conservées dans la chaîne de Nicétas sur l'Évangile selon Luc* in *Revue Biblique* 43, 88-96.

DEFENSE OF DIODORE OF TARSUS AND THEODORE OF MOPSUESTIA

Only fragments of Theodoret's *Defense of Diodore of Tarsus and Theodore of Mopsuestia* have come down to us. Most of the surviving excerpts were the ones used against Theodoret at the Robber Council of Ephesus in 449. Theodoret refers to this work in his sixteenth epistle. In 1957 L. Abramowski published 52 Latin excerpts from Facundus in *Reste von Theodorets Apologie für Diodor und Theodor bei Facundus* in *Studia Patristica* I (TU 63), 61-69.

THE LETTERS OF THEODORET

Many of Theodoret's letters from this period are dogmatic in content. In general, Theodoret's letters are a font of information on the history of the fifth century, of Theodoret's life, and of the history of dogma. Nicephorus Callistus in the fourteenth century still possessed more than 500 of Theodoret's letters. Less than half have reached us. There are approximately 232 letters extant. In 1642 the Jesuit J. Sirmond published 147 of them. In 1885 47 more were first made known by Sakkelion from the *Codex Patmensis*. Preserved in Conciliar Acts are 36 letters which Theodoret probably wrote between 431 and 437 – only four of these are preserved in Greek; 32 in Latin translation. In addition, there is a letter to Abundius and one to John of Aegea. The former is preserved in Migne, *Patrologia Graeca*, 83, 1492-1494. Some Syriac fragments remain of the letter to John of Aegea. The letters discovered by Sakkelion are primarily addressed to imperial magistrates at Constantinople. These letters are remarkable for their pure style and a knowledge that is quite unpretentious. *Epistle* 113 is Theodoret's letter of appeal to Pope Leo in 449.

There are fourteen letters scattered through Migne and Sakkelion which are of interest because they represent a new literary genre. Theo - doret refers to them as *Festal Letters* but they have nothing in common with the *Festal Letters* written by the patriarchs of Alexandria. It appears that the etiquette at Antioch and its surroundings required the exchange of good wishes and blessings to friends on the occasion of the great liturgical feasts. Theodoret's *Festal Letters* were sent after, not before, the feasts, of which he speaks in the past tense (see *Epistles* 4-6, 25, 26, 38, 39, 40, 41, 54-56, 63, 64, and 74). Most important are Theodoret's letters which are dogmatic in content. These are very valuable sources. In twelve of these dogmatic letters Theodoret asks for protection against the false charges that he divided the One Son of God into two Sons (see *Epistles* 92-96, 99-101, 103, 104, 106, and 109).

ERANISTES

Theodoret's most interesting dogmatic and polemical work is his *Eranistes seu Polymorphus*, known in English as *The Beggar*. Theo - doret wrote this significant work in 447 or 448. It is composed as a dialogue. Here Theodoret describes and refutes the then new Mono - physite movement. It is possible that Theodoret used some written Monophysite sources for this work. By the very title Theodoret wants to define the sense of the new heresy: ἐρανιστής from ἔρανον which means "beggar or mendicant," a man who lives by begging and puts together motley, multi-colored cloths out of other persons' scraps. Theodoret sees Monophysitism as just such a "motley and multi-viewed sophistry." The Eranist's orthodox questioner defends the invariability and non-mixing of the unity of the God-Man, and the impassivity of the Godhead in Christ. Theodoret tries to elucidate the true meaning of St. Cyril's opinions and statements and shows the incorrectness of the Monophysite interpretations of "Cyril's beliefs." He repeats St. Cyril directly in many places. As opposed to his earlier works, here Theodoret is freed from his schoolish narrowness and he displays great theological insight. Externally the dialogue is distinguished by proportion and sim - plicity. In the fourth and last address Theodoret sums up the positive results of the debate in "syllogistic form." When collecting evidence from the fathers, Theodoret probably used the *Codex* put together in about 430-431 by Helladius of Ptolemais rather than quoting directly from the 238 passages from 88 different patristic sources.

AN ABRIDGEMENT OF DIVINE DOGMATISTS

To these polemical and dogmatic works one must add the fifth book of Theodoret's *Graecarum affectionum curatio* [*The Cure of Pagan Maladies*] which is titled *An Abridgement of Divine Dogmatists*. This is a concise outline of Christian dogmatics which is supported primar - ily by Biblical texts.

THEODORET'S SERMONS

Theodoret preached constantly from his earliest years – "taught without interruption," as he put it. More than once he mentions his "sermons." He enjoyed great respect and esteem as a preacher. "It would frequently happen that upon completion of my sermon, people would embrace me and kiss my head, breast, and hands. Some would even touch my knees, calling my teaching apostolic," he recalled. Whether or not he ever wrote down his own sermons is still in question. In any case, he never refers to any of his written sermons. Not one of his sermons is preserved in its entirety. The references of his adversaries to expressions in his sermons must not be accepted without verification. St. Photius read Theodoret's five panegyrics on St. John Chrysostom. In St. Photius' opinion they were immoderately eulogistic and he preserved a few excerpts from them. In the Acts of the Fourth and Fifth Ecumenical Councils there exists what is claimed to be the addresses which Theodoret delivered at the Council of Chalcedon in 451. His sermons on Divine Providence are contained at the end of his *History of the Monks* [*Historia religiosa seu ascetica vivendi ratio*].

Theodoret's letters, in conclusion, are rich biographical and general historical material, as previously mentioned. There is no small number of references to works by Theodoret which have not come down to us. The manuscript tradition of Theodoret's writings has not been suf-ficiently studied in a critical light. This is especially applicable to the Syriac literature. In any case, Theodoret was one of the most prolific and versatile writers of antiquity. In St. Photius' opinion Theodoret combined simplicity of style with grace, even though he was not a Hellene by birth.

III

THEODORET'S THEOLOGY

THEODORET'S CHRISTOLOGICAL EMPHASIS

In his Christological confession Theodoret sought the "middle" road – the "road of the dogma of the Gospels." He tried to steadfastly hold to tradition but he was forced to theologize in debate. In this debate he turns out to be a representative of the Antiochene school, the Christology of which proclaimed an intense repulsion of Apollin-arianism from the very beginning. Theodoret gave the first exposition of his Christological views in his work *De incarnatione Domini* [*On the Incarnation of the Lord*]. One feels this brusque repulsion of Apollinarius in this work. First of all, Theodoret shows the completeness of manhood in Christ, its immutability in the union. He proceeds from the fact of Divine *oikonomia* as the fact and revelation of Divine mercy and love. Salvation is achieved only by perceiving the complete manhood along with the reasoning soul. If the Savior had not been God, then salvation would not have been realized. And if he had not been a man, then his sufferings, his "saving passion," would have been useless to us. From here Theodoret arrives at a confession of Christ as God and Man. He conceives the union of natures as indiv - isible. Two natures are joined in one Person, in a union of life, $\xi\nu$ πρόσωπον. It should be noted that Theodoret makes a sharp distinction between the notions of "person" and "hypostasis," and for him ὑπόσ- τασις remains a synonym of φύσις. Theodoret refers to the image of the union of the "Divine nature" or "form" – μορφή – with the human as a moving in, a connection, contact, union – ἐνοίκησις, συνάφεια, ἕνωσις. The Logos mysteriously abides in man, in "the visible," as in a temple, and is manifested in him through his actions.

Godhead is indivisibly joined to manhood but Theodoret primarily stresses the "distinguishing of natures," the "characteristics of each nature." "We do not divide economy into two persons, and we do not preach two sons instead of the Only-Begotten. Rather, we teach two natures, δύο φύσεις – as something learned, for one is the Godhead and the other is manhood; one exists and the other has been made; one is the image of God, the other is the image of man; one is the Receiver, the other is that which is received." Theodoret makes a sharp distinction between these two natures. Thus, of Christ's temptation he writes: "it is not God the Logos which is acting but the temple from David's seed which has been received by God the Logos," the "temple formed in the Virgin by the Spirit for God the Logos." Therefore, Theodoret immediately calls the Holy Virgin both *Theotokos* and *Bearer of Man* – "the latter because she really gave birth to someone like herself, and the former because the image of God was united with the image of a slave." Apparently Theodoret felt that only the combination of both names rules out any hint of an impious "mixing" of natures. In all of these formulations the peculiarity and independence of manhood in Christ is emphasized with excessive sharpness; it is viewed as a special "man." What is more, the notion of a "single Person" – ἐν πρόσωπον – insufficiently expresses the completeness of the union in the language of that time. Theodoret assiduously avoided "transference of names." This made his negative reaction to St. Cyril's Anathemas inevitable.

THE THEOLOGICAL BASIS OF THEODORET'S OBJECTION TO CYRIL'S "HYPOSTATIC OR NATURAL UNION"

What Theodoret objects to in the conclusions to St. Cyril's *Ana - themas* is the notion of "hypostatic" or "natural" union and with this he contrasts the concepts of confluence or conjunction. He suspects that lurking behind the "strange and alien" concept of "union through hypo - stasis" is the idea of mixture, an idea which destroys the features of the conjoining natures, and the idea of something arising that is "midway between flesh and the Godhead," so that God is no longer God and the temple he receives is no longer a temple. Theodoret regards the concept of "natural union" as the subordination of God to *necessity*. In the concept of "nature" – *φύσις* – an element of *inevitability and coercive - ness* abruptly comes to the fore for him: "nature is, by definition, something moved by necessity and deprived of freedom" – that which is not done "by will" is done "through nature." "If the 'natural union' of the image of God and the image of a slave took place in this way," con - cludes Theodoret, "then God the Logos was forced by necessity to join with the image of a slave rather than by being moved by love for man, and the Law-Giver always has to comply to the laws (of nature)."

THE FREEDOM OF THE SON OF GOD'S HUMANITY

In opposition to the notion of "natural conjoining," Theodoret sets off the *freedom* of the Son of God's humanity. He "purposely" joined himself "to a nature which had been taken from us." Conjunction presupposes distinction, and what is being unified is two separate things. Therefore, Theodoret wonders how St. Cyril could refuse "to separate the hypostases or natures." He overlooked the fact that St. Cyril openly understood "person" under the term "hypostasis" or "nature." While professing a "unity of person," Theodoret did not draw the necessary conclusions. By distributing the Gospel phrases between two natures, he weakens the truth of unity. He applies all destructive phrases to the "image of the slave," and thus gives the impression that he understands by this a special "person," a special subject. This impression is reinforced by the fact that Theodoret constantly and insistently speaks of the human nature as an "assumed temple." By this he wanted only to exclude any mixture, transformation, or change. In actual fact, however, he was saying more than he wanted to say: he called Christ a "God-bearing man," stipulating, though, that He "possesses the single Divinity of the Son entirely." "That is why the babe who was born is called Emmanuel – both God, who is inseparable from human nature, and man, who is not devoid of Godhead. The babe is called Emmanuel because he is accepted by God. The image of God received the image of a slave." Theodoret observes that the "assuming" or "acceptance" corresponds with the conception but at the same time he crosses the border of reliability by permitting a parallelism of expres - sions: "God, inseparable from manhood" and "man, not deprived of Divinity." In reality these are contrary and incompatible terms.

THE ASSUMPTION BY GOD THE WORD OF "HUMAN NATURE" OR "A MAN"?

With Theodoret it remains unclear whether God the Logos assumed "human nature" or "a man." He would have us believe the first, by professing a single Person but it was possibly easier to understand him in the second sense. In particular, this is proclaimed in Theodoret's objections to the *Tenth Anathema*. He refused to say that God the Logos himself was the High Priest and Intercessor of our faith. "Who is it who was completed by the working of virtues, and not through nature? Who is it who revealed obedience while not knowing it until he had experienced it? Who is it who lived in reverence, who with a loud cry and tears offered prayers, who did not have the strength to save himself, but who prayed to the All-Mighty to save him and asked to be spared from death?" asks Theodoret. And then he answers: "Not God the Logos who is immortal, impassive, and incorporeal. But it is the One whom he received from David's seed. He received the name of priest through the link with Melchizedek, was clothed in the weakness of our nature, and is not the All-Mighty Logos of God. It is he who came from David's seed and, not being privy to any sin, became our High Priest and Sacrifice, who sacrificed himself for us and carries in himself the Logos of God, who exists from God, and is joined to and inseparably connected to him." "Thus," concludes Theodoret in his notes to the *Twelfth Anathema*, "it was not Christ who suffered but a man taken from us by the Logos." Here Theodoret is defending the indisputable truth of the Logos' incapability of suffering and changing because of his Godhead. And this gives him the opportunity to reveal the fulness and the reality of human feelings in Christ with utmost clarity, and to even disperse remote Docetic shadows. But for all of that, Christ's singleness, the fact that he exists "in God's image" and bore the weakness of the flesh in his own genuinely assumed human nature, remains insufficiently emphasized in Theodoret's thought. As Theodoret depicts it, manhood becomes isolated in a special subject, in a special High Priest.

THE INADEQUACY OF THEODORET'S THEOLOGICAL LANGUAGE, THE IMPRECISION OF HIS IDEAS, AND HIS SUSPICION OF AN UNFOUNDED APOLLINARIANISM

Theodoret's objections to St. Cyril's *Anathemas* show the inade - quacy of his theological language, as well as his great dependence on the terminology he has adopted, and outside of which he cannot think. Schoolish outlines deprive Theodoret of freedom, and the imprecision of his theological ideas is aggravated even more by his short-sighted suspiciousness for imaginary Apollinarian temptations. Theodoret did not notice – and could not notice – that he and St. Cyril are talking about one and the same thing, the true Christ, in whom they believe identically, although they speak about him differently. Carried away by his striving to stress the differences against this imaginary mixture, Theodoret did not see that St. Cyril's form of expression allows him to reveal this singleness more clearly. Even though Theodoret professed this singleness as well, he did not have the words to express it. This is connected with an essential difference in the way they describe psychological facts. St. Cyril and Theodoret both use the analogy of a man whose body and soul are combined into a single living being. For

St. Cyril, however, this analogy explained unity; for Theodoret, it ex - plained duality. Consequently, Theodoret himself confessed that in the struggle with his adversary he lapsed into a certain "immoderation," a certain unevenness but that "necessity alone produced a certain immoderation in the division." He was striving for an extreme logical definiteness and did not have enough of a feel for the antinomy of the God-Man mystery. He did not understand everything in St. Cyril's *Anathemas*. This can be felt in his rejoinders, when he forces, as it were, an open door.

ST. CYRIL'S RECOGNITION THAT THEODORET HAD NOT UNDERSTOOD THE ANATHEMAS

St. Cyril himself noticed this in his critique of Theodoret's objec - tions: "I confess that at first I thought that he understood the meaning of the *Anathemas* and was feigning ignorance in an effort to please someone. *Now I know for certain that he really did not understand.*" Right after the Council of Ephesus Theodoret writes an expansive epistle (*Epistle* 151, *To the Oriental Monks*; in Migne, *Patrologia Graeca*, 83,1416B-1433A] to the Eastern monks (in Syria, Cilicia, Euphrates, Osroene, and Phoenicia). In this epistle Theodoret bitterly complains about "malicious Egyptian handiwork" which came in his opinion "from the bitter root of Apollinarius," and at the same time Theodoret offers a completely precise confession: "We confess our Lord Jesus Christ to be perfect God and perfect man, made of a body and a rational soul, whose Divine nature was born before the ages from the Father, and who was born in these latter days of the Virgin Mary for our sake and for the sake of our salvation, who is *at one and the same time consubstantial with the Father* through his Godhead and con - *substantial with us* through his manhood: for the combination of two natures was completed. That is why we profess One Christ, One Son, One Lord. And we do not divide the union but we do believe that it has been accomplished without mixture. And we offer him a single wor - ship, since we believe that the union took place in the Virgin's womb at the very conception."

But in St. Cyril's *Anathemas* Theodoret still continues to see "impious philosophizing." Theodoret stubbornly stood up for Antio - chene word usage. In many ways Theodoret truly anticipated the Chalcedonian definition. But the Chalcedonian fathers professed a union of two natures in "a Single Person and in a Single Hypostasis." For them the concept of "person," by being directly identified with the concept of "hypostasis," was completely freed from the indefiniteness which it had in the usage of that time, especially in "Eastern" usage. In Theodoret's thought the two-ness of the "natures" or "hypostases" is powerfully expressed, and singleness is expressed vaguely – without any attribute except as a "unity of person" but not "of hypostasis." He provoked the same kind of indefiniteness by constantly combining the names *Theotokos* and *Bearer of Man* and not noticing that the latter expresses either something incontrovertible, or else it says too much.

THEODORET'S STRUGGLE WITH BURGEONING MONOPHYSITISM

In the struggle with burgeoning Monophysitism Theodoret again speaks out in his *Eranistes*, and speaks out more systematically and more fully. The whole meaning of the mystery of the Incarnation is in the "assuming of flesh," without any unthinkable and impossible "alteration" in which God the Logos ceases to be what he was. In Theodoret's thought the Incarnation is perceived in the wide soterio - logical perspective. The Creator had to receive a complete nature in order to restore the decaying form of humanity. Therefore Christ is the Second Adam, and his victory is our victory, and the new life imparted by the union with God the Logos extends to the whole human race. Christ's resurrection uncovers for all humanity freedom from death. Hence the need for the completeness of both natures and the reality of their union becomes clear. "The name 'man'," explains Theodoret, "is the name of a nature and, remaining silent about this, denies this nature; denying this nature, abolishes Christ's sufferings; and abolishing Christ's sufferings, makes salvation illusory." Only through taking the image of a slave from us does Christ become the Inter - mediary, "by combining what had been separate into a unity or union of natures." "Before the union there was not two natures but only one," Theodoret justly maintains, for humanity was not inherent in the Logos from all eternity, "but was formed along with the angelic salutation." Before that there was one nature,which always and everlastingly existed. The Incarnation is receiving something through conception. In addition, only by professing immutability is the completeness of the Godhead in Christ preserved. In union "the natures did not mix but remained whole." But the two-ness of the natures does not violate the unity of the person. By analogy to human personality or personhood, Theodoret even speaks here about a "natural union." In this union, of course, the characteristics of each nature are preserved unchanged – τὰ τῶν φύσεων ἴδια. Theodoret illustrates this "natural union" into a "single person" with the well-known image of red-hot iron. But "this union, which is so tight, this mixture which penetrates through and through, does not alter the nature of the iron," and the iron remains iron. Theo - doret is here almost speaking St. Cyril's language and he refers to him directly.

THEODORET'S EMPHASIS ON THE REALITY OF CHRIST'S SUFFERING

Theodoret goes into particular detail on the issue of Christ's sufferings. "And we do not say that someone else suffered – and not the

Son of God – but at the same time we know from Holy Scripture that the Divine nature is impassive. Thus, when we hear of impassivity and suffering, and of the combination of Godhood and manhood, we say that suffering belongs to the passionate body, while professing that the impassive nature is free from suffering." This body, however, is not the body of a simple person but that of the Only-Begotten. "Because of this union, Christ's person receives all that is inherent in both natures – the Divine and the human proclaim one person. The indivisible unity of natures is not violated in suffering and death, and "the Divine nature was inseparable" from the passionate flesh both in the grave and on the Cross, although it did not perceive the sufferings itself. "By its nature the flesh suffered, and God the Logos assimilated its sufferings as of his own flesh." Through this "assimilation" the Godhead's impassivity and manhood's capacity for suffering are combined, and the sufferings are not imposed on the Divine nature itself, even though they are the suf - ferings "of the body of God the Logos." In the resurrection the Lord's flesh remains impassive and imperishable but also "remains within the limits of nature and retains the characteristics of manhood."

As early as after the Ephesian "murder," Theodoret stated "by professing Christ to be immutable, impassive and immortal, we cannot ascribe to his own nature changes, sufferings, or death. And if people say that he can do whatever he wants, then they ought to say that he does not want what is incompatible with his nature. As much as he has an immortal nature, he also received a body capable of suffering and a body with a human soul. And although the body of the Only-Begotten Son of God is called a body that has been received or assumed, he takes the sufferings of this body to himself." Theodoret is approximating the notion of "*communicatio idiomatum*" – ἀντίδοσις τῶν ἰδιωμάτων – when he substantiates it with the unity of person: "the union makes the names common but the commonality of names does not confuse the natures themselves"; "the union did not cause the peculiarities of the natures to mix," and they are clearly distinguished and perceived. "After all, when gold comes into contact with fire, it assumes the color and behavior of fire; it does not lose its nature but remains gold, even though it behaves like fire. In the same way, the Lord's body is a body but one that is, upon its entrance into Heaven, non-suffering, imperish - able, immortal, sovereign, divine, and glorified by Divine glory. It is not separated from the Godhead and is the body of no one else except God's Only-Begotten Son. It does not appear to us as anything but the body of the Only-Begotten himself, who has received our nature."

Theodoret is now speaking somewhat differently than before, but he is saying the same thing. Suspicious prejudices have been dispelled, and his theological contemplation has become clearer and more lucid. One no longer senses a schoolish or parochial limitedness in him, as one felt previously.

At the Council of Chalcedon Theodoret approved, although in a general form, the epistles of St. Cyril with which he had previously argued. Now he understands St. Cyril's *Anathemas*. This does not mean that he rejected his type of theologizing, but that he stopped insisting on its exclusiveness. Not long before the Council of Chalcedon, Theodoret recalled the "venom enclosed within the *Twelve Anathemas* but he did not attribute the impious conclusions contained in them to St. Cyril, who had brought out his *Anathemas* only against Nestorius, without claiming to settle the mystery of the Incarnation in them. They had to be accepted as an antithesis to Nestorianism, not as a complete creed – this was given in the Chalcedonian definition of faith. By this time the terminological disagreements had been cleared up, the basic Christological concepts had become permanent, and it became possible to unambiguously profess *two natures* in a single person *or* hypostasis of the Logos Incarnate. But Theodoret thought in his own way until the very end. "The Logos became flesh" – this was St. Cyril's Christology. Jesus of Nazareth, a man attested to you by God with mighty works and wonders and signs which God did through him – this Jesus you crucified and killed but God raised him up." (*Acts* 2:22-24). This was the blessed Theodoret's Christology.

CHAPTER EIGHTEEN

THE RISE OF MONOPHYSITISM

The Chalcedonian *oros* became the cause of a tragic schism in the Church. Historical Monophysitism is precisely the non-acceptance and rejection of the Chalcedonian Council, a schism and break with the fathers of the council. The Monophysite movement can in general be compared with the anti-Nicene movement, and the makeup of the Monophysite schism was just as motley and heterogeneous as that of the "anti-Nicene coalition" in the middle of the fourth century. From the very beginning there were always few real "Eutychians" and Apol - linarians among the Monophysites. Eutyches was just as much a heretic for the majority of Monophysites as he was for the orthodox. Dioscorus rehabilitated him and granted him communion more out of indirect motives than because he agreed with him and his beliefs, and mainly in defiance of Flavian. In any case, at Chalcedon Dioscorus openly rejected any "mixing," "transformation" or "cleavage." Anatolius of Constantinople, during the discussion of the *oros* at the council, reminded everyone that "Dioscorus was not deposed for faith." It is still impossible to prove through these words that Dioscorus was not in actuality mistaken. However, it is very characteristic that they judged and condemned Dioscorus at the council not for heresy but for the brigandage at Ephesus and for "human murder." Neither Dioscorus nor Timothy the "Cat" – more accurately, the "Weasel," for he was known as "Timothy Aelurus (d.477) from the Greek *αἴλουρος* [literally "weasel"] denied the "double consubstantiality" of the God-Man – consubstantial with the Father in his Divinity and consubstantial with the human race in his humanity.

The same thing has to be said about most Monophysites. They claimed to be the only faithful keepers of the faith of St. Cyril. In any event, they spoke Cyril's language and his words. The Chalcedonian *oros* seemed to them to be cloaked in Nestorianism. The theology of most of these Monophysites was primarily a systemization of St. Cyril's doctrine. In this regard the theological views of Philoxenus (Xenaias) of Hierapolis (c.440-523) and Severus of Antioch (c.465-538), the two most prominent leaders of Syrian Monophysitism in the late fifth and early sixth centuries, were especially characteristic. It was Severus' system which became the official dogmatic doctrine of the Monophysite church when it finally withdrew into itself. Severus' theological system also became the official doctrine of the Syrian Jacobites, of the Coptic Christians in Egypt and of the Armenian Church. This was, first of all, formal and literary Monophysitism.

These Monophysites spoke of the unity of the God-Man as a "unity of nature" but *μία φύσις* meant to them little more than the *μία ὑπόστασις* of the Chalcedonian *oros*. By "nature" they meant "hypostasis." Severus makes this observation directly. In this regard they were rather strict Aristotelians and recognized only "individuals" or "hypostases" as real or existing. In any case, in the "unity of nature" the duality of "natural qualities" – St. Cyril's term – did not disappear or fall away for them. Therefore, Philoxenus called the "single nature" *complex*. This concept of a "complex nature" is fundamental in Severus' system – μία φύσις σύνθετος. Severus defines the God-Man unity as a "synthesis," a "co-composition" – σύνθεσις – and in doing so distinguishes "co-composition" from any fusion or mixing. In this "co-composition" there is no change or transformation of the "components" – they are only "combined" indissolubly and do not exist "apart." Therefore, for Severus the "dual consubstantiality" of the Logos Incarnate is an indisputable and immutable tenet and a criterion of true faith. Severus could sooner be called a "diplophysite" rather than a Monophysite in the true sense of the word. He even agreed to "distinguish" "two natures" – or better, "two essences" – in Christ not only "before the union" but also in the union itself – "after union" – of course with the proviso that it can only be a question of a mental or analytical distinguishing, a distinguishing "in contemplation" – ἐν θεωρίᾳ, or "through imagination" – κατ᾽ ἐπίνοιαν. And once again this almost repeats St. Cyril's words.

For Severus and his followers "unity of nature" meant a *unity of subject*, a unity of person, a unity of life. They were much closer to St. Cyril than it usually seemed to the ancient polemicists. Fairly recently the works of the Monophysite theologians again have become available to us in ancient Syrian translations and it has become possible to form an opinion about their thought without having to go through biased witnesses.

Now we must not speak of Monophysitism as a revived Apollin - arianism, and we have to strictly differentiate the "Eutychians" and the "Monophysites" in the broad sense of the terms. It is very characteristic that this boundary was drawn with total firmness already by St. John of Damascus. In his short work, *Briefly On Heresies*, which is part two of his principal dogmatic work entitled Πηγὴ γνώσεως [*Source of Knowledge*], St. John of Damascus refers to "Monophysites" directly as schismatics and dissenters but not as heretics – "these Egyptians are schismatics and Monophysites. On the pretext of the Chalcedonian definition they separated themselves from the Orthodox Church. They are called Egyptians because the Egyptians were the first to begin this kind of division during the reigns of emperors Marcian and Valentinian. *In everything else they are orthodox.*" (Heresy 83). However, this is what makes the schism enigmatic and incomprehensible.

Of course, divisions in the Church are entirely possible even with - out dogmatic disagreements. Political enthusiasm and darker passions can also disrupt and shatter Church unity. From the very beginning in the Monophysite movement national and regional motives latched on to religious ones. To the "Egyptians" the Council of Chalcedon was unac -

ceptable and despicable not only because in its definition of faith it spoke of "two natures" but also because in the famous 28th Canon it extolled Constantinople over Alexandria. Orthodox Alexandrians had a hard time reconciling themselves to this fact. It is no accident that "Monophysitism" very quickly becomes a *non-Greek faith*, a faith of Syrians, Copts, Ethiopians, and Armenians. National separatism con - stantly makes itself very sharply felt in the history of the Monophysite disputes. The dogmatic nature of Monophysitism is very much connected to Greek tradition; it is comprehensible only through Greek terminology, the Greek way of thinking and the categories of Greek metaphysics. It was Greek theologians who worked out the dogma of the Monophysite church. However, a keen hatred of Hellenism is very characteristic of Monophysitism as a whole. They use the word "Greek" as a synonym for "pagan" – "Greek books and pagan sciences."

Greek Monophysitism was comparatively short-lived. In Syria there soon began a direct eradication of everything Greek. In this regard the fate of Jacob of Edessa (c.640-708), one of the most remarkable Monophysite theologians of the seventh century and especially renowned for his biblical works – he is called the Syrian Jerome – is quite typical. He was compelled to leave his monastery, where for eleven years he tried to revive Greek scholarship. He was forced to leave "persecuted by the brotherhood which hated Greeks." All of these extraneous motives muddled and stirred up the theological dispute. However, one should *not* exaggerate its significance. Religious differences were still decisive – differences of feeling, not differences of opinion. This explains the Monophysites' stubborn attachment to St. Cyril's theological language and their insurmountable suspicion of the Chalcedonian *oros*, which to them invariably smelled of "Nestor - ianism." This is impossible to explain as a mere difference of intel - lectual cast or mental skills. Neither is it explained as admiration for the imaginary antiquity of the Monophysite formula – "a forgery of the Apollinarians." One can hardly think that Severus in particular could not understand the Chalcedonian terminology, that he would not have grasped that the fathers of the council were using words differently than he but not deviating very far from him in content of faith. But the point is that Monophysitism was not theological heresy, was not a "heresy" of theologians – its soul, its secret is not revealed in theological con - structs or formulas. It is true that Severus' system could be reset almost in Chalcedonian terminology. But only "almost."

There is always something remaining. More than anything else, the spirit of the system distinguishes the Monophysites from St. Cyril. It was not at all easy to reshape Cyril's inspired doctrine into a logical system, and the terminology made this problem more difficult. Hardest of all was intelligibly defining the form and character of the human "traits" in the God-Man synthesis. The followers of Severus could not speak of Christ's humanity as a "nature." It broke down into a system of traits, for the doctrine of the Logos "taking" humanity was still not developed fully by Monophysitism into the idea of "inter-hypostasis-ness." The Monophysites usually spoke of the Logos' humanity as οἰκονομία. It is not without foundation that the fathers of the Council of Chalcedon detected here a subtle taste of original Docetism. Certainly this is not the Docetism of the ancient Gnostics at all, nor is it Apol - linarianism. However, to the followers of Severus the "human" in Christ was not entirely human, for it was not active, was not "self-motivated." In the contemplation of the Monophysites the human in Christ was like a passive object of Divine influence. Divinization or *theosis* seems to be a unilateral act of Divinity without sufficiently taking into account the synergism of human freedom, the assumption of which in no way supposes a "second subject." In their religious experiment the element of freedom in general was not sufficiently pronounced and this could be called *anthropological minimalism*. To a certain extent, there is a similarity between Monophysitism and Augustinianism – the human is pushed into the background and, as it were, suppressed by the Divine. What St. Augustine said about the boundless activity of grace refers in Monophysite doctrine to the God-Man "synthesis." In this regard one could speak of the "potential assimilation" of humanity by the Divinity of the Logos even in Severus' system. In Severus' thought this is proclaimed in his muddled and forced doctrine of "unified God-Man activity" – this expression is taken from Dionysius the Areopagite. The actor is always unified – the Logos. Therefore, the activity – "energy" – is unified too. But together with this, it is complex as well, complex in its manifestations – τὰ ἀποτελέσματα, in conformity with the complexity of the acting nature or subject. A single action is manifested dually and the same is true for will or volition. In other words, Divine activity is refracted and, as it were, takes refuge in the "natural qualities" of the humanity received by the Logos. We must remember that Severus here touched upon a difficulty which was not resolved in the Orthodox theology of his time. Even with Orthodox theologians the concept of divinization or *theosis* sometimes suggested the boundless influence of Divinity. However, for Severus the difficulty proved insurmountable, especially because of the clumsiness and inflexibility of the "Monophysite" language and also because in his reflections he always started from the Divinity of the Logos and not from the Person of the God-Man. Formally speaking, this was the path trod by St. Cyril but in essence this led to the idea of human passivity – one could even say the non-freedom of the God-Man. These biases of thought proclaim the indis - tinctness of Christological vision. To these conservative Monophysites the human in Christ seemed still *too* transfigured – not qualitatively, of course, not physically, but potentially or virtually. In any event, it did not seem to be acting freely and the Divine does not manifest itself in the freedom of the human. What is taking place here is partly simple unspokenness, and in Severus' time Orthodox theologians had also not yet revealed the doctrine of Christ's human freedom – more accurately, the freedom of the "human" in Christ – with sufficient clarity and fullness. However, Severus simply did not pose the question of freedom and this, of course, was no accident. Given his premises, the very question had to have seemed "Nestorian" – concealed by the assumption of the "second subject."

The orthodox answer, as given by St. Maximus the Confessor (c.580-662), presupposes distinguishing between "nature" and "hypo - stasis" – not only is "man" ("hypostasis") free but also the "human" as such – the very "nature" – in all its "natural qualities," in all and in each. An acknowledgement of this sort can in no way be fit into the framework of the Monophysite – much less the "diplophysite" – doctrine. Severus' system was the theology of the "Monophysite" majority. It could be called conservative Monophysitism. But the history of Monophysitism is a history of constant dissension and division. It is not so important that from time to time we meet under the title "Monophysite" individual groups comprised of people who were not quite followers of Eutyches, not quite new Docetists who spoke of the "transformation" or the "fusion of natures," who denied the consubstantiality of humanity in Christ, or who talked about the "heavenly" origin and nature of Christ's body. These individual heretical outbursts are evidence only of the general intellectual ferment and agitation. Much more important are those divisions and disputes which arise in the basic course of the Monophysite movement. These reveal its internal logic, its driving motives, especially Severus' dispute with Julian of Halicarnassos.

Julian also seemed to be a Docetist to Severus. It is true that in his polemic with Julian Severus was not unbiased. Later orthodox polemicists argued not so much with Julian as with his carried-away followers. In any case, Julian's original compositions do not contain that coarse Docetism which his opponents talked so much about when they charged that his doctrine of the innate "imperishability" – ἀφθαρσία – of the Savior's body turned the mystery of Redemption into some "fantasy and dream" (hence the name "fantasiasts"). Julian's system of the "imperishability" of Christ's body is connected not with his understanding of the unity of the God-Man but with his under - standing of original sin, with its general anthropological premises. Here Julian is very close to St. Augustine – this is, of course, a similarity and not a dependence on Augustine. Of the Monophysite theologians Julian is closest to Philoxenus. Julian considers man's primordial nature to be "imperishable," "non-suffering," non-mortal" and free also from the so-called "irreproachable passions"; that is, weakness or the states of "suffering" in general – πάθη ἀδιάβλητα. The Fall substan - tially and hereditarily damages human nature – human nature became weak, mortal and perishable. In the Incarnation God the Logos assumes the nature of the primordial Adam, a nature which is "impassive" and "imperishable." He thus becomes the New Adam. Therefore Christ suffered and died not "because of the necessity of nature" – not ἐξ ἀνάγκης φυσικῆς, but through his will, "for the sake of *oikonomia* – λόγῳ οἰκονομίας, "through the will of Divinity," "by way of a miracle." However, Christ's suffering and death were real and authentic, not an "opinion" or "apparition." But they were entirely free, since this was not the death of a "perishable" and an "impassioned" ("suffering") man, and since they did not contain the fatal doom of the Fall. There is still no heresy in this doctrine. But it comes close to another. Julian's conception of the unity of the God-Man is tighter than Severus'. He refuses to "enumerate" or distinguish the "natural qualities" in the God-Man synthesis. He even refuses to distinguish "in addition" "two essences" after union. For him, the concept of "essence" had the same concrete ("individual") sense as the concept of "nature" *or* "hypostasis." In the Logos' Incarnation the "imperishability" of the accepted body is so secured by its tight unity with Divinity that in suffering and death it is removed by a certain *oikonomic* tolerance on the part of God. As Julian understood it, this did not violate the Savior's human "consub - stantiality." In any case, however, this clearly exaggerated the "potential assimilability" of the human by the Divine by virtue of the Incarnation itself. Again, this is connected with a lack of feeling for freedom and with a passive understanding of "*theosis*" or "divinization." Julian understood "imperishability" of primordial human nature as its objec - tive condition rather than as a free possibility, and he understood "impassiveness" and "imperishability" in Christ too passively. It is this quietism which violates the equilibrium of Julian's system. He did not proceed from an analysis of metaphysical concepts. In his system one clearly senses the deciding significance of the soteriological ideal.

Julian's followers went even further. They were called "aphtarto - docetists" ("imperishable valetudinarians") and "fantasiasts." These names set off well that quietism – rather than "Docetism" – which is so striking in their way of thinking. The human is passively transformed. Others of Julian's followers felt that it was impossible to call this transformation and impossible to call the divinized humanity in the unity of the God-Man "creatural." Thus there arose the sect of *actistites* ("non-creaturalists"). Some of Severus' adherents, in their disputes about Christ's human conduct, came to such a conclusion as well. In the union of God and Man, the limitedness of human knowledge must be removed immediately and passively. Otherwise, a bifurcation of human "ignorance" and Divine omniscience arises, and the "unity of nature" is violated. That is how the adherents of a certain Stephen in Alexandria reasoned. This reasoning reminds us partly of the arguments – not the conclusion – of Apollinarius regarding the impossibility of a union of "two perfect things" precisely because of the limitedness and extreme inconstancy of the human mind. The followers of Stephen found another way out of this difficulty, however – they denied any difference in Christ after the union, in which even the human mind was immediately elevated to Divine Omniscience. Here yet again is pro - claimed a quietistic understanding of human thought. On this question the majority of the followers of Severus were "cryptics" – Christ's omniscience was just not manifested in humanity. It seemed impious to assume that Christ's human "ignorance" – particularly of the Judgment Day – could have been real and not just intentional silence. It is necessary to mention again that for orthodox theology also this was an unanswered question. For the Monophysites, however, it was also unanswerable. In other words, within the limits of Monophysite premises it was answerable only by admitting the *passive assimilation* of the human by the Divine. All these disputes reveal the indistinctness and vagueness of a religious vision damaged by anthropological quietism. There is an inner duality in the Monophysite movement, a bifurcation of emotion and thought. One could say that Monophysite theology was more orthodox than their ideals or, to put it differently, that the theologians in Monophysitism were more orthodox than most of the believers but that the theologians were prevented from attaining final clarity by the unfortunate "Monophysite" language. Therefore, Monophysitism becomes "more orthodox" in a strange and unexpected way precisely when the religious wave has receded and theology is cooling down to scholasticism. It is at this time that Monophysite closeness to St. Cyril seems so obvious, for this is closeness in word, not in spirit. The source of Monophysitism is not to be found in dogmatic formulas but in religious passion. All the pathos of Mono - physitism lies in the *self-abasement of man*, in an acute need to overcome the human as such, and hence the instinctive striving to distinguish the God-Man from man more sharply even in his humanity. This striving can be proclaimed in various forms and with varying force, depending on how lucid and how restrained is this burning thirst for human self-abasement which erupts from the dark depths of the subconscious. It is not accidental that Monophysitism was so closely connected with ascetic fanaticism, with ascetic self-torture and emotional violence. Nor is it an accident that Origenistic motifs of a universal apocatastasis were once again revived in Monophysite circles. In this regard the lone image of the Syrian mystic Stephen Bar-Sudhaile and his doctrine about universal restoration and a final "consub - stantiality" of all creatures with God is particularly significant. Neoplatonic mysticism is paradoxically crossed with eastern fatalism. An apotheosis of self-abasement – such is the paradox of Mono - physitism, and only through these psychological predispositions can one understand the tragic history of Monophysitism. The belated epilogue to the Monophysite movement will be the tragic Monothelite controversy.